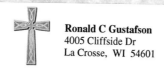

Nature *and* Revelation

Nature *and* Revelation

A HISTORY OF MACALESTER COLLEGE

Jeanne Halgren Kilde

FOREWORD BY
James Brewer Stewart

 University of Minnesota Press
MINNEAPOLIS · LONDON

Published by the University of Minnesota Press
111 Third Avenue South, Suite 290
Minneapolis, MN 55401–2520
http://www.upress.umn.edu

Library of Congress Cataloging-in-Publication Data

Nature and revelation : a history of Macalester College /
Jeanne Halgren Kilde ; foreword by James Brewer Stewart.
    p. cm.
 Includes bibliographical references and index.
 ISBN 978-0-8166-5626-4 (hc : alk. paper)
 ISBN 978-0-8166-5627-1 (pb : alk. paper)
 1. Macalester College—History. 2. Universities and
colleges—Minnesota—St. Paul—History.
 LD3141.M222N47 2010
 378.776'581—dc22
                    2009046764

17 16 15 14 13 12 11 10   10 9 8 7 6 5 4 3 2 1

Contents

Foreword

AS THIS ABSORBING AND BEAUTIFULLY WRITTEN STUDY makes clear, the history of Macalester College involves a highly instructive moral problem familiar to all of us: the paradoxical necessity to negotiate and, simultaneously, to resist. On one hand, ever since Macalester's founding, the college has made a consistent and convincing case for its mission to prepare students for lives that stand against conventional wisdom, question prevailing norms, and act on moral convictions that empower lifetimes of service to the community, the nation, and the world. The college has insisted that its responsibilities extend far beyond providing a classroom education. Students' horizons must be expanded to encompass questions of justice, equity, and human rights. Macalester has always promoted an ethical and empathetic concern for others, wherever they might be found. It has always stoutly resisted the proposition that academic study is simply preparation for the pursuit of personal self-interest, and as unbroken generations of Macalester alumni readily attest, this lesson took hold long ago. The college has consistently graduated an impressive number of resistance-minded people, whose lives have truly made an important difference.

On the other hand, Macalester's history reveals a college deeply sensitive to the necessities of negotiation. Over the decades, it has constantly sought to deepen its mission, broaden its appeal, and bolster its finances by reshaping itself in response to the dominant culture's shifting influences and expectations. At its inception in the 1880s, and during its formative decades, Macalester conformed wholeheartedly to the injunctions of the nation's Protestant establishment by committing itself to evangelizing the world. Close to a century later, a largely de-Christianized Macalester responded to the expectations of a much more diverse America by jettisoning its chapel requirements, overhauling its religion department (revamped as a pluralistic Department of Religious Studies), and abandoning its Presbyterian identity in favor of multiculturalism. By the same token, for most of its history, the college tailored its curriculum to meet the practical needs of its working- and middle-class Minnesotan student body by sustaining a wide variety of explicitly vocational programs that did not require a highly specialized faculty. By the early 1960s, however, the college had eliminated these programs in response to the expectations of increasingly sophisticated donors, the desire to attract a cosmopolitan student body, and the requirements of a higher education establishment that prized the pursuit of knowledge and the fruits of original research for their own intrinsic value. Negotiation, in this instance, ignited the college's aspirations for national preeminence by empowering it to recruit an impressively credentialed faculty, attract an outstanding student body, and finance much improved facilities for scholarship and teaching.

Author Jeanne Halgren Kilde makes plain that this tension between conflicting imperatives—resistance and negotiation—goes far to explain why Macalester's history features such a compelling mix of high ambition; great accomplishment; and, on occasion, stunning volatility. As her analysis of this counterpoint makes clear, there was nothing foreordained or consistent about the college's century-long trajectory toward the elite national status that it achieved in the mid-1990s. Instead, she insists, to understand that trajectory, one must focus, above all, on the ways in which the college responded to the unpredictable world beyond it— to transformations in the nation's economy and demographics, in religious and scientific thought, in educational philosophy, in politics as related to social justice, in wars and their humanitarian challenges, in values that determined student behavior, and in relationships between philanthropists and higher education. Knowing Macalester's past, according to this book, requires understanding how the college developed in negotiation with and in resistance to change within the nation and around the world.

This ambitious approach ensures great rewards for its readers and explains why this volume so convincingly exceeds conventional expectations. In addition to offering absorbing accounts of the college's influential leaders, its defining moments, and the evolving circumstances of students and faculty, this book develops quite substantial encounters with social, intellectual, cultural, and po-litical history. Making no concessions, it assumes that its readers share precisely the attributes of Macalester's best graduates—that they are intellectually criti-cal, alert to moral questions, resistant to easy answers, and personally engaged in lifelong learning. And precisely because this volume is so much more than a conventional narrative, it holds obvious interest for academic readers outside the Macalester community, particularly for scholars of religious and cultural history. Whether alumni or not, such readers will find themselves challenged and instructed by substantial analyses of, for example, American Protestantism's complex spiritual evolution from the 1880s onward, science's ever troubled relationships with claims of faith, and the theory postulating that processes of secularization best explain the emergence of our postmodern condition. For these reasons and many more, this book is a truly substantial scholarly monograph in its own right, even as it doubles as a highly readable history of a unique and truly important liberal arts college.

In the final analysis, this is most of all a book for Macalester people because it addresses head-on the college's most mythology-shrouded questions. For example, during his undergraduate years, did the college's most munificent financial supporter, *Reader's Digest* founder DeWitt Wallace, actually coax a cow into the bell tower? Many decades later, in the late 1960s, did the same DeWitt Wallace terminate his financial support and pitch Macalester into crisis because of his objections to the college's abrupt turn to leftist politics? Was it true that the college's unprecedented initiative to attract disadvantaged minority students, its Expanded Educational Opportunity program, was an academic failure and that its costs drove the operating budget into enormous deficit? While Jeanne Halgren Kilde's answer to each of these questions is an unqualified no, Macalester readers will surely appreciate the careful logic and scrupulous documentation she marshals in support of her conclusions. Finally we possess reliable information that bears on these questions as well as answers that can be evaluated on their merits.

Beyond mythology—and most important, if you were involved in the college from the World War II era to the end of the 1980s—you will find that this book evokes the Macalester you remember. You will come to appreciate as never before the history that makes your memories possible. If you have come to the college since that time, this book will surely invite you to assess the continuing value of the Macalester you have experienced and to consider how the college you carry with you came into being. Whatever one's relationship to Macalester College, and whenever that relationship transpired, this book invites us to reencounter an important part of where we have come from—to understand it; to appreciate it; and in the finest of the college's traditions, to subject it to critique.

—*James Brewer Stewart*

Acknowledgments

THE INSPIRATION FOR THIS BOOK came over lunch in the Kagin Hall faculty dining room several years ago, when members of the religious studies department hosted former Macalester president John B. Davis. During the course of the conversation, President Davis lamented the fact that a scholarly history of the college had not been attempted since the volume by Henry Daniel Funk was published in 1910. As a visiting faculty member in the department very interested in lived religious life, I found the idea of producing such a history immediately intriguing. Several months later, as I and members of the department, including Calvin Roetzel and Paula Cooey, developed a proposal for the Lilly Endowment's Theological Exploration of Vocation Program, we decided that exploring the college's historical vocation should be a central piece of our work. This book is thus very much the result of President Davis's initial idea, collegial support from faculty of the religious studies department, and generous financial support from the Lilly Endowment Inc.

In the process of developing the project, I have benefited from the aid and support of many people—too many, sadly, to name all of them here. I do want to acknowledge a few individuals who have been central to its advancement and completion. First and foremost, Kay Crawford (class of '70) assisted me in countless ways—conducting numerous oral history interviews; transcribing and organizing materials; and, as a longtime Macite, tipping me off to important questions, topics, and issues. Kay hired several excellent research assistants, who transcribed countless documents, mined the Macalester and Minnesota History Center archives with energy and insight, and brought amazing information to my attention: Emily Witsell (class of '05), Sarah Turner (class of '04), Zach Teicher (class of '06), and Michael (Rich) Sheridan (class of '04). I also thank Gail Caligieri and Bobbie Cezinski for their insight and administrative and technical support.

I would like to thank a number of Macalester faculty members for their support of the project. First, James Brewer Stewart generously shared his insights on the institution, gleaned from his many years in the history department, and also shepherded the project through some turbulent institutional waters. His unwavering enthusiasm for the project was a continual inspiration to me. Truman Schwartz provided helpful information and support; Calvin Roetzel and Paula Cooey also have my sincere gratitude. Thanks to Macalester library director Terri Fishel and archivists Beth Hilleman and Ellen Holt-Werle and to Eileen McCormack, associate curator at the James J. Hill Reference Library. I am indebted to Nancy Head (Mrs. Charles Turck), who generously donated important material on President Turck's time in office.

Finally, I express my appreciation to Dale Johnson and Dan Dupre, who offered excellent comments on the initial manuscript, and to University of Minnesota Press editor Pieter Martin, who expertly shepherded this project through to completion.

PART I

Protestant Roots on the Prairie, 1849–1915

1

Identity and Change

AN IMAGE OF TWO WOMEN, classically symbolic in flowing drapery, graces the Macalester College seal. One holds a telescope; a compass lies at her feet. The other holds a Bible. In a peaceful outdoor setting, suggested by a nearby tree and grassy foreground, the two figures carry on a seemingly pleasant conversation. The motto that encircles the scene identifies the two figures: Nature and Revelation, the Twins of Heaven. Although this nineteenth-century image is now no doubt mystifying to many contemporary students and visitors, its message was quite clear when it was designed by the founder of the college: the study of the natural world—science—aligns perfectly with reverence for the Word of God, for Christianity. The laws of nature are one and the same as those of God. Empirical knowledge and belief in divine revelation are fully compatible.

Negotiating a relationship between religious conviction and the pursuit of empirical knowledge ranked among higher education's top challenges from the late nineteenth century through much of the twentieth century. When Macalester College opened its doors in fall 1885, it did so smack in the midst of an ongoing debate about the role of religion—specifically, Christianity—in the modern world and its relationship to higher education and, particularly, science. Could Christianity, which embraced truths divinely revealed in the Bible, be squared with the increasingly sophisticated methods and discoveries in science, historiography, literary criticism, psychology, and other areas? In particular, the work of naturalist Charles Darwin on natural selection as the mechanism for change in nature (rather than divine will) had thrown into question the long-held conviction that God provided the requisite foundation of all knowledge and that, therefore, all learning was dependent on correct knowledge of God and, more specifically, knowledge of Christianity.

This Christocentric epistemology had informed most institutions of higher education in the United States in the nineteenth century, the vast majority of which were founded by Christian religious groups and denominations. Macalester College, too, advanced this position and adopted the previously described seal, which proudly signaled the belief that the natural world, the subject of science, was fully engaged with the revelatory world of the divine. While the founders of Macalester College remained steadfast in this conviction, subsequent generations of college leaders would modify it significantly in light of social, cultural, and technological change as well as historical, social scientific, and scientific developments. Over the course of the twentieth century, a number of new understandings of the relationship between religion and education emerged, flourished, were modified, and waned. Tracing the changing perceptions of the relationship between religion and education is, in broad terms, the goal of this book.

Transformation, then, is a key theme in the following pages. Both factors in the equation—religion and education—changed dramatically and repeatedly over the period to be covered. The basic outline of the transformations in religion and the liberal arts that Macalester College underwent between its opening and the late twentieth century is readily sketched. This small liberal arts college in St. Paul, Minnesota, was born of the efforts of East Coast Protestant migrants to the frontier area to re-create the institutions of the East in the newly opening West. These founders espoused the notion that Christianity undergirded all knowledge and proclaimed that the institution delivered a distinctively latitudinarian Christian education unmarked by the sectarian conflicts that divided Protestant denominations—an education that suited all comers. Yet from its earliest days, the content of that Christianity and its role with respect to the college's mission were negotiated. The college's opening occurred only with the support of the Presbyterian Church, and the first official president of the college, a man who had not worked with the original founders, promoted a distinctive Presbyterian identity and mission for the college, all but ignoring the latitudinarian commitment of the school's original supporters. With its dominant Presbyterian perspective, the institution offered classes that focused on a traditional curriculum that emphasized moral philosophy, Baconian science, Christian apologetics, and classical languages as preparation for the ministry, law, and medicine— a curriculum that was decidedly typical among small colleges during the period.

Its outlook was generally conservative, and its aspirations were more toward piety than intellectual achievement. A century later, religious conviction no longer played a role in defining academic epistemologies or curricula at Macalester College. Its liberal arts curriculum embraced empirical methods in both science and social science instruction; language and fine arts flourished; and politically engaged education predominated. By the 1990s, Macalester had earned a national reputation for its academic rigor and its promotion of international education. Moreover, in contrast to the original conservative character of the institution, the college had developed an ethos of progressive politics and avant-garde student interests and lifestyles.

Exploring this shift from the theologically grounded, politically and educationally conservative institution of the late nineteenth century to the twentieth-century institution apparently unconnected to any religious tradition and with a reputation for embracing learning for its own sake, liberal political views, and international education is our task. This trajectory of profound change raises a number of questions pertaining to the role and mission of the college. What caused these palpable, if gradual, shifts in character and identity? How did changes in the understanding of religion and education contribute to these transformations? What role did social and cultural change play in influencing them? As we explore the changing understandings of the Nature–Revelation relationship, we will shed significant light on the changing character, mission, and institutional identity of Macalester College.

Yet it is not only curiosity about this particular institution that informs this book, for almost all institutions of higher education—particularly small, church-related liberal arts colleges founded in the nineteenth century, many of which are now among the leading educational institutions in the country—experienced similar social, cultural, political, and pedagogical challenges and shifts during this period. Apart from a handful of generalities, however, little is understood about how events of the twentieth century transformed these institutions. Can close examination of the experiences of one college's transformation shed light on changes experienced more widely in the educational community? The answer, at least in the case of Macalester College, is yes, for what we learn from looking closely at Macalester over time is that it experienced multiple periods of rapid and decisive transformation over the course of the twentieth century, usually brought on by social and cultural debate or tension.

Thus, through analysis of one college, we can begin to discern some important lessons about the function of identity, contingency, and change in small liberal arts institutions. This book points to a turbulent history of institutions buffeted by social, political, economic, and religious forces, struggling not simply to define and maintain some sense of self and purpose, a discernable identity and role, but often for their very existence. These influences touched colleges not only through their leaders and faculty, but often through their students, who, as we will see in the case of Macalester, repeatedly nudged, and sometimes shoved, the college leadership in new directions. Macalester College's identity proved to be highly fluid throughout its entire existence. The college's ability to endure has rested not on a static identity maintained over time, but rather on its very adaptability to contingency.

In fact, Macalester's identity has been tightly linked to the cultural crises and changes that have buffeted this era. The values, mission, and identity of this institution have been negotiated continuously from the very inception of the idea of the college to the present day. The major players in this negotiation have ranged from college presidents, trustees, and administrators to students, alumni, and residents of the neighboring communities. All these actors have held strong opinions about the college and its purpose, strengths, and limitations. From their individual stories, this collective story of the history of an institution takes shape.

Several themes emerge from this history. Most noticeably, this collective story indicates that the linchpin of Macalester's identity for over a century—from its earliest inception shortly after the Civil War to the late 1960s—has been its relationship with Protestantism. As the role of Protestantism changed nationally from being an arbiter of cultural meaning to another voice among many in the arena of public discussion, so too did the role it played on campus. This is not to say that it disappeared. Macalester College, to this day, remains in a formal, covenanted relationship with the Presbyterian Church (USA). Nevertheless, of all the changes that occurred over the past 150 years at the institution, its religious identity has been the most profoundly affected.

Another central theme in these pages pertains to the college's relationship to the public arena, both local and national. From its earliest inception, Macalester College has been an institution that has both embraced and been embroiled in public debate. Although modeled on a nostalgic idyll of the New England rural school, sheltered from the world in bucolic peace and filled with young men studiously pondering the truths of the ages, the reality has been an institution deeply and publicly engaged in the municipal, political, and educational debates of the twentieth century. Furthermore, its engagement in public issues has frequently sprung precisely from the religious and ethical convictions of college leaders and, often, the students themselves.

Church-Related Colleges: An American Phenomenon

Although common in the United States, small, private liberal arts colleges like Macalester are an oddity in the realm of education worldwide. Distinctively American institutions founded in all but a few cases on religious grounds, small colleges were established by the hundreds in the nineteenth century and winnowed to a few dozen successful ones in the ensuing century. These colleges were founded on the conviction that education was a moral endeavor with civic consequences. As the new republic called the United States was slowly coalescing in the first half of the nineteenth century, reformers who spurned the European model of aristocratic civil leadership argued that only an educated citizenry could guard against the despotism inherent in top-down rule. Dedicated to governance of the people, by the people, and for the people, advocates of republicanism argued strenuously that such governance would be effective only if the people kept close watch on their elected leaders and understood public issues. This required an educated citizenry. And with the fate of the republic at stake, that education, many argued, needed to rest on the strongest moral principles. At this time, and for these people, those were the principles of Protestant Christianity.

Though education had long been located under the purview of religion, this civic component had not always been a defining feature. The founding model for higher education was the medieval cathedral school established for the education of the clergy. Learning in the medieval period was for the glory and understanding of God, not the good of mankind. The Enlightenment brought the idea that gaining knowledge about the world—economic, political, scientific, and technical—was valuable in its own right and for the improvement of society. A new religious outlook of the eighteenth century, Protestant evangelicalism, which focused on the individual's relationship with Jesus Christ as the necessary component of salvation, merged education and civic progressivism within a distinctive millenarian context, bringing new purpose and activism to education. For nineteenth-century evangelicals, education was a conduit through which one learned of God and the world, and that knowledge was to be put to use for the betterment of society as a whole, which, they believed, would ultimately help to establish the Kingdom of God.

This millennial goal, blended with the idea that the U.S. political experiment in republicanism was a fulfillment of God's plan, energized religious activity and education in the nineteenth century. Protestant leaders were convinced that because God's will and the success of the nation were united, sincere efforts to advance Christianity and education would bring about the culmination of both. Consequently, educated evangelicals not only participated in missionary efforts to broadcast their faith across the nation and the world but also spearheaded civic reform movements from abolitionism to temperance, antiprostitution to Sabbatarianism, and so on. They also founded school after school, designed to provide a properly educated citizenry for the fledgling nation.

This evangelical educational activism grew part and parcel with the nation itself, being among the foremost institution-building movements in this era of nation building in the United States. Through the course of the nineteenth century, the country grew from a collection of small, disparate states loosely linked together in a federation to a continent-wide nation that boasted not only increasing wealth and political power but also a host of internal institutions—local and territorial governments, churches, civic societies—devoted to the improvement and regularization of life in the new country. Education was foremost among the motivations for institution building during this period, and over the course of the nineteenth century, well over two hundred church-related colleges were founded in the United States.

Macalester College, which opened it doors to postsecondary students in 1885, was one among the many—a small, church-related college informed by the desire to bring civilization to the upper Midwest. In many ways, Macalester's development mirrored that of similar institutions of the period. Yet Macalester was also distinctive, not least in the fact that it survived. In the first three quarters of the century, a large percentage of small colleges failed, particularly in the closing quarter. Almost always, these failures were due to insufficient funding. Macalester came very near to this fate on more than one occasion. Indeed, its very founder recommended in 1892 that given its deepening debt and inability to pay its professors, the college be "temporarily suspended until there is sufficient money."[1] Contingency, then, is among the reigning themes of Macalester's founding and first half century. It was against the odds that Macalester College opened its doors at all. That those doors remained open not only through the nineteenth century but also through the next and into the present was not foreordained. That they did sets Macalester apart from the majority of its nineteenth-century peers.

As we shall see, Macalester's success in remaining open through times of financial crisis stemmed in large measure from its willingness to change, to reinvent its institutional identity. Fluidity has characterized the institution's identity as it responded to the shifting historical events and changing cultural and social contexts of the late nineteenth and twentieth centuries.

Change and History Writing

The story told here, then, is one of change, of transformation in the identity of the single college as well as transformation in the understanding of the role of religion in the enterprise of education. Thus this story or narrative is intended to contribute to three distinct areas of historical inquiry, encompassing not only local communities but also national ones.

Most college histories are local in a particular way. Required to justify the ways of the institution to its alumni, their goal is to foster good feeling within this local community. Good feeling, it is assumed, will broaden and deepen financial support. Authors of college histories absorbed in this model tend to be alumni themselves or longtime employees of the college. The narratives they write emphasize the prophetic vision, hard work, and determination that set the institutional ball rolling and culminated decades later in the great institution that currently exists. They might mention a few bumps and obstacles the institution faced along the way, but the general trajectory of the narrative is progressive, even foreordained and inevitable. The story told has but one ending, resounding success, which it reaches through an inexorable set of events, circumstances, and contributions.

This book is not that kind of a history. For one thing, I am neither an alumna nor a longtime employee, though I worked at the institution for nearly seven years. More important, my interest in this subject lies in the phenomenon of the church-related college as a unique and ever-changing institution, rather than in the advancement of this particular institution. The public that I address as an author is threefold and as such places significant impediments on the creation of a triumphal historical narrative. Yes, I do address the Macalester community. But as I have come to know it, this is not a community interested in triumphalism or self-congratulation. Well-educated and thoughtful, the many alumni, faculty, administrators, and trustees to whom I have spoken in the course of researching this book all agreed on one thing: their deep curiosity about the changes that occurred in the institution and their need to understand just how the college was founded, developed, and changed over the course of the twentieth century. Their disdain for a whitewashed, triumphal story has been palpable.

Second, this book is intended for a broader local and regional community interested in the historical development of the Twin Cities. Macalester sprang from one of the first privately funded institutions in the state, the Baldwin School, and over the years, it has benefited from the support and leadership of many of the area's most prominent citizens. While this is Macalester's story, it is inexorably linked to the history of this unique dual-city region.

Last, this study is intended for two academic communities. First, individuals interested in the history of higher education will find this story of Macalester a useful case study of how one institution responded, both in terms of curriculum and policy, to a vast array of cultural events and transformations that took place during the late nineteenth and twentieth centuries. Second, students of religion in America who have been attempting to come to grips with the relationship between Christianity and education will find much of interest in the story of Macalester. As a member of this community myself, I have woven some of its predominant inquiries into the fabric of this text, most prominently the questions of what role the college played in processes of secularization and how it responded to them.

The Role and Meaning of Church-Related College History

The tragedy of September 11, 2001, and the resulting awareness of religious diversity that it thrust on the nation and the world have given new impetus to efforts to understand how religion functions. Though the study of religion in the United States has a long and distinguished history, the institutional context in which most examinations of religion take place is that of the church, synagogue, mosque, or temple, that is, institutions dedicated to worship, polity, and thought. Yet in the United States, religious training has also come through church-related schools, be they Protestant, Catholic, Jewish, or more recently, Buddhist, Hindu, or Muslim. Yet we know relatively little about the role of religion at these institutions—how they have integrated scholarship and new ideas with traditional religious views, how they have shaped the moral character of their students, how they have participated in their communities and in national trends, and so on. With respect to Protestant church–related colleges, the dearth of information is particularly troubling, not only because such schools have trained many who have gone on to become leaders in all sorts of fields, but also because the institutions themselves have played important roles in the changing character of Protestantism and of American culture itself.

Among the important sociocultural transformations in which church-related colleges, including Macalester College, have played a key role is the cluster of changes over the course of the twentieth century that is generally referred to as *secularization.* Recent scholarship on church-related colleges has generally focused on how and why institutions that were originally church related loosened their denominational ties or detached completely from their religious sponsorship over the course of the twentieth century—a transformation that Macalester clearly experienced. Several models of change have emerged to explain the phenomenon, most of which incorporate or respond to the concept of secularization as a category of sociocultural change. Though some of these writers lament the passing of the religiously based education that previously informed colleges such as Macalester, others acknowledge the shift as a necessary embrace of empirical methods and knowledge, and others point out that religious practice remains active in many colleges through student and cocurricular activities.[2]

What the present study aims to examine is how colleges like Macalester contributed to the very construction of the category of the secular as they negotiated the rocky terrain between nature and revelation, science and religion. Just how and why did religiously conceived colleges like Macalester become distinctly nonreligious in institutional outlook and pedagogy while at the same time continuing to foster student religious activities in cocurricular locations and programs? And how did these processes relate to situations or transformations in the broader society and culture? At Macalester, we will see a variety of processes and circumstances that repeatedly, indeed continuously, influenced and transformed the relationship between the college and its Presbyterian identity over the course of the twentieth century. The component that remains consistent is not the institution but rather the students' ongoing search for meaning—transcendent, ethical, social, and cultural—within the knowledge they acquire and the experiences they have during their four years in residence. Macalester students, like students across the United States, have pursued this search for meaning in accordance with, and frequently in spite of, the messages emanating from their institutions. The task of this study, then, is to take the strands of national and cultural change exemplified in these themes and expose their presence in the narrative warp of Macalester's history, thereby not only telling a story about the institution but also exposing its role and the role of other originally church-related colleges within the broader history of education in the United States.

We live in a period in which knowledge about one's heritage is increasingly invested with cultural capital. We seek our roots in everything from immigrant ship manifests to DNA. Thus, at this point in time, there is growing interest in the history of those institutions that have shaped our lives. Yet this is a relatively new development. Rapid change frequently brings a desire to forget, to get past the tension and conflicts and look forward to promising new days. Until quite recently, this has been the attitude that has pervaded the Macalester campus with respect to the college's history.

Those of us who write history know full well that our efforts function not just on the level of the advancement of knowledge, but also on a political level. The writing of a historical narrative has potential use for advancing any number of specific agendas. There will be those who will attempt to use this story of Macalester for their own ends. As a historian, it is not my intention to advance or counter any politically motivated agendas regarding the college. I wish neither to celebrate nor denigrate the institution. My goal has been to put together a historical narrative that accurately reflects some of the major challenges faced and transformations achieved by the institution based on the data available to me.

Noted British historian Eamon Duffy has observed that good historical writing negotiates between narratives of continuity and narratives of disruptedness. Disruptedness, or change and transformation, yields a sense of the "strangeness of the past," he explains, "and sets us looking for narratives to tame and claim it."[3] Disruptedness, which in the current study takes the form of changing identity, can easily evoke anxiety or even fear, a sense of rootlessness. Narratives of continuity, in contrast, can reassure that the important things remain unchanged over time. "History is about continuities," Duffy also writes. "The historian weaves stories that rope together the disparate worlds of past and present, tracing meaning in the arbitrary jumble of what would otherwise be just one damn thing after another."[4] Continuity is not without its pitfalls, however. Bogus patterns of continuity are triumphalist and legitimizing, "fake pedigrees, to demonstrate that this is how things have always been, or how they have to be."[5] Some individuals connected to the college would variously argue opposing sides of this paradox: everything has changed or nothing has changed. It is on ground between these two camps that this historian must plant her flag. Macalester College today is by no means the place it was in the 1890s, yet without its former self, it would not be the institution that it currently is, nor the institution it will become in years hence.

2

Christian Education and
Institution Building in St. Paul

PIG'S EYE, WITH ITS HANDFUL OF RESIDENTS, mainly whiskey traders and a few French-Canadians, was one of only a few white settlements in the Minnesota Territory in 1838. Yet it was less a settlement than a loose collection of people living within a few miles of one another at the confluence of the Mississippi and Minnesota rivers. The majority of the inhabitants in the region were Native Americans—Dakota, primarily, but some Ojibwa—who had long since established winter villages and ceremonial centers on the lakes and rivers of the area, and particularly here, where the two rivers met. But during the period, French-Canadian immigrants and mixed-race peoples, along with a variety of trappers, whiskey traders, and other entrepreneurs, had come on the heels of the U.S. Army, which had established a fort at the confluence in 1825. Pig's Eye came into being only because the U.S. Army's Fifth Regiment kicked the whites off the military reserve's perimeter in the late 1830s. Fed up with the impact of the alcohol trade on the native peoples technically under their charge, the military brass expelled the whites for illegally inhabiting lands that the U.S. government had not yet opened to settlement. Some of those occupants undoubtedly moved on down the river, but the Mississippi is narrow and readily crossed here in its upper ranges, and many simply relocated to the other side (the east bank) of the Mississippi River, a region not controlled by the military. Among those who relocated was Pierre "Pig's Eye" Parrant, perhaps the most notorious of the whiskey traders, who seems to have lent his name to the rough settlement on the east bank. Pig's Eye, then, as the settlement came to be known, was clearly not founded with much thought to permanent settlement, much less institution building.[1]

Soon, however, signs of change became apparent. In 1841, Father Lucien Galtier arrived as a missionary to the region. Welcomed with open arms by the small community, in which, if any religious group dominated, it was French-Canadian Catholics, Galtier set about establishing a permanent church and succeeded in erecting the Chapel of St. Paul on land on the river bluff donated by two of the settlers. The residents, as historian Mary Lethert Wingerd explains, were "so delighted with their first community institution that they rechristened the river settlement in its honor."[2] With these efforts, then, institution building in St. Paul began. Over the next several years, a variety of civic leaders would emerge, intent on establishing the benefits of eastern American cities in this frontier area.

It may seem an unusual choice to begin a study of Macalester College with a portrait of early St. Paul. After all, the college was not chartered until 1874, and it did not open its doors as a postsecondary institution until 1885, all well after the founding of Pig's Eye and even quite a while after the Minnesota Territory had become a state in 1858. Yet the opening of the college was the culmination of decades of work by several individuals deeply involved in establishing the institutions of the eastern United States—the churches, schools, and government structures—in the little river town on the banks of the Mississippi. Though Macalester came rather late in the process of institution building in St. Paul, its roots reach deep into the city's very origins.

Those roots lead directly to Edward Duffield Neill, a man of multiple interests and occupations: missionary, preacher, educator, and historian. Neill, as this chapter will show, conceived of the very idea of a Christian college on the frontier and struggled for decades to make that idea a reality. This conception of a Christian college was part of a broader endeavor on the part of many individuals to build a city through the establishment of government, development of land, and founding of civic institutions. This is the story of how Macalester College fit into that process of early community building.

Institution Building in the Early Years in St. Paul

Neill, a native of Philadelphia, stepped off the deck of a steamboat called the *Senator* onto the Jackson Street pier at St. Paul for the first time on April 21, 1849, at the age of twenty-six. He had boarded the boat two days earlier at Galena, Illinois, where he had been living for the past two years. There he had launched his career as clergyman. The Presbyterian Synod of Galena had granted the young easterner, fresh out of Andover Theological Seminary in Massachusetts, a preaching license and, later, ordination. On the strength of this advancement, he had married his sweetheart from back home, with whom he had corresponded for years: Nancy Hall of Snow Hill, Pennsylvania. She had joined him in Galena, and the two had begun a life together, knowing that they would soon be leaving the relatively settled region of Illinois for the vast reaches of the newly opening frontier, for Neill's vocation lay in missionary work. Within months, the American Home Missionary Society sent him up the Mississippi River to Minnesota, where the tiny village of St. Paul was in need of a Presbyterian presence.[3]

At the time of Neill's arrival in St. Paul, the village was rugged. It had lost its unpleasant original name only a year before. White settlement was growing, as others from the East sought their futures and fortunes on the frontier. Efforts to establish local government in the region had started in 1847, spurred in part by the efforts of the neighboring territory of Wisconsin to enter the Union as a state, a task accomplished in 1848. Minnesota, it seemed, was lagging behind. A coalition of men formed to organize the region to the northwest of the Mississippi as a territory of the United States. On April 9, 1849, the Minnesota Territory, with its capital at St. Paul, was established by the Congress of the United States. Twelve days later, Neill arrived. As one of the few eastern-educated men in town, Neill was drawn almost immediately into the developing leadership group. On September 3, 1849, at the first legislative assembly of the newly formed territory, he gave the opening prayer. Thus began Neill's involvement with institution building, which would eventually lead to the founding of Macalester College.[4]

During the next several years, Neill would come to understand his duty as lying on two fronts: evangelizing and education. His commitment to these tasks grew directly out of his own background and upbringing. Born into the relatively well-off household of Dr. Henry and Martha Duffield Neill in 1823, Edward began his education at the age of fourteen at the preparatory school of the University of Pennsylvania in his hometown of Philadelphia. Two years later, in 1839, he entered Amherst College in Massachusetts, the alma mater of his older brother Henry. Neill's later vision for Macalester College stemmed directly from his experiences at Amherst, a place that served for Neill as an ideal model for Christian education. For our purposes, scrutiny of Amherst not only provides insight into Neill's later thought but also serves as a useful window onto higher education in the mid-nineteenth century.

Amherst College, in west central Massachusetts, had been founded in 1821 by Congregationalists (Congregationalism being a denomination descended from

New England Puritanism) concerned about educating the inhabitants of the new nation. Their goals were at once religious and civic. Indeed, similar motivations underlay the development of all higher education in America in the seventeenth and eighteenth centuries, as Protestants, concerned about bringing education to frontier areas, set about creating institutions to do so. As historian Donald Tewksbury succinctly puts it, "The American college was founded to meet the 'spiritual necessities' of the new continent."[5] The earliest institutions—including Harvard (est. 1636), William and Mary (est. 1693), Yale (est. 1701), and Princeton (est. 1746)[6]—were sponsored by the established churches in their respective colonies and thus enjoyed exclusive claims to providing education within them. Essentially, one college existed per colony, and it was controlled by religious elites. Only with the disestablishment of churches brought about by the First Amendment to the Constitution of the new United States did the field open for the founding of colleges that might compete with these flagship institutions, yet disestablishment itself was a lengthy process, being completed only in 1833, when Massachusetts finally succumbed. Even so, a few hardy exceptions sprang up, Amherst being one of two colleges allowed to open in Congregationalist Massachusetts prior to that state's official adoption of church-state separation.

Amherst would become not only Neill's alma mater but also his ideal of a model college. It provided its students an experience that mirrored the prevailing model of a residential young men's college. Faculty served as both professors and live-in parents. The curriculum emphasized gaining knowledge and training the intellect in what would now be called critical thinking skills. These goals, as articulated by the influential *Yale Report* of 1828, encompassed "fixing the attention, directing the train of thought, analyzing a subject proposed for investigation; following, with accurate discrimination, the course of argument; balancing nicely the evidence presented in the judgment; awakening, elevating, and controlling the imagination; arranging, with skill, the treasures which memory gathers; rousing and guiding the powers of genius."[7] The Amherst curriculum included Latin and Greek grammar, mathematics, natural science, philosophy, rhetoric, and logic.[8]

Most important, though, Amherst emphasized character building through religious study and practice. Colleges of the period were decidedly religious in their outlook and epistemology. The president of Yale had argued in 1743 that "the great End of all ... Studies is to obtain the Clearest Conceptions of Divine Things and to lead you to a Saving Knowledge of God in his Son Jesus Christ."[9]

The source of all knowledge was God, and thus all study ultimately led to greater knowledge of God. And the study of God went well beyond courses. Neill's biographer, Huntley Dupre, quotes a contemporary of Neill's describing the college in his undergraduate years: "There were two sermons on the Sabbath in the college church, and there was a religious lecture every Thursday evening. In 1832, morning prayers were set at 4:45 in the summer and at 5:45 in the winter. These and the first class were held before breakfast."[10] Amherst was steeped in evangelicalism, the belief that even though conversion could only be initiated by God, the church could and should help to prepare the unregenerate individual for salvation. A primary strategy for moving the unregenerate along the path to conversion was the revival, a period marked by enthusiastic preaching, worshipping, and praying. At Amherst, as at most colleges of the time, revivals among the students were frequent, aimed at evangelizing those in their ranks who were not fully committed to Christianity and at deepening the faith of those who were. Such revivals produced strong interest in missionary work and likely gave Neill his first taste of the fervor of his fellow students for evangelizing in undeveloped territories.[11]

Although the purpose of schools like Amherst was to prepare young men for a variety of professions, entry into the ministry was the favored route of most graduates during this period. Neill's much-admired brother Henry, for instance, had gone on from Amherst to a noted career in the ministry. Neill, however, who graduated in 1842, was initially hesitant to pursue such a vocation, and he looked into opportunities in the military and commercial business before beginning a teaching career. The noted minister of First Presbyterian Church in Philadelphia, the Reverend Albert Barnes, seems to have taken Neill under his wing during this period, and the young man soon left teaching to embrace a religious vocation.[12]

Neill's entry into Andover Theological Seminary in northern Massachusetts exposed him to denominational issues that would concern him for the rest of his life and inform his vision for Macalester College. Andover, founded in 1807 by New England Congregationalists as a Calvinist response to the growth of Unitarianism at Harvard, emphasized the orthodox Calvinist belief in individual responsibility for sin, along with an understanding of evangelism that was more liberal than that which held sway a century earlier.[13] Congregationalism and Presbyterianism, both descendents of Calvinism,[14] faced similar theological challenges during this period, though they differed significantly on questions of polity and governance. Though Neill would have been steeped in the Andover Congregationalism—one student said that during his years at Andover, doctrine was "hammered in . . . hammered down tight and the nail clinched on the other side"[15]—he likely retained a strong connection to the more hierarchical Presbyterian practices through his relationship with Barnes. The Congregationalists, however, were more enthusiastic about missionary work than were many Presbyterians, and Andover students firmly embraced missionizing. In addition to sending out dozens of missionaries in its early years, the seminary also graduated the men who founded the influential American Home Missionary Society in 1826. A decade later, the Presbyterians would split into the Old School and New School factions, with the former remaining suspicious of revivalism and the latter embracing it.

Neill's mentor, Albert Barnes, a New School Presbyterian, endorsed a view of the evangelical role of the church within a modified Calvinist theology that the Congregationalist Andover Seminary propounded. New School Presbyterianism was Calvinistic, to be sure, in its emphasis on the depravity of the individual soul and its need for regeneration, yet it was strikingly liberal in its optimistic view of evangelism as the means through which individuals could be guided out of sin and into God's embrace. By seeking conversion, a powerful and personal experience of God's saving grace, individuals could begin the process of achieving salvation, though conversion could only be culminated through supernatural, divine means. Conversion, like salvation, remained God's prerogative, but human agency could play a role.[16]

Alignment of Congregational and Presbyterian thought preceded these discussions about revivalism. Their shared Calvinism had brought the two denominations together in the context of voluntarism as early as 1801, when they had entered into a Plan of Union agreement that allowed interdenominational exchange of ministers and attempted to minimize competition between the two denominations by regulating extension into new geographic regions. An early attempt at what would now be termed *ecumenism*, the Plan of Union was abrogated in 1837 by Old School Presbyterians, a conservative faction that disclaimed the union on the grounds that Congregationalists did not necessarily subscribe to the Westminster Confession recognized by the Presbyterians since 1643. Nevertheless, Neill, exposed to New School Presbyterianism under Barnes's influence and trained in two Congregational institutions, would have found it natural to encourage alliances in fulfilling the important task of evangelizing.

Indeed, his education had exposed him to some of the period's most advanced, ecumenical ways of thinking about religion. Just as the disestablishment of state-sponsored religion was encouraging religious voluntarism and resulting in an explosion of separate religious denominations, Neill was embracing evangelism as his personal mission and launching a career that would be noted for its efforts to unite evangelicals across denominational boundaries.

Neill did not, however, immediately pursue this religious vocation on leaving Andover around 1844. Instead, he was again diverted by his interest in teaching. Though we know little about his experiences immediately following his graduation from seminary, December 1846 finds him resigning from a teaching position in Accomack County, Virginia.[17] Clearly teaching held a strong appeal to the young man in these formative years. By the time he arrived in St. Paul, evangelizing and teaching had become tightly intertwined for Neill, and together they would form the basis of his contributions to the development of the young town. Though advancing Christianity in general, and Presbyterianism in particular, among the new settlers in the region was paramount, Neill deeply believed that if Christianity and St. Paul itself were to be successful, both would need an educated citizenry to take the lead in the coming decades, a view clearly informed by his experiences at Amherst.

From the evangelical perspective, education rooted in the understanding that God made all possible things, and thus all knowledge, served as the fundamental cornerstone for Christian society, and only a Christian foundation would support the unique experiment in self-government that the U.S. Constitution put forth. Missionary work among whites in the western reaches of the republic frequently adopted the tones and rhetoric of Manifest Destiny, championing the extension of Christianity throughout the region as a necessary public good and national right. Religion and education went hand in hand. Thus, even while Neill busied himself establishing Presbyterian services, founding the First Presbyterian Church of St. Paul with eight charter members, he became deeply engaged in efforts to establish public and private education in the region.

As the new territory was being organized, he helped to establish public schools in St. Paul and wrote their mission statement. That statement, articulating ideas that Neill would publicly endorse on many occasions in coming years, emphasized the connections between religion and education in the democracy that he held so dear. Stating that intellectual and moral education was "essential to our present happy form of government, and that virtue and intelligence are the only pillars on which republican governments can safely rest," the mission statement went on to delineate a model of education: "The three great departments are physical, intellectual and moral.... Man should be educated for eternity, and fitted to take his place among those whose employment it will doubtless be to diffuse happiness throughout the sphere in which their Creator destined them to move.... Morality and religion should be regarded as the most essential elements of education, and should hold their due prominence in every institution of learning... and bigotry, fanaticism, and narrow-minded sectarian prejudice alike be for ever excluded from every temple of knowledge."[18] Here, for the first time, Neill set up a rhetorical distinction between sectarian education, which he saw as bigoted and narrow-minded, and another, more authentic religious education. He would come to term the latter *nonsectarian*, a phrase that would inform many future generations associated with Macalester College.

With the writing of this mission statement, Neill established himself as a leader in education in the territory, and his career took off. In December 1849, a month after this statement was produced, Neill participated in a groundbreaking meeting founding the territorial Committee on Schools, and when the legislature voted in 1851 to create an Office of the Superintendent of Schools, Neill was appointed to the position, in which he served for two years.[19]

In 1850, Neill got his first taste of higher education administration, becoming involved in preliminary efforts to form the territorial University of Minnesota. The university was established the following year on a modest basis, but within a few years, growing financial embarrassment closed its doors.[20] When the Minnesota Territory became the state of Minnesota in 1858, the legislature appointed Neill the first chancellor of the new state university. In this position, he would work to reopen the doors of the ailing institution. But times were difficult; the school had accrued significant debt, which only deepened during the depression of 1857. Despite his best efforts, Neill was unsuccessful in improving the financial footing of the institution, prompting his decision to resign the chancellorship in February 1861. Frustrated with the penuriousness of the legislature, Neill remarked in his resignation letter that not only had he served in the dual capacity of chancellor and state superintendent of public instruction "without any compensation" since March 1860 but he had also had to employ a clerk, furnish office supplies, and travel at his own expense.[21] His optimistic forecast that "the day will come when I will be paid in full, with interest" never seems to have arrived, but his efforts would be rewarded with the continuing loyalty of the recipient of the letter, Governor Alexander Ramsey. The university would not reopen until 1867.[22] Unfortunately, this experience of founding an institution amidst severe financial deficiencies, resulting in the delayed opening of said institution, set a pattern that would be repeated in the case of Macalester College.

Neill, a man of enormous energy, was not simply a missionary and an educator; he was also a serious historian. Having done some historical research in Virginia prior to his emigrating to the West, Neill embarked on what would become a lifelong study of the history of Minnesota on his arrival in the region. Like his work for the Presbyterian Church and the public schools, Neill used his scholarship to advance the civic character of St. Paul. In December 1849, he helped to found the St. Anthony Library Association and presented a public talk at its first meeting. The next month, he helped to found the Minnesota Historical Society, lecturing on early French missionaries and voyageurs in Minnesota at that institution's first public exercises.[23] Thus, in these early years, Neill's reputation as an educator, scholar, and minister quickly coalesced into an example of public service based on deeply held Christian principles, and Neill became an important leader in early St. Paul.

This is not to say, however, that Neill's life and work were without obstacles. St. Paul remained a frontier town, and the lack of capital would prove problematic for decades. Neill felt this strongly, for as a missionary, he was beholden to others for his subsistence. Although eastern congregations and organizations, such as the American Home Missionary Society, liked the idea of evangelizing the West and donated significant monies to the cause, almost all missionaries throughout the region found themselves strapped for support for their nascent congregations as well as for their own families. Neill, like other missionaries, looked on his field as his home, and he soon had a growing family for which to provide. Nancy had joined him in St. Paul shortly after he arrived, and we can get a sense of their life in early St. Paul through family stories about Nancy's experiences that have been handed down over the years. For instance, before departing Galena, Nancy had apparently heard that St. Paul was a dirty town, so she had brought a broom with her. Despite her best preparation, though, when she first gazed out at St. Paul from the deck of the steamship, she reportedly asked the captain to take her back to Illinois. Neill's friend Henry Rice, a former fur trader and already one of the prominent political leaders in the region, met Nancy at the landing, shouldered her broom, and walked up Beach Street with her, "chiding her for not wanting to stay."[24] One can readily understand her dismay, however. The boardinghouse in which the Neills set up housekeeping was de-cidedly rustic, particularly for a woman from Philadelphia. Nancy's memories of the place, reported by her daughter some eighty years later, included a vivid recollection of the splinters from the bare floors and the thin walls that hindered private conversation between the couple—particularly given Edward's partial deafness. The Neills soon moved to another boardinghouse and then to a small frame building at Fourth and Washington, in which Edward established the First Presbyterian Church. Soon a brick house was erected on the same lot to serve as a parsonage for the tiny chapel.[25] The following spring, Nancy gave birth to their first child, a girl, who, in a display of the Neills' growing affection for the region, they named Minnesota. Minnie would be followed by four brothers over the next decade.[26]

With a growing family, a paltry income from his missionary and educational work, and insufficient funds to erect a permanent church, Neill embarked on a search for funding that would occupy him until his dying day. In the hope of finding donors in the East who believed, as did he, that establishing Presbyte-rianism on the frontier would be a key to the advancement of the region, Neill journeyed back to Philadelphia—by steamboat, stagecoach, and train—during the summer of 1850 to raise money among Presbyterians there for the St. Paul congregation and other evangelical projects. This first trip, unfortunately, would set the tone for many subsequent ones, for though Presbyterians in long-established eastern congregations were interested in western missionary work and willing to support it somewhat, donations would never be adequate for the task. During the summer, Neill kept Nancy apprised of his progress through a succession of letters, whose tone shifts from optimism to resignation over the course of only a few weeks. For instance, early in the trip, he reported to her that he had seen a nice Gothic building that would be ideal for St. Paul's First Presbyterian Church, and he estimated that such a building could be erected in St. Paul for about fifteen hundred dollars; moreover, the First Presbyterian Church of Philadelphia, under the leadership of Neill's good friend and mentor Albert Barnes, had already pledged $750.[27] As the summer wore on, however, Neill raised little more for the frontier church. The lovely Gothic building would never materialize, and the St. Paul congregation would have to settle for a small, wood-framed chapel instead.

Nevertheless, during this and many later trips, Neill established and kept current relationships with a number of wealthy and leading Philadelphians who would eventually provide support for his projects, particularly his educational efforts. Among the people he met during a fund-raising trip in 1851 was wealthy locomotive maker Matthias W. Baldwin, who shared some of Neill's Presbyterian connections, including acquaintance with Albert Barnes and membership in the First Presbyterian Church in Philadelphia.[28] Baldwin was interested when Neill explained the need for Christian education in the new Minnesota Territory and, in December of that year, agreed to donate fifteen hundred dollars to an academy or prep school Neill wished to establish. Baldwin also loaned Neill ten thousand dollars to erect a building. In response to this munificence, Neill named the school after Baldwin, though the benefactor protested, writing in a letter to Neill that it should be called "Neill College" because "if it is established at all, it would be by your influence and Labour."[29] Albert Barnes, who remained Neill's loyal supporter, also donated to the project and the Baldwin School. Neill requested official status for the school, and the Baldwin School was duly incorporated by the Fourth Territorial Legislature in 1853. He then obtained a lot for the school facing what is now Rice Park, in the heart of St. Paul, and with the help of the first trustees—Alpheus G. Fuller, Henry F. Masterson, William R. Marshall, Henry L. Moss, Gideon H. Pond, Alexander Ramsey, J. G. Riheldaffer, and Joseph C. Whitney—succeeded in erecting a substantial building. This would be the first in a long line of schools that Neill would spearhead in the coming years, culminating in Macalester College.[30] It also established a strong East-West relationship between Philadelphia businessmen and the new Minnesotan minister and educator that would continue for decades.

The Baldwin School, the first educational institution in the Minnesota Territory established through private funding, constituted a significant achievement for the young town, and its opening was observed with a gala dedication celebration held in the new building on the evening of December 29, 1853. Even with a heavy snowfall blustering outside the windows, over three hundred guests arrived to enjoy a late evening of dinner, music, and toasting. Neill opened the festivities with a dedication speech lauding the symbiotic relationship between men of education and men of mechanics and commerce—a topic clearly designed to merge the goals of the school with the source of Matthias Baldwin's fortune, the manufacture of locomotives. Other guests, following a ritual brought with them to the snowy frontier from their colleges and institutions in the East, expressed their sentiments about the new school in lengthy, extemporaneous toasts, which extended the celebration far into the early morning.[31]

These toasts, offered up on such topics as the relationship between religion, education, and the republic, contained ideas that would not only inform the first private educational institution in the region but would remain prominent thirty years later, when Neill and others present at this early celebration would develop Macalester College. Territorial governor Willis A. Gorman, for instance, stated, "Our early forefathers did not forget, while forming written constitutions for government of civilized man, to provide ways and means to educate the people, as essentially necessary to perpetuate what had been thus gloriously begun."[32] Echoing these sentiments, newspaper editor T. M. Newson spoke on the topic, "The Great Constellation of American Freedom—Common Schools and Free Education, controlled by the principles of pure morality and true religion—disconnected with sectarian dictation and sectarian dogmas,"[33] and the Reverend T. R. Cressey, who presided over the event, addressed the topic of "the Common Christianity of the Republic—May its principles ever be maintained by our rulers and the instructors of our youth."[34] As these toasts suggest, for these men, neither the U.S. republic nor the territory of Minnesota could thrive without education, and education was incomplete without a firm knowledge of evangelical religion.

Beyond placing this educational effort in the Manifest Destiny context of the civilizing of the nation through the expansion of republican government, education, and Christianity, two other important themes surfaced that evening. First, Neill and others championed the education of girls and women, the Baldwin school having officially opened only the Preparatory Female Department at that point in time. Neill, echoing then popular ideas about gender difference, assured the crowd that given the "organic differences of the sexes," a girl who attended Baldwin would "not [be] taught how to be *manly*" but rather would "receive that culture of her faculties and sensibilities which will make her fit to discharge all the duties and grace every position that becomes a *true woman*," with the goal to make her an "attractive and intelligent companion."[35] Thus a tone was set for gender-segregated education. The reality of the Baldwin School, however, was somewhat different. The twenty-eight boys who had been admitted to the school (compared to forty-three girls) were not mentioned during the evening. The school catalog, however, noted that the inclusion of the boys aged twelve and under in the female department would be only temporary, until the male department opened, which it did a year later, under the name of the College of St. Paul.[36] Although officially enrolled in two different schools—the girls in the Baldwin School and the boys in the College of St. Paul—the students all took classes together and shared the handful of teachers. The pragmatics of the situation were simply that the number of female students available to enroll overmatched the number of male students. Because operating costs came out of tuition, the more students enrolled, the better. Some thirty years later, this same tension between the desire for gender-segregated education and the fiscal practicality of coeducation would fuel significant debate as Macalester College opened it doors to admit students.

A second theme emphasized that the Baldwin School brought together education and a somewhat generalized evangelical religion. Neill drew on his ecumenical training as he explained to those present that "however some of the Trustees may differ upon non-essentials in doctrine, they are unanimous in the opinion that the great truths taught by the God-Man, the son of the carpenter, should be prominently kept before the minds of the pupil. Nothing but pure and undefiled religion can cleanse the heart, and impart the ornament of a meek and quiet spirit."[37] Ethics and epistemology combine in this view, designed to unite individuals of a variety of religious backgrounds. Action and knowledge together spring from Jesus, a theme prominent in the nineteenth century, and the Baldwin School would present a curriculum laced with daily religious observance and Bible study.[38] This approach, uniting religion and learning, was expressed graphically in the Baldwin School's seal, which portrayed the two themes as classically garbed twin sisters. One sister, representing science, holds a telescope, and near her feet lies a compass; the other, representing divine revelation, holds an open Bible. Around the seal appears the motto *Natura et Revelatio, coeli Gemini* (Nature and Revelation, Heavenly Twins). In other words, God has revealed himself not only in the word of the Bible but also in Nature, which we study through science. An understanding of both is needed to know God. Apparently designed by Neill, this now familiar image remains the seal of Macalester College to this day.

Yet defining the proper elements of theological thought and religious practice was not easy. As mentioned earlier, an explosion of denominations in the nineteenth century indicated a wide range of views on these topics. Protestants did not agree on several fundamental issues. Such disagreement among Christians led to the third theme emphasized during that gala evening: a latitudinarian tolerance of evangelicals of any denomination. Springing from Neill's eclectic religious background, which combined Congregational and Presbyterian elements, as well as from the reality of denominational diversity among the small population of St. Paul, the group was willing to obliterate old theological prejudices and denominational quarrels to present a united evangelical front to the world. Presaging a theme that would become repeated frequently over the next several decades and that would eventually be adopted by Macalester College in the 1880s, Neill explained, "While the Trustees will carefully guard it [the Baldwin School] from being distinctly known as a Baptist, Episcopal, Methodist, or Presbyterian school, they will use their utmost endeavors to make it a Christian school, in the best and highest sense of the term, in which the truly good of every shade of belief will have the fullest confidence."[39] This idea of a Christian school characterized by the cooperation of a diverse group of Protestants unified by their evangelical outlook would be codified in the term *nonsectarianism*, and this term would became embedded in the college's rhetoric for over a century. A remarkably fluid, mutable, and multifaceted term, *nonsectarian* would take on new meanings in the coming years, leaving its original meanings far behind.

The celebration broke up that snowy night at about three in the morning, as the partygoers plunged back into the blizzard to return to their homes. In the next weeks, the Baldwin School, supported by donations from Matthias Baldwin, Albert Barnes, and Nancy Hall Neill, whose inheritance seems to have been put at least partially toward the project, launched evangelical education in the small town of St. Paul.[40]

Not all were pleased with the establishment of institutions like the Baldwin School, however. The St. Paul school was established within a context rife with religious debate, distrust, and discrimination, as tensions mounted between the Catholic majority in the town and the expanding Protestant culture. Two months after the Baldwin School dedication, St. Paul's Bishop Joseph Cretin complained to a friend in France that "the Presbyterians are building at a 1/4 of an hour distance from St. Paul, a college that will cost 500,000 francs; 10 leagues further, the Methodists are building another one costing 600,000. All this money comes from subscriptions collected with the avowed purpose of stopping the progress of Papism in the State of Minnesota."[41] Even more frustrating to Cretin was the Protestant ethos that increasingly pervaded the public schools in St. Paul. In his view, the public schools were "taking the children free of charge . . . expenses covered by Bible societies. They inspire these children with such a hate of Catholicism that it is very difficult afterwards to have them return to us."[42] The only alternative, Cretin urged, was the formation of Catholic parochial schools.

In fact, during the same legislative session in which the Baldwin School was chartered, a contingent of Catholic legislators presented a bill requiring that public monies collected through taxes for schools be made available to "all communities of any denomination, willing to have a school of their own, in which religious instruction will be taught as well as other branches of education"—an appeal that is striking in its similarity to current twenty-first-century discussions of funding private religious schools.[43] Neill, recording the submission of this bill and resulting discussion in his *History of Minnesota*, revealed his disdain for it, writing, "The moderate of all denominations, and the friends of the American system of public instruction, were surprised at the introduction of a bill with such features."[44] His implication is clear: those who supported the bill—Catholics—were neither "moderate" nor "friends" of public instruction. A sermon he delivered on the topic clarified his objections to Catholic complaints against Protestant-oriented education in public school and Catholics' efforts to be released from taxes used for these schools to fund their own schools. In his view, the state owed its citizenry education in American principles, which were wholly antithetical to what he called "sectarian schools," that is, schools in which priests educated children in allegiance to the pope rather than republican government.[45] The bill was voted down, and with the concurrent approval of the charter of the private Baldwin School, Catholic concern for the growth of Protestant education expanded.

A year earlier, Neill had addressed the issue in his 1852 official report on the schools in Minnesota. In that report, he presented a discussion of the selection of textbooks in the public schools and complaints from Catholics that the schools used a Protestant version of the Bible.[46] The texts under consideration here were the Catholic Bible (the Douay Bible) and the King James version used by Protestants. Neill, deploying his views regarding sectarianism, argued that the Catholic position was untenable in an American classroom. He explained that to "receive the support of the *entire community*," the state could not be "too careful in excluding works that have a sectarian bias."[47] In Neill's view, the Catholic Bible was by definition sectarian; the King James version was not.

Around this same time, Neill also argued against public support for Catholic education in an opinion he delivered as superintendent on a request by the Irish and German Catholic residents of a small Minnesota town to be released from their attachment to the local school district and allowed to have their children attend a different school in a nearby town. Though Neill ultimately ruled that the petitioners could send their children to school in the other town if the superintendent of schools and trustees there allowed it, he took the opportunity to again issue a statement against Catholic education. In the statement, he argued that the state could not recognize any relevance with regard to the group's religious outlook and that it "inculcates the morals of Christ in her public schools, simply because they are the best adapted to promote the common weal." He continued by alluding to the nonsectarian argument, saying that the state "also sternly eschews the imparting of the distinctive dogmas of any branch of the church of Christ by any public school teacher." The goal of public education was to teach "the children of Irish, German and American settlers and teach them to sing national songs and love Washington, the Father of the Republic, and a greater than Washington, the 'Father of Spirits,' and the 'author of every good and perfect gift.'" To criticize such as inappropriate to Catholic children was to Neill an opinion based solely on misguided dogma: "A republic can only exist by fostering general intelligence, and urging citizens to lay aside all improper sectional and religious prejudices. In your town it appears that a majority recognize the Pope of Rome as the Supreme and Infallible Head of the church on earth, but in a majority of towns in the State it is far different."[48] Outraged at Neill's public impugning of Catholicism, the author of an article in the *Northwestern Chronicle*, a Catholic newspaper published in St. Paul, lambasted Neill as a longtime anti-Catholic, who had worked for years on a number of fronts to malign the faith.[49]

Because this tension between Catholic and Protestant education would continue for many years, and because Neill would become closely identified with the advance of Protestant education in the region, it is important to examine the relationship in some depth. In the context of this tension, the language of the toasts given at the Baldwin School gala takes on further meaning. One of the toast themes mentioned earlier—"the Great Constellation of American Freedom: Common Schools and Free Education, Controlled by the principles of pure morality and true religion,—disconnected with sectarian dictation and sectarian dogmas"[50]—elicited a response from T. M. Newson that emphasized that America offered a model of democratic freedom based on widespread education, which directly countered what he identified as Old World despotism based on ignorance. Had the "*people* of France" been educated, he opined, they would have "fully comprehended that working of government and the real benefits of Liberty, the yolk of despotism would [have been] thrown off, and France would be regenerate."[51] In the United States, in contrast, the "general dissemination of intelligence among the *people* [through education]" could be traced to the "Pilgrim Father," whose "struggle . . . gave us the inestimable boon of civil and religious liberty." He went on, "How necessary, then (if the intelligence of a people is the pathway to freedom) that the masses should be educated,—how necessary that common schools should be established, and correct information imparted to the young."[52] Here, the use of France as an example alluded to not only its antidemocratic revolution but also to its predominantly Catholic ethos, which, in the view of many Protestants, controlled ideas and education in ways antithetical to American ideas of democracy and freethinking.

The connections between Protestant ideology, freedom, and public education were articulated more patently seven years later by Neill, as he, acting in his official capacity as state superintendent of schools, rejected another plea to establish a separate Catholic school. In a brief article explaining his decision to deny this request, he wrote, "A fruitful source of difficulty in our Public Schools, has been the reading of lessons from the Protestant version of the Bible. It is believed that upon examination, there will be found no extracts in the reading books recommended, calculated to arouse any religious prejudice."[53] In Neill's opinion, Catholic education was by definition sectarian, whereas presenting a Protestant perspective or using a Protestant Bible in classes was not. Having run up against such roadblocks in public education, it is not surprising that Catholics in St. Paul and other communities across the United States feared that private schools like the Baldwin School were purposive volleys aimed at suppressing Catholics and eliminating Catholicism from the country. Indeed, supporters of the Baldwin School seem to have had little sympathy with or tolerance for Catholicism.

The combination of the issues and themes presented at the Baldwin School gala impress on twenty-first-century readers the fluidity and embryonic state of education during the period. At its opening, the Baldwin School enrolled both boys and girls, although it was termed a female preparatory school (a type of school that in the East would have been termed a female seminary) even at its opening. Neill, emphasizing that the boys' department would open later as the College of St. Paul, essentially encouraged a gender distinction that did not initially exist. His use of the term *college* here, however, did not indicate that the courses were postsecondary in nature; rather, it indicated that the courses were intended for boys, perhaps suggesting what the boys were supposedly preparing for, that is, higher education. Neill would use the term *college* in this way for several years, reflecting in part a widespread uncertainty as to the proper role of education on the frontier. Certainly grammar school and preparatory (secondary) education were needed to provide opportunities for the children of new residents. Parents were more likely to send their girls to such schools because their labor could be more readily replaced. For those boys who did attend secondary school, the eastern model of going on to a four-year college to prepare for a profession, though attractive, was less practical. What, then, was the role of a so-called college in the rural West? Further complicating the question was the rise and expansion of public universities, fueled by the Morrill Land Grant Act of 1862. For Neill, during these years, the college occupied a middle period between elementary and university education, equivalent to what we would now call high school, and aimed only at boys. The slippage, however, between Neill's use of the term and the four-year college model that originated in the East eventually rendered Neill's use unworkable. By the 1880s, he would adopt the term *academy* to indicate this middle period, and he would find an entirely new purpose for the *college*, a purpose that would eventually be culminated in Macalester College.[54]

In the meantime, the fortunes of the Baldwin School rose and fell over the next two decades, as did those of Neill. That clouds were on the horizon might have been foreseen as early as 1853, when Neill had suggested to Baldwin that he endow a female college (or seminary), only to be turned down flat due to the manufacturer's unstable financial situation. Though Neill had visited Philadelphia that summer, he had found few people willing to contribute to the new Baldwin School or to the advancement of Presbyterianism on the frontier. In 1854, with the tuition receipts for the Baldwin School and the College of St. Paul not covering expenses, concern grew. Donations from the East remained sparse, and by 1855, even Neill's mentor Albert Barnes pointed to "hard times" as the reason that support for religion and education were waning among his congregation.

Minnesota, however, along with other western states, experienced something of an economic boom in 1856–57, which led to the extension of credit and higher debt loads, creating an economic bubble just waiting to burst. Neill, apparently encouraged by the upswing, took advantage of the easy credit and obtained a mortgage to build a new home for his family. The fashionable house, inspired by architect Alexander Downing, stood atop the ridge just above First Presbyterian

Church and was one of the first to venture into this hill district, an area that would become the most important residential area in the city by the 1880s.[55] With his family settled, Neill continued to lobby for the Baldwin School.

Late August 1857 brought the pin that burst the bubble, bringing financial crisis to the East Coast. Shortly after, in the words of Minnesota historian William Watts Folwell, "panic struck Minnesota with extreme violence. . . . Everyone was in debt, and the territory was literally emptied of money."[56] Real estate that had been sought after in previous months was suddenly worthless. Neill was among those to find his family and his projects in peril. As the country slipped into a deep depression, Baldwin's promised financial support was repeatedly delayed, and Neill's repeated trips east yielded little.[57] By 1861, the Baldwin School had closed.

Thus the early history of educational development that would ultimately lead to the founding of Macalester College exhibited nothing like smooth sailing. In fact, as the country was poised on civil war, the future of Christian education in Minnesota looked decidedly bleak. So, too, did Neill's own future. As the minister of the new House of Hope Presbyterian Church, which he had helped found in 1855, Neill had some steady income, but it barely covered the expenses of his family, which now included five children.[58] In 1860, he was reappointed state superintendent of schools, but that position brought with it little salary. Casting about for other options, Neill had turned to the historical work that would sustain him through the rest of his life. His first monograph, *The History of Minnesota; From the Earliest French Explorations to the Present Time*, appeared in 1858, and his second, *Dahkotah Land and Dahkotah Life*, followed a year later. The books, sold by subscription, brought in some income, but the return was meager.

By the time civil war broke out, Neill was ready to try something new, and in June 1861, he accepted appointment as chaplain of the First Regiment of Minnesota Volunteers.[59] Over the next several years, Neill's need to support himself and his family took him not only far afield from Minnesota but also away from his work to establish Christian education. The idea of establishing a Christian college in Minnesota waned as Neill struggled to support his family.

Though Neill likely accepted the post as chaplain in part in an effort to obtain a regular salary, the post soon proved problematic. By the fall of 1861, he was publicly protesting federal efforts to reduce the salaries of military chaplains, and he began looking for alternative employment. The following July, he resigned his commission.[60] With no certain prospects in sight, Neill went to Washington, D.C., a town filled with refugees seeking employment. In a poignant letter to Nancy, he explained the seriousness of the situation: "As yet I find no opening for myself. It is surely possible that I may obtain a Hospital chaplaincy yet, while I do [illegible] [illegible] my heart upon it. Until I find something to do if you can manage with one servant, it is perhaps advisable to do it. In a month I hope to find employment of some kind, but until then you must manage to live on the [illegible] money and what you have for to be candid I have not a cent. If in a month I do not succeed I will be obliged to borrow to support my family. I am this frank because as my wife I feel you ought to know the true state of my affairs."[61] Within a few days of this letter, Neill's friend Alexander Ramsey, who, by then, was governor of Minnesota, succeeded in using his influence to get Neill appointed chaplain to a military hospital in Philadelphia. In high spirits, Neill shot off a letter to Nancy, telling her of the new appointment and saying that she could keep the servants.[62] Plans soon changed, however, as Nancy rented the house and moved the family to Philadelphia. Neill, then, spent most of the war in Philadelphia, but early in 1864, he was appointed one of several secretaries to President Abraham Lincoln, a post that, though bringing him into contact with a president he admired, turned out to be tedious work.

Neill had not forgotten Minnesota, however, or his determination to establish a Christian school there. About the same time he went to work for Lincoln, he redoubled his efforts to get the Baldwin School going, explaining his plans to Nancy in a letter: "Mr. Baldwin has written to me that he has seen Mr. Barnes and Dr. [Brainard] and that they both approve of my project to unite the two corporations in a Baldwin University. If he would only immediately endow one professorship and designate me, it would be very agreeable as then we would have a fixed income for life and could make definite plans for the future."[63] For a man with a family of five children, such a desire was hardly surprising.

Once again declaring his determination to "build up an institution of learning dedicated to Christ and to Country," Neill entreated on Baldwin with a specific request for funds to endow a professorship at an annual income of fifteen hundred dollars. He was, however, to be disappointed again. Though Baldwin sympathized with Neill's frustrating employment as secretary, saying, "I feel with you, you ought to be otherwise employed, and in a department more congenial to your feelings and more usefull [sic] to the public," he explained that at that time, he could not make the arrangements Neill requested.[64] Neill's search for a new position continued. In March 1865, Ramsey led an effort to have Neill appointed commissioner of the newly created Freedman's Bureau, but after the assassination of Lincoln, this post was given to another.[65]

Though he continued to communicate with Matthias Baldwin during this period, in the hope of reopening the Baldwin School, Neill would not be successful. Baldwin's death in April 1867 came as a particular blow to Neill because the Philadelphia manufacturer left no provision in his will to sustain his namesake institution in faraway Minnesota. Compounding the loss of this benefactor, Baldwin's heir, M. Baird, called in the mortgage of ten thousand dollars that Baldwin had extended to Neill for the construction of the Baldwin School. When Baird had agreed to dissolve the debt for eight thousand dollars cash, Neill and the trustees of the College of St. Paul sold the college property (i.e., the Baldwin School) to the Board of Education of the City of St. Paul for a mere five thousand dollars.

Once the matter was resolved, some assets, probably related to the original donations, remained, for Neill made plans to use them to endow a new Baldwin Lectureship Fund, which would sponsor lectures on the "history of human government, especially as modified by the ethical system of Christianity."[66] This topic had preoccupied Neill for many years; though his stint in the Lincoln administration likely fueled it, his earlier work in establishing several institutions in St. Paul and the Territory of Minnesota and his work on the *History of Minnesota* had no doubt created the foundation on which it stood.[67] His third book, *The Fairfaxes of England and America in the Seventeenth and Eighteenth Centuries Including Letters from and to Hon. William Fairfax, President of the Council of Virginia, and His Sons Col. George William Fairfax and Rev. Bryan, Eighth Lord Fairfax, the Neighbors and Friends of George Washington*, published in 1868, dealt with these topics at length in relation to the Christian ethics undergirding early governance in Virginia.

The next summer found Neill being considered as a candidate for a faculty post at the University of Minnesota, but neither the efforts of Ramsey nor then governor William R. Marshall were successful in gaining Neill a position. Somewhat reluctantly, Neill accepted appointment as consul of the United States at Dublin on September 13, 1869, and packed his family off to Ireland. During his time in Dublin, he would develop close links with Presbyterians and other Reformed groups and complete another book, *The English Colonization of America during the Seventeenth Century*.[68] As Neill journeyed to Ireland, his idea for a Christian college was, for the time being, postponed. It would not, however, be abandoned.

The Contingent Nature of Frontier Development

Looking back on the history of a successful institution such as Macalester College, it is easy to develop a sense of a progressive inevitability about the process: A happened, then B, then C, all in their necessary order and right on time. The picture we accumulate from closely tracing Neill's efforts between 1849 and 1869, however, is characterized more correctly as an ongoing struggle with minimal or at best modest accomplishment. Of course, he and Nancy did successfully raise their family, and Neill contributed a great deal toward the establishment of both Presbyterianism and education in St. Paul, but his dream of establishing a college remained elusive, thwarted, it seems, at every turn due mainly to the lack of capital. As interested as his eastern coreligionists may have been with respect to spreading Christianity on the frontier, they were by no means generous beneficiaries to the cause.

Nevertheless, his vision of an ideal institution, intertwining progressive historical development, education, democracy, and Christianity, remained a powerful motivator. As we will see, the establishment of Macalester College was far from an inevitable occurrence. Although Neill hoped that establishing Christian education would serve as a beacon on a progressive trajectory of the establishment of civilization on the frontier, the reality would be far different. For when the college was at last established, it was less a shining beacon than a testament to the dogged tenacity of Neill and a small group of men who shared his desire to see Protestant higher education in Minnesota.

3

The Idea of a
Christian College

BY 1869, MINNESOTA AND THE NATION were recovering from the wounds of war. Industry began to expand, and completed projects such as the transatlantic cable and the transcontinental railroad were widely hailed. The country seemed to be entering a new era of prosperity. In the upper Midwest, the lumber industry was booming, attracting immigrants and others. International and East Coast investors looked to the region for moneymaking opportunities. The July 5, 1869, issue of the *New York Times* carried an article on Minnesota by a correspondent traveling in the region that claimed that investors from Amsterdam were exploring railroad expansion in the region. E. D. Litchfield of London and George L. Becker of St. Paul were overseeing the development of a project that would extend the railroad across the state and eventually to the Pacific coast. While their efforts were not successful, they do tell us something about the positive mood of the region.

Five years later, George L. Becker would be named in the original charter for Macalester College as a founding trustee. Historical documents do not indicate whether Edward Duffield Neill knew Becker at this time. Nevertheless, Neill, ensconced in Dublin between 1869 and 1871, was in correspondence with friends in Minnesota and likely learned that the financial outlook of the region held promise. His thoughts turned once again to his dream of establishing a Christian college in the region. Yet even now, progress toward fulfillment of that vision would be slow. It would take another fifteen years before the college he envisioned would open its doors.

Jesus College: A Controversy among Presbyterians

By 1871, Neill was ready to resume his efforts to establish a Christian school in the West. In the fall, he took a leave of absence from his consulate post in Dublin, and by December, he had resigned entirely to return to Minneapolis. There, on the urging of his sister Emily, he redoubled his efforts to establish a Christian school. Arriving in St. Paul, however, he learned that, boosterism aside, the financial situation had improved little and, in fact, was worse than he expected. The monies that had remained at the close of the Baldwin School before the war had vanished. "The Baldwin trustees [were] faint-hearted," he wrote in his memoir, "and . . . the treasurer had carelessly invested several thousand dollars."[1] Neill would have to start over from scratch.

He was encouraged, however, by the support of at least some of the original Baldwin School trustees. Though we can only speculate on Becker's participation, trustee Henry M. Knox clearly urged Neill on, writing that although there was some difference of opinion among the trustees, "for my own part I believe our churches are much in fault in not having candidates for the ministry and that a movement in the direction of a school would [bring] the duties & responsibilities of the churches in their regard fully before them & awaken an interest therein." He also pointed out, however, that the timing was somewhat unfortunate in that the St. Paul Presbyterians had other priorities than supporting a new college: "All three of our St. Paul [Presbyterian] churches are now committed to building improvements based upon pledges [obtained] through the year—our own in the sum of nearly $13,000 in addition to our first subscription of some $17,000."[2] Writing about the period several years later, Neill remembered that at this point, he resolved that "if a college for young men was to be established upon a Christian basis in the vicinity of Minneapolis and St. Paul, it would have to be done by the patience, endurance, and pecuniary sacrifice of some one, owing to the apathy of the community upon the subject."[3] What he needed was a new benefactor.

Two years later, Neill reopened the Baldwin School as an academy, but he and Emily paid the school's expenses for some time.[4] The building they rented for the new school was the Winslow House, a large former hotel located on the east bank of the Mississippi River near St. Anthony Falls in Minneapolis. This building would play two major roles in the development of Macalester College. First, its location about a mile from the University of Minnesota sparked a new scheme for the role of Christian education. Second, the building, owned by

Philadelphia businessman Charles Macalester, would eventually catalyze a new and crucial financial arrangement that would significantly benefit the college.[5]

The new conceptualization for the role of Christian education likely fully emerged from Neill's experiences in Dublin. There he was exposed to the English university system, which housed multiple discrete colleges under the auspices of a single university. Here was a possible means of integrating religious education into the new University of Minnesota, an institution whose charter prohibited religious education, a provision that was a source of deep regret for Neill. Using the British model, Neill began to plan an entirely new college, one that would be associated with the University of Minnesota, perhaps eventually a component of the university, but administratively and financially separate. Neill wanted his college to provide university students with what he considered an essential component of a sound education: a thorough understanding of Christianity. No education was complete, he argued, without a deep understanding of "the history of the Bible; of Jesus, the founder of our religion and civilization; and the history of the church of Christ, before it was separated into the Greek and Roman organizations."[6] The new institution would thus provide education "supplemental to the State University which is avowedly secular."[7]

The new college, which he created through expansion of the Baldwin Academy in the Winslow House, encompassed a preparatory school, still called the Baldwin Grammar School (to prepare boys for university), and a School of Christian Literature for University of Minnesota students—the latter effort marking Neill's first actual foray into undergraduate education. Like his earlier efforts, the college was advertised as "unsectarian." Attempting to attract students of broadly Protestant upbringing, Neill enthusiastically asserted that the college did not present any particular denomination or interpretation of Christianity, stating that it would follow neither "Luther or Calvin or Laud" in outlook, referring to Lutheran, Calvinist, and Anglican (Episcopalian) perspectives, respectively. When critics later charged that the college was in effect a divinity school, Neill adamantly denied such an intent: "The Institution is not under the supervision of the Presbyterian or any other branch of the church," he wrote. "It has been founded in truth and love, and desires the confidence of all those who so cling to the teachings of Jesus that it is impossible to keep them from peeping over their denominational fence."[8] In Neill's view, the teaching of a true Christianity could bring down those denominational boundaries with which he was growing increasingly uncomfortable.

Having embraced the British institutional model, Neill also adopted a British-derived name for his new institution, Jesus College, a name that would become immediately controversial and, in the views of some, heralded both Neill's arrogance and the institution's downfall. Just why he chose the name is open to speculation. Neill, who during the period was intellectually moving away from Presbyterianism and toward a more latitudinarian Christianity, likely selected it because it signaled the central figure in all Christianity, a unifying figure that all revered in common. Furthermore, the major British universities in Cambridge and Oxford both housed Jesus Colleges, institutions founded in the fifteenth and sixteenth centuries, respectively. Neill found the name appropriate in part due to the connections of these British institutions to the Protestant cause; Jesus College in Cambridge, for instance, was the alma mater of Archbishop of Canterbury Thomas Cranmer, who compiled the Anglican Book of Common Prayer and thus firmly set England on a liturgical path distinct from that of the Roman Catholic Church. Neill took pains to explain these connections. For instance, a bulletin for the Jesus College chapel service, presumably written by Neill, opens with two epigraphs taken from correspondence between Cranmer and Reformed divine John Calvin, illustrating the intellectual and religious roots of the enterprise. In addition, handbills advertising the new college visually alluded to such venerable medieval institutions. Featuring an ornately illuminated *J* at the beginning of Jesus College, the handbills depicted a Gothic ruin with a tonsured monk wandering among the overgrown foliage, an image that clearly suggested historical connections to Britain or Europe.

Despite Neill's best efforts, Jesus College did not flourish. Only a handful of students signed up for the college course, though the Baldwin School attracted respectable numbers. Apprehensions regarding the name "Jesus College" among both Presbyterians and other Protestant evangelicals seem to have doomed the effort. Many felt that such use of the Lord's name was in fact blasphemous and refused to be associated with the effort. Years later, Neill's critics still charged that selection of the name "Jesus" for the college not only damaged Neill's credibility with the religious community for decades to come but it also put off those who might have contributed to the next institution Neill would champion: Macalester College.[9] Whether this was correct, Neill did make a special effort to explain and justify the name "Jesus College" in response to remarks made by Eugene M. Wilson, then mayor of Minneapolis, who had aired what Neill found to be unacceptable statements about Jesus College at the dedication of the Scandinavian Lutheran Theological Seminary (now Augsburg College and

Luther Seminary) in Minneapolis. When Wilson apparently compared Jesus College to the Lutheran seminary, Neill replied, "Jesus College is in no sense a Professional Divinity School. It is designed merely as a supplemental school to the University of Minnesota, which needs the support of all the good men of the State."[10] He went on to explain that the name "Jesus College" was appropriate for such an institution because knowledge of Jesus, "the founder of our religion and civilization," is essential to a complete education. Furthermore, nonseminary institutions called "Jesus College" existed at both Cambridge and Oxford, and because Jesus is the "name above every other name," he argued, it is far more appropriate than "'Yale,' or 'Harvard,' or 'Washington,' or 'Jefferson.'"[11] Neill concluded his response by expressing his hope that given that the "secular university" was prohibited by Minnesota law from providing religious instruction, the time may come when "we may see clustered around the University, the Divinity Halls of the followers of John Calvin and John Wesley as well as that of the followers of Martin Luther."[12] Here his embrace of the British model of several colleges under the auspices of a single university is clear, though the irony of his efforts to import an administrative model embedded in the class stratification of Britain for republican American educational purposes remains unacknowledged.

Although Jesus College was short-lived, Neill's idea for this institution would become the foundation of later efforts that would see the light of day in Macalester College. Neill remained convinced that a postsecondary institution providing Christian-based education could and should flourish in the region, and by the mid-1870s, other regional models—one might say competitors— were achieving some success. In addition to the Lutheran institution mentioned earlier, Hamline University, a Methodist institution that had been founded in Red Wing, Minnesota, in 1854 but had closed in 1869, was, by 1873, rebuilding in the St. Paul area. Carleton College, founded by Congregationalists at Northfield, Minnesota, as an academy in 1866, had introduced college-level classes in 1870. The time was increasingly ripe for Protestant higher education, and Neill, who still had the backing of several of the original Baldwin trustees, was determined to move ahead with his plans. All he needed was financial backing.

A Hesitant Benefactor, Charles Macalester

The Baldwin School's location in the Winslow House brought about a relationship between Neill and Charles Macalester, a Philadelphia financier, who would play a pivotal role in Neill's scheme to establish college-level Christian education in the region. Macalester, a successful and well-connected businessman and financial broker, had served as the government director of the Second Bank of the United States in Philadelphia during the mid-1830s and continued to advise high-level government figures on financial matters. He had a reputation as a philanthropist, contributing to the founding of the Philadelphia Presbyterian Hospital and the Macalester Presbyterian Church, located near his estate in Delaware. Interested in preserving his Scottish heritage, he was president of the St. Andrew's Society from 1864 until his death.[13] He also lived near Neill's sister Emily in Philadelphia and likely met Neill during his stint at the South Street military hospital in Philadelphia during the war.[14]

Ever seeking financial support, Neill tried to interest Macalester in contributing to the expansion of the Baldwin School to include a Christian college. Macalester responded with little enthusiasm, noting (fairly accurately) that the country was "swimming in educational institutions, most of them crippled and always in pecuniary trouble."[15] Drawing on his previous experience in Philadelphia, he countered that he was more interested in establishing a hospital in the western region. Neill and Macalester continued to correspond through 1873, and Neill eventually won him over, although he never donated funds directly to the project. Nevertheless, in October, Macalester added a codicil to his will bequeathing the Winslow House to establish "Macalester College." Less than two months later, he was dead. Shortly after, the property was transferred to the trustees of Macalester College, on the condition that an endowment of twenty-five thousand dollars be raised within three years. Three and a half years later, the probate court would name Neill the executor of Macalester's will with respect to the deceased's property in Minnesota.[16]

Charles Macalester's death came at a time when Neill was becoming increasingly frustrated in his efforts to establish Christian higher education. For two years, the Baldwin trustees had thwarted his efforts to establish Jesus College, perhaps owing to the enterprise's latitudinarian religious focus, or perhaps owing to its unconventional name.[17] With the legacy from Macalester, he wanted to ensure that the trustees would not misunderstand the purpose of the bequest or misdirect the use of the property. He took immediate and rather covert steps to guarantee that Macalester's wishes for the Winslow House property would be understood as the establishment of a Christian college with Neill as its head, and he did so by emphasizing Macalester's Presbyterian background.

In a condolence letter to Macalester's daughter Lily Macalester Berghman, Neill suggested that she write a letter to himself detailing and clarifying her father's wishes for the use of the legacy. He then went on to draft language for the letter, suggesting that she write something along these lines:

Upon your return from Dublin my father became much interested in your effort of building up a College in the Valley of the Upper Mississippi upon a broad Christian basis but thoughts [well] of your [big] questions [suggestions] that two-thirds of the trustees should be attendants upon Christian worship in the Presbyterian Churches of Minneapolis and Saint Paul. His own catholic [spirit] would not have been in sympathy with an exclusive sectarian college, and he would not wish the Trustees to hesitate in electing a Baptist or Congregational professor provided he would only inculcate the [courses] of Christianity within students. It was also his wish and expectation that you should be the Presiding Officer of the College.[18]

A week later, she responded, thanking Neill for his expression of sympathy and enclosing "a transcript of the letter you sent me with the addition of a few words of my own which I hope you will not think inappropriate."[19] Echoing Neill's prose, she wrote,

Upon your return from Dublin, my father was pleased to hear of your determination to lay the foundation of a college, upon a broad Christian basis, in the valley of the Upper Mississippi, and thought well of your suggestion that two-thirds of the trustees should be pew-holders or attendants upon worship in the Presbyterian churches of Minneapolis and Saint Paul. My dear father's catholic spirit was not in sympathy with an exclusive sectarian college, and he would not have wished the trustees to hesitate in electing a good professor simply because he might be a Baptist or Congregationalist, provided he did not attempt to press his denominational dogmas upon students. With the expectation that the college would remain under your supervision, he made the donation of the building upon the terms mentioned in his will.

Lily Macalester Berghman's letter thus became the legal foundation on which Neill's continuing insistence that Macalester be a "nonsectarian" Christian college rested and on which he would attempt to retain headship of, and later a professorship in, the institution. Although previous historians have traced the blend of nonsectarian Christianity and Presbyterianism to Macalester on the basis of Lily Berghman's letter, it is clear from Neill's earlier letter to Berghman that he was in fact the originator of these ideas, particularly those regarding the religious character of the college.[20] Neill's blending of denominational and nondenominational language was another strategic move to bring together yet another coalition to move forward his dream of a Christian school; that it would ultimately prove successful did not mean that the road ahead was in any way smooth.

Christian Unity and the Meaning of Nonsectarianism

Given that the term *nonsectarian* would become embedded in the outlook and mission of the college for generations to come, it is appropriate that we take a close look at the contexts in which it was originally used and the meanings it carried at that time. It is important to keep in mind, though, that over the course of the twentieth century, the term *nonsectarian* took on new and surprisingly different meanings, as will be examined in later chapters.

By the mid-nineteenth century, sectarianism, or the tendency of Christianity, and particularly Protestant Christianity, to split into a host of competing groups or sects, had become the bane of evangelical Protestants. With the disestablishing of religion required by the Constitution of the United States, with its ratification in 1788 but fully accomplished only in 1833, religious groups—be they Presbyterians, Congregationalists, Baptists, Methodists, Episcopalians, Lutherans, or Catholics—found themselves competing more and more earnestly for members in the new voluntary context. For Protestant evangelicalism, with its emphasis on the necessity of the individual decision to seek a relationship with Jesus Christ, the trend had been moving toward proselytizing and evangelizing for decades, and the added component of competition among groups for converts simply increased their fervor. Many of these groups sponsored enthusiastic revivals aimed at converting nonbelievers and bringing the newly wrought Christians into their particular folds. By the 1830s and 1840s, congregations were using their new and elaborate churches as a means of attracting members, Sunday schools were launched throughout the country as a way of attracting children to denominational identities, and missionaries like Neill were being trained to follow white settlers into frontier areas to spread their particular brand of gospel message.

Yet many like Neill wondered why Protestants had formed so many denominations. If Christianity was indeed a universal religion, why was it so divided?

Denominational distrust and one-upmanship were rampant, and Protestant Christianity, which kept splitting into new forms, seemed to offer so many different understandings of Christianity as to render even core truths suspect. The areas of religious disagreement were legion. What was the meaning of baptism, and who, infant or adult, was a legitimate candidate for it? What constituted a legitimate conversion experience, and who instigated it—God or the individual? What was the meaning of the Lord's Supper, and how should it be presented? What was the meaning of Christ's death and resurrection? What constituted proper worship? What readings, prayers, and music were appropriate? How should congregations be organized? What was the role of the clergy and whence did they derive their authority? What governance structures were appropriate? And what was the relationship between these structures and heavenly governance? Lutherans, Presbyterians, Congregationalists, Baptists, Methodists, Episcopalians, Unitarians, and others all brought distinctive perspectives on these questions to the table. Though Neill, in his latitudinarian optimism, had written of teachings acceptable to "Luther, Calvin, and Laud," in reality, profound ideological issues divided these groups.

Furthermore, in a period in which Roman Catholicism was gaining a stronger foothold in cities across the United States due to increasing immigration, the proliferation of Protestant sects, each with its own truth claims, laid evangelical Christianity open to charges of hypocrisy and inconsistency by leaders of this new "outsider" group. Many Protestants, still steeped in Reformation-era animosities, saw such charges from Catholics as uniquely significant. Moreover, the trend toward ultramontanism in the Catholic Church, or centralizing ecclesiastical power and doctrine in Rome, was seen by many Protestants as incompatible with republican government, American ideas of democracy, and the free exercise of conscience. Catholics, some Protestants felt, could never become "real" American citizens because their allegiance was necessarily to Rome.

Within these contexts, a yearning for so-called Christian unity developed among some Protestants in both the United States and Europe. In Europe, various attempts to form alliances between Lutherans and Calvinists (Reformed Protestants) occurred, including an effort to build a Protestant cathedral in Rome. In England, and later in the United States, an organization called the "Evangelical Alliance" gained members. Intent on bringing Protestant evangelicals together, yet motivated in part by opposition to Catholicism, the Alliance held yearly conferences and worked to advance Protestant religious ideology.

What, then, in this context of a widespread yearning for Christian unity in the face of deep divides, did the term *nonsectarian* mean? The term worked on two different levels, the first referring to a latitudinarian ideal of a singular Protestantism and the second to an anti-Catholic perspective that helped define this unified Protestantism by its negative example.

First, for Neill and many others, it meant a generalized Protestantism that avoided questions of polity (or governance) and focused on a shared view of Christ as the source of all life, knowledge, and salvation. Denominational, or sectarian, particularities could be swept aside as Christians focused on Christ. Yet as eloquent as Neill may have been in advancing an idea of religious education that was not specifically connected to any particular sect, others readily understood that such a dream was absurd. Presbyterians, Methodists, Congregationalists, Lutherans, and others were devoted to their distinctive practices and outlooks.

One new group on the religious scene, however, shared Neill's desire for unity. The Reformed Episcopal Church, organized by George David Cummins, had begun as a secessionist movement within the Episcopal Church but had declared its independence from that body in 1873. Protesting the growing Anglo-Catholicism within the Episcopal Church—that is, the increasing adoption of the liturgical and aesthetic characteristics of the Catholic Mass into Episcopal worship—this group of evangelicals was attempting to carve out middle-ground positions on theology and believed that shared worship could serve as a meeting point for all Protestants. The new church's critique of Catholicism fueled its quest for Christian (read Protestant) unity. As historian Allen C. Guelzo has argued, Cummins's group was "at the center of a fierce struggle between the rationalist impulse of the Evangelical mind in the nineteenth century . . . and the Gothic Romanticism of the Anglo-Catholic, between classical Protestant dogma and gaudy Catholic ritual, and between the symbols of Whig republicanism and the ambiguous antimodernism of an industrial consumer culture."[21] One important feature of the church was its adoption of Bishop William White's 1785 modification of the Book of Common Prayer, which the Reformed Episcopalians felt was unsullied by the Catholic changes to the Anglican and Episcopal creeds and rituals of the nineteenth century.

This effort to reassert the Reformed lineage of the Episcopal Church appealed to evangelicals like Neill, who yearned for a unified Protestant Christianity. As Cummins wrote, "We build in hope, hope of a better day, a day of the re-union of Christians, of a church of the future, that shall not be sectarian, but a confederation of all Protestant churches."[22] Given Neill's interest in Christian unity and his familiarity with the Church of Ireland in Dublin, it is not surprising that the Reformed Episcopal movement captured Neill's attention. He had harbored similar goals and interests for decades. Here was an organization devoted to eliminating sectarian rivalry by offering a rational evangelical alternative. In January 1874, Neill initiated a correspondence with Bishop Cummins, and by March, he was seriously investigating the possibility of joining the church and transferring his ordination to it.[23] For Neill, the attraction of a denomination that would bring together all denominations was palpable.

The Reformed Episcopal Church, however, would never flourish. Despite its efforts to demonstrate its low-church, even antiliturgical, stance, many evangelical detractors seem to have considered the Reformed Episcopal Church a kind of High Church sleight of hand, a refuge for Protestants attracted to liturgical formalism but unwilling to "go all the way" to the Episcopal Church.[24] Indeed, many seem to have confused the Reformed Episcopal movement with the well-established Protestant Episcopal Church. Even Neill's biographer mistakenly explained his interest in the church as an outlet for an interest in liturgical worship.[25] This was as far from Neill's motivation as it was from that of the Reformed Episcopal Church, however. The Reformed Episcopal Church eschewed liturgical formalism. As Neill pointed out in a circular describing specific differences between the Reformed Episcopal Church and the Protestant Episcopal Church, "The Reformed Episcopal Church allows no church decorations, vestures, postures, or ceremonials calculated to teach, either directly or symbolically, that the Christian ministry possesses a sacerdotal character, or that the Lord's Supper is a sacrifice; and also forbids that the communion table shall be constructed in the form of an altar."[26]

Neill's move away from Presbyterianism was fully consistent with his Calvinist background and with his previous pronouncements toward Christian unity and nonsectarianism and constituted an unmistakable articulation of these principles. He took pains to explain that in joining the Reformed Episcopal movement, he "reject[ed] no former belief," and in a conciliatory move, he explained, "The Presbyterian Church must always be a happy home, for very many of Christ's people." He continued, "I shall continue to pray for its peace, and prosperity, to watch the paternal solicitude, the churches of the Presbyterian, which with God's help, I have planted; to maintain cordial relations with those Presbyters with whom, for years, I have been associated; and shall always esteem it a privilege to have them assist me, in the solemn services of the Sanctuary."[27] Neill would go on to found Christ Church in St. Paul as a Reformed Episcopal church in 1877 and would serve as its pastor until his death.[28]

Thus the ideal of Christian unity, vividly displayed by Neill's affiliation with the Reformed Episcopal Church, strongly informed his use of the term *nonsectarian* during this period. A second set of meanings that were also associated with the terms *nonsectarian* or *unsectarian* had less commendable roots, however. These meanings related directly to the context of Catholic growth and suggested a distinct prejudice against Catholicism as a religion and Catholics as American citizens.

As Neill and others advanced the concept of Christian unity through nonsectarianism, the flip side of the message had to do with sectarianism itself. To be sectarian was to be tribal, to hold a closed set of wrongheaded beliefs that favored only those who were members of the group. The term *sectarian* became almost synonymous with *bigotry* or *prejudice*, and to Neill and many like him, those most guilty of sectarianism were Catholics. In the historical record, Neill's disdain for Catholic sectarianism appears almost always in connection with education. As mentioned in the previous chapter, the chartering and dedication of the Baldwin School carried with it Protestant concern for Catholic sectarianism and sparked, in response, growing Catholic concern regarding discrimination. Similarly, Neill was sorely disappointed when, in 1877, the state legislature bowed, in his opinion, to "sectarian interests" and amended the constitution to disallow the use of public monies for schools in which "the distinctive doctrines, creeds, or tenets of any particular Christian or other religious sect are promulgated or taught."[29] Catholics had supported this amendment, arguing that the use of the King James Bible in public schools constituted Protestant sectarian education.

Similar debates occurred throughout the United States during the nineteenth century. In Philadelphia, for instance, the so-called Bible riots of 1844 revolved around Protestant, particularly Presbyterian, efforts to control public education and Catholic efforts to resist the Protestant slant of education in the schools.[30] It is not known whether Neill was present in the city during these devastating three days of rioting, but he must certainly have experienced a certain feeling of déjà vu when the same issues arose in Minnesota thirty years later. As with the national conflict, concerns in Minnesota were as much about the integration of first- and second-generation immigrants—Germans and Irish, in this case—as with religious preference.

To Neill, Catholicism, which he saw as controlled by the arbitrary rule of Rome, was necessarily sectarian and, in his view, unacceptable, whereas a latitudinarian Protestant understanding of Christianity was not. A unified Protestantism was not Presbyterian or Methodist or Congregationalist; rather it was simply agreement among the right-minded and thus was an appropriate basis for education, including public education. An important corollary to this argument was that any claiming of denominational identity was unacceptable. Any educational institution or approach that could be labeled, say, "Presbyterian" or "Methodist" or "Lutheran" could be considered sectarian. Yet if a pan-Protestant or nonsectarian approach were taken, focusing on the moral principles of the Bible and a generalized Christocentric theology, as Neill saw them, such an education would be nonsectarian and appropriate. Thus the terms *unsectarian, nonsectarian,* and *sectarian* functioned as a coded language among Protestants during a period of Protestant–Catholic tension. Neill used this language on a number of occasions in ways that alluded to both of these important contexts.

Though not an attractive component of Macalester College's history, we must not ignore the reality of this language and implicit prejudice. During this period, Catholics in the region clearly understood that *unsectarian* or *nonsectarian,* particularly in Neill's use of the terms over a period of some forty years, connoted anti-Catholic feeling and that the group that Neill most frequently identified as a "sect" was Catholics. In fact, in his dedicatory address for Macalester College, Neill referred to Catholics as not only a "sect" but a "foreign" one at that. In contrast to the propagandistic education found in the parochial schools run by the Roman Catholic Church, Neill implied in his speech, Macalester College would take the moral high ground and not advance a particular religious position.[31] Despite this inflammatory public pronouncement, the Catholic author reporting on the opening in the *Northwestern Chronicle* took pains to separate Neill's prejudicial views from the more liberal ones of other supporters of the college, asserting that "Mr. Neil's [*sic*] bigotry was not partaken of by the many respected citizens who assisted with him at the services, and whose liberal dispositions we have had numerous occasions to serve."[32] This spirit of tolerance characterized St. Paul, a city in which Catholics predominated since the earliest years, far more than did Neill's position.[33]

Thus the terms *unsectarian* and *nonsectarian* worked on a number of levels, connoting a range of meanings. From a generalized, ideally unified Protestant evangelicalism to a perspective supposedly cleansed of religious ideology that served as a counterpoint to sectarian (read Catholic) education, nonsectarianism was a pitch designed to blur the boundaries among Protestant denominations and thereby unify evangelicals while maintaining a strong fence against the Catholic sectarians.[34] These meanings would change significantly as Macalester College continued to use the terms over the course of the next century.

The Presbyterian Synod: Another Hesitant Benefactor

The Macalester bequest renewed the trustees' enthusiasm for the college significantly. A request for a charter was put before the state legislature, and in 1874, Macalester College obtained its official status as an institution of higher education, with Neill as president and the previous Baldwin trustees as overseers. The next step was raising the twenty-five thousand dollars needed to satisfy the terms of the will. By July of that year, some members of the board of trustees and a few friends had pledged a total of seven thousand dollars to the school.[35] Neill, who, as we have seen, was already considering the possibility of greater Presbyterian funding, presented a resolution to the board of trustees that two-thirds of their number be "members or pew-holders in Presbyterian Churches of Saint Paul and Minneapolis."[36] The suggestion, ostensibly from Lily Berghman, that Presbyterians be well represented on the board reassured the trustees that despite Neill's defection to the Reformed Episcopal Church, he was not abandoning his Presbyterian roots and encouraged them to focus their fund-raising efforts on the Presbyterian Synod of Minnesota. Indeed, many felt that it was high time for the denomination to embrace its duty to spread Christian education.

The response, however, was lukewarm. The synod was little interested in establishing a denominational college. Although they had some concern that other denominations—specifically, the Methodists, Catholics, Congregationalists, and two groups of Lutherans—had already established denominational colleges in the region and the Presbyterians were lagging sorely behind, their energies were focused elsewhere. Building up local congregations and home and foreign mission work dominated the synod's energies and expenditures. Between 1874, when the college was legislatively established, and 1880, when it was adopted by the synod, the synod spent a total of $3,621 on "education," whereas home and foreign missions during this period received nearly nine times the funding, for a total of $32,872.[37]

These figures illustrate the choices Presbyterian leaders faced during the period as well as the denomination's reliance on the entrepreneurial activities of lay members to establish institutional strongholds in the region. Despite self-congratulatory discussions of Presbyterian support for education, synod priorities lay with evangelizing. Local congregations, concerned with establishing their own churches on solid financial bases, were similarly little interested in contributing substantially to the formation of a college.[38] Furthermore, the synod had already approved the University of Minnesota and encouraged Presbyterians in the state to send their children to it.[39]

Nevertheless, energetic fund-raising by the Macalester trustees was successful, and in February 1875, they sent the executors of Macalester's will an accounting of the twenty-five thousand dollars they had raised. Many of the pledges were listed simply as "loans," and the executors requested clarification of the meaning of the notation. Furthermore, they required that the whole sum of twenty-five thousand dollars be "actually paid or satisfactorily recurred prior to the conveyance of the property to the college," rather than submitted as a collection of subscriptions.[40] The trustees were apparently able to address these concerns, and by April, the deed of conveyance had been signed by all parties. The Winslow House, Neill's largest asset for the establishment of a Christian college to date, came under the control of the trustees of Macalester College.[41] By no means, though, were the trustees in any position to open the school. As far as Neill was concerned, the college had yet to obtain any assets that could be used either to buy property or to erect a more suitable building, for the twenty-five thousand dollars needed to secure the Macalester legacy was, in his view, to be saved to endow the salaries of the professors.[42] What was needed was additional and significant fund-raising.

Neill, of course, had been laying the groundwork for obtaining financial help from the Presbyterian Church. In April 1877, he laid out his work and arguments to the Reverend H. A. Boardman, a friend from Philadelphia.[43] Boardman responded that he thought Presbyterian participation in a successful Macalester College "would be highly advantageous to the cause of sound Presbyterianism in the North West" and that, in his view, the "Presbyterian Church has a very large interest at stake there [in Minnesota] and if true to herself, will not be indifferent to the plans you now have in hand."[44] In fact, the Presbyterian Synod of Minnesota had considered participation in the project as early as 1872, at which time it declined to become involved in college education, but it did articulate support for Neill's Baldwin School and urged Presbyterian congregations to support it.[45] Yet congregational support was minimal, with the Education Committee of the Synod reporting donations of $553 in 1876 and $361 in 1877.[46]

In 1878, the synod reconsidered its position on higher education, deciding to "consult and cooperate with the Trustees of Macalester College, with a view to the immediate establishment of an educational institution in connection with this synod."[47] Negotiations broke down quickly, however, as synod leaders objected to several of the conditions established by the Macalester bequest. These obstacles included the fact that the name of the college was already determined by the original bequest, as were the requirements that the college be located in the Twin Cities area (the official language was "near the Falls of St. Anthony") and that the board be self-perpetuating (i.e., not appointed by an external organization such as the synod). Furthermore, the Macalester bequest placed Neill in the presidency of the college, but Neill's recent resignation from the Presbyterian Church and new association with the Reformed Episcopal Church was, unsurprisingly, not to the synod's liking. Synod leaders argued that the name, site, and governance of a Presbyterian college should be under their purview, and given that in the case of Macalester College, none of these could be, their representatives broke off discussion of the issue.[48]

Two years later, and still stymied in their efforts to raise sufficient capital to get the college up and running, the Macalester trustees were invited to approach the synod with a compromise offer. Some on the board were not, apparently, thrilled to do so, and Henry Moss, Neill's close friend, wrote an impassioned letter to his fellow board members urging them to enter into renewed conversation and cooperation with the synod. As he pointed out, the board, by their own efforts, had "become irrevocably identified with the Presbyterian Church of this State, and... are entitled to the sympathy, support, and liberal Contributions from its members."[49] In a statement that likely dismayed some of his colleagues, he urged them to "make this institution ... the Educational power, not only of this State, but the Entire Northwest, under the fostering care of the supporters of the Presbyterian Church."[50] For those on the board who sympathized with the nonsectarian theme of Neill's vision of Christian education, capitulating to the Presbyterian Synod could not have been a decision made lightly.

In October 1880, the deal was made. The synod adopted the college, agreeing to the terms offered by Neill and the trustees: Neill would resign his post after the synod raised an additional thirty thousand dollars, and then the synod would be able to appoint a new president. In addition, one-half of the current trustees would resign, allowing the synod to appoint replacements. Thus Neill placed his dream of running the college on the table, willingly sacrificing it for the very future of the institution. With this compromise, Neill relinquished his oversight, and a significant portion of college governance was yielded to the synod. This decision to cooperate would have significant ramifications for the college, both positive and negative.

Yet the nonsectarian theme was not entirely abandoned, for the spirit of Macalester's will, as articulated by his daughter, imbued the trustees with a certain responsibility to advance nonsectarian Protestant education. In the next several decades, the continued devotion to nonsectarianism would remain at times an undercurrent and at times a vital element in the developing institution.

4

Twin Cities Rivalry

THUS FAR, WE HAVE SEEN how the early development of Macalester College grew out of a number of contexts: efforts to missionize the frontier, a belief in Christianity as the foundation for knowledge and democracy, and the desire to transplant the institutions of the East Coast in the newly developing trans-Mississippi Midwest. By the time Neill and the Macalester trustees had amassed sufficient capital to seriously embark on creating their college, they faced yet another set of contingent circumstances that would significantly influence their next steps, that is, the growth of St. Paul and its developing rivalry with its twin city, Minneapolis. During the 1880s, as the trustees struggled to develop capital and buy property, these contexts significantly shaped the institution.

By 1880, St. Paul was a much different place than the rugged village on the Mississippi River that had greeted Neill on his arrival thirty-one years earlier. Now capital of the state of Minnesota, St. Paul boasted a population of nearly 41,500. Transportation had been St. Paul's early strength, and on that basis, the city had grown rapidly, becoming home to a diverse citizenry. In the 1850s, steamboats brought native-born Americans from New England and the Mid-Atlantic regions as well as others migrating from the midwestern states of Ohio, Indiana, Kentucky, and Tennessee. These and subsequent years also brought German immigrants—Catholic, Protestant, and Jewish—many of whom went inland to farm, while others moved into trade, manufacturing, and commercial enterprises in the city. Irish immigrants also stepped off the steamboats, some first-generation immigrants but many second- and third-generation Irish Americans. Ambitious and upwardly mobile, the Irish found important opportunities in St. Paul and soon dominated the political and legal professions. Yet no ethnic political machine ruled St. Paul, for the longtime presence of French-Canadians, Germans, and Yankees made for a highly pluralistic society. By the late 1860s, the new railroads were bringing Scandinavian immigrants, and within a decade, eastern Europeans would also begin arriving. If not exactly embraced, this ethnic diversity was accepted as a fact of life in St. Paul. Religion and politics were highly pluralistic, with no clearly dominant group. Catholics and Democrats occupied just as respectable political and professional positions as did Protestants and Republicans, including participation in the highest social circles in St. Paul.[1]

As bright as St. Paul's future may have looked in 1880, something of a cloud was growing on the horizon, or, more specifically, ten miles upriver. Minneapolis, the upstart town that had not even existed when Neill had arrived in 1849, now outstripped St. Paul in population by over five thousand people. Moreover, the two cities were developing distinct characters, which were frequently at odds with one another. Rivalry and increasingly bitter competition between the two were growing. Whereas St. Paul had established itself as a transportation hub and financial center, Minneapolis entrepreneurs took advantage of the Falls of St. Anthony, the only waterfall on the Mississippi River, to establish a successful milling industry in the 1860s. In 1865 alone, that city produced some sixty-two million board feet of lumber. By the 1870s, with timber resources dwindling, the shift was made to agriculture and grain milling, aided significantly by efforts to attract immigrant farmers to the fertile prairies of the state. Soon "King Wheat" would propel Minneapolis into a world-renowned flour producer, shipping some 1.65 million barrels of flour annually during the 1880s.[2] Even though St. Paul entrepreneurs, including James J. Hill and others, would significantly expand that city's transportation network through the development of railroads, Minneapolis's growing industrial base soon resulted in its eclipsing St. Paul as the leading economic power in the region.

Differences between the two cities were social and political, as well. St. Paul's ethnically diverse population worked together, despite having a variety of religious and political affiliations. City government and the professions reflected this diversity, and although the Democratic Party held something of a stronger position, Republicans were by no means shut out of elections. Minneapolis, on the other hand, was home to a more exclusivist Old Stock Yankee elite, solidly Protestant and Republican, which maintained hegemonic control over wealth, politics, and professional life in the city. Not surprisingly, these differences would set the stage for decades of rivalry between the two cities. By the 1880s, the race was on, and many felt that the advancement of one city could only occur at the expense of the other.[3] In the area of institution building, this rivalry would have significant consequences for the development of Macalester College.

Thus it was that the 1880s brought not only new leadership to the Macalester College enterprise, with Neill's stepping down from the presidency and the adoption of the college by the Synod of Minnesota, but also significantly new urban contexts—demographic, economic, political, and geographical—which would have a great deal of influence on the organizers of the new college and its role in the region. In these changing contexts, the idea of Macalester College would come to fruition.

New Partners, New Interests: The Presbyterian Synod of Minnesota

Edward Neill, as we have seen, spent nearly thirty years, from 1850 to 1880, attempting to establish his particular vision of Christian education on what, for many of those years, had been essentially frontier. He had achieved sporadic success in the area of secondary education. The Baldwin School, despite several openings and closings, had attracted a respectable number of students and demonstrated some desire for Protestant parochial education in the region. Neill, steeped in latitudinarian thought and the idea of nonsectarian Protestantism, realized that his efforts toward inclusive Protestantism had a much greater potential for success than did a distinctly Presbyterian school, given that the total number of Presbyterians in the state remained relatively small. Neill also saw the need for Christian education in broad terms. On the college level, he was convinced, knowledge of Christianity would provide a solid foundation for further study in all the professions, from law to medicine to the ministry. He had been explicit that his college was not a seminary, devoted exclusively to the education of clergy. Within the changing contexts of the growing metropolis, however, new and significantly different perspectives on the mission and goals of the college were emerging.

Most prominent among those different perspectives was that of the Presbyterian Synod of Minnesota. Although the synod adopted the college in 1880, the roots of its reluctance to do so earlier were by no means vanquished with that decision. Prior to the synod decision in fall 1880, Henry L. Moss, an original trustee of the Baldwin School and the college (having been a trustee since 1853), pointed out in a letter to the other Macalester College trustees that significant disparity existed between the trustees' purposes and the synod's understanding of those purposes. He wrote,

For several months past I have felt the necessity of some concerted action on our part that would secure the cooperation of prominent and influential Presbyterians, in our efforts to make this institution successful. . . . It is apparent that outside our own number, only a few have known our true position toward the Presbyterian Church of the Northwest—An apparent antagonism to the promotion of religious education in the interest of that church has been attempted, so that harmonious action with us was impracticable—And it gives me great pleasure, that the present opportunity is given to the clergy and leading members of the Presbyterian churches of Saint Paul and Minneapolis to confer with us, and learn our true position toward them.[4]

Just what the "antagonism" amounted to is not made explicit. It may be a reference to debate surrounding Edward Neill's 1874 conversion to the Reformed Episcopal Church, a move that, despite Neill's best efforts to ensure people that his action carried no aspersions against the denomination, seems to have disconcerted, if not angered, at least some Presbyterians in the area. Alternatively, the antagonism may have stemmed from the synod's urging Minnesotans to send their children to the University of Minnesota or from synod perception that a so-called nonsectarian college would not sufficiently meet their needs for the training of Presbyterian clergy. Or it may have had something to do with the Minneapolis–St. Paul rivalry. In any event, it is clear that Moss saw the need to move beyond the prevailing perceptions to establish a spirit of mutual respect and cooperation. He continued,

The necessity of the hour is co-operation and united effort—As a corporate body, we have not the right or power to transfer our trusts to any other organization—Yet by our own voluntary act under our charter, and in compliance with the wishes of those who have bestowed upon us munificent gifts, we have become irrevocably identified with the Presbyterian Church of this State, and I claim that we are entitled to the sympathy, support, and liberal Contributions from its members.[5]

Having made this claim, Moss presented something of a charge to the troops:

Our charter rights are broad enough to embrace all degrees of Education, from the primary to the highest department, including the scientific, legal and theological—Located as we are at the century of the commercial manufacture and political power of the State why not make this institution also the Educational power not only of this State but the entire Northwest under the fostering care of the supporters of the Presbyterian Church?[6]

He concluded with his desire for cooperation with the synod for the sake of the college: "To the gentleman, who may meet with us on the 30th Inst. I beg to say: 'Inform yourselves of our intents and purposes, and then, heartily, and earnestly unite with us, in our efforts, to make this institution, successful and permanent.'"[7]

Despite the vagueness of the specifics in this letter, Moss's language clearly indicates that the relationship between the college (i.e., its board of trustees) and the synod was in need of repair. Some sort of misunderstanding or difference existed, and in his view, it was time to heal the wounds and proceed together in the enterprise to establish the college. Any previous hostility to the synod or the denomination, whether real or perceived, was no longer relevant. Cooperation would be the mode of the new day.

Yet there is no doubt that the Synod of Minnesota felt something of a divided duty. Although the synod worked closely with Macalester trustees in 1878 as they decided to examine the feasibility of sponsoring a denominational college, Macalester College was not the only institution they considered. Another viable proposal was submitted by the community of Albert Lea, located in southern Minnesota near the Iowa border, under the leadership of the Reverend Russell B. Abbott, pastor of the Presbyterian church in that town. Though the Macalester group boasted an endowment of about twenty-five thousand dollars and property in the form of the Winslow House worth between forty thousand and sixty thousand dollars, the Albert Lea group pledged fifteen thousand dollars, a site worth twenty-five hundred dollars, and twenty-five hundred dollars in railroad transportation. According to synod historian Maurice Edwards, the synod's debate over these two offers revolved around its concern that the Macalester site, to comply with Charles Macalester's will, would be required to be near the Falls of St. Anthony and thus in Minneapolis. Given that there may well have been some friction within the Presbytery of St. Paul, which encompassed Minneapolis, and Minneapolis Presbyterians, who felt underrepresented—the synod would actually split in 1892 into three entities: the Presbytery of St. Paul, the Presbytery of Minneapolis, and the Presbytery of St. Cloud—there was significant hesitancy among synod members to accept the Macalester proposal. The Albert Lea location was, in this regard, superior, but to accept Albert Lea would mean giving up the substantial Macalester endowment. Adopting two similar institutions was seemingly out of the question because doing so would stretch meager Presbyterian resources too far.[8]

Nevertheless, in response to the dilemma, the Albert Lea contingent made a compromise proposal: that two institutions be established, one a men's college (Macalester) and one a women's college (Albert Lea). Guided by this plan, the synod adopted the Albert Lea Female College at the same time it adopted Macalester College.[9] Though its financial commitment to Macalester was set at thirty thousand dollars, its commitment to Albert Lea was fifteen thousand dollars. As things turned out, however, the synod's original hesitance in establishing two schools proved correct. The task of raising forty-five thousand dollars would ultimately be too much for Minnesota Presbyterians, and the two institutions would be placed in an uncomfortable competition for synod funding.

In the meantime, the General Assembly of the Presbyterian Church, the denomination's national governing body, had taken up the question of religious education and had decided, within a clearly sectarian frame of reference, that the denomination was falling short. In 1881, the General Assembly endorsed a proposal calling for the establishment of a College Aid Board, and a year later, spurred by the fear that the Congregationalists were well ahead in providing higher education in the United States and that most who entered Presbyterian seminaries had been educated at Congregationalist or secular schools, it stated that "the Assembly enjoins upon Presbyterian church and ministry the urgent duty of endowing and building up Presbyterian colleges and academies already existing, and of wisely planting, endowing and fostering others as they become needed in order to avert and make provision against the impending dearth of candidates for the ministry, and that the Presbyterian church may overtake its sister church in the work of Christian education and regain the place of supremacy to which it is entitled by its grand system of doctrine and equally grand history."[10] This General Assembly directive, coupled with the synod go-ahead, sparked new activity among the Macalester Board of Trustees. The interests of all groups seemed to be coming together, and Macalester supporters eagerly forged ahead.

The Land Deal: Pursuing Profit in the Highland Area

The first thing to be done was to find a new location for the college. The process of doing so plunged Neill and the trustees headfirst into the growing rivalry between Minneapolis and St. Paul and, more disastrously, into a short-lived land boom that promised quick profits for those who invested in the college.

Five years earlier, the trustees had begun a similar search that was cut short after only a year. At that time, they had announced their interest in relocating the school from its original St. Anthony location in the Winslow House, and over the course of the next several months, a subcommittee of the trustees had considered parcels of land at Summit and University avenues, in what is now known as the Macalester-Groveland area; in the new St. Anthony Park, which had been designed by noted landscape architect Horace W. S. Cleveland; and between Fort Snelling and Lake Calhoun, in what is now south Minneapolis.[11]

As they took up the location question again in 1881, the trustees' previous experience dictated that two concerns must guide their assessment of these properties. First, in the context of the growing rivalry between the two cities, the trustees understood that remaining on good terms with both St. Paul and Minneapolis leaders would be crucial in their bid to raise money and goodwill for the college. For the board of trustees, which included men who resided in and had close ties to both cities, locating the new college between the two cities made the best sense—the college would be associated with both municipalities, yet neither. Second, the trustees were aware that the development of a new institution held great potential for boosting municipal and residential development between the cities. The establishment of a large and attractive institution like a college in an undeveloped area might easily set off, many speculated, a stampede of potential buyers for residential and commercial property near it. Macalester College could be used as a kind of bait to lure buyers, deepen demand, and raise property values. Such speculation was justified given the surge in property values in other segments of St. Paul over the previous twenty-five years. Fortunes had been made by those lucky or shrewd enough to amass property in areas prior to the expansion of the city into them.

For any of these development schemes to be successful, however, a substantial college building would need to be erected on the land as soon as possible. Negotiations with each set of landowners stipulated the minimum expense that such a building should cost—usually, around thirty thousand dollars—as a means of ensuring the desired outcome of attracting further development. That there was some discomfort with these schemes is made apparent by the fact that at one point, Neill's good friend Henry Rice counseled Neill to end negotiations with certain "cold hearted selfish men," referring, perhaps, to property owners' desire to use the college as an inducement to spur residential growth and increase property sales.

As the trustees renewed their search for a new location for the college in 1881, they placed Thomas Cochran Jr., a real estate developer and member of House of Hope Presbyterian Church, in charge of the effort. Cochran had already developed a parcel of land in an area west of downtown on the bluff that was becoming increasingly popular, and he was working with Archbishop John Ireland to develop land several miles farther west, near the Mississippi River, for a Catholic seminary. Cochran's interest in the geographical expansion of St. Paul to the west made sense in the prosperous context of the 1880s. As families sought out residential property relatively close to the heart of the city, they had moved to the top of the river bluff and begun to spread out over the highland area. This swath of land consisted of a wedge of oak savannah produced by a U-shaped bend in the Mississippi River. The main road through the area, Summit Avenue, followed the bluff on the east above downtown St. Paul for half a mile and then shot straight westward to the river some four miles away, traversing the wedge of land formed by a curve in the river. By 1871, this road had been graded as far west as Dale Street, and a horse-drawn omnibus transported people up the hill from downtown and down the avenue. By 1880, the street was attracting the homes of wealthy St. Paulites, with the surrounding streets accommodating a mixed collection of residences and commercial enterprises.[12]

Cochran reopened negotiations with former governor William R. Marshall, who offered the college forty acres of land south of the Manitoba Railroad and north of the Territorial Road at one-third the full price.[13] At least one source suggests that this offer was accepted by the trustees, but by fall 1881, the Winslow House had not yet been sold and thus they had no ready cash or credit with which to close the deal.[14] In any event, the trustees continued their search, and in late January 1882, Cochran and the special committee of the trustees charged with obtaining a site reported that they had purchased from the Holyoke estate 160 acres on the southwest corner of Summit and Snelling avenues. They further reported that "the funds for this purpose were obtained by the pledge of securities [below] [going] to the corporation for leans [sic] from different parties amounting to $11,000; by a loan without security of $8,000 from Rev. Dr. Rice and by a loan of $5,000 from Security Bank of Minneapolis made with the understanding that the land should be held of pledge from the loan and payment be made of this loan before any different disposition be made of the land."[15] Thus was announced the acquisition of the parcel of land on which Macalester College would be built.

Ominously, the day on which the deal was announced was also the day on which longtime trustee George Becker resigned, over Neill's protest. No surviving document cites a reason for his resignation, but in light of later criticism of the profit-making motivations behind the purchase of the Holyoke land, it is not unlikely that either the ethics of the purchase or the decision to renege on the Marshall offer sat ill with the longtime supporter.

Yet the Holyoke deal does not seem to have been the last word on the college's location. Shortly after this purchase was announced, a group of Macalester trustees drew up a manuscript agreement to purchase eighty acres of land just north of University Avenue at Snelling at the price of $205 an acre from the trustees of Macalester College.[16] The intention seems to have been for the trustees to remain in control of a portion of the property and administer it for the college as the site of the new campus, while the group of buyers, which included Neill, Daniel Rice, and others, would each buy five acres for their own purposes. Most likely, they hoped to sell the acreage for their own profit, given that the trustees had already purchased the Holyoke parcel for the college. In the end, it is difficult to ascertain whether this sale of lands by the trustees to the smaller group actually occurred.

What is clear, however, is that the various negotiations regarding the buying and selling of parcels followed common practice among urban speculators convinced that the savannah area was soon to become the hottest property in the region. Many people, it seems, believed that land prices would soon go through the roof as families moved farther west, seeking land for homes in the still relatively rural area, and as transportation options became available. Getting in on the ground floor, so to speak, by buying up the existing farms and undeveloped property seemed a sure route to quick profits. The boom was on. In March 1882, two months after the group of Macalester trustees purchased the Holyoke land, Neill wrote to trustee James McNair, an attorney from Minneapolis, saying, "I have no doubt that each subscriber will realize at the least $100 per acre above the purchase price in twelve months time."[17] The risk was perceived to be minimal, for the city was expanding to the west. In March 1883, the *Globe* had excitedly reported that land from Dale Street to Macalester College had become so valuable that it was being sold by the foot rather than the acre, a clear indication of its transformation from farmland into residential use.[18] Surely the property west of Macalester would soon become similarly desirable. Because such profit was all but guaranteed, buying the land on margin (eleven thousand dollars in third-party loans), many were convinced, entailed little risk.

Others, perhaps George Becker among them, remained skeptical. The recipient of Neill's optimistic note expressed his discomfort with the profit motive, penciling in at the bottom of the letter, "Mr. Neill, Since Mr. Cochran can have all [illegible] I will not subscribe as I would, if I did, only do it 'to help out' and not for the profit."[19]

With the purchase of forty acres at Snelling and Summit, the trustees adopted a two-pronged development approach. First, they opened a competition for plans for the new college building. By January 1883, the Minneapolis architectural firm of Hodgson and Son had submitted plans for a building costing one hundred thousand dollars in total, with the first wing to be built for a cost of twenty-five thousand dollars. Describing their design, the architects explained that "the style in which the buildings, entire group, are designed is the modern Elizabethan and consists of a blending of the picturesque with the semiclassical, which is the prevailing style of the Century."[20] Up-and-coming St. Paul architect Cass Gilbert also submitted plans, but the commission went to the Hodgsons.

Second, the Macalester trustees retained the firm of Elmer and Newell to survey and plat the Holyoke acreage. In October 1883, the plat produced by that company was registered with Ramsey County. The plat reflects the popular interest of the period in emphasizing an organic connection between middle-class homes and the landscape within suburban environments. A common grid plan forms the foundation of the plat, which covers the area bounded by Summit Avenue on the north, Reserve Avenue (now St. Clair) on the south, Fairview Avenue on the west, and the college on the east. This grid is broken up, however, by a cluster of serpentine streets—appropriately named after other colleges as well as individuals and locations relevant to the trustees' Presbyterian heritage—winding through the center of the area.[21] Some three hundred lots of varying shapes appear on the plat. Though not large, they are sufficient to provide for both backyards and front yards—the outdoor space that was particularly attractive to middle-class homeowners.

The Macalester Park plat settles the participating trustees, and particularly Thomas Cochrane, on the leading edge of urban development thought. A few years earlier, noted landscape architect Horace W. S. Cleveland had been hired to develop a similar residential park a few miles north of Summit Avenue. His St. Anthony Park consisted of several estate-sized tracts intended for the homes of the wealthy. This early St. Anthony plat was revised in 1885 by the civil engineering firm of Hawley and Newell to accommodate smaller, middle-class lots and homes, a strategy that Newell had apparently previously used with the earlier Macalester Park.[22]

The Macalester trustees would be sorely disappointed in their expectations for the development of the Holyoke property, however. For one thing, transportation to this remote area remained problematic. The nearest railroad station, which served James J. Hill's Chicago, Milwaukee, and St. Paul Railroad Shortline, had opened in 1880 and was located at Snelling and St. Anthony avenues, about three-quarters of a mile north of the college property.[23] Cochran worked with Minneapolis streetcar owner Thomas Lowry to extend a horse-drawn trolley west on Summit to the Mississippi, but Lowry, deep in debt, was losing money on the trolleys, and the eastern financiers he approached were wary of putting money into St. Paul when Minneapolis was becoming the state's economic powerhouse.[24] The solution seemed to lie in new technology, and in 1887, Lowry built Minnesota's first electric cable car line in St. Paul, but although it ascended the bluff above downtown, the closest it came to Macalester was St. Albans Street, nearly two miles away. Two years later, Cochran and Archbishop Ireland were able to gather a group of investors to finance the extension of the streetcar. Among them was Macalester College, which put up sixty-five hundred dollars and donated a six hundred- by eighty-foot swath of right-of-way through its campus that would become Grand Avenue. By the end of 1891, six years after Macalester opened its doors, the new electric trolley extended from downtown to the Mississippi River.[25] It would be another twenty years, however, before the area would become popular with homeowners, and by that time, most of the Macalester trustees had been forced to divest themselves of their property holdings.

But that was many years in the future. In their original plans for Macalester Park, the Macalester trustees developed an image for the new college and the adjacent area that was almost utopian. Neill's own undergraduate experience at Amherst as well as the experiences of many of the trustees at eastern colleges had instilled in them the idea that a college for higher learning should be located in a rural setting, isolated from the bustle of the city. During a visit to his alma mater in 1853, Neill returned with a picturesque woodcut print of the college in its bucolic setting on the edge of the village of Amherst. The siting of educational institutions in rural areas was an eastern strategy that had been continued in the west. Carleton College, located in the village of Northfield, was a prime example, and some of the trustees' earlier concerns about locating Macalester College near the Falls of St. Anthony also carried with them some discomfort with the idea of locating the college so close to the city of Minneapolis. As the trustees of Macalester chose their site for the new college, they avoided the growing urban centers in St. Paul and Minneapolis and settled on a home in the precincts between the two cities.

The plat of Macalester Park, which transformed the rural location into a residential one, embraced the idea of an idyllic suburban life that was becoming prominent among the expanding middle classes. The residential suburb, isolated from the crime, disease, and diversity of the city, boasted both the benefits of rural life—fresh air and space—and a variety of comforts not common in rural areas: ready transportation, stores and shops, even entertainment. The college itself would become an important amenity of the suburb, lending an air of intellectualism and stability to the surroundings. Illustrating this utopia was an 1886 print of Macalester Park that appeared in the blatantly boosterizing *Northwest Magazine*. This image depicted the subdivision's curving streets and widely scattered houses on spacious lots gently sprinkled with trees and shrubbery, with the college building claiming pride of place, front and center.[26]

As attractive as this image was, the reality was that the subdivision was far from idyllic. The Reverend Thomas A. McCurdy, on being invited by the synod to become the new president of Macalester, visited the site during an interview with the trustees and recorded his distinctively negative impressions:

> The appearance of Macalester College in August, 1883, was beggarly. The building, located almost outside civilization, was unsuitable for college purposes. It had no convenient means of access, and no attractions or inducements such as a school, a church, a post-office, a market, a railroad station, a telegraph or telephone service; nor did it have any furniture for its class rooms, its dining hall, and its dormitories; nor did it have water, or endowment, or student, or President. It was forlorn in its destitution and without means to relieve this impoverished condition.[27]

So much for the utopian ideal. Not only was the site unpromising but so was the building that was being erected for the college. It would take many years before the campus or the surrounding area would come anywhere near to being a pleasant retreat within the city.

Last, one further geographical situation affected the development of the college during this period. The decision to locate the college on the oak savannah reflected the desire of the board of trustees, which contained both St. Paul and Minneapolis men, to carve out an identity for the college literally between the two rival cities. The land west of Dale Street, the St. Paul city limits, and east of the Mississippi River was part of Ramsey County but not held by either city. It seemed an idea location. Throughout the 1880s, the trustees, and particularly Neill, used college stationary that featured a map showing the location of the institution smack between the two municipalities. The founders seem to have been quite aware that given the growing rivalry and a recent decision by the General Assembly to split the Minnesota synod into three synods, with Minneapolis and St. Paul coming under the jurisdiction of the new Lakes and Prairies Synod, whose offices would be in St. Paul (a decision that many in Minneapolis disapproved of), identification of the college with St. Paul could be devastating in terms of support and interest on the part of Minneapolis.

The situation would not last, however. In 1883, the city of St. Paul annexed all of the land west of Dale Street to the Mississippi River. The results for Macalester College were serious; some considered them disastrous. Clearly diminished support from Minneapolis residents over the next several years corresponded with the growing St. Paul identity. Whether it caused Minneapolis supporters to withdraw, as some have charged, cannot be ascertained. Even more important, however, was the fact that the annexation made the college responsible for higher tax rates on the entire Macalester Park area. It would also be assessed for structural improvements over the next several years. These new costs severely strained the poorly endowed college, exacerbating its already desperate financial situation. Moreover, as the college was increasingly associated with the city of St. Paul as one of its important civic institutions, former supporters and potential donors from Minneapolis, according to President McCurdy, refused to contribute to an institution that St. Paul had "stolen."[28]

Struggles of the New President

The financial situation of the college truly was dire, even at this early date. Between 1881 and 1884, three different attempts were made to secure an endowment of forty-five thousand dollars for the college under the leadership of Dr. Daniel Rice, an 1837 graduate of Amherst and Minnesota synod agent. In December 1881, having widely missed this mark, Rice tendered his resignation and raised the question of whether the effort should be abandoned "until the churches of St. Paul and Minneapolis are in a better condition to respond with substantial subscriptions to the college."[29] The synod, determined to persevere, refused Rice's resignation and vowed to continue working. In the race to establish Christian colleges, the Presbyterians did not want to be left behind, despite their slow start. Nevertheless, it took two more canvasses before the sum of $44,621 had been raised for Macalester College; of this, as historian Henry D. Funk points out, Minneapolis sources had contributed $20,409, and sources in St. Paul had contributed $16,400.

Nevertheless, the trustees' confidence in the real estate market continued without abatement, and despite their difficulty in raising endowments or even a spark of interest among Presbyterians in the enterprise, they pursued their plans to open the college. They commissioned the construction of a college building, erected four large houses on Summit Avenue for the use of the new faculty, and began to search for a new president. This latter task was accomplished with significant input from the synod, and an invitation was ultimately extended to a minister from Wooster, Ohio: the Reverend Thomas McCurdy.

On arriving in St. Paul, McCurdy quickly realized that improving the financial footing of the college was imperative. Several trustees optimistically suggested that a canvass of Presbyterians on the East Coast would yield sufficient funds to cover the current debt and establish an endowment. Experienced in soliciting funds for Wooster College in Ohio, McCurdy disagreed, noting that simply too many schools were seeking support among eastern congregations.[30] He suggested stepping up efforts in Minnesota. But having decided to accept the position, McCurdy also took steps to protect himself from financial responsibility for the college, making his acceptance of the position of president contingent on the board's acceptance of three conditions all dealing with the responsibilities of the position with respect to fund-raising:

- First: The board . . . ensures an additional and productive endowment of One Hundred Thousand dollars within a period of time not less than sixty days nor more than six months at the remotest from the date of my acceptance of the Presidency of the College.
- Second: I am to co-operate with the Board of Trustees for a period of time not exceeding six months in helping to secure the [one] hundred thousand dollars aforementioned.
- Fourth [*sic*]: After the expiration of the first six months I am to devote myself wholly to the work involved in securing a faculty, in forming a

curriculum, in arranging for scientific apparatus, in securing students, and in doing work along these specified lines preparatory to the opening of the college in September, 1885.[31]

According to McCurdy, these terms were approved, with the exception of the "sixty days limitation of the First Condition which was changed into 'a reasonable time.'"[32]

McCurdy did launch a campaign to raise funds in Minnesota. As he reported, the canvass "resulted in sufficient money for the furnishing of the college building; in promises of aid in meeting the current expenses; in expressions of interest and sympathy for the college by Pastors." It also, he continued, resulted in his "discovering a pronounced antagonism to the college because of its Founder" and, presumably as a consequence, "no subscriptions to the Endowment Fund."[33] In McCurdy's view, over the previous decades, the whole enterprise had earned a distinctly negative reputation for a number of blunders, most of which he laid at the feet of Neill. In his view, Neill had compromised the project in several ways, which he outlined with some enthusiasm.

McCurdy's first accusation was decidedly personal. He complained that "Dr. Neill had an uncontrolled and uncontrollable temper; that when frenzied by passion he was demoniacal in action and vituperative in speech, and that few escaped his fury in some form or other of its manifestations, are incontestable facts."[34] Consequently, he surmised, "the name Macalester was held by many to be a synonym of Dr. Neill when in passion; and thus it was he 'could not enlist the hearty co-operation of the men of wealth and of the Presbyterian Church in particular.' This is the origin of every objection to the endowment of the college and to the college itself."[35] Furthermore, he charged, "Dr. Neill's influence was hopelessly shattered when he named his 'School of Christian Literature,' 'Jesus College.' His reasons for so doing, although found in the example of Cambridge and Oxford were not and would not be received in justification of what some called 'egotistical sacrilege.' It was felt to be an 'unpardonable irreverence.' It brought the dearest and the sweetest of all names down below the level of common place, and subjected it to the danger of being bandied about as a hilarity in a college song and in a college yell."[36] And last, "when he [Neill] left the Presbyterian for another communion his influence was wholly gone from the Presbyterian Church. Men of the Presbyterian Church would not contribute to the endowment of an institution which would perpetuate the name and memory of a minister of the gospel who had dishonored the 'name above every name' by making it subordinate to his own name in an institution of learning."[37]

Neill was not alone in drawing McCurdy's fire. He also laid responsibility for Macalester's financial woes at the feet of trustees Daniel Rice and Thomas Cochran. Rice, he argued, did a poor job of fund-raising in Minnesota. Cochran, however, besmirched the whole enterprise:

> Mr. Thomas Cochran, a trustee, did his share of harm to the college by using its name in his advertisements of real estate for sale contiguous to the college grounds. It was charged persistently that the ground donated to the college by certain members of the Board was a real estate scheme. The charge was denied by the Board, but Mr. Cochran's persistent use of the college name as aforesaid not only cast suspicion upon the sincerity of the members of the Board in denying the charge, but discounted every appeal for the endowment and current expenses of the college.[38]

In these indictments, McCurdy clearly had an ax to grind. His charges appeared in a lengthy article he wrote that reviewed Henry Funk's 1910 history of the college. McCurdy felt that Funk's examination of the college's financial woes implied that McCurdy himself was responsible for getting the college off to such a rocky start. McCurdy exonerates himself in the review by placing responsibility for the college's struggles at others' doorsteps, particularly Neill's. Despite the vitriol, there is some insight in his charges. Neill's temper was definitely volatile.[39] Whether his temper had become as closely associated with the college's efforts as McCurdy charges is probably a matter of opinion, but that the name "Jesus College" and his decision to leave the Presbyterian Church for the Reformed Episcopal Church did not sit well within Presbyterian circles is evidenced by Neill's many efforts to explain these decisions in public forums and circulars. Furthermore, suspicion of the land development scheme would have been quite normal for the period. If the Macalester Park development was considered at all shady or even a profit-making endeavor, its being put forth by a group of men intent on founding a religious college would have exacerbated the criticism by adding intimations of hypocrisy. Furthermore, as we have seen, at least one trustee seems to have resigned over the issue. That McCurdy, an outsider brought in to culminate decades of work by Neill and the trustees, and faced with the gargantuan task of getting the college off the ground, found in Neill both a continual obstacle and a convenient scapegoat is hardly surprising.

A Grand Opening

Thomas McCurdy met with little success in raising funds for the college; nevertheless, in his first few months of working for the college, he had grown quite determined to see it open, and as the fall date set for the opening (announced much earlier in the year) neared, he decided that the college would, in fact, open. During summer 1885, he hired four men to constitute the faculty (along with Neill) at annual salaries of two thousand dollars.

On the morning of Wednesday, September 16, 1885, a flock of Presbyterian men and women from both Minneapolis and St. Paul, along with a host of other interested parties, including the local press, squeezed into the modest room designated as the chapel in the new college building, many spilling out into the hallway and another nearby room, to witness the dedication of the college. The air was festive, according to historian Henry Funk.[40] A procession of the faculty opened the ceremony, followed by a series of remarks and scriptural readings from local clergy. Edward Neill then gave the keynote address, later published as "Thoughts on the American College." In this talk, Neill stressed the view that Christianity provided the foundation of all education, asserting that "he who leaves college without any acquaintance with the proof that Christ lived on earth, died on the cross, rose from the dead, and ascended into heaven, is a half-educated man."[41] The point was illustrated with reference to the college seal, with its Twins of Heaven, Revelation and Nature. Neill also took the opportunity to take a few swipes at groups and ideas that bedeviled him. Here he lamented the Catholic influence that kept the University of Minnesota bereft of religious instruction and excoriated so-called sectarian education of all types. Here, too, he argued at length for keeping Macalester College exclusively male in student body, a position opposed by McCurdy, for one, as well as some others. But much of the address focused on the need for funding, with Neill pointing to the various benefactors of colleges throughout history. After the benediction, refreshments were served by the women of the Presbyterian churches, followed by formal toasts by several of the guests, trustees, and faculty members.

Only six prospective college students—all freshmen—were present on opening day, along with thirty Baldwin School (soon to be renamed the Macalester Academy) students. By mid-afternoon, according to Funk, the Macalester students had "organized a baseball team" and were on the field battling their collegiate neighbor, St. Thomas.[42]

Financial Hard Times

With income producing an endowment of only fifty thousand dollars and pay-ments on mortgages, tax assessments, and general overhead, the college's debt grew rapidly. Historian Henry D. Funk carefully traces the financial situation in his 1910 history of the college, and there is little reason to retrace his steps here. Suffice it to reiterate the figures he reported from the board of trustees: as of December 1, 1886, the college assets were figured at $159,000 in grounds, build-ings, furnishings, and endowment, and its indebtedness was $27,920.61. During 1887, the trustees violated their own resolution against the erecting of buildings that cost more than on-hand funds and went ahead with the construction of the second wing of the main building (henceforth to be referred to as Old Main), borrowing some forty-eight thousand dollars of the total sixty-eight thousand dollars it cost and mortgaging the college grounds to secure the loan. Over the next several years, yearly expenses, loan and interest payments, taxes, and as-sessments for street improvements produced skyrocketing debt. By the start of the 1888 school year, the college owed over $86,000; by January 1890, the total was near $117,000.[43]

Contributions to the college during this period remained disappointing. Donations from retailer George D. Dayton, a new trustee, went to scholar-ships, and a bequest of land from Sarah E. Oliver intended for scholarships and an endowed professorship was sold for five hundred dollars when the college defaulted on the taxes. An effort to raise capital was launched in the late 1880s, spurred by a proposed gift of twenty-five thousand dollars contingent on the college's finding twenty other donors to give the same amount, but canvassers were not able to raise the needed sum, and the gift was withdrawn.[44]

The human side of this institutional situation is read in the lives of the faculty. As early as December 1884, prior to the opening of the college, the trustees were apparently unable to meet their payroll obligations. At the end of that month, Neill, who had been promised a salary of sixteen hundred dollars per year and fifty dollars per month housing allowance, reported to the trustees that he had not been paid and had been forced to borrow money to pay his rent and living expenses. This letter was the first in a long line of such entreaties that ended only with his death in 1893. In this first instance, a follow-up letter from Neill, dated nearly three months later, reports that he had still received neither salary nor rent allowance. The tone of another follow-up letter in April is distinctly desperate—his loan is coming due and remuneration from the college is no-where in sight. In May, the trustees did come through with sufficient cash to pay Neill, but by September, the month in which the college opened its doors, he was sending new pleas indicating that he had received no summer salary or rent allowance. In October, Neill's friend and trustee J. C. Whitney notified him that the board had passed a resolution directing the treasurer to pay Neill on the first of every month. Whitney indicated that the holdup had lain with the "St. Paul Trustees," an intimation that the board itself was split between St. Paul and Minneapolis factions.[45]

For Neill, his financial situation was not the only precarious thing dur-ing these years. Having resigned the presidency of the college to appease the Presbyterian synod, Neill intended to remain fully engaged in the project as the senior professor of the college in the area of history. When the synod and trustees recruited the new president, Thomas McCurdy, however, he apparently was not made aware that Neill had already claimed the senior faculty position. As McCurdy went about gathering a faculty in the spring and summer of 1884, he offered the senior position to Dr. Nathaniel S. McFetridge as the chair of Greek and Anglo Saxon. Only later, when Neill's objections to being placed last on the faculty list in the 1885 prospectus (course bulletin) were heard by the trustees, did it become apparent that some miscommunication had taken place. Whether this incident marked the beginning of the troubled relationship between the first two Macalester presidents or was simply one of many in a long line of disagreements, McCurdy, as we have seen, clearly blamed Neill for the desperate circumstances of the college in the later 1880s. Neill, for his part, went about continuing his publishing, teaching his courses, and organizing a library for the college, while challenging McCurdy's authority on frequent occasions. But Neill was not alone in this latter endeavor. As early as 1887, the faculty as a group issued a statement aimed at clarifying the relative spheres of influence of the faculty and the president and, in so doing, curbing the influence of the president.

Tension between the president and the faculty would escalate in the next several years. What would become a perennial complaint among faculty emerged as they blamed McCurdy for putting insufficient energy into fund-raising. Mc-Curdy, for his part, was faced from the beginning of his tenure with the reality of rising costs and weak financial support, both from Presbyterian congregations and from the General Assembly.

New Buildings, Growing Debt

In spite of the weak financial situation, the trustees decided to go ahead with improvements to the campus and physical plant, likely in the hope that the more established the college looked, the more students, and tuition dollars, it would attract. The west wing of Old Main, a project that added nearly seventy thousand dollars to the college's debt, was completed in 1889. The new wing added ten classrooms, a museum and reading room, and a modest gymnasium to the college's physical plant.[46]

In the meantime, donations remained low; the endowment was dwindling; and enrollments, along with tuition income, were falling. During that summer, the faculty was warned that a pay cut was likely but that first, positions would be cut. The ax fell on the highly popular William Kirkwood, an ordained minister and professor of mental science and logic. Rumors flew as President McCurdy made the decision to let Kirkwood go—not surprising in a situation in which an increasingly unpopular president was deciding the employment fate of a very well-liked faculty member. Outraged, and likely quite aware that his position would be the next one to be terminated, James Wallace, the next junior faculty member, wrote the trustees protesting the decision. Neill, too, came to Kirkwood's defense, publishing a scathing criticism of McCurdy in the *St. Paul Pioneer Press*.[47] Efforts were made by some community members to raise the one thousand dollars needed to retain Kirkwood, but all was for naught. Kirkwood returned to the ministry. By summer 1890, the salaries of the remaining professors were reduced by 25 percent.[48] Faculty morale plunged. The turmoil over the cutting of faculty salaries, the release of Kirkwood, and the Neill article were too much for McCurdy, who tendered his resignation.

The search for a new president proceeded badly. One candidate asked Neill for advice about the debt situation, and Neill responded quite honestly. The candidate ultimately declined the offer.[49] With few alternatives available to them, the trustees appointed one of their own, David Burrell, the minister at Westminster Presbyterian Church in Minneapolis and a member of the board since 1888, to take the position until a permanent president could be found. Soon the bequest of Sarah E. Oliver, longtime member of the church, arrived, solidifying the relationship between the college and the church. Westminster's congregation, in fact, would remain the most generous congregation in the state vis-à-vis Macalester for many years.[50]

Burrell's approach to the financial crisis was to try to strengthen the relationship between the college and the synod in the hope that the synod would be more generous. In July 1891, the trustees passed a resolution designed to encourage "a more cordial and sympathetic feeling" between the Presbyterian Church of Minnesota and Macalester College. It increased the number of trustees to twenty-four and allowed the synod to appoint nine of them. In addition, the executive committee was refigured with nine members, of which three would be synodical trustees.[51]

Although the financial situation was increasingly desperate, the public face of the college indicated that it was progressing well. It seemed to be under the wing of the synod, it had just opened the west wing of Old Main, and its students were satisfied with their classes. Enrollment in the academy was strong, even if the college's enrollments remained modest. Despite the financial and personal turmoil, the faculty members were committed to providing a quality education for their students. Curriculum and resource development, along with student discipline and well-being, dominated the discussions at weekly faculty meetings.

But telltale indications that things were not right kept cropping up. In summer 1887, Neill reported to the trustees that Macalester's requirements for the junior class in history were not up to the standards of other local schools, including Hamline and the University of Minnesota. Furthermore, the requirements in English and political economy needed greater rigor. Though the trustees' Committee on Instruction passed the curriculum changes Neill suggested, they also stipulated that because no instructor was available to teach the new courses, the changes would not be implemented until 1888.[52]

Macalester, insiders knew, was not getting off to a good start. Neill lamented in April 1892 that "Macalester has been growing less in influence from the day it opened. At present we have no Senior class, and only two in the Junior, about six in the Sophomore, and about twelve Freshmen."[53] Faculty salaries, which, along with payments on the building loan, constituted the major ongoing expenditures, had been paid only sporadically since 1891, and as the trustees, who had been personally sustaining the salaries in the absence of sufficient endowment income, found themselves increasingly stressed by the growing financial criticism, the trickle-down of funds to faculty diminished.[54] By March 1893, Neill's salary was two months in arrears, and he poignantly turned to the new president, Adam Ringland, a Presbyterian minister from Duluth, to intercede with the trustees, explaining that he had borrowed from the bank for household expenses and the note was coming due: "House rent, servants' wages and grocery bills are behind. Relief must be had or I must go to the wall."[55] With the senior professor in such straits, it goes without saying that the junior faculty members were also severely pressed.

The students were feeling the pinch as well. Early in 1891, Neill attempted to raise forty dollars for one Mr. Sundberg, whom he described as "one of the most competent of the graduating class at Macalester," to help pay his board for the term and buy "clothing necessary for Commencement Day." Neill himself pledged ten dollars, as did trustee O. L. Taylor, but the effort came to naught. By May, Sundberg appealed to the faculty for permission to be excused from recitations so that he could find work.[56] Another student who was forced to drop out, Gus Heegaard, wrote Neill requesting reading material: "My Dear Doctor: Not being able to attend college this fall, I naturally feel a certain loneliness and a longing to learn something of Macalester. So I will take the liberty of asking you, If I may still have your historical contributions, for I am always interested in reading them and should greatly appreciate it, if I may continue my valued collection of them."[57]

But there were lighter moments as well. In September 1889, Neill received letters from one of the June graduates, George Achard, who had enrolled in law school at the University of Wisconsin. Achard reported that he was doing quite well in his classes, thanks to his years at Macalester, where he learned to take careful notes and to think clearly. At one point, he was singled out by a visiting lecturer, Wisconsin congressman Robert M. LaFollette, who invited him to his office to discuss possible employment. Achard also inquired whether Neill had read the new utopian novel by Edward Bellamy, *Looking Backward*, and suggested that Neill would find it thought provoking, though not realistic.[58] Achard would stay in touch with Neill for several more years.[59] On campus, students lobbied for recreation space, with the support of the founder. Neill felt that trustee Henry Vanderburgh might be willing to pay for improvements on the field behind the college building, to make it useable for "tennis, Baseball, and other athletic sports."[60] There would be no athletic field, however, for the financial situation was grim.

By fall 1892, Neill, for one, thought it was likely that the school would be forced to close, and he was outraged that the institution was in such financial turmoil. For decades, he had wanted to ensure that the faculty positions were fully endowed before the college opened. This had been achieved, he had thought, in

1885, when the synod put up twenty-five thousand of the thirty thousand dollars they had pledged. Neill thought that this money had been safely invested and that its proceeds funded his position. But since he was no longer a trustee, he was not fully informed of the college's financial situation or financial decisions made after 1885. The college had gone into debt to build the original or east wing of Old Main and, two years later, increased that debt by building the second wing. Payment on the debt, low enrollments and tuition income, relatively little synod support, and only a trickle of donations from local and regional churches proved a near deadly mixture for the young school.

In large measure, the institution's difficulties illustrated on a micro scale the increasingly problematic financial situation of the nation itself. The confidence in land speculation, willingness to accumulate debt, boosterism, and eagerness to launch the project were attitudes prevalent throughout the nation. In 1893, the entire country tumbled into a financial depression. In St. Paul, the bottom fell out of the real estate market as credit tightened, and those who had ridden the earlier wave of expansion were now plunged into debt. Real estate developer Thomas Cochran, for instance, found his very livelihood threatened, as did a number of the trustees. The future of the young institution was very much in doubt.

It would be twenty years, a lifetime in college history, before Macalester College's financial difficulties would ease, and then only temporarily. As we will see in the next chapter, new donors and a successful, if modest, endowment campaign succeeded in placing the college on relatively firm ground. Interestingly, it would be local businessmen, not the Philadelphia and East Coast establishment that Neill had so doggedly pursued, who would come to the rescue of the college.

5

College Life and Identity at the Turn of the Century

DURING THE NEXT TWO DECADES, the 1890s and 1900s, Macalester College would distance itself from the ideals of its early founders, establishing a distinct identity as a Presbyterian institution for higher education serving the upper Midwest. Although the college was not technically an institution of the Presbyterian Church—that is, it was not directly controlled by the national organization or the synod—it was "church related." Two-thirds of the trustees were members of the Presbyterian Church, and the synod could, if it so chose, select their replacements when positions opened. All the college presidents, each selected by the synod, had been ordained Presbyterian ministers (up to the installation of James Wallace in 1894, that is, and he was chosen in a desperate, last-ditch effort to save the college, mainly due to his outspokenness over its financial situation). Presbyterian families in the state and region donated funds to the college through their individual churches, and they sent their children to the new college. By 1905, the first year that records exist on the religious preference of students, 127, or 62 percent, of the 204 students enrolled identified themselves as Presbyterian.[1]

Macalester developed this identity during a period in which the Presbyterian Church, along with such other evangelical denominations as Congregationalists, Methodists, Baptists, and Disciples of Christ, was experiencing significant social, cultural, and scientific challenges to their traditional evangelical beliefs and lifestyles. Rapidly shifting cultural processes, social mores, and educational theories required new responses from religious communities and leadership. As Presbyterianism responded to these challenges over the course of the next several decades, colleges like Macalester were on the front lines of tension between the new and the old.[2]

U.S. historians characterize the years around the turn of the century as a period in which Americans acknowledged, embraced, and sometimes squared off against cultural and intellectual modernism. Spurred by advances in science and technology and the unrelenting incentives of capitalism, *modernism* is a term pointing to such things as the expansion of material life brought on by the greater demand for and availability of material goods, the expansion of scientific knowledge and the development of new technologies, the formation of the social sciences and development of the field of psychology, the alteration of women's roles and integration of women into the marketplace and workplace, the increasing influence of challenges to religious thought and practice, and the rethinking of the role of nations in the world.

Indeed, by the 1890s, and with greater acceleration after the turn of the century, the culture and the institution experienced significant changes. Traditional authorities were losing their power at the same time as commercialization and professionalization raised those with know-how to the fore, eclipsing religious authorities and those with family connections and old wealth.[3] Institutions like Macalester found themselves straddling an uncomfortable position between the new and the old, having to make daily decisions regarding whether to follow traditional ways or embrace new practices. In the case of Macalester, the struggle with modernism is apparent in several areas but particularly in the admission of women, which can be linked to a number of transformations in the college's mission, curriculum, and public image. This chapter will focus on the transformations spurred by the new coeducational character of the college. Macalester's struggles with modernism in other areas—including the role of religion and the nation in the world—will be taken up in the next chapter. In the face of all these challenges, religious belief figured as the guiding principle for institutional change, though as we shall see, it, too, was changing.

Fall 1893 is a useful place to begin examining Macalester's response to modernism and the ensuing transformation of the institution, for it brought not only what can arguably be seen as the most significant change but also the passing of the early founders' generation and the original vision for a Christian college on the prairie.

The Admission of Women to Macalester College

"Coeducation—yum, yum," was the roguish editorial comment that introduced readers of the *Macalester Echo* to the new students who were admitted to the college in September 1893.[4] The admission of women figured as the institution's first brush with modernism—the first, that is, apart from the financial and economic woes stemming from the changing role of capital in the U.S. economic system that had all but bankrupted the school that summer. Beyond that particular set of financial tests, the question of women's education brought its own set of challenges. In fact, women's education contested the ideology of the Presbyterian leaders of Macalester on very fundamental grounds, that is, on their understanding of gender and the normative behaviors deemed appropriate for Christian men and women. Women's education was one of a number of challenges that occurred in and around the turn of the century—challenges that in no small measure reflected significant rethinking of the underlying assumptions on which the institution was originally developed, a rethinking springing from college leaders' inevitable engagement with modernism.

The admission of women to the college in fall 1893 occurred during a time of financial crisis. The economic depression engulfing the country was deeper than any previous contraction, and the college, always vulnerable with its shallow resources, was seriously affected. In the face of the national depression, college leaders' confidence waned that the college would be able to keep afloat with its ever increasing debt. The synod had been of little help. Although that summer the Chicago World's Fair offered some diversion for those able to take the train south—Neill, who had been ordered by his doctor to leave St. Paul and rest, among them—the trip home was a return to despair. By August, it was not certain that the college could even open for the fall term. Students had begun to enroll elsewhere. Neill, always upset about the financial situation, sent a strongly worded description of the situation to the St. Paul newspaper, outlining the failure of the trustees and former president McCurdy in maintaining the financial footing of the institution. This public airing of the college's problems forced the trustees to censure its senior professor—an action that only deepened the feeling of crisis on campus. It hardly seemed the time for a dramatic shift in the direction of the college. Nevertheless, in September President Ringland admitted two young women into the college program.

Admitting women to the college, many later commentators have noted, made good financial sense in the context of financial crisis. Female students had, of course, made up the majority of the Baldwin School students throughout its sporadic existence since that gala opening in 1853. This had remained true as the Baldwin Academy was combined with Macalester College in 1885. Ringland's decision to allow these particular students to matriculate from the academy into the college certainly had to do in part with the economics of the period, but not insofar as women would bring in more tuition dollars and thus help the college during this period of severe financial need. Two economic arguments were put forward at the time. First, junior faculty member James Wallace, who had favored admitting women for several years, argued, "By the present arrangement [admitting only men] we are steadily losing our constituency. When a Pres. [Presbyterian] daughter goes to Carleton or Hamline we not only lose her but we lose her brothers as well if she has any. I have known case after case of this kind."[5] Second, some pointed out, the particular women admitted by Ringland were daughters of Macalester faculty members, and with faculty salaries many months in arrears, offering to educate the daughters as well as the sons of faculty was simply the least the college could do to demonstrate its good faith toward its faculty.[6]

What made this decision so disruptive was the opposition it spurred from the senior faculty member and college founder, Edward Duffield Neill. Neill had publicly opposed all proposals to admit women to Macalester for several years. His opposition to the admission of women to Macalester stemmed not from an opposition to women's education per se, for, as we have seen, Neill supported women's education generally, but rather from a reluctance to violate the many promises he had made over the years to various supporters of Macalester, to the Presbyterian Synod of Minnesota, and to the founders and administration of Macalester's sister school in Albert Lea, the women's college founded by the synod during the negotiations to adopt Macalester. Through all those years that Neill had begged contributions from his Philadelphia sources, he had characterized Macalester as a men's school along the lines of the eastern model of Amherst. In his view, the contributions were made on the assumption of this element, and to change the character of the student body at this point was to act in bad faith with respect to those early contributors. Even more important, however, was the relationship between Macalester, the synod, and Albert Lea. At the time of his negotiations with the synod, Neill had championed the need for a women's college and supported the development of Albert Lea in a number of ways. Since its creation, he had enjoyed a cordial and cooperative relationship with Margaret Stewart, head of the women's college. Stewart had asked Neill to send any young woman "who is capable to college work" to her, and he had cordially responded, "It will give me pleasure to the extent of my ability to present its claims to those who have daughters to educate. . . . Every true friend of education ought to labor for a College for Women in Minnesota with a faculty of its own."[7] For Macalester to now "change its spots" and admit women, who, by the original agreement, should have been encouraged to enroll in Albert Lea, was egregious. Albert Lea's sheer existence depended on increasing its student body, for the Presbyterian Church directed more funds to Macalester than to the women's college. Now, the synod and Macalester seemed to be conspiring to skim off Albert Lea's potential students. Neill was appalled. He accused the administration of violating their moral obligation to uphold the 1874 charter, and he refused to enter the school that fall until the women were banished from the college classrooms, stating that "when . . . the Trustees inform me that college classes exclusively for young men are waiting for instruction, I will be in my class room."[8]

Yet there was more going on here than a new president's desire to bring some faculty children into the college classroom and an elder scholar's wish to honor his earlier promises. The model of the small, rural men's college that had satisfied the educational needs of eastern Americans in the early half of the nineteenth century was becoming outmoded. In the context of the rapid development of the westernmost Midwest states, this model, based as it was on the assumption that only a small segment of society would have access to higher education, was not only proving less than adequate but was also increasingly viewed as undemocratic. The Morrill Land Grant Act of 1862, which funded the rise of public higher education by dedicating tracts of public land for higher education, was a pathbreaking federal recognition that access to higher education needed to become available to more Americans and could no longer be the province merely of the well-to-do. The new public universities, including the new University of Minnesota, brought women into the same classrooms as men and generally allowed them to pursue the same curricula. Thus, whereas the early model of college education had separated classes and genders, the new university model, at least in these years of progressivism, purported to ignore such distinctions. In the context of this new educational model, the Amherst model, which had so dominated the imaginations of Neill and the other founders of Macalester, grew increasingly irrelevant.

Neill's refusal to set foot on the Macalester campus if women were allowed into his college classes was untenable to a young president who had only five faculty members on the dwindling payroll. Ringland sent him a brief note on September 23, 1893, pointing out that the semester had begun and asking when he could expect to see Neill in the coming week. This prompted a return letter from Neill, charging the trustees with dereliction of duty.[9] Three days later,

Ringland visited Neill at his home, and they spoke privately in the parlor for quite some time. Whether they quarreled is unclear, yet given Neill's temperament, it is not unlikely. In any case, sometime later that afternoon, after Ringland had departed, Neill collapsed and died of a heart attack.[10]

Thus, for future generations, Neill's departure from this life would become inextricably and unflatteringly linked to the transformation of the original men's college into a coeducational institution. This connection, however, did not figure large in the minds of those who mourned him that fall. Macalester students memorialized him on the front page of the first *Macalester Echo* of the school year as a respected scholar and favorite professor. The obituary recounts his many accomplishments as both minister and educator, and although it attributes to Neill certain personal qualities that some may have disputed—he is described as "quiet" and "modest"—the language of its conclusion, quoting St. Paul, seems accurate: "I have fought the good fight; I have finished my course."[11] In another, more poignant obituary appearing in the next issue, the *Echo* belatedly reported that student Edward Lacy Darling had died on September 18 and had been laid to rest two days later in a service that "Our Beloved Dr. Neill" had presided over.[12] Thus, although Neill had refused to teach that term, he had still been deeply involved in campus and student life—and death. No one knows what presiding over the sad funeral of his student cost the senior professor, who had been diagnosed during the summer with severe heart problems. Certainly it, as well as the ongoing financial crisis and perhaps the exertion of his summer trip to Chicago and Philadelphia, played as much a part in his demise as did the decision to admit women to the college.

Neill was by no means alone in his opposition to coeducation at Macalester. That fall, the synod addressed the issue along with others in what were described as "protracted meetings" focused on the future of Presbyterian education in the state with respect to Macalester and Albert Lea. One gets an idea of how heated these discussions were by the admission in the official history of the synod that two trustees of Macalester resigned over the matter.[13] Though college records do not indicate any resignations during this crucial period, it is clear that the synod was well aware of the conflict of interest this new policy raised between the two institutions. As the governing body with powerful influence over both institutions, however, the synod allowed Macalester to proceed with its admission of women. Rumors of hard feelings between the two educational institutions were denied publicly, as in a brief piece in the *Macalester Echo* that stated that although reports of the synod meeting "convey the idea that there is some sort of antagonism between Macalester and Albert Lea, . . . as far as we are able to ascertain, [such antagonism] has never existed."[14]

Those who feared for Albert Lea, however, proved correct. In the second semester of the 1893–94 school year, two women from Albert Lea transferred to Macalester. Although Macalester's sister school would plug along for several more years, diminishing enrollments and funds finally forced its closure in 1915. Macalester, on the other hand, was significantly transformed by the addition of women to its student body, for their presence required the Macalester faculty to rethink the role and purpose of the education they were providing. Women's presence in the student body would help precipitate transformations in the curriculum, the faculty, and the religious and educational missions of the college. In this, the college participated directly in the nationwide rethinking of gender roles that characterized the period. In many ways, this change in the student body was modernism's first shot across the bow of the Macalester ship of learning.

Gender Constructs for Women

Whether all of the Macalester students found the new coeducational character of the campus "yummy," a definite shift was coming with respect to how the role of women in the world was perceived by Macalester leaders. A decade earlier, trustee and synod representative Daniel Rice had articulated a Protestant argument for the inclusion of women in higher education that was based on traditional notions of women's role in society. Writing in support of the mission of the Presbyterian women's college at Albert Lea in 1882, he reiterated a Christian-based anthropological argument popular in the period and based on the idea that the elevation of women is a definitive mark of civilization. Christianity, in this apologist view, was superior to other religions in raising women's status. Rice echoed widely articulated arguments when he asserted that Muslim and Hindu scriptures promulgated degrading attitudes toward women and that testimonials of Western travelers to regions in which these religions predominated attested to the shocking depredations women suffered there.[15] The model for Christian women, in contrast, was the ideal woman of Eden, Eve. As the true helpmeet of Adam, postlapsarian Eve could be restored to the highest dignity and beauty of her Edenic existence only through Christianity. Indeed, Rice argued, "nothing is more clearly written on the pages of history than the progressive regeneration of the character and condition of women, by the steady growth of Christianity."[16]

This millennial view championed a progressive understanding of Christian advancement toward establishing the Kingdom of God, which, as we shall see, would undergird much of the Macalester enterprise for several decades to come. Applying this theologically progressive (though, in the long run, socially reactionary) view to women's role in society, Rice explained that

> We live in the dawn of woman's era, an era when, at length, in the foremost nations of Christendom, woman begins to receive all the privileges of instruction in the family, in the church, and in the public school, which are provided for man, and therefore an era when the College is as needful for the higher education of woman as of man; when it has for her an equal value, and when she can as fully avail herself of all its privileges. All the signs of the times indicate that we are beginning to inherit the great promises of the 'last days'; that we are beginning to be borne on the swell of a broader wave of progress, and we can most clearly mark the growing influence of woman as the wave rolls on.[17]

Christian education, and particularly Christian college education, Rice argued, was the crowning accomplishment that would achieve this perfect creature and noble future.

Yet Rice did not support making Macalester a coeducational institution. The education that women required was different from that of men. The latter needed to be trained to take on the mantle of the professions: law, medicine, ministry, education, and business. In contrast, women needed a particular type of education "for her own progressive growth to a higher moral excellence and a fuller restoration to her Eden loveliness."[18] This did not mean relegating women to the home, however. The classroom, in Rice's view, was one of women's crucial domains; because women comprise "more than three-fourths of the teachers in all our best public schools," their education must make them well qualified to enter the classroom. Furthermore, Rice argued, women had a missionary vocation as well and needed education to aid them in their labors to address the needs of the world. "Benevolent associations of women are constantly multiplying in our cities and large towns, to care for the poor and the needy, for the sick and the suffering, for the lost and the ruined," he pointed out, and even more important, "the families of the heathen of the world are opening their inner-doors to the missionary labors of women, that are closed to men."[19] To carry on these important missions, women must have access to college.

Consequently, when Macalester moved into the field of women's education a decade later, it faced an important choice: educate women in the same manner as they educated men or modify the curriculum to take into account the specific educational needs and expected adult roles of women. In his address to the board of trustees in June 1893, Ringland argued that women's education at Macalester should be in the form of a ladies' seminary, which, he felt, wielded a financial advantage over that of an all-boy's school because "paternal pride in daughters" carried with it "a corresponding willingness to pay more for their education."[20] Such a ladies' seminary would provide training in music, painting, drawing, and speaking, all skills required by an accomplished young woman of the period. Ringland, however, did not carry the day. At the opening of the year, and in subsequent college pronouncements, institutional materials proclaimed that women were admitted to Macalester "with equal rights, and on the same conditions as young men."[21]

Would such "equal rights" really apply, however? What did "equal rights" mean in light of the traditional views regarding women's position within Christian society held by people like Rice and Ringland? Here we see some negotiation taking place, as the new students themselves contributed new perspectives on the question of what women's education should consist of. One of the first woman students in the college, Anna M. Dickson, for instance, presented her own views on educated women and their role in society. In an essay titled "The Progressive Woman," Dickson (class of 1898) carefully tread the ground among the idealistic Christian view of women touted by Rice, an even more conservative view that relegated women to purely domestic pursuits, and the radicalism of the "New Woman" espoused by proto-feminists of the period. Dickson begins by arguing that in contrast to the negative example of the New Woman who "clamors and struggles blindly" for "woman's rights," the more positive Progressive Woman, her ideal, seeks to "fit herself" to her own sphere, the home. To do so, however, now requires "greater skill and knowledge for its proper management than does any business occupation," for in the home, the stakes are greatest: "there the manhood of the future is trained to perform its duties to God and man."[22] Given the importance of this role, the Progressive Woman, in Dickson's opinion, must claim her equality to Man, though not her similarity, for her strengths lie in her intuition and moral character rather than in knowledge and judgment. Equality but difference, she suggests, must coexist. As Dickson moves on to address women's participation in other spheres outside the home, her argument moves decidedly closer to identifying with the New Woman. She explains, for instance, that women in business are "proportionately, just as successful as men." Higher education plays an important role in providing the knowledge that women desire and preparing them for these types of responsibilities. Yet, while Dickson admires these abilities, she is troubled by the fact that many fear women's progress, concerned that they will compete with men and become something other than women—a situation that Dickson rejects and associates with the New Woman. It is in the figure of the more moderate Progressive Woman that Dickson finds comfort. For the Progressive Woman does not "sacrifice the dignity and refinement belonging to an ideal American womanhood"; instead, she brings "right relation to Man," a point that returns Dickson to the conservatism of her introduction.[23]

Although these reflections of a young woman may seem a bit naive and waffling, they well characterize the negotiations taking place throughout much of higher education regarding attitudes toward women's education. At many Christian colleges like Macalester, these debates were complicated by their intimate connection with religious views of gender. The key question would remain how to raise woman's knowledge and make her a fit helpmeet for Christian men and a productive member of society without radicalizing her and nudging her toward mannish behaviors or occupations deemed counter to the ideal.

James Wallace, whose role and influence at the college was rapidly growing, had supported women's education and coeducation at Macalester from the beginning and tried to persuade Neill to support it as well. Wallace had, in fact, met his future wife, Janet Davis, in a preparatory Greek course he was teaching at his alma mater, Wooster University in Ohio. Janet, on graduation from the preparatory course in 1876, enrolled as a freshman in the college course but curtailed her studies two years later after her marriage to James, ostensibly due to failing eyesight. Their daughter Helen would distinguish herself academically at Macalester College, graduating in 1902. Wallace, who succeeded Ringland as president of the college in 1894, an office he would hold until 1906, remained a champion of women's full participation in society throughout his life, even lending a supportive voice thirty years later to women's efforts to gain ordination in the Presbyterian Church.[24]

Nevertheless, at the turn of the century, he and other college leaders retained strong views on the proper role of women in society, and despite assurances that women and men were admitted to the college on the same terms, these views necessitated some alteration of the curriculum. Over the next several years, attention to women's educational needs would become an important, though by no means the only, impetus for changes in curriculum, the development of the physical plant, the hiring of faculty and staff, and the accommodation of extracurricular activities.

Gender, Curriculum, and Student Interests

It is with the admission of women that one begins to get a sense of the growing influence of students on college curricula and the parameters of student life. In particular, this influence is seen in the migration of certain activities that had originally occurred outside the classroom—what we would now call cocurricular activities—into the formal curriculum, usually in the form of electives. Here was a new expansion of the model of higher education. This migration of areas of study from the cocurricular to the curricular had begun a generation earlier at eastern universities such as Harvard and the University of Pennsylvania, and its identification with coeducation is readily apparent at many institutions. At Macalester, however, the resulting division of courses into "masculine" and "feminine" categories was not as pronounced as at others, for at Macalester, the curriculum changes were sparked both by efforts to address what were considered women's special educational requirements and by the desires of both men and women students for an educational experience that addressed their needs as they perceived them.[25]

In the area of curriculum, the addition of music and drama as electives and, shortly thereafter, the development of a school of music directly reflected the traditional understandings of the proper education for woman, as expressed by Rice and held by much of society at the time. These elements, popular as extracurricular or cocurricular activities prior to the mid-1890s, migrated into the curriculum both as a means of addressing the particular educational needs of women and as an acknowledgment that higher education should not halt abruptly at the door to the fine arts. The development of a college music course provides a good example. Male students at Macalester had participated in cocurricular musical practice and performance for several years. The college fielded an all-male brass band, for instance, which participated in YMCA events and was given frequent mention in the *Echo*. In addition, the church background of many of the students had nurtured excellent vocal skills among several male students. But in fall 1895, just two years after the institution became coeducational,

Harry E. Phillips was hired to teach instrumental and vocal music. Offered as electives to juniors and seniors only, the courses' arrival corresponded exactly with the first set of women entering their junior year. For these women, it was likely assumed, music would constitute a fitting choice among the elective options, but though the music courses were indeed popular with the women students, men also enrolled.

The admission of women meshed closely with other curriculum changes as well. Curriculum options appeared that allowed students to avoid mathematics. Although all students were required to take math throughout their freshman year, in the sophomore year they could choose to take a course in pedagogy rather than the mathematics course. For women, of course, teaching was the predominant vocational field available during the period, so this option for training in pedagogy may well have been added to address women's particular needs, although, again, it is quite likely that men took the course as well.

Drama and performance courses, including oratory, were also added to the curriculum by the late 1890s. In these areas, the perception that women needed training in proper public etiquette and decorum meshed closely with a broader student-driven desire for training in public speaking and debate. These came together in the new professorship in drama created just after the turn of the century. As with music, students had pursued these areas of performance—oratory, debate, dramatic readings, and theatrical performance—on a cocurricular basis, forming literary societies that they ran with the assistance of faculty supervisors.[26] The first such society, the Parthenon Society, established shortly after the opening of the college, brought student members from the preparatory school and college together to discuss common readings and participate in formal debates and oratorical performances. A year later, a second society, Hyperion, was founded for college members exclusively, and Parthenon was redefined as the preparatory society. With two societies, the debating and oratory elements gained the added incentive of competition, and according to one early student's memory, performers' preparedness and the quality of performances rose dramatically.[27] In December 1893, a third society, the Philadelphian, was formed, a move that likely reflected the growth of the student body, some one hundred in both the academy and the college that fall.[28]

Women who were admitted in fall 1893 quickly became involved in these societies, taking great interest in dramatic readings and performance. Three women —Miss Parks, Miss Dickson, and Miss Hackett—appeared on the November and December programs of the preparatory Parthenon society, and Dickson was elected vice president of the society. Miss Ringland and Miss Winifred Moore appeared on the program of the college Hyperion society in February 1894. A brief review of the women's performances appeared in the *Echo*, with the author opining with some irony that the program was well chosen and performed and that "the parts rendered by the young ladies clearly proved that the ladies are not inferior to the 'lords of creation' in literary ability and force of delivery. Miss Ringland well sustained her part in the dialogue, 'Buying a Feller,' while the declamation, 'The Ruggleses,' by Miss Moore, was delivered with ease and force."[29]

These voluntary literary societies, cocurricular and student led, demonstrated students' conviction that facility in rhetoric, writing, oratory, and performance was among the earmarks of an educated person. As the editor of the *Macalester Echo* argued, "Literary work is a line of labor that should not be overlooked. . . . It is the duty of every student to join some literary society, and strive to develop his powers in composition and oratory, and to give the greatest possible impulse to literary work." In fact, the article continued, a student "should be as conscientious and take as much pride in it as in his studies."[30] Yet students' dedication to these pursuits varied widely, according to pleas published regularly in the *Echo* for society members to prepare themselves more carefully and participate more fully. In regional oratorical contests, Macalester's teams offered Carleton and Hamline little competition for the highest awards. After a particularly humiliating defeat at Northfield in 1894, students began to lobby for classroom training in these skills. The *Echo* argued that "orators cannot be made in a term," particularly when "work is left almost entirely to the literary societies." Other institutions, the editor noted, "have certain hours each week set apart for chapel orations and declamations under one of the professors." During those sessions, "criticism on composition and delivery is made then and there, all in attendance deriving benefit from such thorough criticism." In such systems, "orations and declamations are made a part of the college curriculum, and, as a result such colleges turn out prize winners in oratory and declamations." Thus, the editorial concludes, "Next year we hope to see this matter given more attention, and rhetoricals [*sic*] made compulsory at Macalester."[31]

Though this may well have been the first time that Macalester students launched an effort for curriculum change, it would by no means be the last. Curriculum change throughout the twentieth century was driven as much by student interest as by changes in higher education more broadly. In this case, the students' urging of the addition of rhetorical skills to the curriculum paralleled concerns about providing a proper education for women, forming a powerful justification for curricular change. Drama joined the list of electives by the turn of the century, with the addition of Grace Bee Whitridge to the faculty as professor of drama. As Whitridge's duties developed, they soon included preparing Macalester women, as well as men, for their entry into the higher echelons of public society. Training in social manners, dress, demeanor, and decorum was meted out at special events, including afternoon teas and formal dinners.

Whitridge was by no means alone in these efforts. Macalester's first woman professor, Julia Johnson, professor of English, had taken on responsibility for young women's social behavior as soon as she arrived on campus in 1897. She served as dean of women and housemother for the new women's dorm, the Elms, the former president's house, which had been converted for the use of the growing number of women students. Julia MacFarlane Johnson was a single mother. Her husband, Richard W. Johnson, a Civil War general some thirty years older than she, died in 1897, leaving her with a five-year-old son. General Johnson had been well acquainted with several of the early supporters of Macalester, including Henry Sibley, John Pillsbury, Henry Rice, and Edward Neill, and it is likely that, on his death, those still associated with the college felt some responsibility for his dependents. Prior to her marriage, Julia had pursued a career in higher education. She received a bachelor's degree from Mount Holyoke; studied at the University of Pennsylvania, the University of Cincinnati, and Oxford University in England; completed a master's degree at the University of Minnesota; and taught briefly at Coates College in Terre Haute, Indiana. When the growing interest in studying English literature among students coincided with the general's death, Johnson was hired to teach Chaucer, Shakespeare, and Milton.[32] She became a mainstay of the college, respected and trusted by students and faculty colleagues alike. Students' admiration for Johnson was eloquently expressed half a century later, when in 1950, the class of 1910 organized a fund drive to furnish a lounge in the student union building then under construction. That lounge, they specified, should contain "a big friendly fireplace in the Main Lounge in memory of Julia M. Johnson."[33]

These are only a few of the ways in which Macalester changed with the admission of women. By 1907, the new women's residence, Wallace Hall, named after former President James Wallace, who raised the funds for the building, was completed. Shortly after, the first instance of what would be a recurring concern among college officials occurred with discussions of whether the college was in danger of becoming "feminized." A recruiting flyer distributed around that time proclaimed, "We Want Men! Wallace Hall filled." In addition, Wallace's successor in the presidency, Thomas Morey Hodgman, found himself explaining to the Presbyterian College Board the steps the institution was taking to avoid becoming feminized.

In this concern, the college was strongly influenced by the wider context of evangelical religion, which, for over a quarter of a century, had touted various forms of "muscular Christianity" as a means of warding off undue feminine influence on the church. Such influence, many feared, would lessen the attractiveness of religious participation to men and, in effect, depopulate churches. Indeed, the number of women participating in religious services and activities, particularly within evangelical groups, had always surpassed that of men.[34] That their numbers would surpass men's in a Christian college was hardly surprising. Yet Macalester officials remained diligent and, despite the strength of this trend, managed to keep the gender balance among students weighted in favor of men for most years of the college's existence, with the exception of war years.

Teasing the Watchdogs of Morality

From the earliest days of the college, the concern for shaping the social behavior of students had gone hand in hand with the education of the intellect. Parietals, or rules governing student behavior that placed faculty in loco parentis as substitute parents, proliferated at this evangelical school. Many of these rules aimed at prohibiting activities that might lead to immoral (read sexual) behavior. No drinking was allowed. Smoking, though frowned on, was allowed in some designated areas. Rooms were to be kept clean and tidy. Late hours were forbidden, with lights out at 10:00 P.M. Students, all male in the early years, ate their meals with faculty members, providing the latter with the opportunity not only to monitor students' behavior but to shape it as well. If Macalester students were to take their place among the leaders of society, they would need to shed the manners of their modest homes and learn the etiquette of eastern society, practices that the faculty must impart on them.

Faculty meetings in the early years were frequently taken up with discussion of student transgressions. Student Will Kirkwood earned the wrath of Professor Neill when he persisted in referring to his Latin text during Neill's history lecture. On being reprimanded by the faculty, Kirkwood submitted a written apology to Neill. Recounting the incident years later, Kirkwood (class of 1890) noted that Neill apparently "didn't hold it against me because he awarded me a prize at the end of the term for the best set of notebooks reporting his lectures."[35] The faculty were also kept busy attending to curfew violations; students taking unauthorized off-campus trips; and in one incident, a midnight raid on the college pantry that prompted a crisis in the form of the resignation of the valuable Mrs. Kitchen, college cook and housekeeper.

The arrival of women students brought new concerns. In the first few years, the women students lived off campus, but soon the Elms was converted for their use. Here, both drinking and smoking were strictly forbidden, curfew was at 9:30 P.M., and meals were taken with Dean Johnson and, later, Professor Whitridge. Women were not to set foot in the men's dorm, which occupied several floors in the East Wing of the Main building. Most of these rules were devised to keep the sexes segregated in their living arrangements to avoid opportunities for sexual activities, considered strictly immoral at the time. Yet sexual mores were changing. Men and women throughout American society were interacting in new ways in spaces heretofore off limits for any unmarried couple. One can see that change occurring in an incident that happened shortly after the college went coeducational. A young woman was seen leaving the dorm room of a male student, causing a flurry of concern. She was exonerated of the severest charges, however, when everyone involved maintained that she was simply dropping off a book.[36]

Rules forbidding dancing became a target of student derision shortly after the turn of the century. Dancing was forbidden on a quasi-religious foundation, for many believed that it led to or even constituted sexual activity. James Wallace, for instance, publicly announced that dancing led to "spoonery." The faculty stance on dancing at the college was that women could dance with one another as much as they pleased but that there would be no mixed-sex dances. Yet even evangelical students were pushing back against the sexual mores of their parents' generation, and in 1903 some Macalester students took aim at dancing. First, a literary society hosted a debate on the question of whether the ban on dancing should be lifted. The decision went to the side in favor of eliminating the ban. Shortly after, a group of students surreptitiously held a midnight dance—in the chapel. The *St. Paul Pioneer Press* gleefully reported the incident in detail, emphasizing the subterfuge of the effort:

The trouble arose about two weeks ago when a Y.W.C.A. social ended in a midnight ball. . . . The members of that organization are not in sympathy with the devotees of this giddy pastime, and had announced that the social should under no circumstances terminate in a ball. The others looked at one another and smiled, but secretly arranged for a dance, just the same.

When the evening's entertainment was over the young women were ostensibly taken to the Elms, the girls' dormitory. Instead, however, about a dozen couples walked around the house and down a side street toward the college. One young lad, who was with a theological student, bade his good night at the side door and slipped through the hall and met a second young man, who is not a candidate for the ministry, at the front door, and joined the crowd, which was secretly returning to the college.

"We all walked down a side street," said one of the boys, "for a short distance so that the stragglers could have time enough to get home. Two of the boys returned to the college to see if the coast was clear. They found everybody gone but two of the girls, who were washing the dishes. One of the boys took off his hat and coat and commenced to help, while his companion returned for the rest of us.

"We walked around the building, keeping well within the shade and entered at the main entrance and climbed up to the chapel on the third floor. We locked the door and put a sentry on guard. Our coats were used to cover the windows that were toward the dormitory. Even then we didn't dare turn on the lights for they would have been easily seen from the professors' homes, so we danced in the dark."[37]

The story was accompanied by a photograph of a group of young women sitting in what might be a lecture or chapel service. Male and female students at a Christian college dancing together in secret in the dark in the chapel—it was a story too juicy to ignore, and the newspaper reveled, perhaps justifiably, in exposing this student transgression of both faculty and religious mores. President Wallace, of course, was appalled, not only by the behavior but by the challenge to the policy, which he had strongly reiterated just a few days earlier after the literary society debate. He denounced the escapade as "scandalous and diabolical" in the newspaper but played down the incident later in his report to the trustees, blaming newspaper columnists for not having anything better to write about.[38] None of the participants was disciplined. Once again, the faculty took a lenient view, concluding that the whole incident was perpetrated by two Macalester alumni living nearby, one of whom held a "decidedly pernicious" influence over the freshman girls. The departure of that individual shortly after the occurrence—he ostensibly left town for business reasons—seemed to solve the matter.

Apart from these challenges to sexual mores, pranks and schemes were a normal part of college life. Most were harmless, and the faculty generally looked the other way. A young DeWitt Wallace, the younger son of President James and Janet Wallace who would become a major benefactor of the college in later years, was so proud of a particular prank he had a hand in during his second year in the Macalester collegiate program that he reported on it in detail in a letter to his mother in a misguided attempt to relieve any anxiety she may have been caused by inaccurate rumors about the escapade, which was apparently written up in some form and which his siblings may have passed along to her.[39] Playing pranks and practical jokes on freshmen was common, and at Macalester, as at other schools, initiation was deemed a central aspect of joining the social life of the college.

An often repeated story of the cow in Old Main ranks highest among the Macalester pranks. As the story goes, under the cover of darkness, a group of students, including and most likely led by DeWitt Wallace, led a cow up the stairs of Old Main to the third-floor chapel, leaving it there to greet the community as it assembled in the morning for required service. The question of whether this really happened is repeated as often as the story. This historian is forced to report that with respect to the first two decades of the twentieth century, the period to which the story is generally attributed, the jury remains out on the question. There are many reasons to remain skeptical. While the story enjoys probably the strongest oral history tradition of any told at the college, I have found not a single documentary source supporting its veracity. If it did happen, it was not deemed of sufficient interest to describe in the usual newspapers, either on or off campus. In addition, important details vary widely. The story is variously attributed to an unnamed group of students or to DeWitt Wallace himself. It is variously reported as the cow being led upstairs in Old Main (with the caveat "everybody knows that cows do not mind going upstairs but will refuse to be led downstairs") or downstairs in the same building ("everybody knows that cows do not mind going downstairs but will refuse to be led upstairs"). In at least one version, the beast is a horse, not a cow. In no retelling of the story have I heard or read any discussion of the fate of the animal, whatever it was. Furthermore, the same story is told on many other college campuses, particularly those located in rural or semirural areas.[40]

Yet even if the origin story with its connection to Wallace is apocryphal, in 1923, such an event did occur when several students led a cow into the chapel as a Halloween prank.[41] That event and the connection of it to the earlier period, however, is significant, for its revered place in the lore of the college carries important meaning. It suggests a certain pride taken by the tellers in the transgressive character of the students depicted. Macalester may have been a Christian college, but the students were not wimps. They possessed not only a sense of humor but a certain daring, if not recklessness, as well. A similar if less sensational story of misplaced objects by students does have fairly sound documentation. On a hot summer's morning, students assigned to James Wallace's Bible class on the fourth floor of Old Main got there early and moved all the chairs to the lawn in front of the building. Wallace, not amused by the prank, had them move the chairs back into the classroom before he started class.

Though pranks were one thing, moral integrity was quite another. Clearly the reporting of the dancing incident hinted at the hypocrisy of relaxed moral standards at this Christian college, a charge that would be repeated ever so often over the next several decades. Grace Whitridge, for instance, was accused of contributing to the corruption of Macalester students when she selected the popular play *The Private Secretary: A Farcical Comedy in Three Acts* for a class production in 1911. Written by popular actor Charles Hawtrey and based on a German play from the 1880s, *The Private Secretary* is a story in which a young man conspires with a friend to elude his creditors and an uncle, determined that he should "sow his wild oats." The hero, Douglas, needs no help in sowing them—living alone, playing cards, piling up debt, swearing, flirting with girls, and deceiving his uncle throughout the play—a fact that renders the main premise of the drama, that his uncle is displeased with him, highly improbable; but no matter, it is the ensuing hilarity of the various impersonations that carries the action, not the credibility of the plot. At a weekend house party, Douglas impersonates an effeminate tutor, and the uncle, mistaking the tutor for his nephew whom he has not seen in years, is sorely disappointed in him for not being manly. Improper behavior abounds, with various characters getting drunk at breakfast, one particularly weak individual being repeatedly teased and mistreated, and insults thrown at everyone. When Douglas's deception is revealed, along with his debts and unruly behavior, the uncle is pleased to claim such a manly man for his kin, and the young woman who is the object of Douglas's affection is given to him as his bride.

Not surprisingly, the production of the play drew some fire. Trustee George W. Wishard wrote President Hodgman expressing his distress, saying that he was "mortified and humiliated" by the performance. He found the play lacking in moral character and its language inappropriate—the word *damned* had been used in one scene. The faculty member responsible for the production, he urged, should be severely reprimanded.[42] Hodgman contacted Whitridge for an explanation, to which she responded that the play had been performed on several campuses.[43] The dust-up soon ended. Hodgman took the course of leniency, accepting Whitridge's apology. Nevertheless, the incident underscored the fact that "appropriate behavior" was a concept continually negotiated among students, faculty, administrators, and trustees.

Students, of course, were quick to perceive that the category of moral behavior could also be deployed in their favor. Efforts to obtain amenable exercise space—specifically, a gymnasium, but other spaces as well, including a skating rink and a ski jump/toboggan run—had ensued since the earliest years. The basement of Old Main was designated as the gymnasium, but with its low ceilings and exposed pipes, it was far from ideal. In 1915, students launched yet another in a string of attempts to convince the administration and trustees to build a gymnasium. That attempt, like earlier ones, contextualized the need for a gymnasium within the popular view that physical culture and well-being were as important as their mental counterparts. Paralleling arguments being made nationally by such moral reformers as Jane Addams and G. Stanley Hall as well as by earlier Christian leaders like Dwight L. Moody and James Naismith, the inventor of basketball, the students played their trump card: "Above all we need a gymnasium for the moral and religious safety of our young men at Macalester. To give them a play ground, to keep them from the dance halls and other evils of the city. This need is far greater than either Trustees or Faculty realize."[44] Alas, the students would not get their gymnasium until 1924–25.

They were, however, more successful in their efforts to obtain a skating rink. The rink was available not only to the students but also to residents of the surrounding community, but the college retained strict control over it. For instance, an effort in 1926 by the Macalester Park District to petition the board of trustees to allow skating on Sundays was firmly denied.[45]

College athletics was a breeding ground for conflicts over morality. Though Macalester was not known in its early decades as an intellectual powerhouse, it enjoyed some reputation on the playing fields, thus making such questions of particular import on campus. The football scandals of the 1890s, in which collegiate players suffered increasingly serious injuries, cast a dark shadow on the activity. Calls from the *Echo* to alter the rules of the game appeared as early as 1893. James Wallace was of the opinion that all sports detracted from students' studies, but faculty–student baseball games were a frequent occurrence during the early years. Handball was particularly popular among the men, and the women were playing basketball by the turn of the century.

Around these competitive activities developed a thriving student culture and loyalty to the institution. Macalester alumni boasted in retrospect that on the day the institution opened, they had organized a baseball team by the end of the luncheon and were on the playing field beating St. Thomas by early afternoon. The class yell of 1898 was carefully recorded in the secretary's book: "We're the class; sure as fate; Macalester, Macalester, ninety-eight."[46] The class of 1908 created a more enduring memorial to their class, planting a large elm tree on the lawn outside Old Main and positioning beneath it a half-ton rock that several class members rolled to the site from somewhere near Ramsey School, two blocks west of the campus.[47] The rock remains to this day, repainted regularly by students. In these various ways, then, the faculty and students negotiated the moral landscape created by the adoption of coeducation and by the changing contexts of modern society.

Changing Identity

Such issues, mirrored on campus after campus throughout the nation, were part and parcel of the development of college education at the turn of the century. Macalester was far from unique in its negotiation of these elements of modern American culture. Indeed, from an outsider's view, Macalester was very much one among many, and not particularly distinctive at that. We catch a glimpse of the college's identity from the perspective of an outsider from a 1912 letter written by prospective faculty member Glenn Clark to his parents, describing an interview he had with then president Thomas Morey Hodgman. Clark was living at the time in Aledo, Illinois, where he was teaching English at William and Vashti College. Hodgman, apparently determined to secure the services of this young professor for Macalester, had taken the train eight hundred miles to Aledo to encourage Clark to join his English department. Clark described Hodgman as "a fine looking, strongly built man" who "impresses one as a business man, a broad educator of progressive type and as a strong executive." Hodgman had presented Macalester College as a highly attractive institution, and Clark weighed Hodgman's offer and information about the college carefully in the letter.

In contrast to its first quarter-century, Macalester's strongest selling point was, as articulated in Clark's letter, its financial situation. Clark explained to his parents that not only did the college have an income-producing endowment of two hundred thousand dollars but, he gushed, it also had "the richest Board of Trustees of any college or university in the world, without exception." He explained that "six of them, I believe, are multimillionaires, one Weyerhaeuser being worth 150 million, ranking probably next to Rockefeller."[48] In addition to enjoying financial soundness, the college occupied an attractive urban location. Echoing the sentiments of an earlier generation of Macalester developers, he wrote, "The location of the college is the best thing about it. It is located in the midway district between the two cities. The campus consists of 40 acres fronting upon a boulevard 200 feet wide that connects the two cities. While it is in the suburbs, the center of St. Paul can be reached by the street car in 20 minutes. Minneapolis is not much farther away. Through the state university many famous speakers come to the twin cities. Fine plays are to be seen, wonderful music and fine sermons, etc." After living in Aledo, Illinois, he confessed, "I am hungry for the stimulus of a larger city for a few years."[49]

Yet there were drawbacks. Though Macalester College seemed to have a brighter future than did William and Vashti (1907–19), it did not rank among the first- or even second-class colleges that Clark dreamed of entering: Whitman, Beloit, Lake Forest, and Colorado in the first rank and Coe, Knox, and Carleton in the second. Nor was it among the third-class ones he had more realistically planned on going to: Morningside, Illinois College, and Butler. In fact, he was not sure where Macalester ranked. He surmised, "In wealth, I think it is in the second class but in standing, history, traditions, reputation, etc., it ranks among the third class colleges." A friend had assured him, however, that Macalester "was considered the strongest college in the Minnesota (Presbyterian) Synod."

Clark concluded the letter by asking for the advice of his parents, but he also predicted, "By the time your answer comes, there may be a better offer before me from some other school, which we may all hope for." That better offer did not come, or, if it did, Clark decided in Macalester's favor anyway. He went on to teach at the college until the early 1960s and, during his tenure, launched a parallel career as a nationally acclaimed evangelist.

This letter opens a window onto how Macalester, or at least President Hodgman, presented itself to those it wished to impress and onto an outsider's view of the college in the early years of the twentieth century: a financially sound institution (or at least ostensibly so, given the relative wealth of the trustees), Presbyterian, situated in an ideal urban/suburban location. While Hodgman may have suggested a brighter future than others on campus may have envisioned, whatever embellishments he offered were clearly circumscribed by the fact that if the college had any national reputation at all, it was simply as a fledgling Minnesota Presbyterian institution. Two hundred and thirty students were enrolled in 1912, and of those, 145, nearly two-thirds, indicated that they were Presbyterian. The majority were in the academy or preparatory school. President Hodgman was exactly midway in his decadelong administration of the college.

As we have seen, a great deal of change was occurring at the college during the very period in which Clark contemplated this job offer. None of that ongoing transformation, of course, was apparent to Glenn Clark as he considered joining the Macalester faculty. Yet had he had the opportunity to perceive these aspects of the college, he would have seen something of a pattern emerging in the way that Macalester as an institution was reconciling its religious perspective and the challenges of the twentieth century. In the adoption of coeducation and modification of the curriculum to accommodate both traditional and progressive views of women's role in society, it had signaled concern for a level of gender inclusiveness, while not completely abandoning traditional gender ideals. In its curriculum development, it had demonstrated a willingness to take into account students' opinions and desires, allowing them a modicum of influence in this critical matter. In its efforts to control the moral behavior of students and its responses to transgressions, it had signaled an awareness of changing mores and a tendency toward lenience. Emerging was a pattern of negotiated middle grounds. Macalester was not as strict or as authoritarian as some evangelical colleges, nor was it as indulgent as others. As we turn our attention to the role of religious ideology in other areas of the college mission, we will see similar patterns of negotiation with changing cultural situations and mores.

Also of crucial significance to this changing identity was the gradual improvement of Macalester's financial situation. Presidents Wallace (1894–1906) and Hodgman (1907–17) had worked continuously to raise funds for the college from a range of sources. Donations trickled in from regional churches and individuals. Though most of these donations were fairly small, a few were substantial, including sixteen thousand dollars from one Mrs. McCormick, who routed her contribution through the Presbyterian College Board.[50] The expanding student population brought in much-needed tuition dollars, but the pace of its growth was very slow. By 1903, the institution had 175 students, 66 of whom were in the college, compared to 148 and 59, respectively, in the previous year.[51] Wallace made countless appeals to the Presbyterian College Board, eking out small amounts. Trustees George Draper Dayton and Rufus Jefferson also put up financial support for the college to offer a curriculum in the sciences—physics, biology, and chemistry—allowing the college to offer courses in these areas for the first time.[52]

An endowment campaign launched under Wallace and completed by Hodgman turned the tide, however. Large pledges offered by two longtime supporters and smaller ones from several new trustees relieved the college, at least temporarily, of its financial burden. In summer 1904, the local newspaper announced Macalester's success in raising some $250,000 in its endowment campaign, which was aimed at half a million. Generous pledges from Minneapolis retailer George Dayton (one hundred thousand dollars) and St. Paul railroad magnate James J. Hill (fifty thousand dollars), individuals who had been assisting the college for years, set the pace.[53] Smaller donations, ranging from ten thousand to twenty-five thousand dollars, were pledged by several new trustees: R. C. Jefferson of St. Paul, R. A. Kirk of St. Paul, and T. B. Janney of Minneapolis.[54] A few years later, the college was able to convince Andrew Carnegie to donate fifty thousand dollars toward a new science building, something of a feat in that Carnegie generally refused to donate to religious colleges. In 1910, Hodgman announced the college's financial turnaround in a letter to the Presbyterian College Board, stating that although in 1898 Macalester's debt had been in the neighborhood of $180,000, "now it has no debts, and endowment of $300,000."[55] For the time being, at least, the college's financial woes had been alleviated.

PART II

Engagement with the World, 1915–1960

6

Evangelical Engagement with Modernism

> The church, as well as the world, has entered on the era of the laity. Christianity is girding itself for the conquest of the world. Her call for leaders and workers of all sorts is louder and more engaging than ever before. The world is white unto the harvest and the reapers include not only preachers and evangelists but missionary teachers, missionary physicians, settlement workers, pastors' assistants, secretaries of Young Men's and Young Women's Christian Associations, trained Sunday school organizers, and lay workers generally.
>
> —*Macalester College Bulletin*, April 1915

WITH THIS DESCRIPTION, the 1915 *Macalester College Bulletin* characterized the mission of the Bible Training Department. Its central theme is the role of the church in the world; the time is ripe for Christianity. But how will this conquest be achieved? Not just through the work of clergy but, more important, through the work of laity. And here was where the Christian college, and Macalester in particular, found its central mission in the early decades of the twentieth century: the training of lay Christians who would become the advanced guard in this battle.

Simultaneously invoking metaphors of colonizing militancy and benevolent aid, the paragraph seems a jumble of mixed, even opposite, ideologies: on one hand, militant evangelizing, the mission of traditional evangelicalism, focused on conversion, and on the other, the settlement houses of the Social Gospel, an expression of liberal Protestantism, focused on ethical behavior and the improvement of social conditions. Though historians of religion in the late twentieth century would view these Christian doctrines as fully separate from one another, even paradoxical, the preceding description, along with many other components of Macalester's curriculum, attest to the ways in which these elements—conservative and liberal—functioned together during this period. The blending of seemingly paradoxical understandings of Christianity illustrates the college's determination to redefine evangelicalism itself by renegotiating its role in the world.

The early decades of the twentieth century, during which this renegotiation effort took place, were a time in which scientific, technological, social, and cultural changes challenged traditional ways of thinking and transformed everything from work, to leisure, to education, to religious belief and practice. We have already seen how the students and leadership of the college negotiated challenges to mores and lifestyle. They also found themselves struggling to establish a consistent worldview on which to define their collegiate and religious mission in a rapidly changing world. While a few Christian colleges embraced the theological and social liberalism they perceived in modernism, many, like Macalester, hung back, taking a measured view, determined to retain something of the traditional evangelicalism of the previous generation.

Time after time through the early twentieth century, Macalester found itself searching for a middle ground between the conservative and liberal religious views, adopting some of the scientific advances and humanism of modernism, while attempting to update and thereby keep relevant key elements of evangelicalism.[1] We can trace these negotiations through several areas, all of which relate to efforts to understand or construct a relevant role for evangelicalism within the world. This chapter will examine these efforts as they were expressed through changing approaches to religious education, continued embrace of missionary work and efforts to update it, understandings of the Bible and approaches to teaching it, the relationship between religion and science, and debates over roles of peace and conflict leading to World War I.

The Evangelical Conquest of the World

For the Macalester community, the religious mission of the college could not be separated from the college's mission in the world itself. Although founded as a tiny college on the frontier, the institution was never isolated from the rest of the world. Its early leaders had significant international experience, which invariably occurred within significant religious contexts or resulted in significant religious meaning. Edward Neill, as we have seen, served as U.S. consul to Ireland, where his connections with the Protestant Church of Ireland provided him with a model for establishing a religious college within or associated with a public university. James Wallace, after completing his degree at Wooster University, spent eight months in Greece studying the language of the New Testament and another two months traveling in Europe and the British Isles. Several of the college's early alumni, as we will see, also became engaged with international situations and activities. And several early alumni, as we will also see later, left Macalester for careers in evangelical missionary work that took them far beyond the borders of the United States.

A particular Christian understanding of the progressive character of human history informed the way that the Macalester community engaged with the world well into the twentieth century. This view traced its roots to nineteenth-century postmillennialism, which held that it was incumbent on Christians (specifically Protestants) to work to improve public life and thereby prepare the world for the return of Jesus Christ and the establishment of the Kingdom of God, events they found prophesied in the Bible. For evangelical missionaries abroad or in the United States (home missionaries) in the nineteenth century, including New School Presbyterians, this meant converting nonbelievers to Christianity through revivals and improving or reforming public life by acting against public sins. Protestants of a postmillennial bent were involved in such important nineteenth-century reform movements as abolitionism, temperance, and antiprostitution.

Not all Presbyterians, however, embraced the postmillennial idea. As we have seen, earlier in the nineteenth century, Presbyterians had split into two groups: New School supporters, who accepted postmillennialism and embraced proselytizing, and Old School Presbyterians, who retained enough of the early Calvinist view of original sin to be pessimistic that human endeavor could reform society at all, much less help to bring about the Kingdom of God. Indeed, they argued at the end of the century, certain signs associated with the intellectual life and production of knowledge indicated that not only was society not progressing toward the Kingdom of God but the world was turning rapidly away from God. German universities, for instance, had introduced an analytical approach to the Bible that downplayed and even questioned the divine character of the texts. These scholars, joined by others in the United States, approached scripture as historical documents written by individuals who were enmeshed in concerns of their day. They pointed out errors and inconsistencies within and between texts, arguing that such discrepancies evidenced the Bible's nondivine authors. Similarly, the fields of geology and biology, following the lead of Charles Darwin, were suggesting that the history of the world was not accurately represented in the Bible, but rather that it extended perhaps millions of years before the timeline that appears in the book of Genesis, and that life on earth was not created in six days by God but rather through evolutionary processes of change, guided by natural selection rather than a divine hand over millions of years. Even more troubling was the use to which some representatives of the new field of social science were putting the evolutionary ideas of Darwin, arguing that society itself evolved not progressively through divine plan but rather through biologically inevitable processes devoid of all moral content. The work of Herbert Spencer, for instance, suggested that the underlying motivation of all human action was survival itself within a universe devoid of divine revelation. Whereas liberal Christians generally found a comfortable compatibility between their religious convictions and these new discoveries and ideas, conservatives often rejected them and reaffirmed their belief in the inerrant accuracy of the Bible as the Word of God. For these conservatives, including many Presbyterians, not only was the effort to work toward the Kingdom of God on earth a pipe dream but only divine action would redeem a human race so bent on denying God.[2]

Thus challenges to the mainline evangelical hegemony of the nineteenth century were coming from both sides, liberal and conservative. In the face of these challenges, Macalester championed militant evangelicalism with a progressive bent. As President T. Morey Hodgman explained in a classic statement negotiating the two sides, "The church is at war against the evils of divorce, the strife between labor and capital, the cruelties of war and the saloon, social impurity, city corruption and tainted amusements. The salvation from these evils can come only thru increased intelligence and the application of the principles of Jesus to life."[3] Here traditional evangelical moral thought and faith in Jesus are blended seamlessly with social gospel concerns for social and economic justice. Macalester would do its part in fighting this war, not only by training future clergy but also by expanding Christian education beyond the clergy to provide an ideological grounding for lay work within society. This view rested on the belief that Christianity was the best hope not only for the eternal salvation of the individual in heaven but also for the establishment of human freedom in this realm. Macalester leaders negotiated this millennial view as a middle ground within the debates over historical biblical criticism, evolution, and the role of God in human history that were raging within the evangelical community in general and the Presbyterian denomination in particular.

The YMCA, Missionary Work, and the Evangelical View of the World

Engagement with the world through missionary work interested many of Macalester's students from its earliest years. That interest was likely deepened in 1893, when Macalester welcomed its first international student from abroad. Joseph Koshaba immigrated to the United States from Persia during the summer of that year and enrolled in the college in September. The *Macalester Echo* reported, somewhat ambiguously, that although Koshaba had "arrived in this country from his native land, but a few weeks ago, [he had] already proved himself to be able successfully to compete with the average American college boy, though considerably handicapped by a lack of familiarity with the English language."[4]

Koshaba quickly became engaged with college life. Like the hundreds of international students who would eventually follow him to Macalester, he quickly became an ambassador for his native country, educating his peers on a part of the world that was well beyond their experience. Within weeks of his arrival on campus, he performed a vocal solo of a Persian song during the musical portion of the program at the annual YMCA reception.[5] A few months later, the *Macalester Echo* reported that he had "purchased about one hundred and fifty views of Persia and an excellent magic lantern."[6] Though such a purchase was likely out of the financial reach of most students during the period, it is not known whether Koshaba used his own funds to buy the visual materials or whether he was subsidized by some organization or individual. In any event, through music and visual images he brought knowledge of his Persian homeland to this tiny midwestern school.

Though we know little about his background,[7] it is clear that Koshaba was a Christian because he joined the Central Presbyterian Church in St. Paul in February 1894. It is likely that Presbyterian missionary work played a role in bringing him to Macalester in the first place. Certainly, over the next several decades, many of the international students who would come to Macalester were influenced by Presbyterian missionaries in their homelands. In this case, Presbyterian missionaries had been in Persia since the 1880s, focusing particularly on the Christian Assyrians there and pursuing a threefold mission consisting of evangelizing, medical work, and education. By 1895, they had established over one hundred schools in the country. Koshaba may have been a student in one of these schools or perhaps was aware of the teaching hospital established by Presbyterian missionaries in the Urmia region. In any event, he was likely born into a Christian family, for it was among Christians that the Presbyterians focused much of their effort.[8]

The presence of this Persian student at Macalester very likely deepened students' interest in missionary work abroad. Over the next several decades, Macalester students and alumni would become increasingly involved in missionary work. Much of this work was fostered by the local YMCA and YWCA, on whose meetings and activities the *Macalester Echo* regularly reported. Though not all students belonged to these organizations, many did. Y meetings, described in a weekly column in the student newspaper, included lectures by invited speakers on religious topics, discussions, and social events. The Y's involvement in foreign missionary work grew significantly in the 1890s, and given that the Presbyterian Church had sanctioned the work in 1872 by forming the Presbyterian Board of Foreign Missions, Macalester students were eager to join the movement. In the late 1880s, six or eight Macalester students, under the auspices of the Y, formed a band within its Volunteer Movement, signing a pledge to pursue missionary work abroad on their graduation. Three of those young men likely fulfilled that pledge: James Hambleton went at least briefly to Chile, whereas John Knox Hall and Underwood went temporarily to Rio de Janeiro, Brazil, and then Trinidad and Puerto Rico, respectively. A classmate, Myron Clark, felt a call to missionary work in 1890 after hearing a talk on foreign missionary work at Macalester delivered by one Reverend Chamberlain, and his subsequent letters on his experiences in Brazil appeared in the *Macalester Echo*.[9] Harry Schuler [Schuyler], perhaps influenced by Joseph Koshaba, went to Resht, Persia, to do missionary work.

Missionary work got a boost in the spring of 1894 when the YMCA Student Volunteer Movement held its annual convention in Detroit, adopting foreign mission work for the conference focus. Two Macalester delegates, Charles Petran and Harry Schuler, attended, and the *Echo* provided comprehensive coverage of the event, which included over 170 missionaries from Africa, China, India, and other countries. On their return, Petran and Schuler provided detailed reports to the local YMCA members describing what they had learned about the need for missionaries in China and Africa.[10]

The primary goal of these missionizing efforts was to spread Christianity throughout the world.[11] These Protestant missionaries espoused two important beliefs: (1) no individual soul would enjoy salvation and an afterlife spent in heaven without having first been converted to Christianity and (2) Christianity, the progressive fulfillment of God's plan, was the only religious system capable of establishing societies that could reduce human suffering, poverty, and injustice. Thus, for a majority of Macalester students of the period, to do good in the world was to convert individuals, and thus the world, to Christianity.[12] It is no surprise, then, that the descriptions of the people—and their beliefs, customs, and habits—who were the objects of this benevolence are replete with xenophobia, racism, and Christian triumphalism, the ideologies that fueled most missionary commitment during the period.[13]

Yet change was coming. By the 1890s, the social gospel movement had begun to coalesce, attempting to apply Christian ideals of love, compassion, and justice to social situations of the current day. Social gospel ministers and practitioners attempted to alleviate suffering in modern society, addressing, for instance, poverty among immigrants and laborers through settlement houses, labor organizing, and relief work. This religious view, which gave rise to the progressive movement in the arena of politics, also significantly influenced the thinking about missionary work, deepening the commitment of more liberal missionaries to provide aid—medical care and hospitals, education, clean water, and so on—and lessening the previous focus on converting people to Christianity.[14]

Foreign missionary work through organizations like the YMCA brought together adherents from several Protestant denominations, helping to fuel the growth of a nationwide "collegiate missionary consciousness," as leaders such as the Y's John R. Mott gave lectures at colleges cross the nation.[15] Those students who became involved in these interdenominational groups reflected a host of views on the goals of mission work, and at Macalester both theologically liberal and conservative positions were represented. With respect to the latter, alumnus Myron Clark, for instance, serving as YMCA secretary in Brazil, wrote disparagingly of the Roman Catholicism that held sway in Brazil and published an article on the need to evangelize Catholic countries in the short-lived, anti-Catholic Minneapolis newspaper the *Loyal American*.[16] His position reflected the belief held by many evangelicals that Roman Catholicism itself was a perversion of Christianity. Clark, like most missionaries, achieved few conversions over the years, and he frequently wrote dispiritedly of the difficulties of the enterprise; nevertheless, he stuck with his work and the country, marrying a Brazilian woman and raising a family there.

Though only a handful of Macalester students went on to become foreign missionaries, many would support the work at home through work with Ys and local churches. Both men and women were targeted for missionary work, with women missionaries becoming something of a growth industry: women made up some 70 percent of all foreign missionaries in some regions.

Countries targeted as in need of conversion to Christianity also underwent change after the turn of the century, when the Far East began to loom even larger in the imaginations of students. Perceived as particularly heathen and with a large population seemingly in desperate need of (Christian) spiritual and physical succor, China and East Asia attracted young graduates from throughout the United States. Macalester graduate George Leck and his wife, Francis B. Oakley, whom he had met at Macalester, pursued their interest in foreign missionary work to Korea after he graduated from Auburn Seminary in 1900. On their arrival, they studied language in Pyongyang for a year before moving farther inland. Soon after, however, Leck fell victim to smallpox, leaving his widow to give birth to their only child three months later. Francis would return to the United States and continue her work in the church.[17] Such stories of the hardships of missionary work were legion. Charles Allen Clark, for example, had also pursued missionary work in Korea through the McCormick Seminary, arriving in 1902 during the same smallpox epidemic that took Leck. In his memoir, Clark states that he lost one young son to the epidemic and another later on. He does not mention his wife at all. His poignant understatement that "sometimes that is the cost of being a missionary" attests to the depth of conviction of these individuals. Endlessly repeated, these stories were testimonies to their faith.[18]

As early as 1893, articles on depredations in China and the need for Christian correctives had appeared in the *Macalester Echo*. But China, despite having a reputation among evangelicals for being receptive to the Christian message, proved, like so many other areas, to be a difficult venue for missionizing. Learning the language took time, and foreigners were viewed with great suspicion. Conversions were few. As Chinese resentment against foreign (i.e., Western) influence in trade, politics, and technology grew, resentment against missionaries also increased. With the outbreak of the Boxer Rebellion in the fall of 1899, missionaries were easy targets for rebel aggression. Missionaries and their families were killed or forced to leave. Evangelical colleges across the Unites States mourned alumni missionaries caught up in the rebellions; Oberlin College, for instance, lost thirteen missionaries and their five children.[19] No Macalester alumni were present in China during this period, however.

The rebellion did not stop Macalester students a decade and a half later from laying plans to once again missionize the country. This time, however, their approach echoed the more liberal attitudes toward missionary work brought about by the social gospel. The project that Macalester students developed in 1915 was aimed at education, not conversion, and would bring the benefits of their beloved college to the Chinese people. In essence, the plan, drafted for the approval of the Presbyterian Board of Foreign Missions, was to establish a satellite of Macalester College in China. The purpose of their prospective program was to "crystallize" what they saw as "the vision of Macalester as a powerful missionary force in the world." They wanted "to project the personality of Macalester into the Orient." Just what was this personality? The authors of the plan explained it in some detail, and though the description is lengthy, it appears here in full, for contemporary readers will find much of the present-day Macalester embedded in its language:

> We believe it to be a working combination of three elements: a *faith*, a *policy*, and a *method*. Macalester has the faith to believe that every man or woman who enters her gates is worthy of her fullest measure of service. She has the faith to believe in her own competency to counsel and train that man or woman wisely and efficiently for his life task. She has the faith to believe that God has a worthy, responsible, glorious place for him in His great Plan.
>
> Having this faith, Macalester has also a policy. It is briefly this: (1) to give to every man and woman who enters her gates a knowledge and experience of the true value of human life; (2) to acquaint him with the world's principal present needs; (3) to enable him to build upon the basis of this knowledge and experience and acquaintance, a worthy life-purpose; (4) to give him a fair measure of technical training for his life task.
>
> Having a faith and policy, Macalester also has a method. Her method is: to bring every man and woman into perpetual intimate contact with *typical persons* and *typical experiences*. The teachers, themselves, are types, the literary society, the banquet hall, the athletic field, the laboratory, and the shop, afford typical experiences. And some day in his college career the student is led, perhaps unconsciously, into personal contact with the greatest of all personalities—the Divine Personality—the Christian Experience.[20]

This description rings with the language of contemporary theories of types in the areas of social organization, personality, and logic. Theorizing on the construction and role of *types*, a concept popular in a variety of fields throughout the nineteenth century, reached something of a pinnacle at the turn of the century, pervading the work of Herbert Spencer on the formation of nations in the late nineteenth century, of Max Weber on the notion of "ideal types" as a conceptual category for social functions, and later, of Bertrand Russell on logical systems. Carl Jung applied ideas about types—and archetypes—to personalities. The students who developed the Macalester in China plan seem to have employed such theoretical work, particularly that of Weber, which they likely studied in their social science or philosophy classes, in analyzing the benefits that a Macalester education could bring to students in China.[21]

Their desire to share this privileged context with others springs, of course, from their conviction of the superiority of Christian systems and society. To do good in the world, in China, was to work to make it more like the Christian United States. This would not be the only time that Macalester students would apply the social theories they studied in class to improve real-world situations. Indeed, if one had to identify a single theme that linked Macalester students throughout the twentieth century, it would likely be the conviction that classroom education should be applied to real-world situations in a way that affects people for the better.

In light of the Boxer Rebellion just a scant decade earlier, the Macalester in China plan likely strikes contemporary readers as particularly idealistic. Nevertheless, several Christian institutions, among them a few colleges, such as Canton Christian College, had survived the rebellion and continued work in China. The leaders of many of these institutions, like the Macalester students, felt that only by establishing Christian education within China would the country cultivate the "Christian statesmen" needed to lead China into a bright new future.

Macalester in China would never come about. In fact, the thrust and meaning of missionary work was undergoing even more significant change. If the Macalester plan was to bring foreign populations into contact with typical persons and experiences, including the divine personality and Christian experience, missionaries in the field were increasingly realizing that what people really needed was contact with doctors and teachers and engineers. As this realization was embraced, the importance of being affiliated with a church through a missionary organization declined. While some who embarked on the public service path continued to do so as missionaries, increasingly others, such as Mary J. Rankin (class of 1903), who earned a master's degree at Columbia College and, in 1931, began teaching in Tennessee, were not. Rankin found the needs of those in her community great, and she responded however she could, mainly by offering some medical services, including administering medicines for hookworm and flu and giving smallpox and diphtheria vaccinations.[22] Though teaching school was her primary occupation, she did integrate her religious beliefs into her work, drawing at times on her Presbyterian education to provide a faith framework for those she assisted and offering Bible classes from time to time.

Thus we see that evangelizing and humanitarian service merged with one another and signaled changing understandings of the role of Christians in the world. James Wallace emphasized the humanitarian side of the equation in 1905:

It may justly be claimed for Macalester College that to an unusual degree it is pervaded by the spirit of altruism and of service for humanity. Its graduates are deeply imbued with a desire to be useful and to promote human welfare. One is teaching [at] a colored school in Virginia; one, a school of poor whites in East Tennessee; one is a professor in a farm school near Denmark, N.C.; one is working among . . . Mexicans in Southern Colorado; one is YMCA Secretary in Rio Janeiro [*sic*], Brazil; one is connected with a fine girls' school in old Mexico; one is doing a fine educational work at Aguadilla, Porto Rica [*sic*]; one conducts a mission school at Resht, Persia; one is teaching in Ilo Ilo, Philippine Islands. Three have gone on some mission to Korea; many are teachers or superintendents of Public Schools. Some have gone into the Christian ministry of our Church; others in another. Two are physicians and are devoting much time to service among the poor.

Wallace concluded his remarks by saying, "The fact is the College exists / For the causes that need assistance, / For the wrongs that need resistance, / For the good that it can do."[23]

By the 1920s, the focus of missionizing had shifted sharply toward providing humanitarian aid in impoverished areas. Macalester women became involved in missions in Appalachia and on the Mesabi Iron Range in northern Minnesota. With respect to China, interest remained but actions changed. Memorials donated at the time of James Wallace's death in 1939 were sent to the American Bureau for Medical Aid to China, a New York City–based organization that provided rural areas in China with medical supplies. According to a newspaper account, the donation of over $130 would provide the "medical supplies needed to 'immunize a town of 2,200 Chinese against typhoid, cholera and bubonic plague, or to buy enough quinine to cure 132 persons of malaria, or provide enough anesthetic for almost 2,000 surgical operations.'"[24]

This shift in missionary activities from predominantly evangelizing to predominantly humanitarian aid evidences a transformation of the evangelical view of duty to God. Whereas a vocational call to missionary work in the nineteenth century—such as that which Edward Duffield Neill may have experienced—emphasized spreading the Gospel and converting individuals as a means of helping to bring about the establishment of the Kingdom of God, by the 1920s a vocational call to missionary work emphasized ethical progressivism and the responsibility incumbent on Christians to use their education and knowledge to improve living conditions. To do God's work was now perceived as going beyond saving souls to saving bodies; desire for the Kingdom of God waned. Thus the work of Christians was broadening, and Macalester students and alumni were gradually moving away from the evangelicalism of the college's earlier days toward a more liberal form of Protestantism.

The Social Sciences and Vocational Emphasis in the College Curriculum

The early emphasis on missionary work—the many missionaries who spoke on campus and the abundance of articles in the school newspaper about missionary work—was one component of a broader institutional emphasis on religious careers and leadership. At Macalester, over 50 percent of the students in the first several years entered a religious field, be it the ministry, missionary work, or religious education. Although popular lore at Macalester identifies the adoption of a vocationally oriented curriculum with Charles Turck, who served as the president of the college from 1939 to 1958, this theme was prevalent much earlier in the college's existence. Part of the confusion in identifying this vocational character of the early college lies in changes to the very concept of "vocation" that occurred in the first half of the twentieth century. For during this period, with the expansion of the professions and white-collar work, the contexts to which the word would be applied changed dramatically. Nevertheless, even using the term *vocational education* in its current parlance of indicating a career or job-oriented curriculum, we can readily see that this was precisely how the early founders of the college, and particularly the Presbyterian supporters, understood the mission of Macalester.

As we have already seen, Edward Duffield Neill, steeped as he was in the eastern model of small colleges, viewed higher education primarily as preparation for the three major professions: law, medicine, and the ministry. Young men intending to go into these fields—very few women were allowed into them during the nineteenth century—needed, he believed, a sound Christian understanding of the world as moral undergirding as they took their places as leaders in society. College education as an entrée into these professions has remained prominent at Macalester and other liberal arts schools ever since.[25] By the turn of the century, the expansion of the category of "professions" itself brought additions to the list. Engineering, for instance, was frequently mentioned in the list of professions one could prepare for at Macalester after the turn of the century. Journalism was also added shortly after the turn of the century, when Macalester hired former student Will Kirkwood to teach a news-writing course.[26] And we have already seen that teaching was an approved vocation for women.

Yet for many of the early Macalester supporters, and particularly those associated with the Presbyterian Synod of Minnesota, the primary profession that Macalester was to prepare students for was the ministry. For them, the traditional concept of "vocation" as a special divine call to religious work defined ministry as the highest profession, the highest calling. Preparing students for this calling was Macalester's divine mission. It was for this purpose, some argued in a distinctively millenarian mode, that the institution had been saved from collapse in its early years. The institution's perseverance, perhaps more than anything else, suggested its salvation. Its success in producing ministers proved it. As President Hodgman noted in 1913, Macalester "has been sending somewhere from thirty-three to forty-five per cent of its output of educated men and women into some form of Christian Ministry."[27] For the men, a religious career in the nineteenth century had invariably been seen as ministry, with missionary work as an extension of ministry. But religious vocations expanded enormously in the early twentieth century, adding a number of jobs that welcomed, indeed preferred, nonordained laypeople. If the ministry was reserved for the best and the brightest, there were many other ways believers could serve God short of attending seminary. Proponents of missionary work, for instance, encouraged lay participation.[28] The YMCA and YWCA employed laymen and laywomen who worked with youth groups throughout the country. The bureaucratization of denominations and other religious organizations required a host of new white-collar workers. Renewed emphasis on religious education brought more new job categories, from Sunday school teachers and superintendents to a host of denominational and church workers. Historian of religious education Stephen A. Schmidt notes that Protestant leader and president of the University of Chicago William Rainey Harper "called for multiple ministries, redefining the ministry to include options such as teaching, administration, college academic careers, music, and medical missionary work."[29] As in other professions, Harper urged those going into religious work to adopt specializations.

Harper's view attests to the fact that ministerial work, like many fields of endeavor, was becoming increasingly professionalized, propelled by new academic inquiries. The newly developed social sciences, particularly psychology and social work, shed new light on religious ideas and practices, and progressive educators soon integrated these outlooks into college and seminary curricula. Using empirical methods, Christian practitioners in these new fields confidently blended scientific methods of data collection and analysis into their understanding of God, creation, and being in the world. Here the revelation and science memorialized in Neill's seal for the college remain united. The methods of science, religious liberals argued, would bring to Christianity wholly new, rational, and verifiable legitimacy. It would strengthen the belief in God precisely because it would more closely link the divine to the rational.

Nationally, the work of several individuals constructed new relationships between religion and science, particularly within the new social sciences that were being developed. For instance, Presbyterian George Albert Coe, one of the founders of the Religious Education Association, championed the use of empirical methods in the advancement of religion, arguing that by drawing on the insights of psychology and sociology, pastoral care would "become an art" as pastors used their new knowledge of the processes of moral development in children and adults or of the gendered psychological differences between men and women to guide them in their dealings with parishioners.[30] Coe was joined in his enthusiasm for the new "science of religion" by such people as Harper and G. Stanley Hall, both of whom drew on sociological and psychological models of human development. William James at Harvard did breakthrough research in using empirical methods to investigate religious phenomena, applying, for instance, the methods of psychology to the study of the central Protestant religious experience—the conversion experience.[31] As historian Stephen A. Schmidt asserts, although it was possible that "modern science" would be seen to stand "against religion," these thinkers felt that science, "rather than being threaten[ing]," could be used to "achieve working alliances with the world of modernity and the subject of religion. Historical criticism, sociology, psychology, and educational theory were all companions in the new world they sought to bring into being."[32] And they became the foundation of a newly professional clergy.

These efforts to study religion scientifically, as historian Amanda Porterfield reminds us, "did not draw a firm distinction between the analysis of religious life and its pursuit."[33] Indeed, many located this progressive model of scientific advancement in the understanding of religion within the context of their millennial view of social and political improvement, a view that rested on the widespread assumption that American democracy constituted the only divinely ordained model of political organization.[34] For Harper, for instance, not only was Christianity democratic at its heart but it was the responsibility of all Christians, and particularly of Christian higher education, to advance that democracy. In his words, "the university is the prophetic school out of which come the teachers who are to lead democracy in the true path."[35] Coe was even more explicit in linking Christianity with democracy, explaining, "I use the term 'democracy of God' in place of the 'kingdom of God,' not because I desire to substitute a new social principle for that which Jesus taught, but because the idea of democracy is essential to full appreciation of his teaching."[36] Schmidt summarizes the dominant values of these progressive evangelicals in this way: "truth, including religious truth, is enhanced by scientific method; religion is the essence of democratic life; God is the name for the experience of love and intimate affirmation; and the way to the divine is through social processes of human interaction."[37] For these individuals and the liberal movement, Protestantism exemplified "democracy in religion,"[38] and their goal was to "accept the result of scientific research as data with which to think religiously."[39] Protestantism, for modernists, loosed the shackles of orthodoxy and embraced "freedom in thought and belief."[40] Thus, although the nineteenth-century language of the Kingdom was falling away and the millenarian idea of Jesus's return was given less prominence, the correlation of American society with God's plan remained in place. Now, however, that plan was seen as manifest in the democratic political agenda and the advancement of knowledge through scientific inquiry.

These new, liberalizing ideas within evangelicalism had a significant impact on how Macalester's leaders thought about themselves as Presbyterian educators and about the role of the college. Most important, they understood that to provide the college-level preprofessional education that future clergy would need, these new ideas had to be incorporated into Macalester courses and curricula and, in particular, into the messages the college conveyed about religious vocations. But Macalester leaders did not limit their efforts to preministry students. Following the general trend toward encouraging lay adoption of religious vocations, the scientifically grounded religious training and advising on the host of new religious vocations were made available to all students. An initiative in this latter area was spearheaded by President Hodgman, who wrote extensively on the topic of Christian education, as he attempted to integrate vocational advising into the responsibilities of the faculty. In his view, vocational advising had a critical religious purpose: to assist the student in developing "a clear conception . . . of his ordained place in the world and his consequent duty to society and to God." Hodgman offered the faculty several suggestions for effective vocational advising:

> Time should be taken for analysis of [the student's] ancestral bents, early environments, capacities and tastes as show in studies, recreation, reading. Some never develop a clear bent. Where they do, the Adviser can conserve students [sic] time, energy, enthusiasm and prevent the usual wasteful experimenting of early manhood. Bent once determined, the Adviser should focus student's curriculum, physical exercise, reading, recreation, habits—all on the vocation selected. . . . The Advisers should wage a persistent campaign—through frequent consolation—to graduate students with clearly defined aims, specialized preparation, self-knowledge and therefore self-confidence.[41]

By 1910, a Department of Vocational Development had been formed to assist in the process. A year later, a *Bulletin* article titled "The Study for Vocations" included medicine and law as well as Christian ministry and missionary teaching.

In addition to the new emphasis on religious vocations, a number of curricular changes were brought about by these professionalizing trends in the ministry and academia. One of these trends was the development of new relationships between the social sciences, philosophy, and religion. Courses in mental science and moral science—rough parallels to philosophy of religion and ethics—had been offered by the religion department since the college's opening. By the 1890s, the catalog listed a course in psychology, whose description was very similar to that of the earlier mental science course. By 1915, the college required six credits in mental science (three of which also counted in the Bible training requirement) and six in either social science, political science, or history combined.[42] In 1926, the college changed the name of the mental sciences and philosophy department to the Department of Mental Sciences, Philosophy, and Psychology, underscoring the close relationships between the social science methods of psychology and the religious and philosophical methods of mental sciences.

Other curricular changes came about through a new emphasis on social science. A sociology course was listed in the earliest Macalester catalogs, though whether it was offered before 1893 is not clear. That year, the course focused on "principles of Socialism" and included a set of lectures by Dr. Egbert of the House of Hope Presbyterian Church on the "application of fundamental teaching of Christianity to current social problems."[43] In 1919, the college heralded the introduction of a new degree in social service, explaining that the course grew out of the "point of view of a Christian College" and that "a student with a professional or technical career in view will find it a solid foundation for his later training."[44] The social service curriculum included courses in vocational development and religious education as well as courses in education, anthropology, history, psychology, sociology, economics, the natural sciences, and homemaking (for the women) or applied mechanics (for the men) and led to an AB degree. Designed with a "special emphasis on the application of Christian principles to modern conditions,"[45] the curriculum intentionally used the Twin Cities as a "ready-to-hand" laboratory, where a student could follow the lead of social researchers across the country and "experiment to his heart's content."[46] In the metropolitan area, the *Bulletin* continued, "The industries are liberally represented, and practically all races meet and mingle together in the 'melting pot' where the processes of Americanization can be seen and studied at first hand."[47] A year later, religion professor Farquhar McRae was offering three new courses under the social science rubric: Social Survey, a methods course on the gathering and use of statistical social service data; Settlements, a course on the settlement house movements; and Child Welfare, a course that covered such areas as "child-saving movements in the U.S.," child labor, delinquency, institutions, and so on. All these courses grew directly out of the work of researchers and educational reformers like Harper, Coe, and James.

This new emphasis on integrating the methods of social science into Christian work and training mirrored the shift in missionary work from evangelizing to providing humanitarian aid. Both took the religious focus off of understandings of divinity and salvation, putting it on human ethical conduct. But the shift could be understood in different ways, depending on the liberal or conservative perspective of the interpreter. At Macalester, the general interpretation was fairly conservative. Learning about social and political contexts of a people provided a foundation for evangelizing, to be sure, but more important, it broadened one's outlook and ultimately provided insight into the superiority of Christianity as both an ethical and a theological system. The Macalester in China idea illustrated this idea. Thus, at Macalester, even though the social sciences offered a distinctively liberal approach to understanding Christianity (liberal in the sense that humanity claims a large measure of agency for changing the world), a distinctive conservative element remained important. As much as humanity might change the world, the point remained the glorification of God and Christianity.

The Bible and Religious Education

Neither the purpose nor the form of religious education at Macalester has ever been particularly stable, but one unifying theme emerges: religious education was always seen to have purposes far broader than simply its benefit to individual students—Macalester leaders believed it played a key role in the development of Christendom itself. Just how that role was defined, however, varied significantly from the earliest days of the college through the mid-twentieth century and, like all other aspects of the curriculum, was routinely subject to rethinking and revision. When the college opened, Bible courses were taught under the rubric of religious instruction. By 1910, they were taught through the Bible Training Department, which was restructured in 1919 as the Department of Religious Education. Though the changes in language are subtle here, they do indicate significant shifts of perspective on the function of the study of the Bible at the college and, as we have seen previously, the understanding of the role of evangelicals in the broader world. Knowledge of the Bible, as we will see, shifted from an end in itself, the foundation of knowledge in all other areas, to having a more specialized role in society. Underlying this transformation were significant challenges to evangelicals' traditional understandings of the Bible.

Edward Neill, as we have seen, viewed Christianity as the foundation of all knowledge and therefore as a necessary element within all education. Furthermore, he viewed Christianity as the foundation of the democratic experiment of the nation. Without a thorough education in Christianity, its citizens would fail in their civic enterprises. Despite Neill's early emphasis on the civic role of religion, it does not figure strongly in the language of the early Macalester material. The development of moral character is described as an important goal, but following the denominational practice of the time, this point is presented within the context of Christian formation—of the shaping of believers—rather than within a specifically civic context. Christian formation, in fact, was the focus sanctioned by the Presbyterian denomination. The Reverend Thomas A. Mc-Curdy, chosen to succeed Neill as president of the college, was more clergy-man than scholar and viewed the college as a preseminary experience, a place where students would prepare for seminary education and, ultimately, careers in the ministry. Whether as ministers or pursuing religious endeavors such as missionary work, Macalester alumni would be directly involved in spreading and maintaining Christianity throughout the region, nation, and world. This evangelizing view set the tone of early religious education at Macalester.

For McCurdy and most of his generation of seminary-trained clergy who came of age prior to the Civil War, religious education was perceived as the straightforward conveying of information presented in the Bible to students. The Bible was understood as the precise word of God and therefore fully consistent and completely accurate. Through courses designed to train students in the information and lessons embedded in scripture and through interpretive sermons and worship services, Christian colleges like Macalester would shape students' moral character and thus provide them with the tools to go on to shape the moral character of the country itself. In this way, religious education carried with it a distinctively civic purpose. Given this fundamental role of religion in the education of students, responsibility for it was entrusted to the president himself. Thus it was natural that the presidents of Macalester and most religious colleges of the period were ordained ministers. McCurdy was the first to shoulder these responsibilities at Macalester, teaching the courses in Old and New Testaments, biblical geography, and biblical literature as well as courses titled Evidences and History of Christianity and History of Free Thought. He was succeeded in the position of president by two more ordained Presbyterian clergymen.

McCurdy's view of Christian education and its role in the world can be gleaned from the description of the study of Christianity in the 1885 course catalog. Writing that the "evidences of Christianity" would be the focus of study, his further explanation espouses the widespread view of the authoritative character of Christianity and its exclusive understanding of divine truth: "By critical analysis and historic review the stability and growth of the Christian system are shown in contrast with the corruption and decay of the false systems of religion."[48] Only through Christianity, and particularly evangelical Protestantism, would humanity improve and flourish. Comparison to other religious perspectives, filtered through this particular Christian perspective of progressive change, illustrated the undesirable, indeed horrible, alternatives of non-Christian worldviews. In describing the Literature of the Bible course, McCurdy emphasized the function of the course in encouraging Christian belief within each student: "the *evangelical* views of the Christian religion are reverentially and tenderly pressed upon the hearts [*sic*] of the student."[49]

It was precisely this view of Christian exclusivity and religious education that was on the wane. For several decades, German scholars had been reshaping the study of biblical texts, approaching them not as divine revelation but rather as historical and literary articulations steeped in and shaped by the historical and cultural contexts in which they were produced. Scholars like Johann Griesbach had compellingly argued, for instance, that similarities among three of the Gospels—Matthew, Mark, and Luke—were so distinct as to suggest that either they shared a common origin or that some other literary relationship existed among them. This "synoptic problem" spurred investigation into the processes through which the texts were created, including the search for a common source as well as exploration of editing and redaction. One result of such approaches to scripture—approaches that focused on the documents as produced by fallible individuals—was that the ideas of the exclusive character of Christian truth and biblical authority were challenged, and Christian apologetics began to be separated from the study of the history of Christianity.

It would take several decades for the influence of these new scholarly models of biblical study to fully reshape Macalester's religion curriculum, but signs of change were beginning to appear at the turn of the twentieth century. In 1900, the course catalog offered an account of religious education at Macalester in which Bible classes and apologetics were newly separated into distinct courses. In addition, the study of the Bible is presented first, suggesting at least some preeminence over apologetics. The Bible, the catalog explains, is "the most important book in the whole range of literature"; it can "furnish the most instructive biographies and histories," and it "contain[s] a literature both in prose and poetry unrivaled in excellence." Only after explaining these literary elements does the *Bulletin* description turn to creedal significance, explaining that the Bible is "the only revelation of a perfect law and of a perfect gospel, and to be one of the principal agencies in the development of true moral character."[50] Even here, though, it is the moral lesson that is paramount, not the revelation of Christ that informed earlier approaches. In addition, this period saw the inclusion of new courses on the study of Hebrew and Jewish history, using the material in the Old Testament as historical information rather than as the prophetic pronouncement of the coming of Christ as fulfilled in the New Testament.[51]

By no means, however, had the college fully embraced the German model of higher biblical criticism or the social scientific (historical) study of the Bible as a nondivine text. The study of the Gospels of the New Testament continued to reiterate the progressive, even millennial view of Christianity and Christian living. The same theme was even more directly addressed in the apologetics courses, which examined Christian theism and "the superiority of its philosophy" in comparison to other religions and philosophies. It was also in the apologetics category, not the Bible category, that the religion department began to offer courses examining the scholarly issues and criticisms posed by "historical Christianity" and historical biblical criticism.

James Wallace, the foremost scholar of Christianity at the college, admitted that he was intrigued by much that historical criticism had to offer, but he combined this interest with his firm belief that the text was the inerrant word of God. George Davis, Wallace's colleague in the Bible department, had studied historical criticism at Yale with William Rainey Harper but seems to have taught the approach only peripherally. The question of whether Davis, a self-professed religious liberal, would insist on teaching higher biblical criticism at Macalester raised concerns. Wallace, for one, expressed concern that Davis might "offend the Conservatives of our constituency," particularly when Davis offered a course in messianic prophecy, a position that by then had been declared heretical by the Presbyterian Church but to which some Presbyterians still adhered. To Wallace's relief, though "there were some echoes of opposition," the book Davis had selected to use in the course "was fairly conservative and Dr. Davis put such emphasis on his teaching and his preaching on the great essential doctrines of our faith that what opposition there was died out."[52]

It would not be until the late 1930s that higher biblical criticism would make significant inroads at Macalester, when a junior faculty member, Milton McLean, apparently taught some of its elements to his freshman Bible classes. Wallace, who strove to remain involved in college affairs long after his retirement, was outraged by his efforts. In a long letter to McLean, Wallace charged that his approach to scripture was far more scientific and materialist than Wallace's own examination of "spiritual forces" depicted in scripture. In the letter, Wallace identified himself as a "moderate conservative" on the topic of religion and his colleague Edwin Kagin, the next senior department member, as a liberal conservative. These positions, he asserted, stood in contrast to those of McLean, who Wallace suggested was much more liberal. In an effort to delineate points of ideological and methodological difference, Wallace asked McLean a series of twenty-one questions (labeled "a" through "u"), all of which pertained to the liberal method of applying historical methods to understanding the origin of scripture and to downplaying or denying the veracity of miracles and supernatural acts, the divinity of Jesus, and the doctrine of biblical inerrancy. This is not a letter any junior faculty would welcome from a senior colleague, and how or whether McLean answered it is not known. It does, however, demonstrate the tensions that Bible departments across the country experienced during the period.

McLean's efforts to teach Macalester students to take a more critical approach to the Bible merely confused students, in Wallace's view. The approach particularly confused "the Freshmen who have little or no training in the critical study of the Bible. The majority of them come from Christian homes in which, as in their churches, they have been taught to believe, as Paul affirms, that all Scripture is inspired of God."[53] Wallace's conservatism had beleaguered many at the college for years, but it also seems to have appealed to some of the most loyal college supporters and donors, including Frederick Weyerhaeuser, who endowed Wallace's chair as well as the Bible department itself. Thus, though college leaders were aware of the changes occurring within the study of Christianity and made some move to acknowledge the new approaches in their classes, it would be several decades before they significantly modified the apologetic character of the evangelical religious education offered at the school.

What did change was the way in which religious education was perceived within the curriculum. In 1915, Macalester followed a trend among Christian colleges by renaming its Bible Training Department as the Department of Religious Education. The premise of religious education was vocational—that all Macalester graduates at some time in their lives would be called on to teach Christianity to others. This might come about as the graduate adopted some form of religious education as a career path, or it might be a more avocational occupation. In any case, for a short time, knowledge of Christianity, pedagogy, and administration was deemed essential to the student's college experience.

The Department of Religious Education was founded to great fanfare in 1919. Supported by the John C. Martin Foundation (which, in 1910, had provided an endowment for the Bible Training Department) and the Frederick Weyerhaeuser

Foundation, this was the first (and perhaps only) department at the college with its own departmental endowment. By 1926, that endowment had reached one hundred thousand dollars, half of which had been given by the late Frederick Weyerhaeuser, another quarter by the Weyerhaeuser family, and another quarter by the Martin Foundation.[54] That endowment was further augmented in 1927, when the Presbyterian Board of Christian Education awarded additional funds through the Mary D. Synnott Fund.[55] Initially, the department was called the Religious Education/Bible Training Department, which was shortened by 1925 to the Department of Religious Education. It was in the inaugural description of the department that the words quoted at the beginning of this chapter appeared. The curriculum that first year, however, differed little from that offered in previous years in the Bible Training Department, although Wallace taught a new course on Bible Pedagogy and Sunday School Work.

Within a few years, however, two new courses had appeared: Organization and Administration of Religious Education and International Lessons (which covered the Presbyterian-approved International Sunday School Lessons). Bible Pedagogy, however, had been dropped. By 1930, a range of pedagogical and administrative courses were offered, among them Curriculum Building in Religious Education, Week-Day Religious Education, Young People's Work, Pedagogy in Religious Education, and Principles of Moral and Religious Education. In that year, the catalog identified three levels of religious study: the required courses level, for students who did not plan on becoming involved in education; the service minor, "to give leadership training to those students who wish to devote some of their time to volunteer work in the various activities of the church"; and the vocational major, which provided a "prevocational foundation" for those intending to go into the ministry.[56] These levels reflected concerns raised within national religious education groups regarding the quality and curriculum of religious education programs in Christian colleges. The questions revolved around the integration of the social sciences into the study of religion as well as the proper role of the study of methods, including pedagogy and organizational and administrative methods. James E. Clarke argued that "the Standard Teacher Training Course" was frequently simplistic and filled with "petty details of Organization and Administration" and that it did not belong in the college curriculum. Many, including those who created the Macalester curriculum, disagreed, arguing that methods courses were "worthy of admission in the curriculum."[57] A survey of seven Presbyterian colleges showed that with regard to methods courses, Macalester offered a total of eight courses for twenty hours of instruction, placing it about in the middle of the pack. Coe College, for instance, offered only one course for two hours of instruction, while Trinity College offered ten for thirty hours.

The purposes behind Macalester's approach to the study of religion, then, shifted significantly during this period. From emphasizing understandings of the role Christianity played as the foundation of all knowledge and the well-spring of individual faith, morality, and national political ethics to emphasizing the importance of learning ways to educate others in Christian thought and practice, the curriculum exhibited something of a sea change. Yet grounding this change was a stable set of courses, taught primarily by James Wallace, on the Bible itself and on the lives of Jesus and the apostles. These courses, too, faced challenges but would not significantly change until after Wallace's death at the age of ninety in 1939.

A Host of Vocations

Macalester did not encourage only religious vocations, however. The religious education program was clearly moving toward the model of normal schools in teacher training. Yet other vocations or career paths were also encouraged through curriculum change during this period. As we have seen, in 1919 social service became a favored vocation, with its own curriculum. This program joined several other vocational training courses and programs already in the Macalester pantheon. Courses in education appear in the course catalog as early as 1912. The year 1906 brought Macalester's first commercial program, a three-year curriculum stressing skills needed in the business world. The curriculum included courses in commercial arithmetic and commercial spelling, which were joined by courses in bookkeeping, shorthand, typewriting, and penmanship. The following year saw the addition of courses in "Laboratory Shop Work" to the science curriculum. These courses, which covered the "construction, use, and repair of Physical apparatus," were added "in response to the general demand throughout the state for Science teachers for Secondary Schools who have had a practical training course."[58] A homemaking curriculum was offered as early as 1911, with courses including The Home, a study of the physical and architectural elements of homes; Domestic Hygiene, focused on health issues, including plumbing, heating, and ventilation; Household Art, examining furnishings; and Social Culture, focusing on family and community life.[59] This homemaking curriculum was apparently aimed at women students as well as men going into the building industry.

Thus, though training for careers in religious education was the most visible vocational course advanced by the college in the early twentieth century, it was by no means the only job-specific training available at the institution. These early vocational courses were developed during the administration of T. Morey Hodgman, who struggled to keep the college afloat financially. Student enrollment, which in 1905 was 204, grew slowly through the period, reaching 325 in 1912. During this period, the majority of those students were in the academy, not the college, a fact that may also have influenced these curriculum choices. By the time the curricular revisions that established the Department of Religious Education and the social services course were made in 1919, the academy had closed; the school was on much firmer financial ground, with an endowment of half a million dollars; and World War I had transformed society.

The Bible and Science

Despite the idealistic rhetoric asserting the role of science in deepening Christian faith and knowledge, college leaders, like all evangelicals of the period, were faced with a number of serious challenges that scientific knowledge and methods were raising with respect to Bible-based faith. Conservative evangelicals, increasingly concerned by what they perceived as the growing secular character of society and pressing their belief in the inerrancy of the Bible as a guide to life in all things, launched public challenges to certain scientific methods and explanations in the 1920s. The noted Scopes trial in Dayton, Tennessee, captured headlines throughout the summer of 1925 as a recently passed state law forbidding the teaching of evolution in the public schools was tested by the ACLU in the Twin Cities; Baptist minister William Bell Riley led the fundamentalist charge to banish the teaching of evolution. Riley took aim at the regional colleges, directing his most vitriolic outbursts at Carleton College and the University of Minnesota, both of which advanced scientific study that countered biblical accounts of creation.

For Riley and his ilk, the real conflict was not simply with science; it was with modernism itself. The nation, as they saw it, was dividing into two parties: the modernists, who "enamored of the Evolution Theory, seek to develop the natural good in man, and trust to education and environment for redemption," and the Christians, who "accept[ing] the speech of Jesus as *ex cathedra* [read inerrant], hope for salvation only through the regeneration of the Holy Spirit and by the merit of the shed blood." He continued, "Modernists, clinging to the Descartes philosophy of Divine immanence, count themselves Divine in nature and make the inner consciousness the court of last appeal. Christians, believing the Bible to be Divine revelation, reckon themselves human and sinful, and look to the Christ of the Scriptures as their one and only Lord and to the teachings of Christ, Prophet and Apostle as constituting the authoritative basis of both creed and conduct."[60] His characterization of a divide between modernists and Christians held sway in a period in which it was clear to many that the evangelicalism of previous generations was no longer compelling.

Though Riley was a conservative Baptist, the Presbyterians were equally caught up in the divide. The flagship Presbyterian seminary, Princeton Theological Seminary, which had championed biblical inerrancy throughout the late nineteenth century and well into the twentieth, was inviting modernists who used historical criticism to understand biblical texts to the table. Moreover, it was moving away from the fundamentalist ideas about the end times and Armageddon that some of its faculty had embraced in the 1880s and 1890s.

Though Riley did not direct his attention to Macalester, the college was not immune to these controversies and similar charges. This was hardly surprising given that since its earliest years Macalester had stressed the alliance between science and religion, going so far as to adopt a seal that articulated that very point. As early as 1906, the Macalester leadership had proven adept at carving out a middle ground between liberal and conservative elements on the question of this relationship. The college's success in attracting Carnegie funds to construct a new science building was one instance of this. Carnegie made enormous amounts of money available for education throughout the country but maintained a policy of not funding denominational colleges. James Wallace, however, was able to argue that the nonsectarian character of the college (however much a fiction at the time) mitigated the foundation's concerns about denominational institutions.

Summer 1926, however, found then president John Acheson fielding questions from a concerned Macalester supporter in Virginia, Minnesota, regarding charges by a local minister that Macalester was corrupting students with evolutionary thinking. According to Arthur G. Bailey, the minister of the First Presbyterian Church in Virginia, one Reverend James P. Welliver of the Northern Gospel Mission, headquartered in that town, included the following notice in a newsletter called the *Searchlight*: "We heard a Judge from Kentucky plead for MacAllister [*sic*] College recently. He made an earnest protest against evolution, which would lead his hearers to believe that to support that school would be to fortify against evolution. Probably the Judge thought so, or had never discovered the contrary. The thought is charitable, but oh, to what breadths the cloak of charity must stretch these days, when a school like this, well known to foster evolutionary teaching, must seek such a covering! God restore us just a little common honesty!"[61] Linking support for the school to support for evolution, Welliver succeeded in raising concerns.

Bailey himself was convinced that Macalester's approach to evolution was sound. He explained, "If this is the truth we have been so blind that though we have had two children who have graduated from Macalester we have not made any such discovery. In fact the impression we had has been that at the most there was a passing reference to the so called 'evolutionary hypothesis' as one of the guesses which had obtained some recognition but still was nothing more than the 'evolutionary hypothesis' and in no sense the O. K. of the college upon a godless evolutionary theory."[62] To this inquiry, Acheson responded, "I have this to say and most emphatically: that no Godless evolutionary theory is being exploited at Macalester College in any department of the institution."[63] He labeled Welliver's charges "untrue," "malicious," and part of a smear campaign and clarified that "at Macalester College, fact is taught as fact and theory as theory. All I can say is that the institution in its Department of Biology as well as in its Department of Religious Education is true to the word of God, constructive in its attitude and thoroughly Evangelical in its spirit."[64]

The issue did not rest there, however. By early August, another Macalester supporter, A. T. Gordon of the Oliver Iron Mining Company in Virginia, sent his one dollar pledge check along with a note asking the college to clarify its position on the theory of evolution, as he had read Welliver's charges earlier in the summer. He explained, "I have my doubts in regard to this statement. But if it is true that Macalester teaches or in any way supports the theory of evolution, I certainly would not have pledged my support had I known it."[65] Gordon's concerns were readily addressed to his satisfaction, but the question of how to respond to Welliver remained. With Acheson out of town on an extended vacation through the month of August, Bailey took matters into his own hands, writing Welliver and denouncing his charges as a parent of two Macalester graduates and one current student. In defending the institution, he claimed that its treatment of evolution had even passed muster from a close associate of William B. Riley himself: "An intimate friend of Dr. W. B. Riley, after careful inquiry regarding Macalester College, told me that at first he was prejudiced against the institution, believing it to be like other institutions in the State, but his every inquiry established in his mind the fact that the safest institution in the State and the most free from godless evolution, in his opinion, was Macalester College, and that he could safely send his child there."[66] Thus Macalester, while not denying that it dealt with evolution, confirmed that it did so in a scientific manner, considering it as a theory for consideration, not a fact. For Bailey, at least, this was sufficient, and he concluded that in his opinion, Macalester's best teachers would never put science ahead of faith in God. He concluded, "Such a man as Dr. Wallace could never, in my opinion, be imagined as permitting any man made theory to take the place of God's creative work."[67]

Despite Acheson's assurances, the question remains whether Macalester faculty members were teaching "godless evolution." Indeed, it is quite likely that some were, at least in some form. O. T. Walter, professor of biology, who is remembered by at least one alumna as teaching about evolution in the late 1930s, proposed in spring 1926 that the college establish a summer school combining religious education and natural history study that would offer fieldwork in botany and zoology. Linking knowledge of the natural sciences to good citizenship, Walter suggested that a summer program would give students an "appreciation of the varied life round about them and its influence upon the present and future welfare of this State."[68] Acheson refused Walter's request, saying that the Executive Committee of the board did not feel sufficient funds were available at that time. He did, however, indicate that the plan might be "carried out another year."[69]

Another incident also suggests that evolution may have been taught in some depth at the college. In 1927, Acheson attempted to shift H. S. Alexander's teaching away from geology and toward physics. Given that Alexander was pursuing graduate work in the area of paleontology, this effort may have sprung from a desire to avoid historical controversy over the age of the earth, another area that fundamentalists had targeted for its contradiction of biblical text. In any event, Macalester students seem to have adopted a similar middle-ground position as Acheson. In an editorial published that same year on the occasion of the Minnesota state legislature's rejection of a bill spearheaded by William B. Riley prohibiting the teaching of evolution in public schools, the *MacWeekly* congratulated the legislature on taking the position it did and opined,

> Too few people realize that the conflict over evolution is merely a conflict between ignorance and science, and not religion and science. Religion would

not need to enter the field of battle at all, if unknowing persons would not thrust it out where it can not [*sic*] help itself. Scientists do not seek to unravel the mystery of "ultimate causation," as one professor put it, but leave that for the philosophers.[70]

This writer, taking a position that was a far cry from the linking of science and revelation that informed the early college founders, retained at least the belief that the two were not at odds with one another. Their respective purviews of influence, however, were distinct and separate. This, too, was the message of the commencement address delivered in 1927 by journalist and author S. J. Duncan-Clark, who concluded his classic Christian modernist statement reconciling science with religion with a metaphorical story about ants fleeing the assistance of a person who tried to use a twig to help them push a dead June bug over a ridge. Like those ants, terrorized by the assistance of an even benevolent hand from above,

> so the helping approach of Science frightens us; it sends us scattering hither and thither, rushing madly about in our little world, surrounded by stupendous facts without meaning, overwhelmed by a knowledge as to ultimate things that leaves us without guidance. And then the God who is in Science, comes to us in Jesus, and we begin to understand; we begin to see that there is a meaning in life; that there is something which science cannot yet measure and weigh and fit into its scheme of uniformity. Whitehead says, "The universe shows us two aspects; on one side it is physically wasting, on the other side it is spiritually ascending." And Jesus is Master of the spiritual ascent.[71]

Such reconciliations would satisfy liberal-leaning Protestants for some time to come, but the controversies would remain. A year later, Macalester admissions recruiter Robert Wallace notified Acheson that he continued to hear rumors that "Macalester professors give all the arguments for evolution, and nothing constructive to back up the Bible."[72] Moreover, it is likely that some of the college's major donors also held more conservative views of the relationship between religion and science, views that may have influenced the growing endowment of the Bible curriculum.

World War I and the Great Commission

As important as these debates about religious vocation, religious education, and the Bible were, it was the outbreak of the Great War and disagreement over the role of the United States within it that had the greatest impact on the institutional understanding of the role of Christian education in general, and Macalester College in particular, in the world during this period. Disagreement over U.S. entry into World War I split the campus, creating a rift that mirrored in the microcosm a chasm developing on the macro level throughout evangelical Protestants nationally.

World War I constituted a significant test for evangelicals. For religious liberals still within the evangelical milieu, the question of U.S. entry into the war tapped into long-held postmillennial beliefs in the efficacy of Christian morality. As historian George Marsden has observed, "the most modernistic versions of their [Christian liberal's] gospel saw God as working through the progress of civilization, especially democratic civilization as found in America. War was then for them quite explicitly a sacred cause."[73] It was Christianity that would save the world, and thus it was the duty of America, as a Christian nation, to go to the aid of Europe. Even moderates and some conservatives embraced this position. James Wallace, for instance, strongly endorsed U.S. intervention as a Christian duty. Popular revivalist Billy Sunday argued that patriotic Christian Americans should support U.S. entry into the war to aid Christian England and France and to defend Christianity. Germany, depicted as the enemy of Christianity, was characterized in this position as an ungodly, aggressive nation that had given the world historical criticism and Friedrich Nietzsche (i.e., atheism) and who had threatened peace and noncombatants. It was the duty of the United States as a Christian nation to "save the world for democracy," a phrase used widely during the period to signal not only a political message about a particular form of government but also the idea that democracy was God's ordained style of government, just as America was God's ordained nation.

Most conservative evangelicals, however, advocated for U.S. neutrality and peace. Few conservatives shared the progressive, postmillennial view of the liberals; in fact, some, although clearly in the minority, were attracted to the premillennialism of dispensational writers who argued that only the second coming of Jesus Christ could save the world. A larger swath of conservative evangelicals, among them William Jennings Bryan, advocated for peace on the grounds that the United States had no legitimate role in the war in Europe and that Christianity would not be furthered by participation in a European war that would hit the poor and working classes far more than the wealthy.

Most of these views could be found at Macalester, although evangelical support for the war came to dominate the campus shortly after some students caused a public controversy over the subject that reached the national news. In February 1917, about three years into the European war, Germany resumed submarine (U-boat) attacks on merchant ships headed for Britain in an effort to block armament shipments from the supposedly neutral United States. As the number of ships and crews attacked rose, casualties mounted. Congress, however, refused U.S. president Woodrow Wilson's request to arm neutral American vessels when a small group of congressmen, panned in the press as the "willful twelve," voted against the measure. The country itself was divided. With thousands of first- and second-generation German constituents, many congressmen argued that the United States should maintain strict neutrality in what was a European problem. Many, however, agreed with Wilson, himself a Presbyterian of a fairly liberal, postmillennial bent, that support for the Allies against Germany was imperative.

In response to the vote, an organization of students calling themselves the Macalester Neutrality and Peace Association formed and distributed a circular letter, signed by eighty-seven Macalester students, supporting those who held out against the majority in Congress. They sent the letter to the local press and to all Minnesota congressmen and senators, urging them not to lead the nation into war. The letter explained that the signators "deprecat[ed] the spread of the militaristic spirit over our country and [were] angered at the jingoistic policy pursued by the American press." They listed seven reasons for maintaining U.S. neutrality, including the argument that "the munitions manufacturers are conducting a nation-wide campaign to force war upon the American people." The letter explained that the students felt that "war for honor" would be futile and that U.S. entry into the war would "only result in a prolongation of the conflict and an extension of its horrors to America." It also clarified that "in order to prevent any criticism of lack of loyalty or patriotism, we declare our love of America and the democratic ideals for which she stands, and affirm our willingness to risk or give our lives for America, whenever such a sacrifice may be necessary."[74]

The response was swift and brutal. Representative C. B. Miller of Duluth blasted the students in a response published in the March 21 issue of the *New*

York Herald, calling the students "pro-enemy and anti-American." He continued, "You say the munitions makers are conducting a campaign to get us into the war. That is the cry of the yellow-streaked and coward soul when confronted by duty, seeking to justify its welching by ascribing improper conduct to others." Miller also cast aspersions on the college, suggesting that "if your institution is making citizens of this character, it becomes a matter of public concern."[75] Miller's denunciation launched the story into the public eye, and the story appeared in the evening edition of the *Minneapolis Journal.*

The story set off something of a firestorm on campus. President Hodgman, according to the *Minneapolis Journal*, made no public statement to the press but expressed the opinion that "a free discussion of politics and public matters by students formed a valuable part of their education."[76] Students interviewed by the *Journal* emphasized that they were not disloyal and that Miller's outburst was not surprising, coming from "those who are trying to force this country into war." Several faculty who supported U.S. entry into the war as a Christian duty came together under the leadership of James Wallace to draft a counterstatement. The statement said, "Believing that permanent world peace is impossible until the bloody despotism of the Turkish empire and the arrogant absolutism of the Hohenzollerns are destroyed, we, the undersigned, do urge that the United States owes it to the cause of democracy, the rights of humanity and to its own good name to engage actively in the war and help overthrow those tyrannous and lawless survivals of a barbarous age."[77] All but three Macalester faculty members signed this statement, which was sent to President Wilson and released to the press on March 22. Speaking with the press, Wallace explained that the statement was made "to help correct the miserable showing made by the peace cranks in the college." The *Daily News* also reported that several students who had signed the original peace document had withdrawn their signatures, four having already enlisted in the navy, one of whom acknowledged that he had not read the document carefully before he signed it. Other patriotic resolutions were soon circulated on campus to counteract the peace document.[78]

The overwhelming counterattack launched in an effort to save the reputation of the college signaled the prominence of the millenarian Christian ethos. But the peace document itself hints at a broader range of political and religious opinion, as does the short list of faculty members who abstained on the counterstatement: Henry Funk, F. J. Menger, and Macalester president Morey Hodgman, who, according to the *Daily News*, was a personal friend of William Jennings Bryan.

A year later, the campus situation had changed radically. President Hodgman had resigned, perhaps (as he predicted in a letter to Edward Neill's daughter) forced out over the neutrality issue by a faction of faculty and trustees.[79] In December, the United States had declared war on Germany, and many Macalester students and alumni had already gone into the service. All told, some 320 Macites served in the U.S. military during World War I, among them six women. Nine men lost their lives. In October, Macalester trustees authorized five thousand dollars "to provide for military training," and in 1918 the college became a government-sponsored Students Army Training Corps site, preparing young men for induction into the service. The college provided housing and offered courses in military drill as well as courses in "surveying, map making, military tactics, and war aims."[80] Groups of men or women drill marching with weapons or flags on campus became a common sight, and after the war, the training effort was transformed into a chapter of the U.S. Reserve Officers' Training Corps.

Students felt the war in other ways as well. A war tax of ten dollars was added to tuition, raising it to eighty-five dollars. The number of young men in school declined precipitously. As the United States went to war, a domestic campaign to eradicate the German language and German culture within the nation ensued. An effort was made in March 1918 to include Macalester in this anti-German campaign, but to the college's credit, the faculty spurned it. A motion was presented to the faculty to discourage the study of the German language in the school, allowing it "only by sufferance" and requiring that a disclaimer be included in the course catalog "justifying the attitude of the college toward the language." The motion itself justified the attitude on several grounds, asserting that "the Prussian military party has revealed plans to world conquest.... Germany has revealed a national and dynastic megalomania without parallel in history and which pervades not a little of her recent literature ... [and] it has been policy of the Pan-Germanic party to push the study of German into all the schools, colleges and universities of the United States as part of their wide spread propaganda." Thus, the motion concluded, "until the military party of German is repudiated by the saner German people, her policy of world conquest abandoned, her government popularized and her universities purged of their pagan philosophy," the teaching of German at the college would be frowned on. Likely presented by Wallace, the motion was seconded by Farquhar McRae, professor of Bible. Some discussion proceeded, and Professor Hall made a motion to table the measure, which carried "by a small vote."[81] Though the faculty spurned this effort, anti-German sentiment was not eradicated, but it did not strongly influence policy.

The next year, 1919, brought not only the end of the war but also the transformation of the curriculum and its embrace of religious education and social service. Given its triumph over German imperialism in Europe, Christianity, many liberal-leaning evangelicals believed, had a bright future ahead of it. For Macalester leaders, the Christian "conquest of the world" was just beginning, and the institution was positioned on the front lines. Soon, however, the military metaphors would fade, intellectual pursuits would shift, and the effort to retain a middle ground between liberal and conservative religionists would become untenable.

7

The Collapse of the
Evangelical Consensus

BY THE 1920S, the evangelical hegemony that had inspired the founding of many colleges like Macalester was disintegrating. Liberal and conservative Protestants differed not only over theological questions but also increasingly over political and social issues. These differences inevitably came to inform differing views of education as well. During his tenure as president of Macalester College between 1924 and his untimely death in 1937, John Carey Acheson was able to maintain cooperation among individuals ascribing to a spectrum of religious and political beliefs. Nevertheless, as we will see, despite the delicacy of this negotiation, the college moved away from conservative religion and the earlier college mission of advancing Christianity.

Internationalism and the Growing Differences among Protestants

The evangelical dream that World War I would spread the democracy of God worldwide was dashed in the postwar period. After the war, postmillennial evangelicals like Woodrow Wilson and, closer to home, James Wallace pinned their hopes on the new international organization, the League of Nations, which they saw as the best opportunity for integrating their religiously based understanding of American democracy into postwar Europe. Through the League's influence, they predicted, America's social and political structures, informed by evangelicalism, would be widely emulated and sweep away the depredations and excesses of prewar Europe. But Congress, whose Democratic wing was increasingly focused now on extricating the country from foreign entanglements and whose Republican wing was focused on internal business expansion, blocked U.S. entry into the very organization for whose founding Wilson would receive the Nobel Prize. For liberal and moderate Protestants like Wallace, who had been loyal to the Republican Party despite their support of Wilson's international agenda, it was inconceivable that "their" party, the party of Lincoln, would turn its back on this opportunity to work closely with other Christian nations to broadcast the Gospel and infuse Christian-based democracy throughout the world. The always outspoken Wallace called it "the Great Betrayal," writing in hindsight that a handful of bitter senators had "betrayed the world's hopes of organized peace and of the substitution of international justice for war."[1] Isolationism grew widespread as Republican leaders who had previously supported U.S. participation in international discussions adopted the view that America should focus instead on its own internal problems.

In contrast to the nation's shift toward isolationism, however, Macalester's interest in internationalism grew. In the 1920s, as we have seen in the previous chapter, this interest grew directly out of the missionary agenda of evangelicalism. That missionary interest would continue at Macalester in the postwar period. John Acheson worked diligently as the national chairman of the Layman's Missionary Movement to convince Protestant men and women of the importance of supporting the always underfunded missionaries who brought Christianity to far-flung places around the globe. Guest missionaries on holiday from their work abroad spoke on campus, exposing Macalester students in the 1920s and 1930s to lectures that stirred their imaginations with stories of the spiritual and, increasingly, physical and medical needs of the people around the world. This evangelical component remained an important force on campus through the 1920s and 1930s.

Yet the cohesion between religious liberals and conservatives that Acheson worked so hard to foster was becoming increasingly difficult to maintain. While liberals like Acheson continued to champion the postmillennial work of Christianity as a means of ameliorating social and political strife throughout the world, religious conservatives even more fervently embraced Biblicism, or the belief in scriptural inerrancy, to help them comprehend the destructive impact of the war. The only salvation for humanity, conservatives argued, would come from God and be available only through individual conversion. While the political counterpart of liberal Protestantism was the desire for a worldwide political federation that would foster cooperation among nations and a commitment to improving the lives of American citizens through social work, the political counterpart of Protestant conservativism, and particularly of fundamentalism, was increasing American isolationism and individualism.

With the crisis of the Great Depression and the advent of President Franklin D. Roosevelt's New Deal, the religious Left was challenged in new ways that distanced them even further from their more conservative coreligionists. The main challenge arose from the transformation in the role of government brought about by the New Deal. Roosevelt's actions, which increased government responsibility for the welfare of individual citizens, challenged the belief in individualism that pervaded all but the most liberal wings of the Protestant church. As we saw in the last chapter, the integration of concerns for social welfare in the church had grown out of the intersection of social science, evangelical home missionary work, and an understanding of Jesus's message as one of love and caring for one's neighbors, which had resulted in the development of the social gospel. Yet only the most liberal of congregations adopted this Christian approach exclusively. At Macalester, as we have seen, social gospel work existed alongside evangelical missionizing. The Depression forced many evangelical churches to adopt a more social approach to their congregational missions as they came to the aid of both congregation members and their neighbors within their communities. Given that Protestantism had only recently taken on responsibility for social welfare, many felt that government work in that area was a dangerous step too far, one that threatened personal integrity as well as American democracy. Conservatives and many moderates like James Wallace predicted doom would result from the New Deal as people relinquished responsibility for their personal affairs to the government.[2] Government welfare programs could only lead to socialism, they claimed, which they viewed as incompatible with democracy, and ultimately to totalitarianism—precisely the demon that threatened Europe. Liberals, on the other hand, embraced social programs in both church and government as a necessary counter to the inequalities that resulted from capitalism. Aiding one's fellow citizens, they believed, would create a more caring, Christ-like society.

At Macalester, a wide range of opinion on these issues was expressed. Liberal Protestants like Acheson carefully linked their belief in the efficacy of Christianity in ameliorating strife in the world with a belief in modernism and science. Moderates and conservatives like Wallace retained more of a belief in the moral power of Christianity to critique the excesses of modernism. Fundamentalists who embraced Biblicism and isolationism were not conspicuous within the Macalester community, although, as we have seen in the previous chapter, such voices from Presbyterian sources outside the campus had some influence there. Despite the fact that the modernist–fundamentalist debates of this period have been characterized by historians as disputes between two opposing camps, Macalester's experience demonstrates that differences among coreligionists were marked more by nuances among positions within the center than by a clash of positions at the extremes.[3] President Acheson was well aware that the Presbyterian families of most Macalester students leaned toward conservative politics, even though their religious beliefs might hover in the middle ground between liberalism and conservativism. Many faculty members, particularly the new, younger people coming in, leaned toward liberalism. But the venerable Wallace, who blended a moderate-to-conservative Protestantism with a liberal foreign policy and conservative domestic social policy, could readily dominate the conversation at the college. In addition, as we shall see, the college was home to one particularly renowned evangelical voice—that of Glenn Clark. Acheson, more religiously and politically liberal than Wallace and Clark, operated as a peacemaker, maintaining ties between liberals and conservatives as late as 1937.[4]

Glenn Clark, the New Evangelical

English professor Glenn Clark was a national figure among evangelicals during the 1920s, 1930s, and 1940s. Hired to teach English composition and literature in the 1910s, as discussed in chapter 5, Clark also coached the Discussion League and the track team in the 1920s. He worked assiduously, teaching twelve hours a week, coaching, advising, and putting many more hours into other extracurricular activities. His biographer and son-in-law Glenn Harding explains, echoing a popular evangelical narrative, that the pace took its toll on Clark. After a near mental breakdown, Clark turned to God for solace and guidance and soon devoted his life to evangelizing others.[5]

In a period in which shaping character was seen as an increasingly important responsibility of the college, Clark assigned himself the task of shaping his students' spiritual lives. In 1921, he developed a "scientific" template for vocational selection that used phrenology—the study of physical features such as head shape, forehead shape and size, nose size and shape, and so forth—as a reflection of individual character, aptitudes, and abilities. He self-published his ideas in a series titled *The Master Key Method of Reading Character*, book V of which contained the template with a number of flaps that covered or exposed vocational selections. When set with all the characteristics of the individual, the template aligned to reveal the correct vocation for that person.

Ever seeking new ways to integrate evangelical religion with contemporary life and students' interests to foster students' personal relationships with God, Clark became inspired by the idea that his coaching skills, previously applied to the secular world of the playing field, could also be applied to developing a relationship with God. Individuals, he argued, must develop spiritual discipline and practice prayer just as one would practice a sport. They must develop their "prayer muscles," so to speak. In 1925, Clark made a splash on the national scene with his first book on prayer, *The Soul's Sincerest Desire*, whose main theme was the power of prayer to effect change. Drawing on the language of sport and coaching, Clark became a popular speaker, delivering a number of chapel lectures at Macalester and throughout the country.

In 1930, Clark founded an evangelical retreat, Camp Farthest Out, in northern Minnesota and published a book of the same name. The camp and the book were both vehicles for his message that prayer was the answer to all problems and that developing prayer was a skill. With this book, Clark also founded the Macalester Park Publishing Company, originally housed in a building just off campus at the corner of Snelling Avenue and St. Clair. That publishing house, run by his daughter and son-in-law, published about a book a year of Clark's work between 1930 and 1955 as well as many other evangelical titles.

While Clark was making a name for himself in evangelical circles, Macalester College, as we have seen, was beginning to move away from evangelicalism. Just what the other faculty thought of Clark is difficult to ascertain given the lack of documentary materials, but to hypothesize that some tension likely existed is not particularly outlandish. Just when the Department of Religious Education was turning outward toward social science and the social gospel, Clark was turning inward toward nineteenth-century pseudoscience, individual salvation, and the supernatural power of prayer. In the 1930s and 1940s, Clark encouraged prayer as a remedy for college problems, particularly financial ones, a solution that at least some of the administration and trustees were not likely to take as seriously as he did, though every faculty and trustee meeting began with a prayer.

Clark also claimed to have significant success in his spiritual counseling, particularly with the members of the track team in the 1920s. One student who, he claimed, had "nothing but failures against him" and whose own father had given up on him had been sent to Clark. "We had a talk in which I 'read his character' probed down to find some unknown deeper interests which he didn't realize he had before and the next semester he received nothing but high grades, became the best writer in college among the men, was made editor of the Gateway for this year, played on the athletic teams, and his father and uncle plan to send him to Oxford next year and make a man of letters out of him."[6] Clark's work with this individual exemplified most religious counseling at the college during the period, as individual faculty members connected, often by chance, with individual students.

Clark, who was never ordained, would remain in the English department until his retirement, attracting the confidences of students seeking out and comfortable with his evangelical beliefs. The presence on campus of this well-known evangelical writer likely assisted Acheson in maintaining cohesion among the various constituencies and increasingly diverse religious perspectives represented among Macalester stakeholders. Clark's more religiously conservative views would have reassured certain parents and community members about the college, whose president was understood to have fairly liberal theological views. Indeed, as Macalester Park Press flourished, evangelicalism remained a significant component of the college's public reputation through the 1920s and 1930s.

Liberal Arts and the Small College Mission

Despite Clark's presence, however, the challenges posed by national and international political circumstances and the growing rift between liberal and conservative Protestants played out at Macalester and other church-related colleges in a variety of ways, including through the reconsideration of the mission of these small colleges. During the 1920s and 1930s, the purpose of denominational colleges came under national scrutiny as religion and education increasingly came to be seen as perhaps compatible but essentially separate endeavors. Whereas evangelicals had closely linked the two enterprises, Protestant liberals increasingly saw religion as a private matter that, although an important aspect of life, was not an appropriate component in the study of science or in education generally. The link between Christianity and knowledge was uncoupling. And if Christianity was not the foundation of all knowledge, as, for instance, Edward Duffield Neill and the founders of Macalester had believed, then what was the mission of the Presbyterian college? Should not seminaries handle all necessary religious education, leaving college to provide a broader, scientifically based education?

The University of Minnesota, which did just that and had always vied with

Macalester for Presbyterian students, was gaining a solid reputation, coming into its own just as the function of private religious institutions was coming under attack. The university had much to offer students, including highly trained faculty who could offer a wide range of courses of study. Moreover, its strengths increasingly lay in the vocational realm—in graduate training for careers in the world. Macalester, with its limited funds and fewer and less-credentialed faculty, found itself in the same boat as many other denominational colleges, scrambling to offer a curriculum that would attract good students and struggling to justify its existence. The pressures of students' and parents' desire for practical education that would result in employment seemed almost overwhelming, and some Macalester leaders associated the interest in practical education as evidence of a deepening strain of anti-intellectualism. As Acheson pointed out in a report to the trustees,

> Scholarship in our day unfortunately has fallen into disrepute. It is about the last thing that the average undergraduate seeks when he reaches the campus. He either identifies scholarship with pedantry or considers it rather a questionable virtue that should not be permitted to interfere with his college course.[7]

In this context, college leaders like Acheson turned to the liberal arts as a means of justifying their existence. Vocational training, though important, did nothing to counter the growing "aversion of the intellectual life."[8] Liberal arts education, in contrast, offered the means to demonstrate the value of scholarship and critical thinking. What colleges could offer, argued the leaders of the national Liberal Arts College Movement, a consortium with which Macalester was involved, was a deep experience in the liberal arts—a well-rounded, broad-based education, accompanied by the benefits of smaller classes and individualized attention from faculty. For Acheson, the denominational college must not "surrender its ideals." It must avoid participating "in the popular conspiracy of making learning easy." But here, as in other areas, Acheson sought to negotiate differences. Macalester had, of course, offered vocational or prevocational courses for many years; in fact, in the view of many, its original purpose, as indicated by the desires of the synod and the first official president, had been to provide preministerial training. Yet those courses, Acheson argued, were not "without a certain liberal content."[9] Acheson's commitment to the liberal arts was not compromised by his willingness to maintain some vocational courses, and under his leadership and his involvement with the national Liberal Arts College Movement, Macalester took up these questions, working with other liberal arts colleges to define its mission in a way that would minimize direct competition with larger universities.

In 1929, Acheson submitted to the trustees a comprehensive plan to reorganize the college curriculum and mission statement, develop faculty, and build new facilities to emphasize these liberal arts themes. Among the features of the plan were efforts to move beyond the lecture–examination format to provide learning opportunities that better served different students. As Acheson explained in a letter to the head of the Liberal Arts College Movement, "the chief objection to the lecture method is that it degenerates into formality; the chief objection to the objective examination is that it measures only one kind of intellectual progress; the chief objection to the essay examination is that it promotes a careless attitude toward writing."[10] In contrast, he cited the example of an experimental interdisciplinary course taught through the English and history departments that drew on pedagogical strategies designed to counter these pitfalls. Titled Modern World Cultures, the course integrated, in Acheson's words, "history, a social science" and "English, a social art," with the goal of integrating and balancing three educational objectives: "factual knowledge, skill in interpretation, and power of socialized expression."[11] Each week, students in the course heard two lectures, participated in a writing laboratory and a two-hour student-conducted conference, and took an objective quiz. The course, in Acheson's view, served as a model for the type of intensive learning environment that liberal arts colleges could offer.

Acheson's 1929 plan included other strategies to raise the intellectual rigor and reputation of the college through testing and other means. For one, admissions requirements would be raised above the previously required fifteen high school credits to include entrance examinations. Furthermore, comprehensive exams would be administered at the end of the sophomore year. Other strategies to enhance academics included the creation of honors courses for those juniors and seniors who performed at the highest levels on the sophomore exams. The plan also proposed the creation of fellowships to be awarded each year to seniors to be used for graduate study. With respect to faculty, the plan made provisions to enhance their financial security with higher salaries and to offer retirement and insurance. With respect to the physical plant of the college, the plan called for the construction of at least six new buildings: a library, a classroom and administrative building, a science building, a chapel, a fine arts building, and a student activities building, each of which would be equipped with the most modern of facilities.[12]

Despite its focus on academics and intellectual development, Acheson's plan was no secularizing document. Concern for the religious life of the campus was also addressed in the plan, in which Acheson argued that "the only sufficient and justifiable reason why the Church is engaged in the business of education rests on the moral and spiritual values that should be emphasized in the Christian college,"[13] that is, on the development of students' Christian character. Though the development of Christian character had always figured prominently in the college's mission, that the role of Christianity in this plan was limited to character building is significant. Just as the emphasis on vocation building in the 1910s required new faculty to guide students in that area, this new emphasis on character building would require a new position within the college, that of campus minister. The person who filled this position would attend to the religious life of the campus and the pastoral needs of the students. This role had previously been assumed by the faculty, many of whom were ordained, and by the ministers of local churches, particularly the nearby Macalester Presbyterian Church. But the new position would bring an added dimension to the college, now to be increasingly focused on academic rigor. As Acheson suggested, the campus minister should be an individual who was "primarily a man of heart rather than of head—sympathetic, kindly and approachable, who possesses spiritual vision and leadership."[14] This recommendation, eventually instituted as the campus chaplaincy, would consolidate religious life in a central office.

Though endorsed by the board of trustees in 1929, Acheson's visionary plan suffered from poor timing. As the economic situation worsened the next year, the plan was shelved. Nevertheless, Macalester was on the cutting edge of this movement, which would be recognized in fall 1931 by U.S. president Herbert Hoover, who labeled liberal arts colleges the "seed beds" of the nation's leadership in a speech during national education week.[15] Acheson's plan for and vision of Macalester as an intellectual and academic leader would be revived several years later, when the financial situation of the college improved. Sadly, its author would not live to see its implementation.

Internationalism in the Post–World War I Period

Macalester had more to offer than pedagogical flexibility. The course titled Modern World Culture illustrated another growing area of interest in Macalester's curriculum: internationalism. By the early 1930s, this course was not alone in its focus on international topics. Others included International Law, taught through the political science department, and a new course in the Spanish language. In October 1932, the history department, at the instigation of new professor Rob Roy MacGregor, organized the formation of the International Relations Club (IRC) for "those students in the college interested in contemporary international questions."[16] With a strict membership requirement of the completion of six semester hours of history or related subjects, club membership remained relatively low, but its work quickly spread across the campus and into the larger community. The club affiliated itself with the Carnegie Endowment for International Peace, which brought together similar clubs throughout the United States. In 1933, Macalester's IRC staged a model assembly of the League of Nations and a Pan-American Day conference. In 1934, it hosted a meeting of the IRCs of the Twin Cities, which included papers on "The Challenge of Fascism," "The Cost of War in Dollars and Sense," "Cuba, the Platt Amendment and Reciprocity," and "American Students in Tomorrow's World."[17] The club also sent Macalester representatives to similar gatherings sponsored by other colleges and groups, participating, for instance, in the fifth annual meeting of the Mississippi Valley International Relations Clubs Conference, held in 1935 under the auspices of the St. Paul Council of International Relations Clubs.

Professor MacGregor, deeply involved in the activities of the club, advanced international engagement in other ways as well. In 1933, he introduced a new course titled The Rise and Development of Central and South American Republics to the history curriculum, lectured widely on topics related to South America, and was involved with Pan-American Day activities.

Through these activities, the institution began to develop a reputation for its international focus. The local press covered several of these events, resulting in the college's growing public profile as an institution involved in international studies and activities.[18] The March 1935 issue of the *Macalester College Bulletin* highlighted the college's efforts in the area of internationalism, focusing on "languages, social sciences, and world citizenship."[19] As the *Bulletin* announced on its cover, "The Liberal Arts College Teaches its Students to be Internationally Minded and Encourages them to Enter Governmental Service, Either Domestic or Foreign." In his introductory remarks in the periodical, President Acheson claimed that it was the responsibility of colleges and universities to be apprised of "our vital international relations" and to take the lead in "creating that spirit of good will and sympathetic understanding which alone will guarantee for us a peaceful and happy world."[20] Expanding on this point, he explained that the institution of higher learning had a "responsibility in preparing its students for intelligent citizenship and effective diplomatic service" as a means of avoiding such historic, "stupid and blundering" actions as the Chinese Exclusion Act "and our immigration policy which refuses to put races from the Far East on a quota basis." Education on international situations was something that the colleges could develop effectively, "through properly coordinated curriculum and the inspiration of scholarly teachers in the field of the social sciences and languages." Thus, he concluded, "It is my sincere conviction that the colleges in the United States, efficiently organized and manned, constitute the most hopeful sources from which we may draw recruits for diplomatic service and for the enlightenment of our future citizenship in the whole field of international problems."[21]

Articles in the issue included a brief history of the IRC and a description of its newest project, an electrified wall map of the world in which small colored lights on the map lit up to identify certain world hot spots and were linked with explanatory text. This Current Events Board was placed on display in Old Main. Other articles in this issue of the *Bulletin* included a piece on the first intercollegiate Model Assembly of the League of Nations; a description of the work of visiting expert on Hispanic-American history W. S. Robertson, who was being sponsored by the college's Funk Memorial Foundation; and articles on the study of Spanish, German, and French. In addition, it included vocational articles on political science and government service; economics and foreign/domestic service; and sociology, history, and social work.

Apart from an initial epilogue on the cover of the issue, which stated, "God Divided Man Into Men That They Might Help Each Other," this *Bulletin* did not link international concerns with the religious mission of the college, a marked difference from the earlier interest in internationalism spurred by missionary work. The new impetus for engagement in world actions was a sense of the interconnectedness of nations and the desire to avoid armed conflict rather than a desire to advance Christian ideology. The goal was to shape Macalester students into good citizens of the world. Though missionary work remained a topic for chapel services and a vocational option connected to the religion department, it was clearly on the wane in the 1930s. As Macalester's social and political interest in world affairs expanded in the next decade, the missionary impulse would eventually fade entirely.

The IRC attracted both native-born American students and international students. In fall 1939, for instance, it sponsored a convocation featuring a discussion by Macalester international students hailing from Czechoslovakia, South America, and Germany.[22] Among the organizers and presenters was new student Gunther Theodore Mitau, a German-Jewish immigrant who had arrived on campus a year earlier, having completed a year of study each in Prague, Czechoslovakia, and at New York University before heading to the Midwest. Mitau quickly became a high-profile student, writing for the *MacWeekly*, taking on a leadership role in the IRC, and shining in his classes.

Likely due to Mitau's influence, interest in Judaism surged on campus. The week after the IRC convocation on international students, a week that marked the one-year anniversary of the Nazi rampage of Kristallnacht in Mitau's native Germany, Macalester held a convocation on Jewish-Christian relations featuring a talk by Herbert L. Seamans of the National Conference of Christians and Jews. In place of its regular Wednesday service that week, the chapel held a "Jewish weekday service, in which students took part, conducted by Rabbi Albert G. Minda of the Temple Israel in Minneapolis." Marking what was likely the first non-Christian religious service to take place on campus, the *MacWeekly* coverage of the event noted that the Temple's men's choir that performed at the service included as a member Hollis Johnson, the head of the Macalester music department. The order of the service, outlined in the article, echoed categories that would have been very familiar to Macalester's Christian student population: Call to Worship, Affirmation of the Unity of God, Sanctification, Prayer for Peace, Silent Devotion, and Adoration.[23]

In this way, interest in internationalism began to foster a parallel interest in other religions, an interest no longer rooted in a desire to demonstrate the superiority of Christianity, as had been the case in the early years of the college, but in a desire to better understand people throughout the world and at home on campus.

The Great Depression

The Great Depression of the 1930s brought a new period of financial strife to the college, though not this time so severe as to threaten the college's existence. In 1933, 41 percent of the college's endowment investment was nonproductive, with the rest returning at a rate of 3.5 percent. The number of enrolled students dropped significantly, from 553 in 1931 to 471 in 1932. The college reduced tuition to bring enrollments back up, and by 1933, 576 students were enrolled. Over the same period, the return on rents from college-owned property (mostly farms in north central Minnesota) dropped from $1,604 to $326, and their interest return dropped from over $54,451 to just $12,403.[24] In 1933, Acheson appealed to the Presbyterian Board of Christian Education for assistance, only to learn that the previous year their budget had been cut by a fifth and that year had been cut by nearly a third.[25] In 1935 and 1936, the college's investments in farms in central Minnesota earned nothing because of crop failures associated with the drought, and the college was forced to cut salaries and amenities to keep its doors open.[26] The timing of the financial crisis was particularly awkward in that the new liberal arts curriculum had to be put on hold until the financial situation eased. Nevertheless, Macalester leaders had reason to be hopeful: a new and unexpected donor was emerging—the newly wealthy son of James Wallace.

DeWitt Wallace had gone on from an ignominious Macalester career in the early years of the century to found, with his wife, Lila Acheson Wallace, *Reader's Digest*, a monthly periodical that condensed articles from established publications to present them to a broader audience.[27] Founded in 1922, the *Digest* experienced extraordinary growth, which continued through the Great Depression. Between 1929 and 1935, its circulation grew over 400 percent, reaching 1,457,500 in 1935 and outselling, as historian John Heidenry points out, *Time*, *Newsweek*, the *New Yorker*, *Vogue*, *Harper's Bazaar*, and *Popular Science* combined.[28] As DeWitt and Lila's success grew and news of it became public, they soon became important donors to Macalester, largely due to James's efforts. Their initial donations came in 1931.[29] As the *Digest* grew more profitable—an article on corporate salaries printed in the *St. Paul Pioneer Press* on January 8, 1935, listed the *Digest*'s business manager and managing editor being paid at the astonishing rate of $102,467 yearly apiece—James Wallace pressured his son to support the college even more. Perhaps not coincidentally, later that year President Acheson announced that Macalester would embark on a capital campaign with the goal of raising one million dollars, some of which had already been pledged, likely by Wallace.[30]

In fall 1936, *Fortune* ran an article about *Reader's Digest* that described DeWitt and Lila as among the wealthiest business owners in the country.[31] Shortly after the publication of this article, James Wallace, astonished at the wealth of his son, urged him to do more for the college, writing in a letter, "I wish you both to know that I fervently hope and pray that you may be able and willing to build on the foundation I have given most of my life to lay here in Macalester."[32] He went on, somewhat prophetically, "I am often told that Macalester College is my monument. Would it not be glorious if you both would make Macalester your monument also? Your support will give great impetus to its up-building. Who knows but you were born for such a high calling?"[33] Sadly, DeWitt's response to his father's letter, if he wrote one, has not surfaced.[34] The relationship between the pointedly nonreligious DeWitt and his staunchly Presbyterian father was often strained; nevertheless, DeWitt would grow increasingly interested in sustaining the work of the college over the next several decades. In this case, it is clear that he did act on his father's wishes, for by Christmas, James was thanking him profusely for his donation to the college, some of which was used to provide pensions for elderly professors Anderson and Kingsley, allowing them to retire.[35]

DeWitt and Lila preferred that their names not be linked to their contributions to the college. In 1936, they refused Macalester's efforts to honor them with Doctor of Letters degrees. They also formed the Byram Foundation, named after the lake near their newly built home, High Winds, at Pleasantville, New York, and by 1938, all donations from the Wallaces to Macalester came through that foundation, which made yearly donations to the college beginning in 1938, when they donated seventy-five thousand dollars.[36]

In the late 1930s, then, with Wallace donations in hand, the board of trustees was in a good position to demonstrate the worth of the college and seek out further funding. With the Acheson liberal arts plan in hand and ready to be implemented and the promise of rising income on the horizon, it was an exciting time, though meeting current operating expenses continued to be problematic given the lack of income from the college's major investments. The capital campaign rolled along quite successfully. In mid-November 1937, President Acheson took a ten-day trip to Washington, D.C., Philadelphia, and Chicago seeking contributions to the college. On his return to St. Paul, he became ill and entered St. Luke's Hospital on the morning of November 24. He lapsed into a coma later in the day and passed away that evening. Acheson was sixty-seven years old at the time of his death.

During his thirteen years in the presidency of Macalester, Acheson had been a strong presence on campus, an energetic advocate of college advancement through improved intellectual rigor and interest in internationalism. Unlike earlier presidents, he envisioned a college that could compete academically with the likes of Carleton, Hamline, and the University of Minnesota. Presiding over the college at a critical time, when the relationship between religion and education

Top, "Nature and Revelation, the Twins of Heaven." Baldwin School seal, created by Edward Duffield Neill, 1853. Image from Baldwin School handbill, 1859. Courtesy Macalester College Archives, DeWitt Wallace Library.

Bottom, Macalester College seal. Courtesy Macalester College Archives, DeWitt Wallace Library.

Above, Minnesota State Officers, 1861–62. Promotional handbill. Note Edward D. Neill at no. 10, top of star. Courtesy Minnesota Historical Society.

Opposite, top, Edward Duffield Neill. Photograph ca. 1885. Courtesy Macalester College Archives, DeWitt Wallace Library.

Opposite, bottom, Edward Duffield Neill and family at home. Stereograph ca. 1860. Courtesy Minnesota Historical Society.

EDWARD DUFFIELD NEILL, 1823 - 1893
Founder and First President

JESUS COLLEGE,

At the FALLS OF SAINT ANTHONY is CHRISTIAN, but unsectarian. It will comprise for the present Two Schools.

1. The SCHOOL OF CHRISTIAN LITERATURE, supplemental to the State University which is avowedly secular.

2. The BALDWIN GRAMMAR SCHOOL designed to prepare Students for the University of Minnesota.

The College will have ample accomodations. Any University Student who complies with the Rules may obtain a room. The fall term will begin on 5th of SEPTEMBER. At least a month before, Students should apply for admission, by letter or in person to the PROVOST

REV. EDWARD D. NEILL,
St. ANTHONY P. O., MINNESOTA.

Opposite, top, Winslow House, St. Anthony (Minneapolis), Minnesota. Photograph ca. 1870. Courtesy Minnesota Historical Society.

Opposite, bottom, Jesus College Handbill, ca. 1871. Courtesy Minnesota Historical Society.

Above, Charles Macalester, photograph undated. Courtesy Macalester College Archives, DeWitt Wallace Library.

VIEW OF AMHERST COLLEGE, WITH THE NEW CABINET & OBSERVATORY. (FROM THE SOUTH WEST.)

MAP OF
MACALESTER PARK
SURVEYED AND DRAWN BY
ELMER & NEWELL
FOR THE
MACALESTER PARK SYNDICATE
—OF—
ST. PAUL & MINNEAPOLIS.
SCALE 180 FEET=1 INCH

D.S.B. Johnston, President
Jas. F. Brown, Vice President
Thos. Cochran, Jr. Secretary
R.M. Newport, Treasurer

SUMMIT AVE.

DARTMOUTH ST.

HAMILTON ST.

PRINCETON

CAMBRIDGE

RUTGERS ST.

RESERVE AVE.

COLLEGE GROUNDS

FOR FULL PARTICULARS APPLY TO
COCHRAN & NEWPORT,
ST. PAUL, MINN.

THE NEW ELECTRIC LINE—MACALESTER COLLEGE AND SUMMIT AVENUE BOULEVARD.

Opposite, top, Amherst College, Amherst, Massachusetts. Woodcut ca. 1853. Courtesy Minnesota Historical Society.

Opposite, bottom, Plat map of Macalester Park by Elmer and Newell, 1883. Courtesy Minnesota Historical Society.

Top, Macalester College and Summit Avenue. *Northwest Magazine,* April 1886. Courtesy Minnesota Historical Society.

Bottom, Intersection of Summit and Snelling avenues, St. Paul, Minnesota. View is to the west, down Summit, showing Macalester faculty housing on the left. Photograph ca. 1886. Courtesy Macalester College Archives, DeWitt Wallace Library.

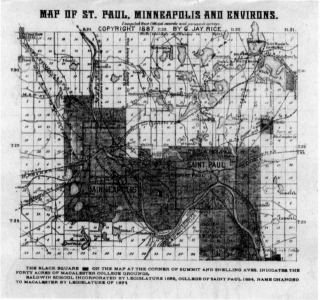

Top, Macalester College, original East Wing. Photograph ca. 1886. Courtesy Macalester College Archives, DeWitt Wallace Library.

Bottom, Map of St. Paul, Minneapolis, and environs, which was used on the Macalester College stationary in the late 1880s. Courtesy Minnesota Historical Society.

Opposite, top, Thomas McCurdy. Photograph ca. 1885. Courtesy Macalester College Archives, DeWitt Wallace Library.

Opposite, bottom, The East and new West Wings of Macalester College (left), shed, President's house (1586 Summit Avenue), Wallace house (1596 Summit Avenue), Eutrophian Hall (Grand Avenue), Faculty House (1620 Summit Avenue), and Ramsey School (Grand Avenue). Photograph ca. 1890. Courtesy Macalester College Archives, DeWitt Wallace Library.

Opposite, Macalester College class of 1889, the first college-level graduating class. Photograph ca. 1889. 1. George Achard, 2. Joseph W. Cochrane, 3. Benjamin W. Irwin, 4. S. W. Kirkwood, 5. William P. Lee, 6. E. P. E. McCurdy. Courtesy Macalester College Archives, DeWitt Wallace Library.

Above, Macalester College class of 1890. From left: T. T. Creswell, J. L. Underwood, W. P. Kirkwood, J. K. Hall, A. A. Randall, M. A. Clark, W. H. Humphrey. Photograph 1890. Courtesy Macalester College Archives, DeWitt Wallace Library.

Above, James Wallace. Photograph ca. 1890. Courtesy Macalester College Archives, De-Witt Wallace Library.

Opposite, top, Women students of Macalester College. *Front row*: Frances Blair Oakley Leck, Almira Fulton Lewis. *Second row*: Nellie Flanders Sherwin, Hulda Eckern, Katherine McMillan, Mable Emma Dunlop, Belle Campbell. *Third row*: Florence Julia Watson, Anna Moore Dickson, Winifred Viola Moore, Louise Pederson, Mary E. Mackin. *Back row*: Miss Kellogg, Alma Dodds, Janet Watson Dade, Mary Ella Borchert, Clara Jackson Kingery. Photograph ca. 1896–97. Courtesy Macalester College Archives, DeWitt Wallace Library.

Bottom, Wallace Hall dining room, Macalester College. Photograph ca. 1907. Courtesy Macalester College Archives, DeWitt Wallace Library.

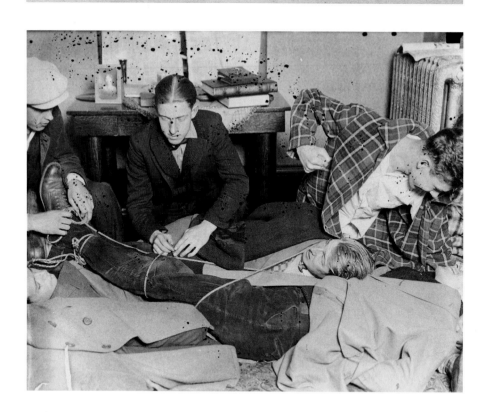

Opposite, top, "We Want Men." Promotional handbill ca. 1912. Courtesy Presbyterian Historical Society, Presbyterian Church (USA), Philadelphia.

Opposite, bottom, Student hazing prank, Macalester College. Photograph ca. 1923. Courtesy Minnesota Historical Society.

Above, Margaret Doty and Clarence Ficken (right) celebrate Macalester's Golden Jubilee with Donald Cowling (left), President of Carleton College. Photograph 1936. Courtesy Minnesota Historical Society.

Above, James Wallace being pinned with a homecoming button by Macalester students Fern Stolberg [?], Frances Solman [?], and Elizabeth Thornton [?]. Photograph ca. 1938. Courtesy Macalester College Archives, DeWitt Wallace Library.

was being challenged on several fronts and undergoing enormous change, Acheson guided Macalester toward progressive politics and liberal religion, while working to minimize conflict with those who held more conservative outlooks. What all could agree on was the importance of his effort to enhance the college's academic life and his leadership in the capital campaign. At the time of his death, Acheson had accumulated pledges of over $560,000.[37] James Wallace, delivering the eulogy at Acheson's memorial service, noted that "the cross which Dr. Acheson had to carry all the time was the discrepancy between what the college was and what he knew it should be."[38] His "indefatigable efforts" to accomplish this, Wallace argued, "undermined his strength and brought him to the grave," but his sacrifice was not in vain, for "all through his administration, the college steadily grew in influence and prestige."[39]

His death in office hit the college hard. Acheson's successor would not be named for nearly two years; in the interim, Dean Clarence E. Ficken, professor of French, would serve as Macalester's top-ranking officer. The delay, though not fully surprising given the suddenness of Acheson's death, was protracted, in large measure because of the eruption of conflicting aims and priorities among several constituencies. With Acheson's death, the on-campus groups that he had so deftly negotiated among found little reason to continue working together. Divergences of opinion emerged on the mission of the college, on the role of religion and the Presbyterian Church with respect to the college, and on the curriculum, creating great tension on campus and making the trustees' job of finding a replacement for Acheson difficult. Complicating the situation was the rapidly increasing influence of the college's new benefactor, DeWitt Wallace, whose newly developed interest in and willingness to support the college would prove infectious among the Macalester trustees and supporters.[40]

The Deevangelicalization of Macalester

The need for a new president, along with the promise of new and substantial funding, created an ideal situation for college leaders to assess and reenvision the goals, priorities, and identity of the institution. Macalester in the mid-1930s was a respectable but hardly outstanding school. A survey of incoming freshman history majors revealed that the majority had carried a B average in high school; the average grade point average of Macalester students was in the C+ range. A few faculty held PhDs, but most did not. Curricular changes, as we have seen, had been guided chiefly by the religious mission of the college and its role of serving Presbyterians in the state, although Acheson had worked diligently to implement the new liberal arts model. This is not to say that it had no academic successes. The speech and oratory programs, in particular, had distinguished themselves early on, winning accolades in state and regional contests. Also, as we have seen, the international relations program was making a name for itself. But these successes did not necessarily elevate the reputation of the college as a whole, and in comparison to the more premier private schools in the area, Carleton and Hamline, Macalester was a poor cousin indeed.

The faculty, under the leadership of Dean Ficken, began the reassessment in a systematic way, gathering information on other "distinctive college plans" and "trends in higher education." They identified three innovative institutional plans currently being developed within liberal arts colleges: plans that had a "function emphasis, such as Antioch, Hobart, and Sarah Lawrence"; those that "emphasiz[ed] intellectual contest as Chicago, Swarthmore, and Reed colleges"; and those that "emphasiz[ed] individualized or socialized instruction, such as Bennington and Rollins colleges."[41] These exemplary new programs were described by the authors in terms of their avant-garde educational character and the "outstanding" reputation of the colleges. The reforms being put into place at Sarah Lawrence College, for instance, incorporated the theories of educational pragmatist John Dewey, whereas those of Rollins instituted conference or seminar classes and individualized courses.

Perhaps the most distinctive feature of the selection of colleges is that religion appears not to have been a criterion for inclusion in the sample. Sarah Lawrence, Reed, and Bennington, for instance, had never had any religious connections. For a college that had previously linked knowledge and Christianity so tightly, this was an unexpected approach. As we will see, the centrality of Protestantism to the mission of the college was entering a period of significant transformation.

As the faculty collected information to help reassess the college's educational mission, the trustees also set about articulating their ideas for Macalester's future as they began their search for a new president. Despite the seemingly secular direction suggested by the faculty's interest in the preceding programs, for the trustees, under the leadership of the Reverend William H. Boddy of Westminster Presbyterian Church in Minneapolis and chair of the search committee, religion figured prominently in their discussions. Boddy, expressing the general consensus of the trustees three weeks after the death of Acheson, circulated a list of eleven points titled "Suggestions as to the Future of Macalester College" that stressed their desire to make Macalester distinctive, for "at present it is just one more denominational Christian College."[42] The document called for a more systematic and centralized approach to curriculum; stronger academic quality; elimination of preprofessional training; and echoing Acheson's plan, a focus on the liberal arts of the humanities, science, and literature, with an emphasis on "philosophy committed to the Christian world view." The document addressed religion at several points. The selection of faculty, for instance, should take into account their "earnestness" and "exuberance" in religious life, although denominational lines should be of little importance. Displaying an admirable religious tolerance, Boddy explained, "If I happened to find a broad-minded and devoted Catholic who was equipped in a field in which I needed him, I should not hesitate to elect him."[43] In addition, though teaching religion in separate Bible courses was no longer seen as necessary ("religion cannot be taught, it must be caught"), it was expected that the Bible would be included in history, literature, and philosophy courses. Finally, in describing the type of individual who was needed for the Macalester presidency, Boddy emphasized the intellectual ambitions of the trustees: the new man should be a "widely known scholar whose very name and reputation would give academic standing to the College and whose presence as its administrative head would announce to all that we are committed to the highest academic and Christian ideals."[44]

The most innovative elements of this statement are directly related to religion. The elimination of vocational programs would specifically include religious education and social work, and Boddy recommended that the college should not be "an especial training ground for ministers." Chapel services should be redesigned to be more "stimulating and attractive" and attendance made voluntary. Religion would be transmitted through personal enthusiasm rather than courses and requirements. Though these views projected a strongly religious institution, it was not an evangelical one. The trustees were conceiving of the role of Christianity and Presbyterianism at Macalester in liberal Protestant terms that were very different from their forebearers' understanding of the primary mission of the college as advancing both in the world. Traditionalists who retained the earlier view would soon be heard from.

Even before Acheson's death, questions regarding the evangelical character of the school seem to have been raised, with James Wallace leading the rear-guard action. Two days before the president's death, James Wallace had written the Presbyterian Board of Christian Education asking for clarification on Macalester's relationship with the Presbyterian Church. "Can you or your Board give me a definition of what in the judgment of the Board a Presbyterian College should be?" he wrote. "What are our Presbyterian Colleges formed for? . . . Is Macalester College fulfilling the mission for which it was founded, for which your Board has given it money? Wherein (if at all) is it failing? What kind of a faculty is a Pres. College expected to have?"[45] Sidestepping the questions about mission, General Director Charles C. McCracken noted that "one of the most essential things in making a college Christian is to have a faculty that is imbued with Christian ideals of thought and action."[46] Later the next summer, as the discussions surrounding the hiring of a new president intensified, Wallace took the opportunity to write a letter to the Macalester Board of Trustees outlining his views on the historical background of the college's relationship with the Presbyterian Church and arguing strongly that the current efforts by some faculty to redefine that relationship were illegitimate, in part because faculty were employed at the will of the board and had no authority in the matter. But even more important, he argued, forces in the world currently threatened to defeat Christianity, making Christian education more important than perhaps ever before. As he explained,

> The emergence of rank paganism in the forms of new gods, new despotisms, and new philosophies of might, war and conquest in Europe and Japan is the most defiant challenge to the Christian interpretation of life that the Church and its colleges have witnessed in centuries. The world cannot remain static, half defiantly, aggressively pagan and the other half complaisantly Christian. It will be a fight to the finish. The world of men and nations is dynamic. Christianity is dynamic, or it is no candidate for supremacy in this world.[47]

But the threat, for Wallace, was not only from external forces; there was also a threat from within, particularly now that, in his view, the importance of the "place and mission of the Christian college" was so "vastly greater" than ever before. His fear was that the Christian college would lose its religious mission of advancing Christianity and its religious foundation for the pursuit of knowledge, succumbing to a "purely secular view of education." The threat, he warned the trustees, was that "there is always a danger in the administration of our avowedly Christian institutions that some men and women get into the faculties to whom the dreadful moral conflict going on in the world means little or nothing."

As the leader of the old guard, Wallace's perspective clearly had weight with the trustees as well as some support among faculty. Dean of Women Margaret Doty, for instance, responded to Wallace's letter to the trustees by declaring that she "heartily agreed" that the trustees needed to understand and take into consideration the denominational mission of the college. She continued, "I am just as much in accordance with your insistence upon . . . securing only members of the Faculty who are not only in accord with the whole program [the college's original Christian mission] but are aggressively interested in promoting it."[48] A flyer most likely written by Wallace circulated during this period, asking, "Why Should the Denominational College Live?" and outlining twenty-one reasons that it should.[49] Though the ostensible purpose of the flyer was fund-raising, urging Presbyterians to donate to the college, it spoke directly to the fate of the college at an important crossroads. Would it retain its avowedly evangelical character, or would the denominational association be modified in some way, or even eliminated?

Wallace was convinced that "powerful tendencies are at work all the time to drag the college down to a purely secular view of education."[50] The committed evangelical faculty of his generation, individuals whom he felt best exemplified the trustees' vision of a college composed of committed and enthusiastic Christians, had all died: Henry Funk, Julia Johnson, R. C. (Farquhar) McRea, George W. Davis, and even John Acheson. With the passing of these individuals, Wallace felt, "the college has lost heavily" with respect to Christian exemplaries. Furthermore, its willingness to contemplate hiring less-than-enthusiastic Christians suggested to Wallace that the institution was embarking on a slippery slope toward secularization. In particular, he opposed the naming of M. W. Boggs to the permanent chair in political science on the grounds that Boggs had left doubts in the minds of his students as to his religious views.[51] The Reverend Boddy, far more moderate in his position on the religious commitments of faculty, attempted to assuage Wallace's fears about Boggs, suggesting that if a single agnostic faculty member could so "disturb the spiritual equilibrium of the college," then the Christian faculty were not fulfilling their role. Furthermore, he asked Wallace, "[Must] the Macalester students be so coddled and cuddled that they have no contact with an agnostic even though they must meet so many in graduate school and in life?"[52] Wallace remained unconvinced. As names were put forth in the presidential search, he presented Boddy with a barrage of insinuating questions regarding one of the potential candidates, John W. Nason. Nason, who had not only a "Quakeress" wife but also a Congregationalist mother and a Harvard (read

Unitarian) education, was clearly unsuitable in Wallace's view, and the synod and the Presbyterian Board of Education would be terribly lax to allow such an individual to be seriously considered for the presidency of the college.[53]

Wallace, semiretired, quite hard of hearing, and champion of an evangelical Christianity that no longer held sway among younger Presbyterians, was not party to the ongoing search committee discussions regarding the selection of the president, which indicated that it was not only the college that was changing but the Presbyterian Church itself. He was correct, though, in his fear that he was seeing his view of Christianity waning at Macalester. The college, particularly with the death of the mediator Acheson, was rapidly deevangelicalizing. A more liberal Protestantism grounded in Christian ethics, rational reflection, and tolerance for other religions had all but replaced the evangelical conviction that Christianity must be the center of one's commitment and carried out into the world.

Yet even though the college was losing its evangelical character, it was certainly not losing its Christian perspective or its Presbyterian identity. College leaders and the general director of the Presbyterian Board of Education were in frequent communication regarding such topics as the financial situation, the number of required Bible courses, and the number of chapel sessions and their content. In addition, financial arrangements were being made that would guarantee that the "adoption," as the relationship was frequently called, would last for several more generations. Two conservative Presbyterian benefactors of the college, Frederick K. and Rudolph M. Weyerhaeuser, made donations of one hundred thousand dollars each to the capital campaign at the close of 1937, but rather than giving the funds directly to the college, they deposited them in a trust with the Presbyterian Board of Christian Education, which became responsible for paying the proceeds to the college. The Elizabeth Sarah Bloedel Trust, named after a relative of the Weyerhaeusers, and the Synnott Trust, set up a decade earlier, helped guarantee that the relationship between the college and the church would continue.[54]

Searching for a New Mission

Macalester received an extraordinary boost in early 1939, when DeWitt and Lila Wallace's Byram Foundation announced that it would award the college half a million dollars over the next four years. This astounding donation, it was hoped, would attract further major donations, particularly from local and regional benefactors. The resulting infusion of funds would allow the college to pursue goals that neither its founders nor current leaders had ever imagined. In fact, the foundation specifically challenged the college "to become one of the leading liberal arts colleges of the country."[55]

The time had come to take stock, to carefully reassess the goals and mission of the college, and to plan a new future. How would it go about taking the lead among liberal arts colleges? Again, Ficken led the way, outlining his views on how Macalester should change in an article that appeared in the *MacWeekly* in spring of that year. To rise to this challenge, he argued, Macalester must consider its mission, its pedagogy, and its curriculum within a broader national context in which the stakes were high: "America," he opined, "is ripe either for a revitalization of democracy, or for chaos born of confusion."[56] Macalester was at a crossroads, and new directions were needed.

Macalester's new mission, Ficken held, must support and actively contribute to the "revitalization of democracy." The Presbyterian Church, he noted in passing, was already engaged in efforts to support democratic education, and Macalester must follow, using its propitious location in a state capital as a foundation for engagement with urban issues. Curriculum and pedagogy would change as Macalester focused on this mission. As Ficken explained, Macalester College had previously "tried to make itself indispensable by being 'all things to all men,'" the result being "an instinctive and perhaps laudable tenacity" in hanging on to a "traditional book-centered curriculum."[57] In place of these old approaches, he argued, the institution needed to address the needs of students. Only then would it be able to develop not simply the "*philosophy* of democracy" but also the "*psychology* of democracy," the latter being the "psychology of democratic patterns and procedures in social interaction."[58] Developing this psychology was, in Ficken's view, the central pedagogical problem; democracy must be practiced on campus, not simply studied. Students' growth as knowledgeable and committed democratic citizens must be the focus of education. Pedagogically, the college should demonstrate its commitment to democracy at every opportunity. Thus, he explained, "we may find that the organized conference class as it has been in vogue at Macalester for a number of years is our basic pattern for the best democratic procedures."[59]

To these ends, the college would also need to adjust its admissions policies, for, as Ficken lamented, it was frequently guilty of admitting students from the bottom third of their high school graduating classes who had little chance of getting through the current curriculum, much less a more rigorous set of classes. The new mission and the Byram challenge required a more rigorous intellectual focus as well as academically strong students committed to and capable of doing such work. The college would become more selective, accepting only students "who have the ability, personality and inclination to invest themselves in four years of broad and intense training which is in most areas frankly non-terminal."[60]

Ficken's article obliquely addressed a number of issues that were swirling around the college. Should the college retain its many vocational or job-training courses or eliminate them and focus on academic subjects—or "cultural" education, as it was being called? Ficken staked his claim with the latter, though he did not entirely dismiss vocational training, perhaps to head off tension among the faculty or with the synod, explaining that the cultural-vocational dichotomy was artificial and frequently inaccurate, that "a given course may at the same be vocational for one student and cultural for another. A course in Shakespeare may be cultural for a biology major, but serve a very crass occupational purpose for an incipient English teacher."[61] Thus, he suggested, tweaking the present curriculum, the college might "approach . . . our goal by evolution rather than revolution."[62]

With respect to religion, Ficken made mention of Christianity at several points in his essay, indicating that he did not foresee the elimination of the Christian focus of the college. He did not, however, discuss Christianity as a foundational component in knowledge, mission, or curriculum, taking a position that was a far cry from that of James Wallace. He did, however, indicate in his conclusion that he was well aware of the tensions that had been generated around these issues in previous years. If the college adopted a new focus on students' personal development, on their growth as citizens in the world, rather than the "sorting and re-arranging of curricular antiques, or of displaying them in more impressive settings," it is likely, he concluded, that "culture, vocation, citizenship, religion, athletics, and a dozen other battlefields will be demilitarized."[63]

Inventing Traditions: or, How to Be "Not Just Another Denominational College"

The Reverend Boddy was right: when Macalester students looked around their campus in the 1930s, they did not see a great deal that was distinctive. Yes, the physical plant had improved significantly from the days of the dusty and muddy prairie, now boasting seven buildings. Old Main, Carnegie, and Wallace Hall remained the centerpieces of the campus. Several new buildings demonstrated the growing character of the college: the Gymnasium (1925), Macalester Presbyterian Church (1925), the Kirk Hall (1927) residence for men (replacing the old Edwards Hall), and the new President's House (1927) at 1644 Summit. Yet the campus had an oddly linear feel, with its line of buildings along Lincoln Avenue.

About one-third of the students lived on campus. Others, many of whom were from either Minneapolis or St. Paul, lived with their parents and took the streetcar to campus. A few drove, carpooling with other students who lived nearby or on the route to campus. Still other students rented rooms in the area surrounding the campus. Dining halls were located in the dorms and were gender-specific until World War II, when men and women were allowed to dine together. Off-campus students brought their bag lunches with them and made the third floor of Old Main their on-campus haven. Student activities varied throughout the school year, with Y meetings being the most broadly consistent tradition across campus.

Each fall brought a new batch of freshman, and the upperclassmen, particularly the sophomores, began the ritual initiation of the newcomers. Freshman initiation, carried out in the first two months of the school year, attracted a great deal of attention, though the level of actual participation is not clear. A Frosh Rules Committee was charged with overseeing freshman observance of campus rules as well as the more playful side of initiation. The central theme of the initiation was that "Froshes" were to defer to upperclassmen. Easy to spot on campus, the men wearing green beanies and the women sporting green ribbons, froshes were the target of usually mild, good-natured hazing—it was a Christian college, after all. The official rules dictated certain requirements, including the wearing of the green, the use of side doors only in the chapel, and strictures requiring froshes to hold doors for upperclassmen, to enter the dining halls after upperclassmen, and to run errands for them.[64] Other assignments could be given by any sophomore, junior, or senior willing to enforce his or her demand. A woman might be forced to wear an apron—a badge of domestic servitude—to class. A man might be made to clean the streetcar tracks on Grand Avenue with a toothbrush. As punishment for snubbing an upperclassman in 1938, Hal Susie was made to wear a large sign saying "I insulted an upperclassman," and a picture of him in the outfit appeared on the front page of the *MacWeekly*.

These festivities ended the last week of October or the first week of November with Freshman Fryday. On that day, the usual freshman Friday morning convocation was canceled to allow the class to appear in the Freshman Court, a tribunal in which they would be required to respond to a series of inquiries: what are the names of all the campus buildings? What are the words of the "Mac Hymn and Rouser"? Name at least five noted alumni. Name all Macalester championship teams. When was Macalester founded, and by whom?[65] Later in the day, the initiates entertained the college in the Freshman Follies, gender-segregated events in which the froshes performed a variety of humiliating actions. In 1937, several male students of the class of '41 were thrown in the pool wearing only shorts and shirts. They climbed out to find their trousers tied in knots and their shoes hidden. That same day, female froshes were seen directing traffic on Snelling Avenue, and several men were hopping aboard streetcars to inquire of riders, "Who won the World Series?" In addition, women were seen on campus stockingless and wearing their dresses backward, and barefoot men had their trouser legs rolled up and their shirttails dangling.[66] Fryday, however, marked the end of the initiation period. "Surviving" freshmen had proven themselves by their endurance. And early November marked the time to refocus on one's studies in time for upcoming examinations.

Concerns with appearance, gender relations, and dating preoccupied many students. Freshman women were invited to fashion shows organized by up-perclasswomen to teach them how to dress like modern college women. Dean Doty dispensed lessons in manners and social etiquette at every opportunity. The YWCA was also involved in bettering the appearance of the female population, offering instruction in, for instance, makeup application. Articles in the *MacWeekly* frequently addressed dating, usually taking a decidedly tongue-in-cheek tone as they dished out advice in response to inquiries or surveyed student opinion on such topics as "things I can't stand in a date." By the 1930s, dancing was a popular pastime, but Macalester dances tended to be formal affairs, requiring elaborate preparation by the dance committees as well as by those who attended. The Kirk Hall residents, for instance, held a Thanksgiving "Jitterbugs Jive" dance during their annual Kirk Jamboree in 1938, printing their guest list (couples only) along with the playbill (Tommy Dorsey, Benny Goodman, Hal Kemp, and Glen Gray on the phonograph) in the *MacWeekly* ahead of time. The *Lil' Abner* comic strip launched the idea of Sadie Hawkins Day activities, in which women chased men in a footrace. The theme quickly caught on, with women free to pursue men throughout the designated Sadie Hawkins Day. At Macalester, a Backwards Day was also launched, with women taking on male activities—holding doors for men, helping them with their coats, picking them up for their date to the evening dance.[67]

Athletics also flourished during this period. Baseball, which had been eliminated from campus in 1926, was reinstated in summer 1938. Football, basketball, and track remained the prominent varsity sports for men. Though women's sports did not include intermural competition, they did participate in a synchronized swimming team. As college athletic competition grew in the 1920s and 1930s, so, too, did interest in team spirit and campus identity. Student Harriet Pankhurst founded the Macalester cheerleading squad. But something was missing: Macalester had no mascot. The 1920s, the heyday of college athletics, had seen institutions across the country create new mascots and institutional identities. Close to home, the University of Minnesota's Goldy Gopher appeared frequently through the 1920s and 1930s, though the mascot was not adopted officially until the early 1940s. Hamline University asked the *St. Paul Pioneer Press* to publicize a contest to create a Hamline mascot, their subsequent Piper being suggested by a woman from the city. Macalester, however, had no mascot, at least not until November 1937, when Staples High School students gave the Macalester football squad MacQuack, a duck intended to bring good luck. Sadly, the duck did not adjust well to college life. Although its fate remains mysterious, the gesture by the high schoolers was well appreciated by the team.[68]

Not only did Macalester lack a mascot, but it did not boast much of an identity, either, apart from its Presbyterian connection, and even that was rather misleading because a majority of the student body was not Presbyterian.[69] It is not coincidental that Macalester's first effort to develop if not a non-Presbyterian identity, then at least a less self-consciously religious one, came during this period of institutional reassessment and transformation. The creation of Macalester's Scottish tradition would be not only James Wallace's final legacy to the college but also an effective compromise between the traditionalists like Wallace and the educational progressives.

Macalester owes its Scottish identity to Wallace, who, in 1930, had compiled and written a book on the history of his own Scottish ancestors, the Wallace and Bruce clans.[70] Scotland, being the birthplace of Presbyterianism, provided an apt metaphor for the institution, whose first benefactor, Charles Macalester, had also been of Scottish descent and an active member in the Philadelphia-based St. Andrews Society (though it is unlikely that this was known by the Macalester community in the 1930s).[71] The effort to "establish a Scottish tradition," as the

MacWeekly put it, occurred in the spring of 1938, when the college celebrated James Wallace's eighty-ninth birthday with the first Founders' Day celebration. A small notice in the student newspaper explained that the celebration committee was "asking that all Macites wear plaid neckties, dresses, or any other plaid effects available."[72] Highland bonnets (tams) would be available for sale in the gymnasium for ten cents apiece. All that was needed was the music, and the article assured the campus that "a search of the Twin Cities for bagpipe players is being made."[73] Plaid and clans were indeed the toast of the evening, and slowly the Scottish theme grew.

With these types of activities and traditions, Macalester started to carve out an institutional identity beyond its Presbyterian parentage. That parentage would remain an observable theme on campus for many years. But just what it meant to be a Presbyterian college was changing rapidly. No longer predominantly evangelical, the college by the late 1930s had taken on a more liberal Protestant bent than ever before and, in the next several years, would move even further in this direction. While we have seen individuals like Acheson and Ficken laying the groundwork for this shift, it would be the next president who would move the college even further toward religiously and politically liberal positions. He would be able to do so in part because the need to mediate between religious liberals and conservatives abruptly ended with the death of that venerable "old man" of the college, James Wallace. Wallace's death on August 23, 1939, at the age of ninety, marked not just the passing of one of the most important figures in the college's history but also the passing of the original generation of founders. The new generation did not share the New School–Old School theological debates or the evangelical beliefs of the nineteenth-century Presbyterianism of their forebearers. For them, the cultural and sociopolitical changes surrounding them required serious reflection on Christian ethics and the role of Christianity, not as an imperial force but as a foundation for compassion and human aid. In the hands of the new president, Macalester would complete the transformations that had begun in the 1920s and 1930s.

8

Liberal Arts in Service to
the Nation and the World

THE FRONT PAGE of the September 21, 1939, *MacWeekly* heralded an extraordinary turning point in the life of Macalester College. On the left side of the page, a headline announced the upcoming memorial service for the recently deceased James Wallace; on the right, another announced the new presidency of Charles J. Turck. One of these men was the aged patriarch of the institution and champion of evangelical Protestantism, the other was a forty-nine-year-old liberal Protestant eager to move the college in new directions. Here was the institutional equivalent of regime change, a literal out with the old and in with the new.

Historians wisely hesitate to identify watershed events that precipitate broad change for the simple reason that change is always the result of multiple influences and developing situations. But naming an event a watershed can be tempting, for certain events can illuminate transformations in ways that crystallize their significance. This particular watershed, an event that abruptly and decisively changed the trajectory of Macalester, is implied by this front page, for the death of Wallace and the arrival of Turck would finalize the most significant transformation of Macalester's brief history: its deevangelicalization. With the passing of Wallace, the defender of the old guard and watchdog of the evangelical position throughout his long association with the college, the founding generation of evangelicals relinquished its grip on the college's identity. With the arrival of Turck, a new Christian perspective gained ascendancy. Turck was a committed Christian, a leader in the national Presbyterian organization, but he was not an evangelical. Like his predecessor, John Acheson, Turck embraced liberal Protestantism. Unlike Acheson, he would not need to negotiate his views with the old guard evangelicals who had run the place for years. With Turck, Macalester moved well beyond its evangelical roots.

The ramifications of deevangelicalization were many. One of the most obvious changes was that missionary work no longer took center stage at chapel lectures and among campus speakers. A new language of tolerance, a willingness to learn about and respect other religions, and a move toward working with non-Christians eclipsed the language of Christian preeminence. These changes were relatively easily made, but another transformation would prove more complex, as the liberal Protestants strove to develop a new vision of the college's mission that would be as powerful as the earlier evangelical linking of education and Christianity had been. If the mission of the college would no longer be to advance Christianity, what would it be?

Liberal Arts in the Service of Democracy

In conducting the presidential search, the Macalester trustees had sought a high-profile educator who could bring Macalester to a new level. In finding Charles Turck, a respected intellectual and experienced administrator who was relatively well known in Presbyterian circles, they seem to have succeeded. A native of New Orleans, Turck had trained in law at Columbia University and had taught law at Tulane and Vanderbilt before becoming the dean of the University of Kentucky Law School in 1924. Four years later, he became the president of Centre College, a Presbyterian institution in Danville, Kentucky, and he remained there until 1936, when he became director of the Department of Social Education and Action of the Presbyterian Church's Board of Christian Education.

In fall 1938, almost a year into the presidential search, Turck spoke on campus at a chapel session. Chapel lectures had always been something of a sore spot with Macalester students. In the 1920s, disgust with the all-too-frequently uninspiring, not to say downright tedious talks led to one of Macalester students' earliest on-campus protests and to President Acheson's suspension of the requirement for part of a semester.[1] In addition, discussions over how to improve chapel sessions arose from time to time. The sessions in fall 1938 had begun on a promising note with University of Minnesota philosophy professor George P. Conger speaking on "My Visit with Gandhi." That lecture was followed, however, by such character-building fare as the executive secretary of the YWCA, Mrs. Bradshaw, speaking on "Making Choices," Miss Doty of the YWCA speaking on "Making Friends," and Professor Kenneth Holmes of the Macalester history department speaking on "What I Believe." Though we have little information on the response to these lectures, they are of a type that, at least in previous years, had spurred some measure of revolt in Macalester students. Chapel had become noted for being a nice time to catch up on one's sleep, read the newspaper, or finish knitting that scarf. In this context, Charles Turck's topic, "Problems of Social Education and Action," was somewhat out of the ordinary.[2]

The talk seems to have resonated. Turck, a moderate Republican interested in the intersections between law, education, and liberal religion, introduced a new kind of activism to the Macalester campus that November morning: social action. Though Macalester students were no strangers to helping others, having embraced years earlier the idea of improving the lot of others through missionary work, Turck raised the stakes, imagining education in a partnership with other institutions, including government, to work for peace and justice. On this historically Republican campus, Turck's progressivism would have appealed to the moderate Republicans who were gaining strength in the state.[3] Yet many Macalester supporters identified with the more conservative wings of the party. Just before they offered Turck the presidency, for instance, the trustees had voted to oppose federal legislation to broaden old age pensions (the forerunner of Social Security) unless those provisions were separated from unemployment insurance legislation. If the separation were made, they agreed they would support some of the changes in the old age pension legislation "which would place the college under the provisions of the new Act." Support for the elderly was an issue the trustees had dealt with for several years as its faculty aged and were forced to continue teaching because they had no resources on which to retire; thus, by supporting old age pensions, the trustees demonstrated both enlightened self-interest and some social progressivism. Their opposition to unemployment insurance, however, showed that they were far from stepping into the liberal camp.[4] Moreover, the new campus benefactor, DeWitt Wallace, who was becoming increasingly involved in campus affairs, was gaining a reputation for his conservative Republican views.[5] Nevertheless, Turck's chapel lecture, whose text has not survived but which likely examined the United States' responsibilities in light of the growing hostilities in Europe, must have appealed to some influential members of the community, most likely William Boddy, the chair of the trustee's search committee, for eight months later, Turck was offered the presidency.

An alliance between an avowed religious and social liberal like Turck and

Macalester must have surprised not a few, but Turck not only held a vision of education that accorded well with the aspirations of the trustees to improve the institution; he also brought a philosophical foundation and justification for change that could propel the college in that direction. Whereas Acheson and his immediate successor, Clarence Ficken, had moved the college in the direction of embracing the liberal arts for the sake of broad-based learning, Turck would face head-on some of the hardest questions of doing so and would provide new answers that could be widely embraced throughout the institution.

Turck took office in September 1939 but was not formally inaugurated until May 17, 1940.[6] By the time of that event, Turck, having been on campus for over eight months, was well aware of the issues that faced the college, and he crafted his inaugural address to raise and respond to them. The question of what was then widely called a "cultural" (or liberal arts) education versus vocational education, which had preoccupied the college for several years, took center stage in Turck's remarks. But unexpectedly, Turck did not set these two educational philosophies in opposition to one another. Instead, he placed cultural or liberal arts education in the context of an even more important question facing the college: how the institution would use the new opportunities for advancement proffered by the promise of greater institutional income. The question was a serious one. By embracing the liberal arts and doing the things needed to improve the academic reputation of the college—tightening admissions, improving the physical plant, and raising faculty credentials—many wondered whether Macalester would become just another exclusive college for the wealthy. If Macalester was not preparing its students "for life" by offering vocational classes, what would be its contribution to society? Given its diminishing religious mission, how would the college justify its existence in a way that would not surrender to shallow materialism? Turck insisted that the institution's embrace of liberal arts education itself would guard against collegiate exclusivity by locating the institution squarely within the American democratizing project. Liberal arts education, in his view, was not part of the problem; it was, in fact, the solution.

Opening his inaugural talk, Turck summarized the popular argument of the period that claimed that the liberal arts, or "cultural education," were antithetical to contemporary American society based on democratic ideals because it had originated within an aristocratic setting that excluded the masses. The leisured classes might study culture in their exclusive colleges, but middle-class people who would be working for a living after college needed a more practical education in areas such as business or education. Philosophy, history, and logic, people like R. Freeman Butts argued, did not "fit them [students] for life."[7] Training for careers was the true province of higher education: vocational education.

Turck then took issue with this view, arguing not only that its narrow and exclusivist understanding of "culture" was untenable in a democracy but also that the liberal arts had in fact long since broken free of their ancient and aristocratic roots and "expanded as political rights and economic opportunities have increased." For Turck, steeped in classical political liberalism, the American Revolution itself, the quintessential struggle for democracy, was led by individuals who had been culturally educated. For him, cultural education was "the mother of democracy," not its antithesis, for liberal arts education focused on culture as "the ultimate goal of all humanistic endeavor," in the words of Theodore Meyer Greene. Because its subject matter was human society, the effort was necessarily democratic. He opined, "All the facts about man and his world are the subject of a liberal education, and the effort to place these facts in the time sequence as the historian does, and to interpret them and evaluate them in relation to all other facts, as the philosopher does, is the essential task of the liberal arts college." Moreover, he argued, the liberal arts should never limit the scope of inquiry to a particular group or civilization. Intellectual inquiry into culture should not "be limited to a particular age, aristocratic or democratic," and it should not "be identified with the set of facts or theories that a particular age of the world accepted as true."[8]

The ancient aristocratic roots of liberal arts education as presented in the opening paragraphs of Turck's inaugural speech served as something of a double metaphor, a subtle two-pronged allegory of the current situation at Macalester, alluding at once to the institution's past and its future. On one hand, his denouncing of the exclusivist understanding of cultural education could easily be read as a thinly veiled attack on the evangelical Christian viewpoint of the college. Imagine his words being pronounced on campus a quarter century earlier, when the role and purpose of a Macalester education was very intentionally to demonstrate the superiority of Christian civilization and beliefs. Yet in Turck's view, all civilizations made equal claim to "culture" and thus had equal claim on the attention of those who would be liberally educated. Macalester's past, he seemed to imply, was precisely that: its past. Moving far beyond the former evangelical mission, Turck indicated that no longer would Christian civilization hold an exclusionary status at the institution.

The second prong of this double metaphor of the aristocratic and democratic pointed toward the future, for Turck's condemnation of the aristocratic nature of some colleges uncomfortably hinted at Macalester's unexpectedly flush financial situation. Turck was hired to use the infusion of dollars from the Byram Foundation, the Weyerhaeusers, and others to take Macalester to a new academic level. He was hired because the trustees felt he was precisely the type of innovative educational leader who could make Macalester into a national leader. Plans were afoot to improve facilities, hire new faculty, better support current ones, and narrow admissions requirements to bring in academically stronger students. No longer, college leaders hoped, would Macalester seek the majority of its students among the rural communities of Minnesota. No longer would Macalester courses be taught by faculty lacking advanced degrees. Given these new aspirations, many people must have asked how the character of the college would change. Again, would it become an elite college for wealthy students like those ivy-covered institutions in the East?

A quarter century earlier—that is, in Wallace's heyday—this question could hardly have been fathomed. While Ivy League schools might have been growing increasingly elite, private denominational colleges like Macalester struggled to survive. Evangelicalism in the nineteenth and early twentieth centuries was the religion of the upwardly mobile middle classes, not wealthy elites, particularly in the Midwest, where wealth came from economically modest and even hardscrabble beginnings. Any thought of aristocracy was out of the question. The development of Macalester College is a good example. Founder Edward Neill grew up in a family that had been comfortably provided for, but he arrived in the Midwest with little money, and his eastern connections proved to be less than generous. Even when the college got going, donors were scarce and salaries were minimal, and the leadership found more inspiration in God than in personal advancement. Through the 1930s, Macalester admitted just about anyone who applied and could pay the tuition. The children of ministers were admitted free of charge. During the Depression, when enrollments dropped, the college reduced its tuition rate significantly to retain enrollment levels. The college's emphasis on learning proper social behavior also belied its social position, indicating that the faculty aspired for their students to rise on the socioeconomic ladder but also that those students had far to go to do so. Consequently, the new infusion of dollars in the late 1930s raised unprecedented questions about the college's goals, character, and mission. Turck's second metaphorical prong acknowledged this troubling issue, asking how the college would negotiate this new terrain, in which exclusivity threatened like a sinkhole on the prairie.

His answer lay in the populism of the democratic tradition, which, he claimed, was not antagonistic to culture but in fact sprang from it. Through the advancement of democracy, he argued, the liberal arts would participate meaningfully in the betterment of humanity. In his words, "We need the liberal arts colleges to keep alive the humanistic tradition of culture that insists that the whole is greater than any of its parts, that freedom for all is the concern of each, that man as man in a free society has sublime possibilities of achieving great moral and social goals beyond our present dreams."[9] Upholding "individual freedom, the foundation stone of a true democracy," resting on "the love of humanity," and "express[ing] that love in the untrammeled search for truth in every field in which human beings have walked," the liberal arts played a key role in the betterment of society. Macalester, by advancing the liberal arts, would lay claim to a new mission, the advancement of democratic ideals.

In its implicit critique of the institution's previous narrow mission and embrace of a new politically based one, Turck's inaugural speech signaled a new Macalester. His language of democracy likely found favor not only with moderate Republicans but also with the populist Farmer-Labor Party members in the state. But had any of the old guard evangelical Macites been present, surely they would have been disturbed, for in addition to the implied critique of the institution's earlier narrow (read Presbyterian) mission, Turck's inaugural speech signaled a new Macalester by barely mentioning religion. Only in his closing remarks did Turck turn to the topic of religion, and he bracketed these remarks by saying that his thoughts on the subject were of a personal nature, thus implying they were distinct from his previous discussion. Favoring the political above the religious, Turck asserted that it was the duty of every man and woman to explain "our principles of freedom" widely and to "crusade" for them by "unmask[ing] half-truths and deny[ing] untruths." Religion, he continued, was the instigator of this duty, the "power that can drive us to this service and perhaps to the sacrifices incidental to this service." Jesus Christ, in his view, was "the great motive for lofty action and pure idealism," and having been raised in the Christian faith, he personally would "continue to look [to it] for light upon the way."[10]

This view of Christianity as a motivator, not an end in itself, was a far cry from the earlier evangelicalism that had informed Macalester College. For Turck, religion motivated the search for truth, but the goals of the search were not personal or individual salvation but rather human betterment, and betterment came not through the intervention of the divine but through human effort. Similar to the earlier postmillennialists in his view that human work could improve society, but lacking the conviction that the purpose of that improvement was to establish the Kingdom of God, Turck's argument rested on a humanism, a confidence in human action, that the earlier evangelicals would have rejected. As for the post-millennialists, service was seen as a central component. But whereas for them service was for the advancement of God, for Turck service, though driven by belief in Jesus Christ, was for the advancement of humanity.[11] Thus Turck and the earlier generation spoke similar words, but the meanings of those words had shifted. "Service" was the link between Turck's new philosophy of liberal arts deployed for democratic advancement and Macalester's evangelical heritage, and it was to the spirit of service that Turck urged the college to rededicate itself that day. Here, indeed, was a new vision.

Reconstituting Christianity during Wartime

The deevangelicalization of the college went hand in hand with the move toward cultural education. The 1940 catalog, which announced the new liberal arts focus of the college, addressed both religion and curriculum in the new mission statement. It also clarified the institution's new attitude toward religion, ensuring that the college *was* religious on one hand, while asserting that it did not endeavor to *spread* religion on the other. For the first time, however, language in the catalog directly linked the college to the church, boldly stating that it was "maintained under the auspices of the Presbyterian Church of the USA."[12] This statement strongly suggests that Turck had a hand in drafting the language, for he had the closest ties to the national organization of any president since McCurdy. Immediately after this statement, the former qualifier of "nonsectarian," which had not been used for some time, was reinserted. The college was "Christian in its spirit and purposes, but nonsectarian in its instruction and attitudes."[13]

But what did *nonsectarian* mean in this new context? Further explanation of the religious character of the institution came a few paragraphs down the page in a section describing the objectives of a Macalester education. Asserting that "the primary need of all persons is to learn a way of life and to achieve spiritual integration," the catalog explained that the college met this need by emphasizing the study of philosophy and religion. But, it carefully vowed, "the college does not seek to impose specific religious ideas on its students"; instead, Macalester "students are encouraged to examine the life of Jesus as a pattern for living and his teaching of justice and good as the highest wisdom."[14] Thus the college was maintained by the church and embraced the need for spiritual inquiry and a Christian understanding of ethics, but it did not seek to impose that perspective on students. Inquiry into spiritual matters, like inquiry into philosophy, was deemed the most suitable approach. *Nonsectarian*, we can then surmise, now meant something akin to "liberal Protestant," with its emphasis on humanism and action. Furthermore, we can see that the role of religion, or more specifically, Christianity, at the college—now conceived of more as the subject rather than the foundation of inquiry—had been transformed. Within this new framework, the study of religion, equated with the study of philosophy, was rapidly being demoted to a mere component of the liberal arts.

The liberal arts agenda was the second new theme in the 1940 mission statement, which explained that "Macalester College seeks to be a place of culture, where intellectual horizons are widened and young men and women find a reason for living and a source of joy in living. It stresses the humanities, science, and philosophy." The undergraduate years were to be "a period of intense and comprehensive cultural training" through which students would develop "self-realization," skills in "cooperative experience," and exploratory acquaintance with various fields and would also cultivate the art of thinking and communicating and develop a philosophy of life. The goal of such an education was at once personal and social: to "make life a joyous experience for the individual and a source of strength for society." Macalester, which had always embraced character building as a central aspect of its Christian mission, now retained character building, while bracketing spiritual life as a specific segment of a full life.

Nevertheless, Christianity remained the lens through which both students and faculty viewed the world, even as it was diminished in the disciplinary studies they undertook. But again the liberal Protestant brand of Christianity was a far cry from the earlier evangelicalism. In an effort to make this distance clear, assistant professor of religion James Hastings Nichols wrote an article for the *MacWeekly*, distinguishing the "cosmopolitan" Christian perspective of the college and, he hoped, its students from the lingering "frontier" perspective of much of the state of Minnesota. It would be the duty of Macalester graduates to gently guide the less enlightened churches in the state away from the uniformed "primitive" perspective, which, when "maintained artificially in a world society, however, becomes provincial and reactionary."[15]

Nichols's critique of evangelical or frontier religion, published four days after Japanese fighter planes bombed Pearl Harbor, explicitly understood Christianity as having an important role on the world scene. Indeed, in the years leading up to the Second World War, Christianity informed both students' and faculty's positions on the question of U.S. involvement. The desire for peace was predominant on campus between 1938 and 1940. A national student poll taken in spring 1938 showed Macalester students favoring neutrality, disarmament, and either an optional Reserve Officers' Training Corps or its elimination.[16] During the fall semester, Charles Turck, then director of the Social Education and Action Unit of the Presbyterian Board of Christian Education, argued in two nationally broadcast radio talks that Christians must continue educating for peace with full knowledge that the aggressors in Europe were not likely to be swayed by their arguments.[17] A few weeks later, as mentioned earlier, Turck appeared on campus to discuss social education and action, a talk that likely included his views on the need for Christian-based peace activism.

By 1940, as the Nazis swept through Europe, pacifism and peace activism at Macalester continued, with the general focus being opposition to U.S. entry into the war. At least one Macalester student, Ruby Erickson, attended the National Youth Anti-War Congress at the University of Chicago over the Christmas holiday in 1939. Late that spring, a group of peace-minded students and faculty (including religion professor James Nichols and English professor Glenn Clark) used the pages of the *MacWeekly* to encourage their peers to attend their meetings.[18] The group's leader, Beverly Werbes, harked back to the fall 1938 chapel lecture by George Conger when she stated that it adopted "the policy of non-violence [of] Mahatma Gandhi as the only method of resistance to evil which can settle conflicts satisfactorily and lead toward a real and lasting peace afterwards."[19] Throughout the year, students voiced their thoughts on the war and U.S. entry into it in the new "My Views" letters-to-the-editor column of the *MacWeekly*. In letters printed in this column, William Bergh wrote on Christian selflessness and love, and Erickson urged greater financial support for China, arguing that the outpouring of Christian support for Finland in the face of Nazi aggression was an "enigma" given that the Chinese people were far more in need of aid.[20]

Christian activism against the war also extended to faculty. With the September passage of the Selective Service Act of 1940, all males between the ages of twenty-one and thirty were required to register for the draft. Faculty member Nichols initially refused to register on religious grounds, declaring, "In my present understanding of the will of God, there is no place for the profession of soldier-ing." Five days later, he did register, stating that his "opinion of the act remains as it was, but the positive side of the Christian practice of brotherhood and service can be better carried out by constructive work under civilian direction."[21]

The faculty and students involved in the peace movement shared a belief in the power of Christianity, and religion in general, to serve as a prophetic voice, a voice that could steer the nation and world toward the values of peace and brotherhood. From President Turck to faculty members like Nichols to students like Erickson and Werbes, the lessons of Christianity served as a lens through which to view the growing conflict in Europe. Working for peace was seen as the only viable response, not because it would result in divine intervention or help to spread Christianity but because its principles of love and compassion were the only route to human cooperation.

Attitudes changed, however, as the war grew closer to home. Fall 1940 had seen the reelection of Franklin Roosevelt as president of the United States. Macalester students polled by the *MacWeekly* demonstrated their loyalty to the institution's Republican heritage, with 331 of the 509 respondents (out of 677 students) indicating their preference for Wendell Willkie. Roosevelt received 120 votes among the student respondents, and Socialist candidate Norman Thomas received 38. Among the polled faculty, a similar breakdown was evident, with sixteen indicating a preference for Willkie, eight for Roosevelt, and three for Thomas.[22]

Both Roosevelt and Willkie favored sending aid to the Allies, and the Ger-man aggression that brought massive air attacks on England in the fall, escalated war in North Africa in January, and continued attacks on U.S. shipping in the Atlantic led the country to publicly move beyond its neutrality position. President Roosevelt signed the Lend-Lease Act in March, thereby "loaning" U.S. military equipment to the Allies. These events also produced a shift in Macalester's dis-cussions on the war and a growing distinction between those who supported aid and those who supported U.S. neutrality. On March 6, 1941, Turck used his regular *MacWeekly* column, "The President's Corner," to urge students to become engaged in study of the international situation. Faculty, he reported, felt that students were "apathetic" and held "indifferent attitudes when 'democracy' is discussed."[23] A student editorial in the same issue, however, indicated not apathy but rather interest in isolationism. Countering Turck's argument, the editorial suggested that what the faculty took as disinterestedness was actually opposition to aid to Britain and to the war itself, a position consistent with "the conserva-tive influence of the people in this area."[24] Appealing to arguments of old guard Republicans in the state, the author linked student support for isolationism to conservativism and suggested that it "reflect[ed] an appreciation of the horrors of war rather than a lack of appreciation of the dangers of totalitarianism."

The debate soon heated up considerably, casting strong echoes of the con-troversy that had surrounded the First World War. In May, a group of students drafted a petition opposing U.S. entry into the war and gathered signatures from 180 men. The petition was to be sent to Minnesota senator Henrik Shipstead, one of the most outspoken isolationists in Congress, under the college's name. Turck, however, intervened to ensure that the Macalester name was not used. A mass meeting of the campus community was held, and the petition was withdrawn.[25] Student supporters of the petition argued that the incident indicated that the president was curtailing their free speech. Although the petition was not sent to Shipstead, some students attempted to promote a letter-writing campaign by individuals to Congress, urging them to keep the country out of the war.[26] The situation brought the political character of the internationalism–isolationism debate to the fore, and Turck wrote a hurried note to DeWitt Wallace trying to head off the benefactor's possible displeasure on hearing of the incident, which he no doubt soon would.[27]

A week later, Turck came out publicly against isolationism, warning students that "it is not possible to maintain a neutral course," and in light of this, each student would need to make a choice. Using words seemingly designed to head off the kind of antiwar debacle on campus that had preceded World War I, Turck wrote, "If the war comes to America, I hope that the nation which we rightly call the land of liberty and which of all nations has the best chance of helping liberty throughout the world will not call in vain upon Macalester College for support and defense." To serve the nation, he argued, was to do so "in the way the nation itself commands."[28] Turck's statement contained only a single, oblique reference to religion as he mentioned, almost in passing, that he would accept the responsibility of defending the nation because "that is my faith." Whether this referred to faith in God or faith in the nation is not made explicit. What is clear in Turck's letter, however, is his view that national service, which he undoubtedly knew would claim thousands of lives, rests not so much on Christian principles as on the responsibilities of citizens in a democracy. A not unexpected retort came from a student in the next issue, pointing out that "obedience to the state," when construed as a primary duty, may well conflict with Christian principles.[29]

At the same time that this discussion of the responsibilities of democracy on the international scene was reaching a peak, an effort to create greater student democracy at Macalester also emerged. Students increasingly became involved in the issues and situations that faced the institution. With strong encouragement from Turck, the development of a student government ensued. Turck also instituted informal weekly meetings with faculty and students at which campus problems could be discussed.[30] Faculty committees buzzed with activity, and faculty contributions to the *MacWeekly* demonstrated a strong commitment to communicating their ideas to students not only in the classroom but through other means as well.[31] Leadership broadened during these years. This is not to say that the previous model of trustee–presidential decision making was abandoned, but with a larger and more educated faculty, more perspectives entered the conversations and were becoming influential. In fact, the institution was adopting more of a community-based approach, a style that Turck hailed as a model for all society, writing in 1943 that "the days are at hand when life outside of college will also be community-centered, not individual-centered." And the liberal arts college student, he concluded, is "prepared for that kind of life."[32]

War College: Macalester's Service to the Nation

At Macalester, Christianity, cultural education, vocation, and now democracy all teetered on the fulcrum of service. In the early twentieth century, service to God and religion at Macalester had tipped the scale toward missionary work, religious education, and eventually, social science. Soon other vocational paths were added. By the 1940s, as college leaders embraced the liberal arts, the rhetoric of religious service was already diminishing, and the expectation was that vocational courses would soon go as well. Yet as much as Turck argued for the liberal arts and the study of culture as the foundation of democracy, service to society demanded applied knowledge and methodologies, the stuff of vocational courses. As the United States entered World War II, the delicate balance shifted again, and Turck's own convictions regarding the responsibilities of citizenship in a democracy moved him to champion the vocational side of the equation. Macalester became a war college, assisting the federal government in pursuing the war.

As discussions of neutrality, isolationism, and service swept through the campus in spring 1941, several Macalester students had already been called up for

National Guard duty.[33] By the fall, at least fifty Macites, both recent graduates and current students, had volunteered for service, and twenty more had been called up by the Selective Service. Turck urged the remaining students to correspond with those men, and a list of their names and addresses was placed on a bulletin board in Old Main.[34] As Congress debated the neutrality act, student and faculty views were shifting toward entry into the war. A faculty–student poll showed that 86.7 percent of respondents favored the United States remaining nonbelligerent but supplying the Allies, although it showed an almost even split on the question of whether the United States would be able to stay out of the war (yes, 48.4%, and no, 44.4%).[35] A letter to the editor written by a student who supported neutrality placed support in the context of earlier peace efforts and stated that in an informal poll of students, most opposed repeal of neutrality, attributing this view to students being "more peace-minded than the general population."[36]

By the first week of December, however, a new *MacWeekly* poll showed that 53.9 percent of respondents felt that defeating Germany was more important than the United States remaining a nonbelligerent.[37] Moreover, the poll suggested that the question of whether entry into the war should be considered through religious categories was also quite divisive, with 51.5 percent of those who responded agreeing that the war should *not* be "discussed from the pulpits of American churches."[38] Unlike the situation during the First World War, efforts to cast World War II in a religious context were minimal, supplanted as the causes of democracy and liberty took the place of Christianity.[39] Macalester students' views on U.S. entry into the war were also influenced by those who had recently attended the first Canadian-American conference sponsored by Macalester and United College in Winnipeg. Thirty-nine Macalester students had traveled to Winnipeg, where they quickly learned that isolationism was a marginal viewpoint in a country that had declared war on Germany in 1939.[40]

As Macalester students prepared for their Christmas break in December, the United States was plunged into the war by the Japanese attack on Pearl Harbor. Students returned to classes in January 1942 to learn that major challenges and transformations were in the offing. Foremost on the minds of college administrators was maintaining enrollment levels in the face of mass enlistments and inductions. Though women students generally remained available, college leaders around the country sought ways to attract new male students fresh out of high school and to enable some men to finish their degrees before entering the service. One way to do this was to bring the military to campus rather than sending men away to it. Earlier that month, representatives of several higher education organizations—among them the National Conference of University and College Presidents, the Association of American Colleges (AAC), and the National Conference of Church Related Colleges—met in Baltimore to analyze the situation. Each of these organizations passed resolutions in support of the war and outlined ways in which their institutions would contribute to the war effort. Charles Turck, who attended these meetings, endorsed the AAC's statement, saying, "We believe it will be greatly to the advantage of the government to provide for those institutions which it is not yet utilizing fully, a training corps, in which selected physically fit male students may be given military and other specialized training for the war effort, in connection with their college course, and may thus finish their course."[41] By developing such training courses, campuses would contribute expertise in technical areas, help men finish their education before entering the military, maintain at least some male student presence on campus, and bring in some federal dollars to replace lost tuition. President Turck announced to the campus that Macalester had "pledged to the government its complete support. Our equipment, our staff, our grounds are at the service of the government." He also set out to find "specific work that we can do for the Army or Navy."[42]

The military required service of the exact age group that kept colleges like Macalester in business. Pearl Harbor spurred thousands of enlistments, and with the Selective Service already in place, young men were leaving college for military duty. Like all colleges, Macalester scrambled to find ways to keep young men in the classroom, and it embraced the new identity of "war college" with enthusiasm. The first component of the new war college strategy was the introduction of new courses in January 1942. Marion Boggs, in political science, offered War and Peace. A variety of new technical courses were offered, including International Morse Code, taught by physics professor Russell Hasting and admissions director George Scotton; Map Reading, taught by geology professor Hugh Alexander; Meteorology and Celestial Navigation, taught by University of Minnesota astronomy professor W. J. Luyten; and Mechanical Drawing. College leaders encouraged students to take more classes in mathematics and science to prepare themselves for technical war work. While these courses were aimed at men, women students enrolled in them as well, and the following year brought new technical courses especially for women: Red Cross First Aid, Nutrition, and Canteen Service.[43]

Macalester also developed two new quasi-military programs designed to give graduating high school seniors and current freshmen an opportunity to start or continue their studies at college with the possibility of deferring military service for a year or two. Under the navy program, announced in March 1942, a student would enlist in the naval reserve and then be assigned to the college for two years. If he did well on certain examinations, he would be forwarded for aviation or officer's training. Under the army version, the student would take courses for one or two semesters, enlist, and then go on to training at an aviation center.[44] While neither of these plans guaranteed deferments—the government did not announce a deferment policy until May—they seemed to offer reasonable options for young men of eighteen and nineteen years of age. The college offered courses in such areas as navigation and telegraphy, trigonometry and spherical trigonometry, maps and weather, astronomy, physical mechanics, and electricity and magnetism. During the first summer session, in 1942, 127 students, including over twenty freshmen, enrolled in the accelerated plan.

With these courses, a distinct shift occurred toward the very education that the rhetoric of the liberal arts had attempted to downplay in previous years: vocationally oriented education. Again, the fulcrum of service played a key role, for it was in service to the nation that these courses entered the Macalester curriculum. Macalester would help prepare the young men who would go on to lead the U.S. fighting forces. Young women were not excluded from the new vocational turn either, though courses tended to be gender segregated. College recruiting material predicted "shortages in secretarial and stenographic areas" and an even "more critical . . . need for technically trained women in chemistry, biology, nursing, medical technology, mathematics and physics."[45] Faculty also encouraged women students to keep an eye on vocational options. Sociology professor Ruth H. Koontz, for instance, asserted that demand was rising for trained social workers. In the next few years, courses in other female-oriented categories would be developed, most notably home economics.

Other efforts to keep students in school also surfaced. With the aid of the Byram Foundation, the college instituted an earlier plan to offer scholarships to those students who achieved top grades. Cash prizes of fifty dollars were given to the top ten students in grade point average rank in each but the freshman class; the second ten were given twenty-five dollars. Remaining monies in the scholarship fund each year were given to individual students on the basis of both ability and financial need.[46] Despite these measures, enrollment of males plummeted.

Not only male students were leaving the college, however. Faculty also left for military service. That summer, Kenneth Holmes (history) enlisted, Marion Boggs accepted a position in the State Department, and Frank Meserve (biology) left to take a commission as first lieutenant in the army air force.[47] Several months later, in late December, Macalester administrators met to decide which of their number should go to war. According to Turck, who reported on the deliberations to DeWitt Wallace, the decisions were made on the basis of family responsibilities. Treasurer F. N. Budolfson and Student Personnel Services director Fred Repogle had young children, and thus their absence was deemed out of the question. Dean Ficken's children were older and his knowledge of French could be useful, so he agreed to go if asked. Turck's own children were also grown, and he, too, agreed to go if called.[48] Shortly after, Charles Turck, a recent grandfather at the age of fifty-three, accepted a commission as major in the U.S. Army and left for Charlottesville, Virginia, where he assumed teaching duties. Soon more faculty and staff would leave for military service, including Margaret Adams, Kenneth Brown, Norman Elliott, Howard E. Gustafson, Herman Petzold (speech), William Verhage (political science), and Robert Waite; secretaries Mary Jane Atcheson, Betty Jane Peterson, and Lorraine Stegner; engineer Earl Douglas; and bookkeeper Elmer Ojamaki.[49]

For the women on this now predominantly female campus, the war was a period of extraordinary negotiation among a host of traditional and new gender roles. On one hand, messages abounded that women could advance the war effort by becoming more serious about family life and fulfilling the traditional roles of wife and mother. Macalester women were encouraged to take the new home economics courses to learn more scientific and efficient means of homemaking. Efforts to build menus and prepare meals that made effective use of rationed foodstuffs like butter and sugar were publicized in the *MacWeekly* with photos of happy, apron-wearing students working in kitchens. Women students were also depicted in the student newspaper caring for young children at the Baby Clinic at Wilder Day Nursery and knitting socks for soldiers. Dating was covered assiduously in the *MacWeekly*, with commentary on how to reduce costs by skipping the movie and enjoying a game of Scrabble at home instead. And marriages, which had long been announced in the student newspaper, gained their own section.

On the other hand, messages that subverted traditional female gender roles were also prominent. Foremost among these was the need for continued academic work. Women students were repeatedly told that continuing their studies was central to their duty to the nation. Dean Margaret Doty, for instance, who strongly encouraged women to take up teaching careers, asserted that "no girl can make a greater contribution to the nation than teaching if she has the intelligence and aptitude." Acknowledging that college women were likely to question whether their labor would be more useful to the nation elsewhere, Doty claimed, "No woman who is seriously and earnestly preparing for teaching need feel that she is serving her country any less than one who is moulding [sic] a bullet."[50] As we have seen earlier, women were also encouraged to take up science and math and to carry the torch of the liberal arts in aid of the nation.

Women's accomplishments as community volunteers were also praised as national service. Accompanying the previously mentioned baby clinic photos were others depicting women's community service. The caption read, "War not only determines accelerated academic programs for coeds—but it also demands specific attention during extra-curricular activity hours. Preparing for civilian work essential to the war program, women students here have reached out beyond the campus and volunteered for community social service."[51] One photo in the story depicted a Macalester student in the medical technician program practicing taking a blood sample from another student in the program. Macalester women, including theater professor Grace Whitridge, also participated in the national boycott of silk stockings as a protest against Japanese aggression in China.

Women students were also exposed to a number of distinctly gender-transgressing activities during the period. A number of Macalester women, featured in the pages of the MacWeekly, took flying lessons and earned their pilot licenses. Advertisements for the Women's Army Air Corps were common in the student newspaper, and at least nine Macalester women, graduates from the years 1920–45, went into military service.[52] Austrian Linda Littlejohn, lecturing on campus in 1943, argued that before the war was over, U.S. women would be drafted for military service and for industrial work.[53] Rather than a single message regarding women's role in society, then, these examples demonstrate a variety of messages being sent by and to women students. They attest to the negotiations among tradition roles and new opportunities that Macalester women likely found both confusing and exhilarating.

One of the most long lasting of the war-inspired gender-role shifts occurred in the area of women's physical fitness. In a period in which German leaders' desires to create an uber-race were well publicized, the physical character of

American society came under scrutiny. Were Americans sufficiently fit to fight? Concern that many of the young men going into military service could not pass minimal fitness tests resounded widely. The *MacWeekly*, along with many other newspapers across the nation, printed statistics on the numbers of men rejected for physical incapacity. Although the statistics purported to describe male physical weakness, women, too, became the target of nationwide campaigns to improve physical coordination and stamina. Despite the condescending attitude these campaigns often took, young women students welcomed the expanded opportunities for physical activity they produced. Not only was the physical education requirement increased, but women were generally encouraged to become more active. The first women's basketball team at Macalester was organized. Recreational sports like archery, horseback riding, and bowling were introduced. Almost any physical exercise, from energetic tom-tom beating to stretching exercises and calisthenics, was touted as a significant contribution to the war effort. U.S. citizens needed to be fit, and Macalester women were in the forefront of this effort. Hand in hand with this emphasis on physical fitness came an emphasis on nutrition. Eating right, even in times of shortages, was important, and women were seen as having a particular responsibility to become knowledgeable about nutrition and skilled in food preparation. The new home economics courses provided this training.

Men did not escape fitness concerns, of course. In their case, the emphasis, particularly among college leaders and in the pages of the *MacWeekly*, took a distinctively moralistic tone. Good study habits, regular meals, eight hours of sleep, lights out at ten o'clock, and early dates were the themes aimed at male students in the pages of the *MacWeekly*. Fear of uncontrolled behavior in the face of war swept the country, and containment of sexual activity, as historian Elaine May has noted, emerged as a national theme during the period.[54] President Turck, still on campus in fall 1942, urged the War Department to better acknowledge its responsibility for the spiritual and moral development of the young eighteen- and nineteen-year-old men in its charge. Colleges, he asserted, have had years of experience in guiding young men away from such temptations as "liquor, immorality, gambling and kindred vices," but the military, in his opinion, had not sufficiently acknowledged that they now were obligated to take on these responsibilities. Military chaplains were available, he admitted, but far more needed to be done to steer these young men away from harmful influences.

On campus, containment of sexuality mirrored national patterns, particularly in the paradoxical visual construction of women as at once virginal and objects of desire. Following the lead of popular magazines of the period, the *MacWeekly* provided coverage of a variety of beauty contests among Macalester women. An article in 1941 conveyed the results of one such contest, in which the "perfect girl" was "assembled" from the hair, hands, legs, smile, and profile of five different students. Close-up photos of these body parts ran diagonally down the front page.[55] Two years later, as the country was deeply embedded in the war, the *MacWeekly* announced the Mac Sweetheart contest, identifying five girls whose photos servicemen "from North Africa and Iceland . . . to the South Seas and camps all over the country . . . on land . . . on sea . . . and in the air" would be delighted to carry in their billfolds.[56] A glamorous headshot of each woman was printed on the front page of the newspaper, and an article explained that all servicemen who had ever attended Macalester College were invited to vote for their favorite. An accompanying article described each woman in detail: height, weight, hair and eye color, interests, and activities. President Turck, back in St. Paul on leave from his position at the School of Military Government in Charlottesville, Virginia, diplomatically attempted to vote five times, once for each student, saying, "Just between us, if it were a nationwide contest, I think these five would still get my vote." Updates on vote totals were announced in the newspaper on April 9, infusing the contest with a sense of suspense and drama, and the results were announced the following week. Some three hundred votes had been cast, the majority for sophomore Polly Johnson.[57] The contest, supported enthusiastically by both men and women students, was a success.

Between the time the contest was announced and its conclusion, the campus had experienced another profound change. As the war continued, the U.S. government accepted offers by private colleges and public universities to use their facilities to billet and train recruits. In late March, army air corps trainees arrived on campus, under the command of Captain Edward D. Sickler. To make space for the trainees, the men students of Kirk Hall vacated their dorm, and a few women moved out of Rice Hall, part of which would be used as a hospital. The resulting doubling up on housing brought another key change as men and women were allowed to dine together in the Wallace dining room rather than in the previously sex-segregated Wallace (women's) and Kirk (men's) dining halls.

Faced daily with reminders of the war emergency—friends leaving for the military, the air corps on campus, classes in military drilling, food shortages, gas rationing, courses on the international situation, and announcements of casualties—Macalester students displayed a "new intellectual maturity," according to visiting professor of English and former president of Reed College Norman F. Coleman. Gone were the frivolous weeks of freshman hazing in the fall. Fund drives like the Macalester Service Fund campaign and the World Student Service Fund campaign topped their goals and then topped the revised goals. Community service commitments abounded. Students were looking to the future, searching out ways in which they, too, could contribute to the war effort and to American society; the theme of service on campus acquired a new intensity.

By the end of the war, thirty-seven Macites—alumni and students—had lost their lives in service to the nation. On Armistice Day in 1947, Charles Turck dedicated a plaque in Old Main, listing the names of each of these individuals. Their fellow students remaining at the college were urged by Turck to take inspiration from their commitment to dedicate themselves to the causes of freedom and justice:

> I hope that your voices will always be raised on the side of freedom and justice for all, for all the people of America and for all the people of the world. You pass through this way but once, and you can make your life count either on the side of freedom or against freedom, either on the side of justice for everybody or for injustice.[58]

Thus the war brought many changes to the college. The most significant, however, may well be that Charles Turck, who had only just managed to establish a liberal arts curriculum in 1940, was forced by the war and his conviction regarding the college's responsibility to the nation to sacrifice that curriculum— or at least significantly modify it—in favor of vocationally oriented classes. It would be several years before the liberal arts identity would again be embraced by Macalester.

The Macalester Triad: Service, Internationalism, and Political Engagement

If service to the nation resulted in participation in the U.S. military effort, the desire for peace was never far from the minds and hearts of Macalester students and leaders. Peace, however, is always a political issue. Discussions surrounding peace would prove as discordant as those surrounding the war, primarily because the topic could not be separated from that nagging polarity of isolationism and internationalism.

With the world at war in the late 1930s and 1940s, it would have been difficult for any college campus to ignore international situations, for the entire nation was wrestling with the question of America's role in the world context. At Macalester, the groundwork for studying international situations had been established in the 1920s and 1930s, which placed the college in a position to proceed rapidly in the direction of international involvement and inquiry in the 1940s. With the arrival of Charles Turck, who was convinced of the need for students to learn about and understand the perspectives of others and the complexity of global situations, many speakers on international topics were brought to campus, including the prime minister of Belgium, Paul van Zeeland, and the former president of the Norwegian parliament and League of Nations, Carl J. Hambro. Foreign exchange students continued to study at Macalester as well, and Turck attempted to expose Macalester Minnesotans to a larger and more diverse community. The Canadian-American conference took Macalester students to Winnipeg for ten days to get a taste of perspectives from north of the national border, and the Institute of Pacific Ocean Relations focused their attention on that part of the world. As Turck explained to DeWitt Wallace, his desire was to "creat[e] among our students an international attitude of mind," an attitude which, he continued, "is certainly needed out here in the Northwest and which I hope we can continue to foster."[59]

The so-called Northwest, and Minnesota in particular, had a deeply entrenched tendency toward isolationism. Conservative domestic politics translated for many into an unwillingness to support U.S. involvement in world contexts. Yet with the United States becoming the largest global financial creditor and military power, it was growing increasingly involved with other countries. In Minnesota, as in other parts of the Midwest, isolationism crossed party lines. When the Farmer-Labor Party moved away from isolationism in 1940 and endorsed U.S. cooperation with other nations, isolationists like Minnesota senator Henrik Shipstead left the party to join the Republicans. Yet the Republicans were by no means monolithically isolationist. In Minnesota, with a prominent moderate Republican wing, internationalism was strong. On the national scene, the party also endorsed internationalism, such as with the nomination of Wendell Willkie for president in 1940. Willkie had supported international cooperation during the mounting conflict in Europe.

Peace activism of the late 1930s and early 1940s, much of which, as we have seen, was rooted in Christian convictions and emphasized cooperation among nations and U.S. dialogue with the Allied nations, predominated at Macalester. The other wing of peace activism hailed from political isolationism, and it, too, as we have seen, had a vocal following on campus. The mood of the nation, however, was moving toward internationalism, and the attack on Pearl Harbor ended the debate over entry into the war. The question of how to pursue peace, however, remained unresolved. With the specter of the failures that followed the First World War looming in the public mind, many on both the national and local scenes, including Macalester leaders like Charles Turck and Clarence Ficken, placed their hope in international cooperation among friendly, peace-loving nations.

In summer 1941, shortly after the isolationist petition incident at the college, the European Allies signed a peace declaration stating that "the only true basis of enduring peace is the willing cooperation of free peoples in a world in which, relieved of the menace of aggression, all may enjoy economic and social security. . . . It is our intention to work together, and with other free peoples, both in war and peace to this end."[60] That fall, the college launched its four-year citizenship curriculum, a series of courses in history, philosophy, religion, literature, art, and music, disciplines "that form the background of our modern world," designed to "build civilian morale soundly based on understanding of the problems arising from the world crisis."[61] Such curricula, adopted around the country during this period, would become the forerunners of interdisciplinary American studies programs, aimed at educating students in democratic ideologies and American distinctiveness within broader world contexts. At Macalester, the curriculum demonstrated the institution's commitment to international dialogue.[62]

Further moves toward international cooperation were soon to come. The Moscow Declaration, signed by the United States and other Allied nations in October 1943, established an international organization for the "maintenance of international peace and security."[63] That fall, a bipartisan resolution drafted by four senators, including Republican Joseph Ball of Minnesota, calling for U.S. cooperation with other nations to create a world organization of nations that would work together for international peace and security was introduced into the U.S. Senate. The Ball-Burton-Hill-Hatch Resolution was overwhelmingly endorsed by the senate by a vote of 85–5, but it was highly divisive in Minnesota, where isolationism remained strong. The Minnesota senatorial delegates split, with Ball voting for the measure and Henrik Shipstead casting one of the five negative votes.

Shortly after the resolution's passage, the *MacWeekly* addressed the topic. Acting president Clarence Ficken expressed dismay over Minnesota's unwillingness to approve the measure wholeheartedly but cheered its passage, urging continued work to change public opinion in the state:

> One way of doing so is to make a contact with such organizations as the Minnesota United Nations Committee or the Foreign Policy Association. Above all, today's studious preparation may result in tomorrow's effective cooperation. If our public opinion becomes truly enlightened, Minnesota will not long remain 50–50 toward the only hope of a lasting peace.[64]

Clearly Macalester, in his view, would lead in the "studious preparation" of leaders who would bring about "tomorrow's effective cooperation."

The Moscow Declaration and approval of the Ball-Burton-Hill-Hatch Resolution signaled a turning point in the isolationist–internationalist debate. Within a year, at the October 1944 Dumbarton Oaks conference, the groundwork was laid for this international organization, and by June 1945, the details were honed. The United Nations was thus formed. Among those who anticipated and welcomed this series of events in fall 1943 was a new visiting professor of political science, Hubert H. Humphrey. In an article printed on the same page as Ficken's response to the Ball-Burton-Hill-Hatch vote, this new faculty member argued that given the failures of isolationist America First and imperialist Britain First policies of the previous decades, a new Humanity First effort was needed, predicated on the acknowledgment that "today we are living in 'One World,' where our mutual interdependence is the only real fact of social organization." Touting a "political democracy" based on "a belief in the dignity of the individual and an acceptance of the brotherhood of man," Humphrey articulated ideas that resonated deeply with the Macalester leaders, fusing his populist Methodist background with political liberalism in a way quite similar to Charles Turck. The crux of his article came as he championed the development of the United Nations, noting that its formation was not only inevitable but held the greatest promise for warding off the kind of struggle between national interests that followed the armistice of World War I. The United Nations, he told his student audience, would "become the embodiment of democratic principles applied on a world scale" and would ensure that the "rights of nations are not to supercede or destroy the rights of people." This world organization would ensure that "humanity has a priority over nationality."[65]

This bold statement contributed to a reputation for dynamic and inspiring teaching that was already forming around the new professor. Humphrey, a graduate student at the University of Minnesota at the time, held a master's degree in political science from Louisiana State University and had taught political science there for a year. At Macalester, he found a welcoming home. Given the international and local situations of the time, politics necessarily emerged as a central component of the international inquiries undertaken by Macalester students. Political science itself, as a field of inquiry, was increasingly seen as central to the liberal arts project, particularly as it was being construed as a cornerstone of democracy. Turck, with his background in international law, taught in the political science department on his arrival at Macalester. Marion Boggs, professor of political science, who had finished a doctoral degree at the University of Chicago on the strength of a dissertation on practices of aggressive armament in 1940, had launched the department into the international debate, giving a number of lectures on the war situation, writing for the *MacWeekly*, and working with the International Relations Club.[66] When the war took first Turck and then Boggs away from campus, Humphrey was hired to carry on the leadership of the important department. As a visiting instructor during the 1943–44 academic year, Humphrey was welcomed by students, who found his classes stimulating and challenging. His afternoon seminars, for instance, were renowned for going on through the evening, with the students taking a quick break for dinner and returning to the classroom to continue discussion. Political science and internationalism were quickly gaining ground at the college.

In Summary

The pre–World War II and war years, then, crystallized a multipronged set of themes that would come to define the institution's reputation for decades to come. The first of these themes was service. In his earliest appearances on campus, Charles Turck began to translate the former religious language of service into a new language of national service in the interest of democracy. This concentration on democracy, shared by a number of national figures, including DeWitt Wallace, who devoted many of the pages of *Reader's Digest* to articles on the efficacy of American democracy, infused the college mission and curriculum with new meaning apart from its earlier Christian commitment. It would become the ideological glue that would hold the college together for at least two more decades. As Turck explained in 1951,

We are endeavoring to make the college of use to the community and to the state and a wider region without diminishing its loyalty to the cultural and religious ideal on which it was founded. My hope is that our community will come to understand that these essential principles of integrity, of faith, of self realization and unselfish service are the only principles on which a democratic society can rest.[67]

The second theme, internationalism, had been prominent well before the Turck era, but during the war years it crystallized into a modern form in large measure because it existed hand in hand with the third theme, politics. With Hitler's invasion of Europe, internationalism could not be discussed apart from political questions. James Wallace had understood this after the First World War, when early support for the League of Nations fizzled rapidly in the face of what was relatively shallow opposition. While missionary-based international engagement was not seen as political by pious individuals convinced that their efforts to spread Christianity were in the best interests of foreign nations, the League of Nations had been something of a shot across the bow of this complacent attitude. Those same pious families from Minnesota who would eagerly send their children to convert the Chinese or the Brazilians were highly suspicious of entering into cooperative political relationships with other countries. Isolationism ran deep in Minnesota, and Macalester's students often reflected these attitudes. Macalester faculty, however, leaned toward the progressive when it came to international relations. Drawing on the theme of democracy and deploying the strategy of service, however, they carefully yet successfully impressed on their students the political ramifications of international engagement and isolationism. As theater professor Mary Gwen Owen reportedly exhorted her inexperienced students, "One of these days you'll realize that everyone in this world is not white, Republican, and Presbyterian."[68] World War II brought this message home with a vengeance.

9

DeWitt Wallace's Ambition

THE POSTWAR PERIOD saw not just an influx of new GI Bill students into the educational system but also an extraordinary transformation of higher education. The role of education in the new "superpower" nation was in flux. Education questions were on the front burner, debated in localities across the nation. Liberal arts colleges, for instance, were called on to add education curricula to their offerings. Macalester, in response, entered negotiations to merge with the long-standing experimental kindergarten founded in Minneapolis by education innovator Stella Louise Wood. In 1949, Miss Wood's School relocated to the Macalester campus, becoming the college's elementary education department.[1] Other changes were also occurring as the nation reassessed the role of higher education within the new international context. Most significant for Macalester was DeWitt Wallace's increasing interest in the educational goals of the college and willingness to financially support new initiatives. Through this benevolence, Wallace, in the next several years, would sometimes lead, sometimes push the institution in new, even unexpected, directions.

A New Era of Beneficence

The effects of DeWitt and Lila Wallace's beneficence on the college were apparent as early as 1939. A portion of the Wallaces' large 1938 donation to the college funded scholarships for new students, and those new scholarship students were making a difference—at least in terms of the institution's numbers. In 1940, Charles Turck reported to DeWitt Wallace that a University of Minnesota study of all freshmen in the state showed that those who entered Macalester in 1939 had "a higher ranking in their high-school classes than the freshmen entering any other college in the state." According to Turck, Macalester students' rankings were 10 points higher than the university's and 2.7 points higher than Carleton's, a remarkable accomplishment given that only two years earlier, Macalester was 8.3 points behind Carleton.[2] Turck attributed the change to Wallace's scholarship funds, which, he explained, "allowed us to find worthy students among many families of moderate circumstances who but for the scholarship grant could not have come to Macalester College."[3]

Wallace's contributions were substantial. His donation of five hundred thousand dollars to the capital campaign of 1938, of which one hundred thousand dollars had been given up front, was being paid in yearly installments of fifty thousand dollars that were to continue until 1947. Furthermore, Wallace was contributing ten thousand dollars per year for pensions for emeritus faculty, along with other grants ranging from five thousand to twenty thousand dollars for specific purposes.[4] Wallace was a donor with agendas. Though he never completed a college degree, he was deeply interested in education. Wallace believed that Macalester could and should become the premier private college in the upper Midwest, and he was both willing and eager to put his time and money toward making it so. During this period, he became a public booster for the college, using his influence on the East Coast and in the Twin Cities to encourage others to financially support Macalester as well.

Over the next several years, much of this money went toward buildings. In 1942, the college erected a new library, which would later be renamed Weyerhaeuser Hall, for a total cost of $122,000. Fifty thousand dollars of this sum came from the Wallaces' Byram Foundation and twenty-five thousand dollars each from board members R. M. Weyerhaeuser and F. R. Bigelow. Seven years later, Bigelow Hall, a new women's dorm named after its principal donor, was opened. Trustee David Winton and his family donated funds for the new Winton Health Services building, completed in 1951, and the next year, the new Student Union building was completed. Concern about the physical character of the campus also resulted in a wave of landscaping, driveway paving, and tree and shrub planting in the mid-1940s, a project funded by Weyerhaeuser and Lila Wallace.[5]

DeWitt Wallace's primary agenda was to make Macalester into a nationally recognized institution and a leader among colleges in the Midwest. He challenged Turck to "make it one of the conspicuously outstanding small colleges in the country."[6] Together, they kept a close eye on publicity attached to the college. Mention of Macalester in the *New York Times* occurred twice in the early 1940s and did not go unnoticed. Wallace and Turck congratulated each other on the college's growing reputation outside the state.[7] Soon there was other evidence of advancement to report. Admission requirements were being tightened, and the college "regularly turned down applicants who are not in the upper half of their high school graduating class." Over five hundred applicants were rejected in fall 1946. The new "selective admissions" process, in Turck's view, was helping to establish the reputation of Macalester. In addition to admitting better-prepared students, the college was also attracting better-trained teachers. He noted that the University of Minnesota sent "its best young graduates with advanced degrees to teach here (if we want them), and I have seen letters from heads of the University departments telling their graduates to choose Macalester as a place to teach, if they can get contracts from us."[8] Nevertheless, establishing a national reputation required breaking into the eastern lines of communication, and Turck feared that Macalester lagged behind not only Carleton, which was miles ahead in developing a national reputation, but also Lawrence and Beloit colleges in Wisconsin. Not to be dismayed, however, Turck trusted that "if a job is well done the large public finally comes to appreciate that fact."[9]

Yet there were doubters, particularly within the Macalester community. Both Turck and Wallace felt that some members of the board of trustees remained lukewarm, unconvinced that the institution could—or even should try to—achieve significant national stature. Turck expressed his frustration with the board in a private letter to Wallace, complaining that "our Trustees *assume* that Macalester is still an average kind of college, yet I am told by countless people in the cities that everybody here recognizes what Macalester College has done."[10] Wallace stated a similar view publicly.

These frustrations with the board of trustees stemmed in part from uncertainties about the role of the board in this new era of donor largess. Whereas previously the board had been primarily in charge of overseeing investments and the financial well-being of the perennially underfunded college, with the advent of Wallace's largess their responsibilities in these areas diminished, or at least shifted. Giving large amounts of money, Wallace, not surprisingly, tried to keep a close eye on the college's financial situation, repeatedly requesting financial reports from Turck and the new treasurer, F. W. (Buddy) Budolfson. In the process, he seems to have hijacked a significant portion of the board's work. Wallace's financial acumen and that of his financial advisors was grounded in eastern strategies and techniques, which were relatively foreign to the midwestern businessmen who populated the board. Given such a powerful and involved benefactor, it is not surprising that the board deferred to Wallace.

What the board needed was a new role, and Wallace was eager to define one for them: giving to the institution and urging their friends to do the same. His encouragement launched a new era of board benevolence, with Weyerhaeuser, Bigelow, Winton, and soon George D. Dayton II leading the way.

The Blended Liberal Arts and Vocational Curriculum

So just what should education at this small Presbyterian college look like if it were to fulfill these grand aspirations? Acheson's 1929 plan had emphasized liberal arts, and a decade later Turck had championed a similar focus in his early years at the helm. But the war interceded. In the heat of the national emergency, a strong and deeply rooted belief in service drove the college away from the liberal arts and toward vocational education, that is, job or career training, as Macalester eagerly stepped in to provide courses that would aid young men as they entered the military and young women as they entered the working world.

The service-oriented sentiment did not lessen after 1945. With unemployment high during the postwar recession, Turck grew increasingly committed to the need for colleges like Macalester to step in to provide the type of education that young people in the region needed: education that would lead to productive careers. Claiming that "private colleges are public-service institutions," he applauded the GI Bill, which had boosted private colleges, giving them "an enlarged recognition and usefulness."[11] Macalester, as a designated participant in the GI Bill educational programs, welcomed hundreds of veterans and, in many cases, their families onto campus. In fall 1947, President Turck reported that of the record-breaking 1,558 students enrolled, 642 were veterans. He also noted that 909 were men and 649 were women, figures that silenced concerns about female predominance that had arisen during the war and earlier.[12] Parallel concerns about this significant male predominance among the student body were not raised. Indeed, Turck expressed some pride in the fact that the football team had tied Carleton and beaten St. Mary's College 7–0 in the first two games of the season. Focused on getting an education as quickly as possible and finding a job that would support or allow them to start families, these older male students appreciated the opportunity to gain expertise in areas that would give them a leg up on the job market. Macalester strengthened its vocational offerings in areas such as education, business administration, medical technology, and journalism, offering a cluster of new bachelor of science degrees.

This postwar continuation in the vocational direction did not mean that the college was leaving the liberal arts behind, however. Of the fourteen new members of the faculty appointed in 1947, twelve were in liberal arts departments (including physical education). More specifically, the college attempted to unite vocational and liberal arts education with a blended curriculum. As Turck explained in 1955, he envisioned three primary educational concerns for the college: (1) it "should maintain a curriculum suitable to the Christian tradition, the Christian gospel and the Christian purpose"; (2) as a liberal arts college, it should continue to "keep at the core of its course offerings an emphasis on those studies that interest and concern human beings in their dealings with one another and this world, such as literature, history, philosophy, natural science, social science and the fine arts"; and (3) given its location "in a great and growing metropolitan area, Macalester should offer in almost each department series of courses that have vocational outlets."[13] This last theme, that given its urban location, the college had a special responsibility to provide vocational education, was put forward as a qualitative difference between Macalester and such liberal arts colleges as Carleton and Swarthmore, which were isolated in rural areas and did not have the same responsibilities for engaging with the surrounding community.[14]

In Turck's view, the relationship between the liberal arts and vocational education was not a zero-sum one: "the inclusion of vocational emphases or overtones does not destroy the essential elements of the liberal education program of the college."[15] In fact, the two supposedly opposing sides sprang from the same impulse and were therefore both appropriate: "there is no reason why any vocation that has an intellectual base may not properly be admitted into the curricula of a liberal arts college."[16] As was so often the case with Macalester leaders, binary constructions of opposing ideas were once again blended into a both-and unity.

Interest in vocational courses sprang from the populism that Turck had exemplified for years. In an article on liberal arts education, he pointed out that prelaw, premedical, and preministerial courses were never considered "vocational" in character, hinting that the privileging of these professions drew legitimacy from their longtime aristocratic associations. The vocational courses that Macalester had developed in home economics, medical technology, business administration, journalism, and education were created to respond to the needs of the Macalester students and addressed the needs of the city and the region. As a "public-service institution," the college had an obligation to serve these needs; doing so was central to its mission.

It appears that the college's primary donor and campus booster, DeWitt Wallace, likely agreed with this position, insofar as he considered the curriculum at all in the decade following the war. In the mid-1960s, when the college eliminated all bachelor of science degrees along with the journalism department and the religious education program, he expressed dismay that these useful programs had gone. Wallace, whose political conservatism was well known by the mid-1950s, also expressed suspicion of the very concept of a "liberal" education, asking Turck on at least one occasion to explain just what the phrase meant.[17] In the early 1970s, Paul H. Davis, a development and educational consultant who had joined the Macalester administration in 1956 at the behest of Wallace, wrote that he, too, felt that the "abandoning of those [vocational] principles and substituting the pure liberal arts motif" had been an "error."[18]

Indeed, Turck's blended curriculum would not last long, for it held significant consequences in an academic world that itself was attempting to regain professional ground lost during the war. Turck's very discussion of the topic in his 1955 article on the liberal arts was occasioned in part by the college's unsuccessful bid for one of the prizes of liberal arts colleges, a Phi Beta Kappa chapter. In his view, the Phi Beta Kappa's on-site reviewer axed the college's chances by criticizing its courses in home economics, journalism, and medical technology.[19] Yet there were other things that excluded the college from serious Phi Beta Kappa consideration—perhaps most important, that only a small percentage of the Macalester faculty held doctoral degrees. When fourteen new faculty were hired into professorships and part-time instructorships in 1947, only one, geographer Hildegard B. Johnson, held a PhD. Six held master's degrees as their highest degrees, and five held only bachelor's degrees.

The necessity of hiring nondoctoral educators was in part a consequence of the scarcity of doctoral-level faculty available nationwide in the postwar years and in part a consequence of the abysmal salaries that Macalester offered.[20] Finances were tight in the postwar recession. Turck expressed relief in balancing the budget in 1951, calling the year "the most difficult . . . we have ever had."[21] He may have spoken too soon, however, for he would repeat similar sentiments on just barely achieving balanced budgets in 1953–54 and 1954–55.[22] The college was about to receive another shot in the arm from the Wallaces, however, which would launch the institution on a ten-year plan that would significantly change its mission and curriculum.

New Development Initiatives: The Paul H. Davis Plan

DeWitt Wallace was no educational expert. He was in a position, however, to call on leaders in the field, retaining educational consultants as early as 1944, when he secured Willis A. Sutton, superintendent of the Atlanta public schools, former president of the National Education Association, and executive officer of the Georgia Education Association, to advise him on educational matters. Sutton was replaced in the early 1950s by Paul H. Davis, an educational entrepreneur who was making a name for himself in higher education funding and development. At Columbia University, Davis had served as general secretary and later as vice president of development during Dwight D. Eisenhower's presidency there.[23] Davis led highly successful capital campaigns at Columbia and Stanford, racking up references from the likes of Herbert Hoover, among others.[24] In 1953, he advised University of North Carolina president Gordon Gray on fund-raising methods, providing him with synopses of the methods used at ten other universities.[25] That same year, he also published an article in the *Los Angeles Times* decrying the sorry state of higher education's financing and urging institutions to take a more market-oriented sales approach to college and university development.[26]

Wallace, who had beaten the streets himself as a salesman in his youth, was attracted to Davis's "modern" approach of "selling" colleges, and by 1955, he and Davis began to lay plans for the improvement of Macalester College. That summer, Wallace recommended Davis's services to Charles Turck, who quickly invited him to campus. Davis arrived within the week. He outlined a number of strategies for raising funds among local business and civic leaders, with which Turck expressed his "complete accord."[27] By August, a plan to hire Davis at six thousand dollars a year with a two thousand dollar expense allowance was formed, with Wallace agreeing to pay half of both amounts. Turck proposed the arrangement to board of trustees chair Arnold Lowe, minister at Westminster Presbyterian Church, and vice chair Archibald Jackson, president of St. Paul Fire and Marine Insurance Company, prior to the board meeting in mid-September. The board approved the plan, and Turck offered Davis the position in early December, fully expecting him to accept. But it would not be that easy.

Rather than accepting the position, Davis wrote Turck, thanking him for the offer but indicating that Macalester was not yet in a position to hire him, for it had not fully committed to the fund-raising project. Davis's plan was to head up a full-court press, a year-round continuous campaign of volunteers aimed at business leaders and alumni. It would cost close to two hundred thousand dollars to implement, and the trustees, he pointed out, had not committed to this. Nor had they indicated to his satisfaction that they were determined to make "the major strides" needed to move "Macalester forward and upward." He explained, somewhat condescendingly, that "if Macalester is just to carry on with its continuous efforts to balance the budget and construct occasional buildings, the trustees would not be wise in committing the college to a long-term contract with a high-priced consultant in institutional finance and public relations."[28] Given that these efforts were precisely what the trustees had been doing for several years, Davis's demands were not outlandish, yet the situation does indicate that his knowledge of the institution went beyond the casual. Wallace had very likely informed Davis of his dissatisfaction with the trustees' relative inaction in raising the profile of the college. Davis then used this information to leverage a greater level of commitment out of the trustees.[29]

Turck was left to break the news to the trustees. Wallace, observing that "the Board, of course, will have to decide whether Paul's plans are too ambitious," sweetened the deal by assuring Turck that "Lila and I will contribute *substantially* to Macalester only if there is a concerted and determined effort to make the college a recognized leader among small liberal arts colleges."[30] Then he sent another gift of four hundred shares of *Reader's Digest* stock to the college.[31] Placed in this awkward position, Turck put together a report for the board, outlining "the kind of problems with which we are faced" in several areas: "endowment, buildings and grounds, faculty status, student admissions and guidance."[32] The trustees agreed to take the matter under advisement.

On February 5, 1956, Wallace and Turck met at the Palmer House in Chicago. Turck presented a ten-year plan for the college, along with a plan of giving. In the course of their discussion, Wallace agreed to fund certain projects at the college on a scale unimagined even by Turck. He would give the college one hundred thousand dollars (in the form of Reader's Digest Association preferred stock) each year for the next ten years, and if the college would commit to a capital campaign target of ten million dollars, he would give the last million dollars when the total pledges reached nine million dollars. In addition, he would contribute five hundred thousand dollars for a science building costing at least one million dollars, meet the current deficit on the Field House (approximately seventy-five thousand dollars), and pay up to twenty thousand dollars a year toward the expenses of the capital campaign.[33] In total, Wallace was offering the college some $2.75 million.

Wallace authorized Turck to pass the specifics of this confidential agreement on to four trustees—Lowe, Jackson, Winton (then vice chair of the board), and George Mairs (treasurer)—intending, most likely, to enlist their help in convincing the rest of the board to commit to Paul Davis's campaign plan. On returning to St. Paul and consulting with the selected trustees, Turck reported to Wallace that they all expressed "great delight in hearing of such magnificent benevolence" and assured Turck that they would help persuade the board, although they were sworn to secrecy on the specifics. As Wallace required, the full board would not be told of his munificence until their commitment was secured. On April 12, DeWitt Wallace sent a telegram to Turck expressing his delight that Paul Davis had accepted the board's unanimous invitation to lead the college's "new continuous volunteer development program."[34] The board had made the commitment. DeWitt Wallace's relationship to the college had thus dramatically evolved from generous benefactor to something more akin to a puppet master. Soon he would lead the board itself in another unprecedented direction.

Donor Relations in a New Era

Macalester publicly announced its ten million dollar capital campaign in October 1956 to great fanfare. Articles appeared in all the local newspapers, giving strong support to Macalester's new commitment to "make the college known the nation over for its outstanding scholars in both student and faculty ranks."[35] Soon attention turned to the major donor, DeWitt Wallace, whose support for the program was announced in conjunction with the upcoming release of a new biography of Wallace's father, James Wallace, written by Macalester professor Edwin Kagin. These joint announcements, combined with a poignant introductory endorsement by DeWitt Wallace that appeared in the James Wallace biography, cast a nostalgic, sentimental aura over Wallace's support of the college. The estrangement that had existed between father and son, which had continued to the death of the elder, never hit the newspapers, despite its depth. After leaving St. Paul for New York in the early 1920s, DeWitt Wallace returned to visit his father on only a handful of occasions. James Wallace's letters frequently pleaded with the son, urging him to come, and rebuking him for not attending church regularly and a variety of other misdemeanors. Nevertheless, once *Reader's Digest* started making an income, DeWitt had been generous in his financial support for James and other members of his family; he also wrote James regularly, keeping him apprised of family matters, if not financial ones.

He was stingy only with his presence.[36] But this story was not presented in the newspapers. The public story claimed that from reading Kagin's book, Wallace had come to understand the depth of his father's commitment to and sacrifice for the college during those years of DeWitt's carefree childhood. In tribute to this sacrifice, he was taking up the standard his father had carried so many years earlier.[37] This heartwarming story, although a publicity coup, overlooked nearly two decades of Wallace gifts to the college.

Wallace's contributions in this period focused on the same areas that he had been supporting for years, but now efforts to enhance those areas were ramped up considerably. The physical plant was to be beautified on a grander scale, with a new landscaping plan, shrubbery, and redwood fence enclosing the campus. Funding for faculty projects continued, but now salaries were increased enough to approach some level of parity with other schools to make Macalester competitive. Most important, the development of relationships with potential donors was to be taken to a higher level.

Wallace's gifts during this period were heavily weighted toward "restricted" giving, that is, dollars earmarked for specific projects or uses. This project-oriented giving stemmed not only from the historical pattern of Wallace's earlier donations but also from new, strategic thinking on benevolence that became popular during the period. Paul Davis wrote frequently on the topic of institutional giving, arguing that restricted or designated donations were the most attractive to wealthy funders precisely because they wanted to know what their money was doing, to feel that their gifts were "tangibly important, significant and appreciated."[38] In his view, organizations like the Red Cross, with its Hungarian Refugees program, and the *New York Times*, with its "100 Neediest Families" program, owed their success to the immediacy of the stories they broadcast about individuals in need. Potential donors saw at once how their dollars would help. Colleges, he argued, should offer donors an array of projects from which to choose. Scholarship programs, for instance, were proven winners because, as he claimed, by freeing up monies for other uses, they did not necessarily tie colleges' hands in the use of such restricted donations.[39] Wallace took this message to heart, proposing that the college launch a competition among faculty to come up with exciting project ideas. He personally would underwrite a one hundred dollar award for each of the five best ideas suggested.[40] Those projects would then help bring in new donors.

Turck, though grateful for the Wallace support, had other ideas about college giving. As he explained to Wallace shortly before his retirement was announced,

"I still believe, DeWitt, that the most important single material element in the strength of a college is the endowment. . . . We put into endowment still here at Macalester every bequest that is not specifically designated otherwise."[41] In this same letter, he thanked Wallace for sending his final payment on his pledge of one hundred thousand dollars for the endowment made eight years earlier. In June, the book value of Macalester's endowment for 1956 stood at $2,250,000, much of which, including the Bloedel Trust, was restricted. Two weeks after Turck's note about endowment, Wallace turned over five thousand shares of Reader's Digest Association second preferred stock, worth some $350,000, to be applied to the endowment but designated for faculty salary raises.[42] By June 1957, the endowment stood at $2,656,000.[43] Had all of Wallace's intended donations over the next ten years been applied to the college's endowment, they would have doubled it.

But to make Macalester into a top-flight school, Wallace felt that new ideas, new practices, and new programs were needed, including greater foresight and daring than anyone at the institution had yet displayed. While the capital campaign and campus beautification would surely benefit the college, the real, on-the-ground impact of this period of funding would occur with the faculty salary increases. Concern over faculty salaries had been sparked by Phi Beta Kappa's rejection of Macalester's request for a chapter two years earlier. Although Turck was convinced that the vocational curriculum was the reason the application was rejected, other factors were also identified as problematic by the scholarly organization. In particular, faculty salaries were still not on par with other liberal arts colleges already in the fold, and the percentage of PhDs among the faculty was woefully deficient.[44] Turck announced a new salary program to faculty in early December 1957. At the highest level, the maximum full professor salary was raised by one thousand dollars a year to eight thousand dollars. Other individuals received salary increases ranging from $250 to $1,000. Yet these increases would not solve all of the college's financial woes with respect to faculty salaries. As Turck pointed out, instructor salaries remained very low. "The whole scale must be lifted and will be lifted, but it cannot be done this year. Everyone of us on the teaching staff of Macalester College can look forward to the day . . . when we shall be paid on a scale of salaries that compares favorably with any college in this region, and ultimately with any college in our land."[45]

To further address the faculty situation, Wallace set up five "named" professorships at ten thousand dollars a year, intended to attract top-flight scholars. There were other perks for faculty as well. Wallace created a fund of twelve thousand dollars to assist faculty with obtaining their PhDs. During summer 1959, nine junior faculty members received one thousand dollars each toward their graduate work. Merit pay bonuses were also instituted to recognize scholarly achievements. In addition, Wallace launched what would become the High Winds program, buying up houses near the campus and making them available to faculty at reduced rents.[46] All these programs aimed at improving faculty standing with respect to other institutions.

Raising the academic level of the student body also emerged as a strategy in developing the new Macalester. New Wallace-funded scholarships of five hundred dollars each for National Merit Scholars attracted twenty-eight students to the college during fall 1957, and the next year, another thirty such scholarships were offered.[47] Larger grants-in-aid packages were also offered. Turck reported on the accomplishments of Macalester students, writing to Wallace that at the end of the 1956–57 academic year, two Fulbright awards (to Oxford and Greece) and two Ford Foundation grants (one to study Russia at Columbia and one to study behavioral science at the University of Michigan) had been awarded to Macalester students that year. Fourteen graduates were planning to enter graduate school, and seven were planning to enter theological seminaries.[48]

Ideas for improving the college and campus seemed to abound, particularly in the mind of Wallace, and he wrote Turck frequently, making suggestions for a host of improvements. Very little escaped his notice. At one point, he complained that students were not sufficiently friendly to strangers on the campus and asked then president Harvey Rice to talk to them at convocation about being more welcoming.[49] After a rare campus visit during spring 1957, he wrote Turck that "at the basketball game we attended, it was my impression that the bloomers the five . . . cheer-leaders were wearing were not particularly attractive nor becoming" and suggested that Turck might enlist Lila Wallace to arrange for a New York designer to create new outfits for them.[50] Turck soon contacted Lila, who approached Mainbocher, a New York–based designer whose strapless evening gowns had recently taken the fashion community by storm, to design the cheerleading costumes. DeWitt suggested that a "snappy Scotch kilt costume" would be appropriate and set the *Reader's Digest* research department on the task of finding some color photos of possibilities. The next spring, the new outfits, designed by Mainbocher and featuring a Scottish kilt, sash, and tam made out of imported Scottish tartan fabric, were premiered to an admiring public.[51]

Throughout this period, Wallace corresponded with Turck on almost a daily basis, sometimes sending two or three short letters a day, making suggestions, raising questions, asking for reports, and congratulating him on achievements. Turck's responses to these frequent letters were consistently polite and frequently enthusiastic, though he did differ with Wallace on occasion. Wallace was not necessarily demanding, but he was always persistent. And as the major benefactor of the college, he had enormous power. Just the fact that Turck responded to almost every letter from Wallace, a task that took not just precious minutes but likely hours out of his workweek, attests to the importance Turck placed on keeping Wallace engaged in the campus.

McCarthyism Hits Home

Negotiating between Wallace, the board, and the faculty took some skill, but this likely was not the biggest challenge Turck faced in his relationship with Wallace. There were growing political differences between the two men. During a period in which both political parties were undergoing enormous change, Turck and Wallace would increasingly find themselves in opposite camps, and Wallace was becoming increasing vocal about the political alliances on campus. Though Wallace praised Turck's selection of faculty—and at this time, faculty hires were accomplished almost exclusively through the action of the president—he began to drop hints that Republican candidates were to be preferred. Of course, Macalester had always favored Republicans, but in this period of political transformation, Wallace understood that the academy was moving toward the Left. He opined, "Many professors tend to be leftists," in part, he conjectured, because they had no contact with businessmen. He therefore suggested that Turck bring faculty together with board members. Such contact might also "stimulate the interest of the Board in Macalester if they felt they had at least a slight acquaintance with the leading professors at Mac."[52] Overall, though, Wallace's general feeling was that Republicans were "probably scarce in most colleges."[53] Turck countered that among twenty-six Macalester department heads, he counted twelve Republicans, eight Democrats, and six independents but promised that he would "do the best I can" in adding more Republicans to the faculty.[54]

Turck's own political views were rapidly becoming disassociated with the Republican Party as a new social and international conservatism developed within it. He lobbied for diplomacy toward China and congratulated Eisenhower on overriding the decision of the Joint Chiefs of Staff to authorize an air attack on the Chinese mainland in 1954.[55] He supported international nuclear disarmament, testifying at a hearing held in Minneapolis.[56] These positions, through quite consistent with his earlier views on democracy, Christian brotherhood, and international cooperation, were being negotiated within the Republican Party between two increasingly divergent wings: the moderates, who supported an engaged foreign relations and individual liberty on the domestic front, led by individuals like Senators Margaret Chase Smith of Maine and Edward John Thye of Minnesota as well as Dwight Eisenhower, and a new wing of conservatives fueled by a growing anticommunism and led in part by Richard M. Nixon.[57]

Turck's identification with party moderates during this period resulted in his being considered by the Eisenhower administration for the post of staff director of the Civil Rights Commission. The White House background check noted Turck's support for both Democratic senator Hubert Humphrey and Republican senator Thye, the latter individual indicating that Turck might at some point be of interest to the party for a presidential candidate.[58] But the moderates were not in ascendancy. As anticommunism spread, Turck's views were increasingly associated with idealistic liberalism. Even the Democratic Party would not embrace them for decades.

In the context of growing anticommunism and cold war ideology, idealism and progressivism were the targets of a series of red-baiting essays by J. B. Matthews published in 1953 in the popular journal *American Mercury*. The first article attacked colleges, arguing that the Communist Party had "enlisted the support of at least thirty-five hundred professors—may of them as dues-paying members, many others as fellow travelers, some as out-and-out espionage agents."[59] Particularly egregious evidence of the Communist activity of college faculty included participation in peace activities, which, in the author's view, essentially provided aid and comfort to the enemy through appeasement. Among the individuals Matthews named as involved in peace activities and, even worse, a former president of the American Association of Colleges, an organization by implication rife with Communists, was Charles Joseph Turck, "a familiar name on the lists of the Communist-front apparatus."[60]

Turck viewed this national effort to smear his reputation as a serious threat to his relationship with Wallace, a relationship that must have been increasingly strained as the two men took up opposing views on a number of international and political situations. Wallace, as historian John Heidenry points out, used the pages of *Reader's Digest* to fuel the flames of anticommunism, urging U.S. entry into the civil war in China and debating "the advisability of launching a preemptive atomic attack on Russia."[61] These positions were diametrically opposed to those of Turck, who was not hesitant about expressing his views publicly. In addition, that Turck was considered for a position at the head of the Civil Rights Commission, attesting to his belief in equality among all Americans, contrasted significantly with *Reader's Digest's* editorial position, which, according to Heidenry, favored "de facto segregation and separate but equal rights," that is, when it was "not mak[ing] them [African Americans] the butt of dialect humor."[62]

In these positions, we see the national negotiation of new party lines. Racial equality was shifting from a reformist element in the Republican Party to a platform plank of the Democratic, in large measure because of the work of the new Democratic senator from Minnesota, Hubert Humphrey. International cooperation, a position that had previously existed across party boundaries, shifted toward the Left as anticommunism grew, yet both positions continued to cross party lines for another decade. Wallace and *Reader's Digest* leaned toward the Right, although as Heidenry points out, the magazine "showed sympathy" toward some individuals subjected to "McCarthyite suspicion," including George Kennan and Joseph Oppenheimer.[63]

Publication of the Matthews article also threatened Turck's relationship with the board of trustees. Meeting prior to its publication to discuss the situation, the board, under the leadership of chairman Arnold H. Lowe, minister at Westminster Presbyterian Church, decided to issue a public statement expressing their support for Turck and "affirming their confidence in the integrity of Dr. Turck as a patriotic American and a Christian gentleman."[64] Lowe's leadership here was likely not coincidental, for two months later Matthews published the lead article in *American Mercury* condemning liberal Protestantism. That piece, with its sensational opening sentence—"The largest single group supporting the Communist apparatus in the United States today is composed of Protestant clergymen"—attacked the premises of liberal Protestantism outright.[65] Lowe, a champion of liberal religion, had likely felt the sting of anti-Communist innuendo himself. Turck, as a college president and a leader in the Presbyterian Church, took the hits on both sides.

Turck was no ideologue. He worked assiduously to present all political perspectives on campus, pointing out to Wallace in a letter that Professor Mitau of the political science department was regularly called on for addresses by both the Young Republicans and the Young Democrats.[66] But given his activism and the anti-Communist accusations, the handwriting must have been on the wall. Turck's moderate-to-liberal political views were becoming problematic for a college whose main benefactor was moving in the opposite ideological direction.

Wallace had received at least one letter indicating that Turck's "liberal viewpoint" was hindering fund-raising among certain businessmen.[67] In fall 1957, Turck tendered his resignation, some three years earlier than he had previously indicated he would.[68] There would be no delay this time in selecting a replacement. In January 1958, Dr. Harvey M. Rice, then president of the State University College for Teachers in Buffalo, New York, was announced as the incoming president of Macalester College.

Academics and Curriculum Revision: Revisiting the Identity Issue

For faculty, accepting Wallace's contributions and the changes they brought with them during this period was hardly a difficult choice. Nothing about the proposed improvements of the mid-1950s capital campaign was particularly controversial. Of course, a few trustees would need to be replaced, but on campus, among the faculty and students, these changes could only be seen as advantageous. None of the Wallace-driven changes had yet touched on curriculum, however. As curriculum revision was eventually taken up in the next several years, it would become the battlefield on which the faculty competed for influence in, if not control of, Macalester College. The struggle, rooted in this earlier history of the college's curriculum and views of its identity and mission, revolved once again around the question of whether Macalester should offer vocational education.

The board of trustees took up discussion of "what is Macalester College" in its first meeting of 1958. They agreed on several components: (1) it was a liberal arts college; (2) it had a mission to provide "useful citizenship" and a responsibility to the world, nation, and community; (3) its curriculum provided undergraduate preparation for graduate work or specialized training for professions, along with special programs designed to prepare students to go directly into careers; and (4) it had a mission to develop Christian faith and character, though it was nonsectarian in spirit.[69] These points were descriptive of the then current mission, which reflected a college that the war had shaped in the last fifteen years.

Despite Wallace's enthusiasm for raising the college to new heights of academic repute, the college was not universally despaired of in 1958; not everyone agreed that it should strive for a stronger position in the national arena. In many areas, the college was steadily gaining strength and reputation. Interest in international study, for instance, had increased apace during the previous twenty years. The Mexican Caravan, a summer study trip for Macalester students, was highly popular when it was launched in 1946, though sadly, the program had to be curtailed a year later after a typhoid outbreak.[70] During the war, as we have seen, faculty commentary and courses, in addition to the national emergency, kept discussion of the relationship between the United States and other countries prominent.

As the student body changed in the postwar period, with its influx of GI Bill veterans and a continuing influx of international students—according to college sources, Macalester ranked in the top four or five U.S. schools in the ratio of international students—the college saw even greater interest in international studies. Following a national trend set initially by the U.S. military during the war and quickly emulated by universities, Macalester became involved in area studies, an approach to international education that emphasized language, culture, and institutions in subject countries. Under the auspices of funding provided by the Louis W. and Maude Hill Family Foundation of St. Paul, Macalester joined Hamline, the University of St. Thomas, and the College of St. Catherine in a cooperative area studies program.[71] The first two years of the program, under the leadership of Macalester history professor Yahya Armajani, focused on the Soviet Union and the Middle East. Subsequent years focused on the Far East and again on Russia and the Middle East. The program provided support for the development of an integrated curriculum on these focus areas among the participating schools as well as funding for guest speakers and for library books and curricular materials, including films. In summer 1954, this cooperative area studies program sent seven faculty members to the Middle East for study.

According to Armajani, the program had unexpected benefits. As the study of Russia was taken on by the program, other faculty shifted their lesson plans to include study of the country. A total of ten departments at the four colleges were involved in the program, even though faculty participation was on top of regular workloads. Visiting lecturers also united interest across disciplinary fields, and as Armajani pointed out, "in some cases . . . the area study program was responsible for bringing together colleagues from the same field for the first time in the history of the four colleges."[72] This flowering of a citywide intellectual community was unprecedented. In particular, the cooperation between two Protestant schools (Macalester and Hamline) and two Catholic schools (St. Thomas and St. Catherine) did not go unnoticed.

Macalester students were earning national attention in other areas as well. The speech and oratory program, which had grown out of the early literary societies, regularly won high honors at regional and national competitions.

In 1956, for instance, student debaters Henry Ruf and Karlyn Kohrs placed second in the national invitational tournament held at West Point. A year later, Ruf placed first in the Phi Beta Kappa contest, and in 1958 the team tied for first place in a tournament of one hundred colleges. Similarly, the journalism program, and particularly the *MacWeekly*, took home honors in regional and national competitions.

These successes and advances had been achieved not through an infusion of funding by a wealthy donor but through dedicated faculty who strove to bring the best education to their students by engaging them in the educational process. Of course, there was a range of ability as well as expertise among the faculty, and as new methods and ideas developed, differences of opinion on how courses should be taught arose. But given the general soundness of the college's work, it is not surprising that some faculty raised concerns and opposition as the plan to "move Macalester forward" took shape under the new president.

In the final month of Harvey Rice's inaugural year at Macalester, May 1959, the new president organized a landmark conference that led to dramatic changes not only in the curriculum but also in the activities of the board of trustees. The conference brought together the trustees and a few faculty members, including Donald Butler, chair of the religion department and professor of Christian education/philosophy of education, for two days of discussions on the future and direction of the college. It was held at the well-known Lowell Inn in Stillwater, Minnesota, on the St. Croix River.[73] During the course of the conference, the participants engaged in sessions reviewing the current educational activities and mission of the college, examining a variety of alternative college models, assessing the financial structure of the college, and planning for the future. The conference did not yield immediate results but triggered a two-and-a-half-year-long process of institutional review and ultimately curriculum revision, which, in the end, turned the college quite dramatically away from the vocational and blended curriculum paths it had carved out over the previous fifty years.

A year after the conference, the board of trustees met to consider a proposal for the college's redevelopment based on points raised at the earlier conference. The proposal recommended focusing on the liberal arts and eliminating most of the vocational programs, including all the bachelor of science degrees, the education program, the secretarial courses, the journalism major, and the religious education track. Rice, reflecting on the events some twenty-five years later, remembered the meeting as a make-or-break one, not only for the proposal but for his own future at the college.[74] Several board and faculty members strongly opposed this new direction for a variety of reasons. Some of these individuals felt, as Turck had, that the service mission of the college demanded that it respond to the needs of students in the region, and that doing so meant retaining the blended curriculum. Others felt the college would be inexorably changed by the new curriculum; Macalester would no longer be the Macalester of earlier times. Still others felt that the religious mission of the college would be diluted by the new focus.

Rice, Dean Ficken, and board members like David Winton, however, backed the plan for refocusing on the liberal arts. The desire for a Phi Beta Kappa chapter figured into some of this support, and Rice, for one, felt that if the college was to become a first-rate institution, obtaining a Phi Beta Kappa chapter was simply a necessity. By the time he arrived on campus, the college had applied twice for the honor and had been rejected both times. It was clear that some of the new recommendations, including the elimination of vocational courses, targeted areas that Phi Beta Kappa had identified as weaknesses. Similarly, preliminary recommendations for establishing new hiring procedures and a tenure system addressed the faculty problems that Phi Beta Kappa identified. Other recommendations were aimed at changing the student body, including one to expand it and house more students on campus and thus reduce the number of Twin Cities commuter students.

By the time the full board of trustees considered the recommendations developed out of the initial conference, the various "sides" of the argument had been distilled. Rice remembered the meeting as something of a marathon, lasting from noon to seven in the evening on a spring day in 1960. By the end of it, three board members had resigned and three faculty members had been urged to resign. The remaining board gave the go-ahead to pursue the changes recommended.[75]

By no means were the issues resolved. An Advisory Council on Aims, Practices, Policies and Plans of Macalester College was formed to make specific recommendations for transforming the college. By spring 1961, the council forwarded a number of recommendations to the full faculty, including the closing of the education department and the elimination of the art and religious education programs; the evening college for adults; the summer school; the journalism program; the nurse's training program; and the business administration, preengineering, medical technology, and secretarial studies programs. A survey conducted by the advisory council provides a window into faculty feelings about the proposed changes. Some sixty-four faculty members responded to the survey, which asked them whether they "Approved in Principle" or "Disapproved in Principle" to the changes recommended in a range of programmatic categories. Among the faculty, strongest agreement existed around a handful of recommendations: eliminating the fifth-year program, the summer school program, and the medical technology program. Elimination of the art education and the preengineering programs was also widely supported. However, over 20 percent of the faculty opposed eliminating the elementary education program (the partnership with Miss Wood's School), reducing the physical education requirement, and eliminating the business education and secretarial studies programs. And just under one-fifth opposed eliminating the evening college, the journalism program, and the nurse's training program. Similarly, about one-sixth, or nine of sixty-three respondents, expressed disapproval of the effort to pursue a Phi Beta Kappa chapter.[76]

Comments accompanying the survey expressed a wide range of reasons for both dissenting and approving positions; clearly the faculty entered this curriculum discussion with serious concerns for the health of the college. In defense of the blended curriculum, one individual wrote,

> In the past Macalester gained a national reputation purely with its own genius—no money. It tailored a curriculum to the desire of the best group of students in the world. These students are characterized by poverty, character, ambition, and a desire for knowledge. They and the Macalester faculty and administration came up with the new liberal arts.[77]

The writer continued, perhaps alluding to Charles Turck's earlier pronouncements on the democratic responsibilities of higher education: "There appears to be a movement started to close out the present Macalester and buy a new group of students who will become excited with the education of 100 or more years ago. It can't be done with the best students. The best students want the new, practical liberal arts, which Macalester now gives."[78]

Several individuals objected to the fact that the measures significantly altered the historical trajectory of the college. One anonymous responder wrote, "It seems to me that we have been developing at Macalester a valid and valuable integration of liberal and vocational education which does not need apology but does need assertion." Another claimed that the college would end up pursuing unwise goals:

> Consciously or unconsciously, the measure of our increased efficacy seems to have been such operational devices as 5 who go to grad schools . . . [the] number of Ph.Ds, publication, research of faculty. Grant that operationally measurable devices are easier to attain and to talk to, they also tend to become *the* goals for this very reason. Small Christian liberal arts colleges have multiple functions, some of which are less tangible than being a "prep school" for graduate training. The graduation of terminal students imbued with the best of widespread education, and therefore the preparation for a general high level interest as a citizen of the world should not be overlooked. This may not be coterminous [*sic*] with all of the above recommendations of the Advisory Council.[79]

Similarly, another responder wrote more dramatically,

> I feel I must register a vote for responsibility and deliberation as a dying gasp of a small voice from one who would look back momentarily as he is swept along by the invincible surge of humanity plunging madly onward in search of utopia, wildly casting aside its old and tried as it grasps upward and outward for the elusive glory which seems always just beyond reach.[80]

Despite these counterarguments, the faculty approved the recommendations, stripping the curriculum of the vocational components. In September, the board of trustees met once more in Stillwater to officially approve the college's new direction. The liberal arts had won. All bachelor of science degrees were to be "modified to meet the requirements for the Bachelor of Arts degree." Students interested in education would complete an academic major and take a minimum of education courses. The medical technology, journalism, and engineering programs were eliminated, as were the nursing program, the evening session, and the secretarial courses. The religious education major and the master of education program were to continue but were to be closely reviewed. The new plan also identified specific goals for faculty, including raising the percentage with doctoral degrees to fifty "as quickly as possible." It also established a six-year tenure process and a system of faculty sabbaticals as well as a number of other support structures. Measures regarding the student body specified a goal of attaining at least 20 percent of admissions from outside the upper Midwest and at least 3 to 5 percent from outside the United States.[81]

These changes significantly affected faculty. Courses needed to be adjusted and some eliminated. Teaching loads shifted, and research was to become a requirement rather than a personal pursuit. Neither teaching nor pedagogy were mentioned in the document.[82] This may have been in part because faculty had responded strongly against suggestions for peer reviews of teaching earlier in the reassessment process. But taken at face value, this missing element also indicated that improved teaching was not considered a critical component of the reorganization. What needed to be improved were the faculty themselves, not their teaching techniques.

Significant changes for the student body were also outlined. Macalester, which had been a commuting campus for the majority of its students, was to become as residential as possible. Two new dorms were to be built: one to house 150 to 200 women and one for 250 men. The male-to-female ratio was to be kept at approximately 50/50, although the board had discussed securing it at 60/40. In addition to new residence halls, dining facilities that would allow male and female students to eat together would be constructed. Off-campus students were to be encouraged to eat some of their meals on campus. For the first time, the campus was to become a "seven-day" campus, with meals available through the weekend and programs developed to encourage students to remain on campus during the weekend rather than going home, which was common practice. The feasibility of developing new student spaces—recreational space and a snack bar, meeting rooms, and offices for student organizations—was to be explored.

These changes in student life, which would occur over the course of the next several years, were every bit as transformative for the college as the curriculum changes. Placing a larger percentage of students under the care of campus administrators and reducing the role of parents and home life, Macalester launched into a new experiment, creating a residential campus based on the rural model within the urban context. Of course, this is precisely what Edward Duffield Neill had sought to do back in the 1880s when the college opened, his own college days at Amherst guiding his vision. But Macalester had never been able to achieve this, nor had it really attempted to, knowing full well that with the majority of its students coming from the Twin Cities, students wanted to save the cost of housing by living with their parents. The new residential model, as we will see, posed significant challenges, and few campus officials had much experience in administering such large groups of students without the aid of local parents.

Last, the reorganization also transformed the duties of the board of trustees, which was charged with initiating these new policies. The board, through its new subcommittees, would take up the reins of the college, guiding its curriculum, faculty, and student life as well as its fiscal components. The board, strongly influenced by the college's major donors, including DeWitt Wallace, would lead the campus, assisted by the administration—a governance model that would have been untenable under the independent-minded previous president, Charles Turck. The consequences of these changes would play out over the next decade, leading to near-disaster in 1971. As we shall see, this new model, developed from the initial Stillwater Conference, planted the seeds of that calamity.

PART III

Revolution and Redirection, 1960–2000

10

The Religion–Education
Intersection Transformed

THE DECADE OF THE 1960S significantly transformed the role of religion at Macalester. Two events, one at the beginning of the decade, the other at the end, serve as bookends of this transformation. The first came in 1960, when the Macalester Board of Trustees voted to eliminate the requirement that two-thirds of their members be practicing Presbyterians. The second came in 1969, when the college dedicated a new chapel, the first building on campus devoted fully to religious work. While the first raises questions about whether the college was moving away from the church and becoming more secular, the second implies almost the opposite—a strong connection to the church. Taken together, these events point to a distinct ambiguity, even ambivalence, in the evolving religious identity of the college during the period.

Of course, the religious identity of the college had changed several times during its relatively brief history: by 1960, Macalester College had created, embraced, and then moved on from several understandings of how religion and education intersect. Edward Neill had championed the idea of a unifying Protestant education based on the belief that Christianity undergirded all knowledge; for him, such education was a cornerstone for all professions. Thomas McCurdy, his successor as the college opened, believed more strongly in the unique perspective of Presbyterianism and the responsibility of the college to provide the region with educated young men prepared to go on to seminary. By the late 1890s, missionary zeal and a stronger evangelical tone shifted the college toward preparing students for religious vocations of various sorts, spurring the development of the religious education program. By the 1920s, the college adopted a middle-of-the-road approach to reconciling different views of religion's proper impact on education. Charles Turck translated Christian ideals into an activist focus on service, redefining Christian education as that which served the broader society (read democracy) and world in the 1940s.

The 1950s would bring further transformations in how the college administration and students conceived of the relationship between religion and education, setting the stage for the more radical shifts of the 1960s. As with the earlier changes in the prevailing models, the transformations that occurred during this period affected many aspects of campus life, from the institution's relationship with the Presbyterian synod to curriculum requirements and student religious life.

Traditional and New Institutional Structures to Instill Religion in the Postwar Period

The decade following World War II had brought a few new features to religious life at Macalester, the most important of which was the creation of the position of chaplain of the college. The college hired its first chaplain, Dr. John Maxwell Adams, in 1947. This fact may strike readers as somewhat strange. Would not a Christian college have employed a chaplain from the start to look after the spiritual well-being of the students? The answer to this question hints at how the college viewed itself vis-à-vis the Presbyterian Church prior to the creation of the office of chaplain. As the office of chaplain had historically been conceived, Christian colleges were *not* in need of such a position precisely because of their denominational affiliation. Chaplains, like missionaries, were assigned to constituencies distant from the structures of the church: institutions such as prisons or hospitals or military units, for instance. Denominational colleges, closely tied to the church itself, were not in need of special clergy.

In the 1920s, however, denominations grew increasingly concerned about the role of religion on campuses, as Christian college and university students began to critique the ineffectiveness of the church during World War I and participate in parachurch activities outside the control of specific denominations. Students at both denominational colleges and secular state universities were deeply involved in a variety of religious organizations, many of which welcomed a broad range of evangelical participation and functioned outside of denominational purview. The YMCA and YWCA, the Student Volunteer Movement, Christian Endeavor, and later a host of organizations, such as the Macalester Christian Alliance, shared at least an implicit critique of the territorial character of denominations and the inability of Christians to unite. These student organizations also tended to be informed by social concerns and a strong service (sometimes missionary) ethic, and for many students the theological conundrums of the denominations paled in comparison to the need for Christian activism in the world.

Such ideas challenged denominations. By the 1920s, several denominations had created chaplaincies at universities, in large measure to provide a denominationally educated and ordained clergyman to oversee these student organizations and activities. Asserting denominational identity as well as attempting to consolidate this diffusion of religious activity, colleges began creating chaplaincies and often erected impressive chapels on their campuses to house the new college clergy. Carleton, for instance, erected its Gothic Revival–style Skinner Memorial Chapel in 1916 for its new chaplaincy.

Macalester, waiting until after the war to hire a chaplain, was slow in following this trend, which suggests that there was little anxiety about the Presbyterian character of the college or its students. The religious needs of Macalester students had for decades been addressed by the clergy at the various churches that students attended; by their parents, as many lived at home; by the faculty in the religion department, most of whom were ordained; by other Christian faculty; and by the president. Most students attended a local church, with many Presbyterian students attending Macalester Presbyterian Church, which had been founded in 1887, two years after the college opened its doors. In 1925 that congregation, in cooperation with the college, erected a new church at the corner of Lincoln and Macalester avenues that was used for college assemblies, including daily chapel services. In 1929, President John Acheson recommended that the college create an office of the chaplain, but this recommendation, along with the rest of his curricular plan, was put on hold by the Great Depression. By the postwar period, however, with the influx of GIs and their families and the larger student population in general (the Mac student population soared from less than seven hundred in 1940 to over sixteen hundred in 1949), the administration decided that it was time to hire a chaplain.

The man they selected for the job, Maxwell Adams, had served since 1934 as the director of the Department of University Work of the Presbyterian Church, so by the time he reached Macalester, he was well aware of the responsibilities, issues, and debates surrounding campus ministries throughout the country. Just what was the role of a campus chaplain? As the first occupant of that position at Macalester, Adams carved out his own role, taking on responsibility for weekly chapel worship services, overseeing student associations, working with students interested in religious vocations, teaching Bible courses in the religion department, interpreting Christianity for students and faculty, providing pastoral counseling for students, and connecting with local religious groups. Over the course of his twenty-year tenure at the college, Adams provided a formidable voice in defining the Christian character of Macalester.

The religion department also served as an important component of students' Christian experience at the college. As previously noted, the department had experienced significant transformations during the prewar years as ideas about Christian education and vocation changed. By the early 1950s, the faculty in the department taught a host of required courses on the Bible (eight credits were required for graduation) along with religious education courses for students intending to pursue religious vocations. Most of these courses retained a distinctly apologetic Christian perspective and were intended to guide students in their development as Christians. In addition, the religion faculty, most of whom were ordained, were also entrusted with the development of students' Christian character.

Thus, through the 1950s, the chaplaincy and the religion department worked in concert to teach students the stories that comprised the Protestant Christian mythos, the tenets of Presbyterianism, and the moral components of Christian life and character. Whereas the department took an educational approach, the chaplaincy offered required daily chapel lectures that, as we have seen, often focused on topics such as Christian character formation and service.

Student religious life on campus in the years following the war remained centered around a variety of voluntary organizations, including the YMCA and the YWCA as well as denominational groups such as the Canterbury Club for Episcopalians, the Mac Catholics, and the Mac Lutherans. Religion-in-Life Week, a college event sponsored yearly since the early 1940s, encouraged a campus-wide focus on living one's faith. During the week, a variety of speakers, chapel convocations, discussions, and services were held. The events were organized in part by the Mac Christian Association, an interfaith organization founded in 1947–48. Attendance at chapel and course requirements in religion provided an institutional religious structure.

Early Signs of Change: Rewriting the College–Synod Relationship

With respect to the role of religion in the institutional identity of Macalester, the 1960s started with a profound change. As the trustees reassessed the college that year following the first Stillwater conference, among the issues raised was that of the Presbyterian representation on the board of trustees. Since the original "adoption" agreement with the Presbyterian Synod in 1880, two-thirds of the board members were required to be members of Presbyterian churches. As the board reconsidered this stipulation in 1960, at least part of their motivation was that Phi Beta Kappa looked suspiciously on denominationally controlled colleges, viewing them as attempting to serve two masters, one academic and one religious. Moreover, as the board took on new responsibilities in the areas of curriculum and campus life, it ran the risk of its efforts being viewed by outsiders as a Presbyterian takeover of the college. Attempting to ward off such charges, the board considered and by October unanimously passed a resolution to eliminate the two-thirds requirement from the Articles of Incorporation.

Despite this action, the board had no intention of abandoning the Presbyterian denomination and took pains to reassure both the synod and the public of this. At the same meeting in which the two-thirds requirement was axed, a resolution affirming the college's relationship to the church was passed:

> The Board of Trustees of Macalester College, impelled by the conviction that Christian faith and learning should be inseparable, reaffirm their devotion to the cause of Christian education and the ties of Macalester College to the Christian faith. Macalester College was founded as a Presbyterian college and has had a noble and close relationship with the Presbyterian Church in Minnesota and with the Synod of Minnesota. The Trustees affirm the historic relationship of the College to the Presbyterian Church and pledge to continue that relationship in the days that lie ahead.[1]

Although this statement implies that nothing had really changed in the relationship between the college and the church since the former's founding, certainly much had changed, and the elimination of the two-thirds requirement marked the beginning of a twelve-year period in which the institution slowly shed itself of its Presbyterian identity and its identity as a Christian college.

The preceding statement clarifying the ongoing relationship with the Presbyterian Church appeared in the 1961 long-range planning document "Macalester College Challenges the Future," a document that, despite this statement, set the course and the method for loosening the ties between Christianity and the college through the careful use of some distinctively new and highly ambiguous language to address the religious goals of the college. The shift hinges in part on the use of the term *faith*, a term that rarely appeared in pre–World War II documents. In the preceding section, "faith and learning" are "inseparable," an idea that diverges not only from Neill and his cohort's understanding of Christianity as the foundational element in all knowledge but also from Turck's understanding of Christian morality as the motivator of social or political behavior. Here, a link is present—faith and learning are inseparable—but just what constitutes that link remains unspecified. The final paragraph of the "Purpose and Goals" section refers again to "faith," saying, "Taking good will rooted in faith to be basic, the College seeks to constitute a community exemplifying the spirit of Brotherhood." Here, the term *faith* is linked to goodwill and brotherhood, but again the nature of that link is not made explicit. Nevertheless, a statement about brotherhood in this period of cold war politics and growing interest in internationalism on campus made perfect sense. Looking too deeply into how religion ought to function may well have jeopardized this goal.

Last, the statement revisited the term that had come and gone at various times over the past century: *nonsectarian*. This time the use of the term pointed to a whole new meaning: "Christian in spirit and Presbyterian in background, but not sectarian in outlook, Macalester endeavors in its instruction, activity, and worship to enable the student to develop a philosophy and way of life rooted not only in knowledge and useful capacity, but also in character, sensitivity, and reverence." Here, again, relationships are implied but not defined: the "spirit" of the college is Christian but "not sectarian"; it aids students in personal development "rooted" in "reverence," but reverence for what is not articulated. The term *nonsectarian* has clearly lost the anti-Catholic overtones of its original use as well as the veiled call for Protestant unity of the turn of the century. It has also lost the connection to service and citizenship that grew out of the Second World War period. Here, it seems to mean that the college's "outlook" favors no denominational perspective; indeed, despite the reference to "Christian spirit," the phrase is sufficiently broad to be interpreted as encompassing any religion, for the central point, articulated in the goal for students "to develop a philosophy and way of life," is disconnected from a specific religious outlook and linked to "knowledge and useful capacity . . . character, sensitivity, and reverence." In the context of ambiguous references to "faith" and "brotherhood" and "reverence," then, the use of the term *nonsectarian* seems to indicate that the college favors no religious or philosophical perspective at all.

The statement ends with a civic ideal that had grown out of the war years:

"Macalester seeks to cultivate in all its students constructive citizenship and aspires to bring out in many fearless zeal for justice, freedom and human well-being." Thus qualities and interests that were in earlier years linked explicitly to Christianity and then by Turck to spiritual sources were in the 1961 long-range planning process only vaguely mentioned, together with acknowledgment of the Christian heritage of the college. Yet, as we have seen, that heritage itself had never been a static set of components or relationships.

Overall, then, this statement, and others that would follow, inserted a new ambiguity into the institutional relationship with Christianity. One could read the statement as endorsing a Christian identity of the college, or one could read it as an acknowledgment of the institution's friendly attitude toward a generalized "faith."

In the face of the elimination of the two-thirds requirement and the ambiguous language in the planning document, the Presbyterian community began to raise serious questions about the college's commitment to the denomination—to them, the statement of affirmation regarding the college's relationship with the church was not sufficient. It fell to Chaplain Adams to translate the board's action for the Presbyterian public. The Synod Committee on Christian Education, for instance, took up discussion of the relationship between the college and the synod early the next year and invited Adams to address a meeting. The chairman of the committee pointed out that the "'public image' of Macalester is that it is a 'Presbyterian' college and the college from which our church leadership springs."[2] Adams, in clarifying how the college saw its relationship with the church, responded that though the church and the college were related "historically," the college had always been "independent," even while it "look[ed] to the Presbyterian Church more than to any other for understanding of what the word 'Christian' means in its objectives."[3]

The committee chair returned that given the historical link as well as the many donations that Presbyterian families had made to the college through their churches over the years, the college owed something to the denomination. In fact, a certain amount of outrage was growing among some Minnesota Presbyterians as the college denied admission to some Presbyterian students from smaller communities, even ones who placed at the top of their rural high school classes. Macalester was turning its back on its loyal supporters in favor of a new exclusivity, the committee charged. Adams's response was realistic, if blunt: given the new direction of the college, he explained, "the synod would have to decide what kind of a college it wants to be related to—a mediocre college that more young people can get into, or a nationally respected institution."[4]

In a follow-up effort to assuage contention, Adams wrote a lengthy letter in which he argued that Macalester's recent efforts were more of a reclaiming of its initial trajectory rather than something new. The roots of the liberal arts went as deep as founder Edward Duffield Neill, he claimed, and the relationship between the college and the synod, while cordial and mutually supportive, had never been one of synod ownership. In effect, nothing was changing. He pointed out that even after the recent round of additions to the board of trustees, two-thirds of the members were still Presbyterian. Furthermore, he argued, the percentage of Presbyterians among the faculty (36 percent Presbyterian and 20 percent of these ordained; 91 percent of the faculty identified themselves as Protestant of some kind) remained strong, as did the college's relationship with the national denomination, based on the amount of funds the Presbyterian Church contributed to the college (approximately one hundred thousand dollars per year, exclusive of contributions to the capital campaign, which was over two hundred thousand dollars since 1958).[5] Given these figures, Adams argued, there was no reason for alarm.

Revisiting Required Courses and Compulsory Chapel Attendance

But clearly the institutional commitment to earlier mechanisms for religious education and participation was diminishing. By May, the faculty Curriculum Review Committee was considering reducing the number of religion courses required for graduation. This concerned even Adams, who pointed out to the faculty that the number was set through agreement with the Presbyterian Board of Christian Education as a requirement of the Synnott and Bloedel trust funds set up years earlier. Those agreements stated that the college would require "a minimum of six semester hours of Bible study for all students for graduation." Furthermore, the college would "encourage students to elect such other courses as will provide for the development of a Christian philosophy of life."[6] To reduce the requirement or to alter the teaching of Christianity risked, in Adams's view, the income from those funds.[7]

President Harvey Rice agreed, notifying the committee that he felt the trustees would be loath to alter those agreements, either in fact or in spirit, and thereby "to lessen the academic as well as the spiritual results of the teaching of the Bible Courses in accordance with our contracts to the Board of Christian Education."[8] Nevertheless, when the new curriculum revisions went into effect in September 1963, the religion requirement had been reduced to one course in biblical studies and a yearlong course titled Man and His World, which would be taught by faculty throughout the college and would cover, among other things, the role of Christianity in the world.

In addition to these curricular revisions, the chapel program also came under scrutiny as debates around compulsory attendance at weekly chapel services was discussed. As with earlier discussions of the topic, this debate was raised by students, who were growing more outspoken in their questioning of the role of religion on campus. Throughout the 1962–63 academic year, they took up the debate over compulsory chapel, a debate that, as we have seen, had been raised repeatedly since the 1920s. Even though some college leaders felt that the students were becoming more sophisticated in their arguments, it is clear that their point closely echoed those of their earlier counterparts. In a society in which religious observation is voluntary, institutional requirements for such seemed to violate basic individual rights. The Student Chapel Review Committee argued that

> for many students compulsory chapel is not a worshipful experience . . . because students are required to attend chapel, those who resent this may act immaturely by reading, studying, knitting, etc., and by doing so distract those who want to worship, . . . destroying the desired worshipful atmosphere.[9]

The students also pointed out that being forced to attend services "does not seem compatible with Christ's method of teaching."[10] Furthermore, they argued that the overwhelmingly Protestant character of the services did not meet the religious needs of Catholics, Jews, and other non-Protestants among the student body.

College officials negotiated a number of components of attendance, raising the number of cuts allowed per semester and lowering the number of additional convocations students were required to attend. But the uneven quality of chapel programs was among the most problematic issues. Student Larry Demarest, for instance, asserted in a letter to the editor in the *MacWeekly* that the talk on "The Power of Protestantism" by the Reverend Irving A. West, minister of House of Hope Presbyterian Church and a member of the Macalester Board of Trustees, was in his opinion focused more on the weaknesses of the Catholic church than on the strengths of Protestantism and thus violated the effort to create a "community exemplifying the 'spirit of brotherhood.'"[11]

This is not to suggest that all chapel sessions were irrelevant, inflammatory, or even boring. In November 1962, for instance, the Reverend Wyatt Tee Walker delivered a chapel address on the civil rights movement. Walker, one of the founders of the Southern Christian Leadership Conference and its executive director from 1960 to 1964, had been involved in the freedom rides of the previous spring and summer, challenging the by then illegal segregation on interstate buses. During the month of May, in which buses filled with black riders in front and white riders at the rear traveled through Alabama on their way to New Orleans, the freedom riders were met with firebombs, beatings by angry white mobs, and ultimately, arrests and convictions. Walker had been among those who served time in jail for civil disruption.

Struggling to recast the weekly gatherings in a more relevant light attuned to current issues, the student Chapel Review Committee recommended in March that rather than required chapel services, a weekly "religious confrontation" session, at which student attendance would be required, should be organized with student input. These confrontations would consist of "an address, a reading from a religious work, and a period of silent meditation."[12] No worship would be involved, and the address and reading might focus on any religion, not just Christianity. In addition, two voluntary worship services would be offered each week for those students who wished to attend.

Adams, during this period, supported compulsory attendance at chapel services, believing that Macalester students simply would not attend if not required to do so. Most colleges, in his experience, achieved in the neighborhood of 10 percent attendance with voluntary chapel services,[13] although a few exceptions existed, such as nearby Concordia College, which reported a 90 percent attendance rate during their voluntary twenty-five-minute chapel session. Given Macalester's high commuter population, Adams predicted that few students would attend should the policy change. The issue would not be resolved for another three years, when the compulsory chapel attendance requirement would be dropped.

Reconsidering the College–Synod Relationship

Throughout the next several years, the relationship between the college and the local Synod of Minnesota, on one hand, and the national Presbyterian Church, on the other, would come under increased scrutiny. With respect to its relationship to the latter, things were relatively clear. Macalester was and had always been church related, but just what that meant had shifted from time to time over the years and was now in need of clarification. Again in 1965 stakeholders in the synod tried to clarify the situation, turning this time to the national Presbyterian leadership for a definitive answer. The response, from Harold H. Viehman, secretary of the General Division of Higher Education of the Board of Christian Education of the United Presbyterian Church (USA), was clear: "Macalester College has no legal tie to the United Presbyterian Church in the U.S.A."[14] The college did not "belong" to the denomination.

As we have already seen, at the synod level, the situation was more complex, however. Viehman had written the preceding clarification in response to an inquiry made by a member of the Minnesota Synod's Higher Education Committee, one William J. Van Dyken of Fergus Falls, Minnesota, who was concerned by the information he had heard at a recent meeting of that committee. Van Dyken's concern stemmed from comments made by Harvey Rice in an address to the synod committee, in which he had implied that the college had little need or interest in its relationship with the synod. Minnesota Presbyterians, Van Dyken countered, felt a special relationship to the college; they had been sending their children to it for decades, and now it was closing its doors against them, increasingly excluding Presbyterian students from around the state. Van Dyken wrote to Rice, "I realize how difficult these matters become when someone is emotionally involved over a letter or notice of rejection. These problems, for the most part, arise out of the fact that the people of the Synod feel they have a special claim on the college." In a sharply insightful set of questions, Van Dyken asked whether "they really do have a special claim," and "if they don't, then would it be better to be simply a college without being a Presbyterian college?"[15]

The new admissions standards were indeed designed to eliminate many of the students who the synod represented; thus, though the college had no issues to settle with the national denomination, its relationship with the synod was undergoing significant strain. In a long response, likely intended to be diplomatic, Rice pointed out that he could find no documentary evidence of any legal agreement with the synod and that despite the fact that the financial contribution of the synod amounted to "about 20 cents per Minnesota Presbyterian per year," "other kinds of support were of far greater importance and significance."[16]

The problem, as we have seen, had deep historical roots. Edward Neill was adamant that the college was not controlled by the Presbyterian Church but ultimately compromised with the synod in exchange for financial support.

Thereafter, a close connection existed between the synod and the college. As early as 1885, with the installation of Thomas McCurdy, Macalester's presidents (almost all of whom were Presbyterian ministers) and trustees (who included the ministers from the largest Presbyterian churches in the Twin Cities) formed a close alliance with other synod leaders. The original hesitancy to call the institution a Presbyterian college had long been overcome, and the college had viewed itself as clearly Presbyterian for decades. As we have seen, even as the college deevangelicalized in the 1930s and 1940s under Charles Turck, it continued to claim that it was "maintained under the auspices of the Presbyterian Church."[17] As admissions expanded from the 1930s through the 1950s, it was Presbyterian students who frequently benefited. The percentage of Presbyterian-identified students averaged in the 1950s between 28 and 35 percent and in the 1960s between 30 and 35 percent until 1965.[18] Nevertheless, these figures are nowhere near the 50 percent figure in the 1920s and the clear predominance of Presbyterians on campus before then.

Now, however, as the college attempted to distance itself from the church to raise its academic standing, Neill's early efforts to remain independent provided a convenient precedent that was easily deployed as a "tradition." As we have seen earlier, the term *nonsectarian* was also redeployed, this time with very broad meaning.

In 1967, two years after Van Dyken and Rice's initial exchange on the topic of the college–synod relationship, Van Dyken was won over by Rice's and Adams's arguments, and he submitted a new report to the Higher Education Committee of the synod clarifying the relationship between it and the college. Unlike Lutheran colleges or Catholic schools that were owned by the denominations, he explained, the relationship was one of "mutual cooperation and helpfulness," in which the synod, through limited financial support and "voluntary relationships," seeks to minister to the college, and the college, through cooperation with the synod, seeks to educate its leaders and benefit from its counsel.[19] The document went on to explain, most likely for the benefit of local ministers, that the college, recognizing the "impossibility of being a College for anyone who graduates from high school," had made a decision to "concentrate on those students of high academic ability" and to focus on liberal arts education. Such decisions, he explained, were not in the purview of the synod, precisely because the synod had refused to accept full responsibility for the college back in 1880, when it was originally offered. Nevertheless, Van Dyken continued, the college and synod hoped to "go beyond" their current relationship, to work toward increased understanding of one another, to "explore new structures by which 'Education' and 'Mission' can be supported effectively as a united concern," and to develop new "strategies and tactics" for ministry in higher education.[20] A year later, Macalester College received a charter in Phi Beta Kappa.

The Transformation of the Study of Religion

At the same time that the Christian identity of the college was being negotiated in the ways described earlier, the role of Christianity in the curriculum and the methods used to study it and other religions were also changing. As we have seen in previous chapters, the way Christianity was studied on campus had shifted a number of times since the college had opened. The religion department, charged with the primary responsibility for teaching about Christianity and other religions, was also transformed many times throughout the century, but until the late 1960s the thread that remained constant was that the department was primarily a service program, providing the courses in religion that all students were required to take. In 1885, all freshmen and sophomores were required to take two three-term courses each year, and all juniors and seniors took one three-term course. These courses were primarily in the study of the Bible and were intended to familiarize students with Christian stories and Protestant perspectives. By 1900, the number of semesters of study was reduced for all students (to one three-term course for freshmen and sophomores and no requirement for juniors and seniors), although electives, including Christian Apologetics, were offered. In 1905, the requirement for graduation was four semesters of Bible, which was doubled to eight semesters in 1910. By 1920, the influence of the social sciences was being felt, and the requirement was changed to include courses in religious education, mental science, and vocation. A decade later, it was rolled back to eight credits in "religion," which could include courses in religious history and experience and/or religious education, and essentially remained so until the early 1960s. As we have seen earlier, the requirement was then changed in 1963 to one course in biblical studies and one Man and His World course. This was altered in 1967, when Man and His World was eliminated and replaced with a two-credit requirement in religion. A year later, the requirement was one course in Judaic-Christian Heritage, and in 1970 the religion requirement was eliminated entirely.

The relationship between these changing requirements and the ways in which the study of religion was developing into a discipline within the academy is central to the slow transformation of Macalester's religion department. By the 1950s, scholars influenced by social science methods turned their attention to the phenomenon of religion generally, using the term to focus on what was considered a universal category of human experience. The study of non-Christian groups moved away from the former focus on demonstrating the superiority of Christianity to collect cultural data that could lend insight into human behavior. In effect, scholars of religion attempted to move away from the Christian ideological (and apologetic) components that had heretofore driven the study of religion and to understand other religions on their own terms. They also began to turn these more objective methods of study back on Christianity itself, asking questions about history, myth, and practices that made more traditional believers nervous.

By the early 1950s, Macalester's increased hiring of religion faculty with PhDs (as well as seminary degrees and ordination) suggests that a more critical perspective on the study of religion was beginning to appear. Robert McAfee Brown, for instance, who had just finished his PhD in the joint Union Theological Seminary–Columbia University program, launched the first Introduction to Religion course at Macalester, a course that focused on categories relevant to comparative study across religions—God, myth, ritual, and so on—an approach gaining influence through the work of Mircea Eliade at the University of Chicago. Brown also offered a Jesus in History course, which took a historical rather than confessional approach to the life of Jesus.[21]

When Brown left Macalester in 1953 to accept a position at Union Theological Seminary in New York—he would go on to become a celebrated Protestant theologian—he was replaced by A. Leland Jamison, another University of Chicago graduate who had spent the war years serving as a U.S. Air Force chaplain. Jamison would also work to increase the rigor within the study of religion at the college, but his tenure, like that of Brown, was short-lived. He left for Syracuse University within four years. Thus the religion department seemed to be serving as something of a training ground for talented scholars who then moved on to better positions.

It is not surprising that these professors did not stay long, for despite efforts to incorporate new scholarship into the study of religion at the college, most of the courses offered, particularly the Bible courses, were service courses: every student was required to take eight credits in the department, and as a result, upper-level offerings that challenged students intellectually were not a priority. Moreover, most of the courses were taught from a nonscholarly, insider perspective. Nevertheless, it was clear that the religion department had begun to move away from what became known as the "confessional" model of teaching about religion and toward a more academic model. Donald Butler, an ordained Presbyterian minister who held a PhD from New York University and was hired as the James Wallace Professor of Religion in 1961, would transform the program from its earlier service orientation to a scholarly major alongside the other humanities disciplines. "We assume that there should be religion in a church-related college," Butler observed in 1967, "but to what extent and of what nature?"[22] For Butler, though study of Christianity and the Bible remained a central part of the Macalester curriculum and the mission of the Department of Religious Studies (as he renamed it from the earlier Department of Religion), the approach to these topics was steeped not in faith but in historical and social science methods. "All of our courses are academic in character. While the teacher may express his own beliefs when and as indicated, they are not intended as the presuppositions of the course. There is no indoctrination of the student, telling him what he should believe. The teaching of religion in our College is as open to free inquiry as well as the freedom of the student to draw his own conclusions responsibly as in any other discipline."[23] No longer were Christian apologetics central to Macalester's curriculum. Under Butler's leadership, the PhD and the scholarly approach became the norm among religious studies faculty hired in the 1960s, a transformation that was mirrored in religion departments in church-related liberal arts colleges across the country during that period.[24]

The Weyerhaeuser Memorial Chapel

Of the many disruptions to the religion program created by the 1961 long-range planning recommendations, the decision to erect a chapel on campus resulted in the most heated dispute. According to Maxwell Adams, the long-range planning document recommended the construction of a chapel most likely as part of the effort to make Macalester's campus a seven-day residential environment. In 1962, Margaret (Mrs. Frederick) Weyerhaeuser, along with other members of the Weyerhaeuser family, offered to build the chapel as a memorial to the late Frederick Weyerhaeuser, a longtime trustee and benefactor of the college.[25] Delighted with the offer, Harvey Rice encouraged Margaret Weyerhaeuser to proceed with plans for the building.

In the meantime, the chapel requirement had again surfaced as a source of conflict for, as it turned out, the last time. In 1966, the board once again took up the question of compulsory chapel attendance. The context had shifted somewhat since the previous discussion of chapel, for now the college was putting together its third Phi Beta Kappa proposal and criticism of the denominational character of religious instruction had come under scrutiny. Complicating the question even further was the establishment of a religious speaker's fund a year earlier by DeWitt Wallace and Howard Pew. If required chapel attendance were to be eliminated, the status of that fund would no doubt be put in jeopardy.[26]

In April, an ad hoc committee of the college recommended that compulsory chapel be discontinued and called a special meeting of the board for May 19. The recommendation would find support at the highest levels. On the morning of the 19th, Macalester trustee Arthur Flemming, then president of the University of Oregon, at home in Eugene, dictated a message for Harvey Rice over the telephone to Rice's secretary. The message echoed the students' argument and supported the ad hoc committee's recommendation, stating, "Whenever any institution in society, whether it is government or a college or university, endeavors to force people to participate in religious meetings of any kind, it is doing something which is in direct conflict with the concept of freedom that lies at the heart of our Christian religion." He suggested that the elimination of chapel sessions be taken as an opportunity to demonstrate the true power of Christianity:

> The resources that have been made available to Macalester College to bring the Nation's outstanding religious leaders to the campus plus the prospect of a worshipful chapel provide Macalester College with the finest opportunity confronting any institution of higher learning to demonstrate that Christianity has a message which when presented effectively attracts and holds young people.[27]

Other trustees agreed, and later that day, the board voted to eliminate the chapel attendance requirement, except for three ceremonial events each year. The chapel would offer weekly services on Wednesdays. The board also approved a requirement that each term students attend five "religious confrontations," discussions of important issues pertaining to or involving not just Christianity but other religions as well.

In September, when the new rules went into effect, Adams reported that he was "ringing the College bell at 10 A.M. every Wednesday for our Chapel services and have nothing but favorable comments from students and faculty."[28] Attendance through the year averaged around 170 participants, or about 10 percent of the student population, a figure that was consistent with other church-related colleges that had dropped their chapel attendance requirement.[29] Confrontation attendance, still required, averaged around fourteen hundred to fifteen hundred students.[30] A year later, Wallace grew concerned that the attendance at chapel no longer warranted the cost of bringing in major speakers; gathering only small audiences for major figures was embarrassing and wasted the time of the speakers. Throughout 1967, Wallace investigated the impact of the speaker's fund, consulting with Pew and Paul Davis on whether to retain it. Davis recommended (perhaps in response to criticism raised when journalist Harrison Salisbury, who opposed the Johnson administration's handling of the situation in Vietnam, appeared as a convocation speaker) that Wallace require that a least a third of the Pew-Wallace chapel fund be used to bring in "conservative evangelical men of the type approved by Mr. Pew."[31]

Just as the chapel requirement fell, the new chapel building rose. Spring 1967 brought the unveiling of plans for the new building designed by architect Duane Thornbeck of Cerny and Associates of Minneapolis. Intense debate ensued. Many faculty and students questioned whether a new chapel building was needed at all. Others took issue with the location of the new building, fearing that were it to be placed on the main campus, it would break up the mall, the main axis and unifying feature of the grounds. Some held what Adams called "an ideological objection" to the building. "They just don't want a visible reminder that this is a Christian college and that we intend to continue to be a Christian college."[32] Still others expressed concern about the lack of transparency in the process by which the trustees decided to allow such an important addition to the campus.[33] Supporters argued that the building would fill a need for a focal point for religious activity on campus. Professor Hildegard Johnson, for instance, argued that "on this campus where there is a building for the specific sciences, one for the administration, the Fine Arts Center, and a gym, why should there not be a building which says we are a part of the outside civilization? We will be poorer by not having this architectural symbol of the function of the mind."[34]

Although these discussions and several student demonstrations against the chapel dismayed donor Margaret Weyerhaeuser and her family, Harvey Rice and Maxwell Adams, who would soon retire, as well as his successor, John Bodo, continued to assure her that the vocal minority did not speak for the majority of Macalester students, who welcomed the new building and appreciated her generosity.[35] Completed in 1969, the chapel would be the strongest institutional statement made by the college in years that it embraced, or at least acknowledged, a Christian identity. Yet the college and synod continued to move apart. By spring of that year, as the chapel was near completion and plans for its dedication were being prepared, the college was again negotiating its role vis-à-vis the Synod of Minnesota, and this time the college's interest in that relationship was deemed to be even less than it had been earlier in the Rice administration.

Nevertheless, not all were comfortable with the decreasing attention paid to religion on campus. Political science professor Yahya Armajani, a Christian originally from Persia who joined the faculty in the 1940s, argued that the college's unwillingness even to discuss the role of religion on campus was intolerable and not a little cowardly. In his view, the Protestant identity of the institution did not preclude ecumenism, in which all were welcome under the Protestant umbrella. This type of ecumenism, in which the context was defined by one outlook, was precisely what many critics railed against. Long years had demonstrated that, for instance, practicing Catholics, though welcomed and tolerated, were not supported in their religious lives at the college. Jews were treated similarly, though Judaism was also a subject of study. Religious support was reserved for Protestants.[36]

At least two other faculty members weighed in on the question of church relatedness during this period. Self-described "secularized, nonobservant Jew" and "fairly devout Sociologist" Irwin Rinder argued that the college served as a bridge between the church and secular society and that the church should not be deprived of this important connection. Furthermore, the college "permit[ted] the continuance of real types of beliefs and memberships which can serve as the basis for identity and outreach toward others," and those for whom the institution thus functions should not be deprived of that function.[37] Taking a different tack was mathematics professor and evangelical Christian Wayne Roberts, who argued that the institution should more publicly demonstrate Christian practice and commitment. In his work with the Macalester Inter-Varsity Christian Fellowship, an evangelical group, he saw growth in students' interest in developing a deeper Christian life, demonstrated by attendance at meetings (increasing from about fifteen in 1968 to twenty-eight in 1969) and participation in "dormitory Bible studies, the operation of the Kurios House on Friday and Saturday nights, and participation in conferences with other schools."[38] These types of programs, which Macalester students had created and participated in for decades, would continue to be the most prominent and broadly meaningful religious activity on campus.

Required chapel attendance had always been problematic, its elimination more than anything an acknowledgment that forced participation had never accorded well with the democratic aspirations of the institution. Despite Armajani's insistence that the college was avoiding a real discussion of its religious identity, the chapel controversy did precisely that. And what that controversy revealed was that there were deep divisions within the Macalester community regarding just what course the college should take. In coming years, many of those divisions would again be played out in discussions of the use of the chapel and of the role of the chaplaincy itself. The controversy also affirmed the historical tie between Presbyterian financial support and the college, a tie that had informed the college–synod link since 1880 and, although loosening, still remained.

The Uncoupling of Christianity and the Liberal Arts

The changing role of Christianity in the institutional mission of and student life at Macalester College sheds some light on the ongoing academic debate regarding the so-called secularization of higher education in the twentieth century. As mentioned in the introduction to this book, some historians have argued that secularization is apparent in the transformation of colleges from being wholly religious in the early part of the century to being not religious at all in the latter half. Others have called for more sophisticated approaches to and understandings of the quite complex processes of change within religious institutions. In the case of Macalester, where the religious mission of the college changed many times over the century, was indeed diminished during the 1960s, and would all but disappear in the 1970s, the term *secularization* oversimplifies changes within religious life and how Protestants perceived the role of religion in public life and education. The case of Macalester provides some detail into those processes as over the course of the twentieth century, the role of religion with respect to the educational mission of the college shifted significantly, from being all encompassing to functioning within a narrowed field.

Through the first half of the twentieth century, Macalester, like most church-related colleges, used a four-pronged approach to infusing religion into the institution and campus life. The first prong consisted of the nineteenth-century conviction that Christianity provided the foundation for all learning and for knowledge itself. Education was therefore infused with Christian (in this case, Protestant) ideology through the curriculum itself. This understanding of the link between Christianity and education or knowledge was the first of the four prongs to be challenged and eliminated. As we have seen, by the 1910s almost all vestiges of this were gone, except for some residual concerns about the teaching of evolution, which would be dispelled in the late 1920s.

The second prong was the study of religion, initially imparted in required Bible courses and later at Macalester in the religious education curriculum. This specialized curriculum meshed with the third prong of church-related service, particularly the encouragement of vocational work in religion. Though preparation for the profession of the ministry remained relatively stable throughout the century, the emphasis on lay preparation for religious vocations, either professional or volunteer, grew stronger in the 1910s and 1920s but ebbed significantly in the post–World War II period. With the elimination of the vocational curriculum in the mid-1960s and the religion course requirement in the late 1960s, these two prongs of the institutional support for religion also faded.

The fourth prong of the religious mission of the college was to develop the Christian character of its students. In the early years, this was accomplished through close contact with faculty, most of whom were ordained. Students were carefully guided into Christian life in three ways. First, they were to be immersed in a climate of Christian morality, which was most frequently imparted through rules and regulations such as separation of the sexes in living and dining arrangements and strict control over their movements off campus and their daily routines on campus. Second, Christianity was fostered through meticulous behavioral training. Faculty despaired at times of the backward behaviors of the students, whom they felt must be initiated into more civilized activity. Lessons on table manners, how to dress, and how to interact socially brought the manners of middlebrow society to the mostly rural students of the college. Last, character training came through the biweekly lectures delivered at the chapel and convocation services on Tuesdays and Thursdays. During these lectures, speakers imparted the benefit of their Christian experience to students, discussing such aspects of Christian character as how to make and be a friend, the importance of missionary work, and later the need for Christian activism. These efforts to instill Christian character were the last vestige of the Christian mission that remained on campus by the late 1960s, and even they had been significantly diminished. Within the next decade, they would be all but gone, resurrected only once a year in the graduation convocation lecture.

Change in each of these areas must be understood within the context of the close relationship between how people live and experience their religious life and the social and cultural contexts in which they live it. Religion and culture are inseparable. As scientific models of knowledge developed at the turn of the century, Protestantism adapted to accommodate them in a new epistemological model that redefined God's role. As Western Christians interacted with peoples and cultures around the world, a new model of Christian responsibility to others emerged, as did new approaches to the study of religion. As religious life changed, the educational needs of religious workers shifted as well, moving toward more sophisticated forms of knowledge. And last, as the experience level of students changed and as the perceived need to "civilize" them diminished, the need for overt moral training transformed into encouragement of student independence and responsibility.

These changes on campus provide a unique window into how Protestantism itself was changing. Religion is never static; it responds to and transforms in the face of ongoing and changing cultural situations. Colleges like Macalester were not changing on their own but rather in a dialogue with Protestantism and culture. As we shall see in coming chapters, the relationship between Macalester and Protestantism would continue to evolve over the next several decades.

11

New Approaches to Academics, Internationalism, and Service

IN SEPTEMBER 1967, Lucius Garvin, Macalester's vice president for academic affairs, opened the academic year with a stirring convocation lecture highlighting the great strides made by the college. Using the metaphor "steeples of strength," borrowed from Frederick E. Terman, recent provost of Stanford University and a national leader in scientific and engineering education, Garvin singled out the science program as among the college's most impressive "steeples." Not only was it run by first-rate scientists, many of whom Garvin himself had recruited, but it also boasted such advanced equipment as an electron microscope, a high-energy particle accelerator, and a computer. Garvin also highlighted the many successes of the college's social and international programs: it ran successful student and faculty exchanges with several historically black colleges, including Knoxville, Tuskegee, Lane, Bishop, Huston-Tillotson, Virginia Union, and Bethune Cookman; its work–study abroad program put students to work as teacher assistants, hospital orderlies, waiters, farm laborers, and factory workers; its Student Leader Scholars program hosted ten international students; and the Foreign On-the-Scene Confrontation with Unusually Significant Developments (FOCUS'D) program sent students abroad on independent research projects. He underscored the many projects being pursued in collaboration with other regional and national colleges and universities.

By the time Garvin concluded his talk with a charge to the students to "put your revolutionary zeal and off-beat (innovative!) ideas into the total work and counsels of the College" and a prediction that "Macalester can look ahead with strengthened confidence in its future," the audience was convinced. There were simply too many wonderful things happening at the college for Macalester to be anything but a leading institution. Within a few months, Macalester would also win that academic prize it had so longed for, a Phi Beta Kappa chapter. Surely, given that the college had come "so far, so fast," the Macalester community could rest assured that a glorious future lay ahead.

Change had indeed proceeded rapidly at Macalester after the approval of the new liberal arts curriculum in 1961. In the span of a few years, as we shall see, the new curriculum was implemented, dozens of new faculty were hired, an array of new programs to foster academic excellence were launched, and the traditional components of the college mission regarding internationalism and service were redefined within new social and cultural contexts.

Those new contexts themselves became central players in the new character and identity of the college. The nation was undergoing a variety of social, cultural, and technological changes during this period that would reshape the parameters of life in the United States and abroad. In many cases, these social and cultural changes called into question the purpose of a liberal arts education, challenging the role of education in a world increasingly troubled by war, the arms race, poverty, racism, sexism, and other disturbing situations. Macalester looked to its leaders, particularly Vice President Garvin and trustee and soon-to-become president Arthur Flemming, both of whom helped to formulate the college's new mission and to articulate the mission and identity of the college in this tumultuous context.

New Leadership, New Academic Programs

Over the course of the 1960s, a new leadership coalition emerged at Macalester, bringing together its major donor, a handful of trustees, two administrators, and outside consultants in a delicate coalition of unequal partners. The primary and most powerful partner in the new leadership coalition was, of course, DeWitt Wallace. As we have seen in previous chapters, Wallace's determination to raise the national visibility of the college was the primary motivating force behind the curricular revisions of the early 1960s. Just who would lead the college into this new educational frontier was also of great concern to Wallace. As we have seen, he successfully engineered the replacement of President Charles Turck with Harvey Rice in 1959. Dean Ficken was also on the way out, replaced in 1961 by Lucius Garvin, about whom we will learn more shortly. The most prominent leaders of the new regime, however, did not arrive on campus until the mid-1960s, and they came together as something of an educational super-duo: Arthur Flemming and Paul Davis.

The name Arthur S. Flemming appeared on a list of suggested convocation speakers for Macalester College generated by an editor of *Readers' Digest* for DeWitt Wallace in February 1957.[1] Flemming, then president of Ohio Wesleyan University but destined to become the most inspiring and controversial of Macalester's presidents, would not appear at the Macalester convocation lectern for another seven years. In the meantime, he would serve as secretary of the Department of Health, Education, and Welfare under Dwight D. Eisenhower, as a member of John F. Kennedy's National Advisory Committee on the Peace Corps, and as president of the University of Oregon.

Flemming and Charles Turck were cut of similar cloth. Both were deeply religious in the liberal Protestant vein, Flemming an ordained Methodist minister. Neither man was evangelical. Both were moderate-to-liberal Republicans, comfortable with working across party lines; both held strong convictions about service to the community and nation; both were dedicated educators; and both believed that education sprang from and carried with it responsibilities for the democratic advancement of the nation. Flemming's early career had focused on public service on a national level, serving in the U.S. Civil Service Commission, the War Manpower Policy Committee, and the First Hoover Commission on Origination on the Executive Branch of the Government under F.D.R. and Truman. He had also served on the International Civil Service Advisory Board, the Advisory Committee on Government Organization, the Second Hoover Commission, and the National Security Council and had directed the Office of Defense Mobilization under Eisenhower. Later, he moved into higher education administration, serving as president of Ohio Wesleyan University from 1948 to 1953 and again from 1957 to 1958. In 1961, Flemming became president of the University of Oregon.

Higher education in the early 1960s was in crisis. The Soviet launching of Sputnik in 1957 had made Americans fear that they were trailing this cold war enemy not only on the technological front but in education generally. Americans, they feared, were not sufficiently educated to excel in the new technological age. In response to these fears, university leaders around the country, including Flemming at Oregon and, as we have seen, Dean Ficken and others at Macalester, strove to increase the rigor of the educations their institutions delivered. An array of new approaches and agendas for higher education, including the advancement of the liberal arts, the strategy that Macalester adopted, was proposed by educators across the country.

A new figure emerged in this crisis: the educational specialist, private consultants who made themselves available for a fee to assess current practices and suggest new directions to institutional leaders. By 1962, Flemming was among many college and university presidents who solicited the expertise of educational specialist Paul H. Davis in their search for more effective educational strategies. Within a few years, Flemming hired Davis as his consultant at the University of Oregon. The two men became close friends, their families vacationing together, fishing on the McKenzie River in Oregon.[2] They agreed on the fundamental ideas that higher education in the United States had not fulfilled its potential, that educators had a long way to go to deliver high-quality education to students, and that administrative measures frequently hindered rather than helped the cause. Flemming, with his enormous energy and access to Davis's vast store of information on current practices in higher education (Davis paid regular visits to over forty institutions yearly, gathering and dispensing information and consulting with top-level administrators), moved the University of Oregon in several new directions, acquiring significant federal funding, establishing two new professional schools, and expanding the student body by nearly 60 percent.[3] This effective partnership would set the agenda for Macalester by the closing years of the decade.

Davis brought Flemming and the Wallaces together sometime in 1963, initially recommending Flemming's work to Lila Wallace, an alumna of the University of Oregon. Clearly impressed with his work, she sent Flemming a check for ten thousand dollars in November of that year, to be used at the university as he chose; soon after, she contributed ninety thousand dollars for the university's social work programs.[4] Davis and Flemming worked closely together during 1965 and 1966, with the Wallaces increasingly involved. Flemming was just the kind of man Wallace was looking for to lead Macalester into a new, more glorious future. He had national visibility, a proven track record in higher education administration, energy, dedication, and ideas. Furthermore, he was a Republican and religious to boot.

Flemming's direct relationship with Macalester dates to March 1964, when he delivered a chapel talk on "The Role of the Presidential Cabinet." The next year, he was appointed to the board of trustees, and he delivered the commencement speech.[5] Paul Davis pronounced his participation in both activities "highly successful and much appreciated."[6] Taking his fiscal responsibility as a trustee seriously, Flemming donated five hundred dollars to the college each year for the next two years; at least one of those gifts was matched by the Wallaces. On the occasion of his being elected president of the National Council of Churches in December 1966, Flemming received congratulations and glowing endorsements from Macalester president Harvey Rice and from DeWitt Wallace, with the latter gushing uncharacteristically, "It is a privilege just to know you."[7] Clearly Flemming's was a welcomed presence in the Macalester community. A knowledgeable, experienced, dedicated, and charismatic man, he quickly became an educational leader to whom the administration, the trustees, and Wallace looked for advice and guidance.

Macalester's "inside" academic leader during this period was Dr. Lucius Garvin, a professor of philosophy who was hired in 1961 as academic dean, a position soon renamed Vice President for Academic Affairs.[8] Thus, by 1965, a new leadership coalition was in place: Garvin, Flemming, and Davis, working to accomplish Wallace's dream of making Macalester College a national leader among private colleges.

Thirty Million Dollars' Worth of New Ideas

Beginning that summer and continuing through 1967, Garvin, Flemming, and Davis led a team of faculty in the development of proposals for thirty-three specific educational programs explicitly aimed at enhancing Macalester's teaching and research abilities to move the college into a higher tier of liberal arts schools. The programs, requested by DeWitt Wallace, who intended to provide the necessary funding, ranged widely over a variety of areas. Among them were programs focused on salary supplements for "new major [faculty] appointments," which were estimated to cost $517,500, funds expected to come from income on an influx of $1.5 million in endowment.[9] Other programs aimed at strengthening the institution, departments, and research and teaching. Institutional research programs and the purchase of new scientific equipment aided the first two. Faculty were further aided by programs to foster research innovation, to support travel to the meetings of scholarly societies, to endow visiting professorships and acquire books and new media (audiovisual equipment and materials), to create a "Great Teaching and Learning Program" designed to partner new faculty members with more experienced faculty teachers, to support an award for distinguished teaching, to provide funds for faculty research, and to support new staff.

Internationalism also received a significant shot in the arm from these new programs, which built on earlier efforts to emphasize international learning and exchange within the Macalester curriculum and campus life. Programs were developed to support international visitors, to increase student participation in the Student Project for Amity among Nations (SPAN) program, to strengthen financial aid, to establish a simulation computation center for the behavioral sciences, and to create International House. The internationalism proposals included programs to create an Ambassadors for Friendship program, summer work-abroad opportunities for students, continued funding for the Canadian-American conference, and an international visitors' program.

The total estimated costs of the package of programs proposed in 1965 reached well over twenty million dollars.[10] Though a fairly astonishing sum, Davis assured Garvin and Flemming that it would be forthcoming, for these were the plans, everyone agreed, that would put Macalester firmly on the path toward regional dominance and national acclaim.

January 1966 brought an attempted raid and a new clarification of the leadership model. Hiram College in Ohio wanted Garvin for their president. On receiving the offer from Hiram, Garvin consulted with both Paul Davis and Arthur Flemming. Davis dashed off a telegram, urging him to stay at Macalester because he was unequivocally "the central person in what may become one of the great educational advances of the decade."[11] A special meeting of the executive committee of the board of trustees was called. With assurance from DeWitt Wallace that he would personally "provide financial aid necessary to meet the offer from Hiram," the committee agreed to do all they could to persuade Garvin to stay.[12] What they ultimately offered Garvin was unprecedented: a guarantee that then president Harvey Rice would delegate "complete administration of every phase of academic affairs" to Garvin and would not interfere with his authority in these areas.[13] Rice, although involved in the initial curriculum revisions, had taken little part in the development of the 1965 programs. As we will see, though popular among faculty, he was experiencing increasing trouble with the board, other administrators, and Wallace. Garvin agreed to stay.

Later that summer, Garvin, Davis, and Flemming met in Los Angeles to discuss DeWitt Wallace's growing interest in expanding Macalester's international affairs program.[14] This trio, along with two members of the board of trustees' education committee, David Winton and Archie Jackson, was developing a shared outlook on the future of the college and, in particular, its relationship with Wallace.

Together, they developed plans to bring Macalester and the University of Oregon into partnership in the pursuit of "educational innovation and experimentation." This partnership would focus on, among other things, improving undergraduate teaching, incorporating new technologies into teaching, and emphasizing international study. In Flemming's view, such a partnership would allow "each institution . . . [to] profit from the strengths of the other institution."[15]

A year later, in 1967, the trustees' education committee, led by Winton, appointed a subcommittee on education that came to be known as the Flemming Committee. Another education specialist, Gilbert Wrenn, who was already a member of the board of trustees and would eventually be hired by the college in 1968 to help lead the new programs, was appointed head of the committee. The Flemming Committee developed a number of further proposals, including the formation of the Office of Educational Research and Experimental Innovation, which, among other things, would apply to a variety of federal and private organizations for grants to support innovative educational practices. The committee also recommended the formation of an Office of Planning, Institutional Research, and Evaluation, with the latter component being stressed. Other recommendations included a postdoctoral fellow program designed to bring to campus bright young educators just out of graduate school. An overhaul of the dorm residence programs was also called for, with the recommendation that the traditional housemothers be replaced by young educators able to lead informal discussions among students on important topics of the day. The committee also recommended closer relationships with the University of Minnesota and the University of Oregon, the formation of a program to aid students in identifying career options, more effective use of Twin Cities cultural resources, the development of an interfaith institute at the college, and the formation of the Macalester Foundation for Advancement of Higher Education, which would coordinate investigation of and develop policy in regard to questions of educational administration. The sweeping scope of these programs, coming on the heels of the thirty-three new programs three years earlier, attested to the committee's and the trustees' eagerness to use the college as an institutional petri dish, a place to test new ideas and experiment with programs.[16]

With these leaders at the helm and several innovative and well-funded programs poised to begin, Macalester's prospects seemed to be skyrocketing. The liberal arts curriculum went into effect in 1964. Over one hundred vocationally oriented courses were trimmed from the catalog. More than two dozen faculty members were hired in 1965 and 1966, creating a cohort of young PhDs who increased the excitement and energy of the college. Student applications were strong and admissions standards were tightening. Plans were being laid for a new library, and another set of academic proposals was being prepared for submission to DeWitt Wallace.

Redefining Internationalism in a Cold War Context

Perhaps most effective in helping Macalester achieve a national reputation were various efforts to enhance international programs at the college. As the cold war raged in the early 1960s and fears of Communist influence wracked the country, many institutions of higher education across the nation became involved in programs to enhance understanding across national borders by internationalizing the curriculum, admitting greater numbers of international students, and sending American students abroad. At Macalester, two programs in the latter category, both funded by Wallace and other donors, were the SWAP program, which placed students in summer jobs abroad, and the SPAN program, which combined research on campus with a trip to the country under investigation. In 1963, for instance, some sixty Mac students spent the summer abroad working at Conrad Hilton hotels in Istanbul, Amsterdam, London, and other cities and studying through SPAN in Brazil, Finland, Lebanon, Yugoslavia, and other countries.[17]

Wallace's participation in the international programs at Macalester extended beyond funding these particular programs. In 1960, he sent soon-to-be Rutgers political science graduate Harry Morgan to campus to extol an idea for fostering understanding among nations and particularly for countering negative images of the United States being instilled abroad through Communist-inspired propaganda. Morgan's idea was to take foreign students enrolled in U.S. institutions on tours of the United States, stopping to talk with "ordinary" Americans, staying with farm families, and seeing America from a grassroots perspective. His program, called Ambassadors for Friendship, became a favored cause of Wallace's, and Macalester was a ready-made location for its growth. Macalester's first Friendship Caravan toured during that summer. Four international students—Nasser Mazaheri, Manuchehr Movassaghi, George Lymburis, and Kofi Annan—along with Morgan and his wife, Catharine Johnston, drove some fifty thousand miles together in a single car.[18] Wallace, delighted with the program, printed articles on it in *Reader's Digest*, which resulted in a steady flow of public donations, prompting Wallace, according to historian John Heidenry, to incorporate the Ambassadors of Friendship as a nonprofit corporation. Six years later, the Macalester Ambassadors for Friendship program had grown to a caravan of fifteen cars filled with international students.[19]

On graduating from Rutgers, Morgan was appointed by Harvey Rice as special assistant to the president in charge of international programs. With Wallace bankrolling his effort, he relocated to St. Paul, taking up residence in Macalester's International House. Still seeking to improve the image of the United States abroad, the next year, Morgan invited, with the financial support of Wallace and the presidents or chairmen of Pan American World Airways, American Motors, National Cash Register Company, IBM, and NBC, twelve young foreign journalists to campus for a Foreign Journalists Institute. The intention was for the journalists to spend a year at Macalester studying such subjects as American civilization and social studies and touring the country, again staying with farm families and learning about the nation literally from the ground up.[20]

This program, soon renamed the World Press Institute, or simply WPI, not only served Morgan's and Wallace's goals of countering Communist propaganda about the United States but also became a conduit for information about Macalester College to flow throughout the world. Whereas previously interest in Macalester among students abroad had been linked primarily to the Presbyterian missionary connections, WPI, by targeting young journalists (initially, participants had to be under twenty-six years of age) with the greatest promise of becoming influential writers in their home countries, raised the profile of the college in influential international circles. Many future Macalester applicants would learn about the school from WPI participants.

WPI was not alone among educational programs founded during this period explicitly aimed at polishing the image of the United States. Federal organizations, such as the U.S. Information Agency, also sponsored programs on college and university campuses, developing a U.S.-based strategy to accomplish the same goals that the Voice of America radio network aimed at overseas. For Wallace, an ardent anti-Communist, Morgan and WPI were an effective means of steering Macalester's international agenda in a direction he favored. Others on campus, however, were less interested in the anti-Communist ideology than in fostering good relations with other countries for the sake of peaceful relations, echoing earlier articulations of Macalester's role in the world. Several faculty members, for instance, including Huntley Dupre, were deeply involved in organizations such as the International World Federation as well as peace and nuclear disarmament activism. Internationalism at Macalester cut both ways during this period, providing at least a temporary bridge between the political conservativism and anti-Communism of the major donor and the growing liberalism of others on campus.

Public Service and Macalester's Response to Racism

In addition to this transformation in the motivations underlying the institution's commitment to internationalism, the college's long-standing though frequently redefined dedication to service also shifted, in large measure because of changing social and cultural contexts. The instigator of many of the changes that occurred in the service mission during this period was Arthur Flemming.

Flemming arrived at Macalester with an established reputation as a public servant that fit neatly with the civic understanding of service instilled at the college during the Turck years. As mentioned earlier, he had served three U.S. presidents before heading up the largest public educational institution in Oregon.[21] He was deeply engaged in the social and political debates of the period, and during the late 1960s those debates were taking on public proportions never before seen. Flemming was a moderate-liberal Republican of the old school. During his years as the head of the University of Oregon, he gained a reputation as being outspoken on political issues, one newspaper calling him "a public employee who is not going to abdicate the full responsibilities of citizenship."[22] He supported civil rights and criticized John F. Kennedy for not pressing for racial equality in federal housing. He was outspoken in his criticism of the handling of the Bay of Pigs incident. In 1962, he was vilified by the anti-Communists when he allowed Communist Party leader Gus Hall to present a lecture on the University of Oregon campus, a situation in which he defended Hall's right to speak though not his positions.[23] In 1966, he participated in peace marches organized by interfaith religious groups in Portland, Oregon, and he also taught a course on the Vietnam War.[24] As a result of these activities, Flemming gained a reputation as a progressive defender of free speech.

Flemming also championed students' rights at Oregon. He made himself available to students, allowing walk-in conferences without appointments, and appointed students to a range of faculty and administrative committees, arguing that their perspectives and input were highly valuable to the decision-making process. He taught courses to connect with students, and believing that adult students should take responsibility for their own actions, he worked to eliminate the in loco parentis rules that governed student life on campus.

Flemming's reputation and activities were well known among the Macalester trustees and to Paul Davis and DeWitt Wallace when they invited him to become president of the college. Indeed, the college's press release announcing the appointment hailed his work in politics and education. The announcement quoted the presidential search committee chair, Archie Jackson, himself quoting from the University of Oregon's student newspaper, praising Flemming "for defending students' rights to have discussion of any sort on the campus . . . a decision based on his belief that without complete freedom to seek information the objectives of a university cannot be reached."[25] Flemming's public service and pro-student views were not liabilities; they were the strengths of this extraordinary candidate, even though many of his actions conflicted with Wallace's anti-Communism and conservative politics.

Flemming took office at Macalester in what was one of the most domestically turbulent years in the history of the nation, 1968. Even a short list of the events of that year is unsettling: the Tet offensive in North Vietnam in January; release of the Kerner Commission report on racism in America in March; the assassination of Martin Luther King in April, sparking riots in Washington, D.C., Baltimore, and other cities; the assassination of Robert Kennedy in June; rioting at the Democratic National Convention in Chicago in August and on the campus of Columbia University in September; and the black power salute of Olympians Tommie Smith and John Carlos at the summer Olympic games in Mexico City. In this charged national atmosphere, college campuses found themselves squarely at the center of the fray, and Macalester, with a new president committed to free speech and public participation and a history of open discussion of political and international topics, become increasingly involved in the divisive issues of the day. Just what service did a college owe the nation?

The new president was drawn into the local political scene almost immediately on his arrival in the Twin Cities. The predominantly African American Selby-Dale neighborhood of St. Paul, like so many other inner-city areas across the nation, was experiencing increasing unrest. One disturbance had resulted in significant property damage already, and the city was searching for ways to ward off further violence. The St. Paul Urban Commission appointed a committee to investigate the situation and asked newcomer Arthur Flemming to serve as chair. His work on this committee thrust Macalester's new president immediately into the public eye, at the center of an already volatile situation. Race relations and achieving racial equality through education would become prominent themes for Flemming and the college alike during the next several years. Although much of white America, including white St. Paul and Minneapolis, wished simply to ignore the issues of racial equality that had been raised by the civil rights movement, transformed by the black power movement, and most recently brought more militantly to the streets by groups of black activists, Macalester took steps to address the issues head-on.

The college's initial efforts to advance racial equality had been launched four years earlier, in 1964, when Louis W. Hill, president of the Louis W. and Maud Hill Family Foundation, approached Harvey Rice and the presidents of Hamline, Carleton, and St. Thomas with the idea of starting a faculty exchange program between their colleges and several historically black colleges participating in the United Negro College Fund. Rice endorsed the idea, and Macalester faculty helped to develop the program, called the Inter-College Faculty Exchange Program, which began a year later. During the program's first academic year, Macalester hosted three faculty members—Clarence Epps (history), Tuskegee Institute; Mary Stewart (English), Knoxville College; and Thelma Washington (mathematics), Tuskegee Institute—and sent two, Murray Braden (mathematics) and David Hopper (history and philosophy), to Tuskegee and Lane College. The next year, four new visiting faculty members arrived from Bishop College (Herbert Alexander, biology, and Nathaniel Williams, music), Huston-Tillotson College (June Brewer, English), and Virginia Union University (Robert Walker, chemistry), and three Macalester faculty members—Paul Berry (sociology), David White (English), and Hugo Thompson (religion and philosophy)—went to Virginia Union University, Huston-Tillotson, and Bishop.[26] The goals of the program were to offer all participants educational opportunities—several visiting faculty in Minnesota took courses at the University of Minnesota—and to encourage cultural enrichment and dialogue, thus "furthering good human relations."[27] In July 1965, President Rice, a strong supporter of the program, presented a paper on the topic at the conference of the American College Public Relations Association, which was later published in the organization's journal.[28] Lucius Garvin served as chairman of the Inter-College program after its first year.

Macalester students were also becoming involved in the civil rights movement. Across the nation, activism with respect to civil rights among students at northern universities is generally traced to the 1961 freedom rides and continued through 1964 voter registration efforts. White students at Macalester were shocked to learn in 1962 that off-campus housing landlords in St. Paul regularly discriminated against African and African American students, resulting in what appears to be the beginnings of an institutional consciousness raising.[29] Soon the Student Action on Human Rights organization focused more attention on race issues nationwide, raising funds for the freedom schools in Mississippi and inviting speakers to campus.

Fall 1967 saw the formation of the Black Liberation Affairs Committee, or BLAC, the campus's first African American student organization. Many of the thirty-nine African American students on campus that year deeply felt estrangement and difference from the hundreds of white students. BLAC organized a week of consciousness-raising activities, BLAC Week, during February 1968, which included a lecture by Floyd McKissick, national director of the Congress of Racial Equality; a screening of the film *A Raisin in the Sun;* a black talent night; and a Soul Day featuring Afro-American cuisine in the cafeteria and an evening dance. The next spring, several African American students published essays, short stories, and poems describing their experiences and feelings in a collection of works distributed throughout the campus. The pieces speak to the false expectations and stereotypes faced by the African American students; open discrimination they encountered as they sought off-campus housing; deep differences in religious life, music, recreation, and relationships they found in relation to their white counterparts; awkwardness in white students' efforts to relate to black students; and strength they found in community with other black students.[30]

When Flemming arrived that summer, he readily took up the standard passed by Rice to use the institution to advance racial equality. Earlier that spring, just days after the college announced that Flemming had been chosen president, President Lyndon Johnson's National Advisory Commission on Civil Disorders, widely known as the Kerner Commission, released its report analyzing race relations in the United States. The study was prompted by the race riots that had continued to erupt across the nation since 1963. Starting in Birmingham, Alabama, in summer 1963 and spreading to dozens of cities in the next four years, racial violence in the 1960s claimed some three hundred lives and millions of dollars in property damage. The Kerner Report concluded that the nation was "moving towards two societies, one black one white—separate and unequal" and that the underlying cause of this separation and of racial unrest was racist attitudes on the part of whites. This conclusion, itself highly controversial and still debated to this day, implicated the entire society in the problem and suggested that everyone shared a level of responsibility for addressing the situation. The problem of the urban ghetto, in effect, was everyone's problem.

Macalester took this message to heart. The Kerner Commission pointed to the lack of educational opportunities available for African American children in the ghetto, and Macalester, with its well-established faculty and student exchange programs with black colleges, was eager to use its resources to address the issue. Doing so related strongly to the college's history of service to others and belief in brotherhood, and Flemming fueled the campus's moral conviction that this white, Presbyterian, historically Republican institution needed to be among those leading the nation toward racial unification. The Kerner Report prompted Flemming, who was still working in Oregon at the time, to commission a President's Committee on Racism at the University of Oregon to make recommendations on how the institution could make a "contribution . . . to the solution to the problems in inter-personal relations growing out of the prevailing racist attitudes in our society."[31] The several subcommittees reported to Flemming in May, offering recommendations touching on all aspects of the university, from student life in residential halls and cafeteria offerings to admissions, advising, and curriculum to athletics.

Colleges and universities across the country were doing the same thing, scrambling to create ways to address the problem of racism outlined by the Kerner Report and evidenced in the everyday experiences of African American students. At the University of Minnesota, where African American students were not allowed to stay in the dorms and the campus was particularly inhospitable, students took over the university's records office in Morrill Hall on January 14, 1969, expelling the staff and refusing to leave. The students presented a list of demands that included the creation of scholarships and tuition reductions for black high school students, the recruitment of and counseling for black students, review of policies regarding black athletes, and integration of the study of the "contributions of black people to the commonwealth and culture of America." Negotiations with the university's top administrators proceeded through the night, with an agreement being reached the next day. Most of the demands would be met; most significantly, the university would develop a program in African American studies.[32]

Macalester was also searching for ways to address racism and the problems that African American students faced. On campus, a group of faculty developed a program aimed at providing higher education to young African Americans trapped by ghetto conditions. By December, the group had written a proposal for the Expanded Educational Opportunities program, which would "provide total scholarship aid for 75 new students each year whose parents can provide them with no financial assistance and whose backgrounds limit their opportunities for higher education." Of these seventy-five, sixty of the fully funded students should be members of racial minorities. The language harked back to Turck's populism and represented a challenge to the ten-year effort to focus admissions on academically high-achieving students. The plan also called for the hiring of an African American admissions counselor, rigorous recruiting efforts, a special effort to recruit National Achievement Scholars, the creation of compensatory courses in communication and mathematics to raise students' skills in these areas, a new cadre of advisors, cocurricular programs designed to showcase African American culture, and a facility to serve as a "cultural and social center for black students."[33]

The original proposal contained no cost estimates, but in the spirit of service that had characterized the college in the Turck years, the trustees ensured in January that nine hundred thousand dollars of unrestricted funds over a period of three years would be available for the program. Funding from external sources, particularly from the new federal programs that many expected would soon be introduced, was to be pursued.[34]

Service and Civil Disobedience

As we have seen, the cold war implicated college campuses in national and international political debates to an unprecedented extent. Among the issues that centered on institutions of higher learning was free speech. As cold war anti-Communism polarized interest groups, what was the role of colleges and universities with respect to the idea of free speech? Who would be granted access to college speaking platforms? Who would be denied?

In 1962, George Lincoln Rockwell, who founded the American Nazi Party in 1959, gave a lecture at Carleton and appeared at a smaller gathering at Macalester. Soon after, Ben Davis, a Communist Party member and African American politician from Harlem, was prohibited by the trustees from appearing at Macalester. Students were quick to point out the double standard. Many asserted that the college should provide a platform for a variety of positions—that a liberal arts education was predicated on full consideration of all points of view, a position that echoed Charles Turck's earlier conviction that the heart of the liberal arts was the advancement of democracy. In the face of public challenges to free speech, he had claimed, the liberal arts and liberal arts colleges could offer the national service of providing for the fair airing of multiple perspectives.

But service to the nation went beyond providing—or at least working toward providing—a platform for and considered reflection on the views of many. Increasingly through the 1960s, it meant taking action on one's political convictions or, even if one's convictions were less than firm, still participating physically in causes of national concern. While in 1961 a few students raised funds for civil rights workers in the South, by the late 1960s significant numbers of students were participating in a variety of causes, including free speech, racial justice, and, particularly, peace. The Vietnam War became a lightning rod for student political activism by 1967.

As we have seen in previous chapters, antiwar activism was nothing new to Macalester, as significant peace activism had arisen during each of the world wars. Much of the earlier activism had stemmed from religious convictions regarding peace, and during the Vietnam War, some of those who opposed the conflict also did so out of religious convictions. More crucial for many, however, was that this unpopular war to curb Communism in Southeast Asia seemed to have no end, its appetite for young men voracious. Over the course of the war's escalation between 1965 and 1968, the number of American troops in Vietnam rose from 25,000 to 543,000.[35]

Members of the Macalester faculty and administration were deeply involved in the antiwar movement. Teach-ins on the war and peace demonstrations began at Macalester in 1965. History professor Huntley Dupre organized Macalester's Concerned Democrats, a group opposed to Lyndon Johnson's Vietnam policy. Dupre, Yahya Armajani, and other faculty members participated in antiwar protests on and near campus, along with many students. In February 1967, eight current and former Macalester students and Assistant Chaplain Alvin Currier traveled to Washington, D.C., with a Minnesota delegation of state legislators to attend a peaceful protest of clergy and religious laymen.[36] Days later, the Reverend William Sloane Coffin, Jr., who had moderated the Washington demonstration, appeared on the Macalester campus for a series of talks on the responsibilities of the church in addressing Vietnam, racism and discrimination, and other contemporary situations. Coffin, called "Yale's version of Al Currier" by student Dave

Nordstrom in the *MacWeekly*, argued that churches and educational institutions both had a responsibility to teach the issue. Later that spring, the college awarded an honorary degree to Minnesota native and *New York Times* journalist Harrison E. Salisbury, who had written in opposition to the Vietnam War.

By spring 1970, campuses across the United States were in turmoil. At Macalester, the Vietnam War was one of a host of political issues that loomed large: pollution and the environment, aid to Biafra, and the viability of African American businesses in St. Paul were just a few issues that garnered attention in the *MacWeekly*. A great deal of interest centered on a potential means for leveraging some power in a number of issues, including the use of the college's proxy votes as a shareholder in such corporations as Northern States Power Company, Honeywell, General Electric, and General Motors, which accepted federal contracts for war-related products and research. Perceiving that by exercising its proxy rights as a shareholder, Macalester could have some influence on issues ranging from the expansion of the military industrial complex to corporate treatment of workers, students sought to negotiate student, faculty, and alumni participation in the process of deciding institutional proxy votes at shareholders' meetings. Support for the idea was relatively deep throughout the campus, but when the trustees turned to alumni, likely seeking voices opposed to the plan, they found significant contempt for it.[37]

In mid-April, the Executive Committee of the board of trustees reported their opposition to a student-led plan to gain a voice in proxy voting but recommended that the full board take up the issue at their May meeting. Several students rallied in the chapel to discuss ways to express their disapproval. An effort to again bring more students together later in the evening proved ineffective, sparking stronger efforts—dorm-to-dorm canvassing for supporters—to raise support (about 250 students participated in planning discussions that evening) and eventually a decision to occupy the business office of the college for exactly three hours "to make their point." From 9:30 P.M. to 12:30 A.M. on the evening of Thursday, April 16, students occupied the business office, located in the building at 77 Macalester Street, spending the time drafting a statement of their position and telephoning trustees to invite them to a special meeting to discuss the issue further. Administrators responded calmly, allowing the demonstration to proceed, largely because it was peaceful and no damage was done to the buildings or offices. The demonstration proved to be more theater than protest, however, given that the trustees had not denied broader participation in proxy votes (though the students' statement claimed they had) and had put the topic on the agenda for their next meeting.[38]

Such physical demonstrations themselves caused a great deal of anxiety and anger across campus (as well as across American society generally), in part because their radical version of pubic democratic activity challenged deep-seated perspectives long associated with the institution. As Mary Gwen Owen had observed years earlier, Macalester had been for so long a white, Presbyterian, Republican institution. The college's white element could be profoundly insular. Whereas some within the Macalester community were unsympathetic to efforts to challenge racism or advance minority equality, many others were simply indifferent.[39] The Presbyterian element, like all the mainstream denominations, was divided between those whose support for racial justice grew from their Christian commitment, those who wanted to retain the status quo, and those who wanted the problem to go away. With respect to the Vietnam War, the denomination was similarly divided. Perhaps most important, the Republican element was changing dramatically. As the Johnson administration became associated with the passage of the Civil Rights Act of 1964 and the Voting Rights Act of 1965, the war on poverty, and the desegregation of schools, the Republican national leadership increasingly appealed to those whites uneasy with racial change and with government efforts to aid African Americans as a group. Moderate Republicans who were sympathetic to racial equality found their party shifting beneath them as more right-wing perspectives, such as that of Barry Goldwater, candidate for the Republican presidential nomination in 1964, argued that respect for civil authority must be maintained, by force, if necessary, as a condition for any dialogue—a position that often masked an underlying antipathy to racial justice.[40]

Thus speaking out against problems in the nation, civil disobedience, and agitating for peace were perceived by many as central to the problem itself even as such disruptive challenges to the status quo were seen by others as an effective means of challenging deep-seated habits of thought and getting specific agendas and viewpoints into the public sphere. It is hardly surprising that Macalester students, having for years been encouraged to become engaged in public and national issues, did so during this period. Moreover, many Macalester faculty and administrators—the president among them—joined students in their critique of certain situations and authorities. The presence of these sympathetic campus leaders created an on-campus environment quite different from that of other colleges and universities where students aimed much of their dissent at internal institutional authorities.[41]

Though short-lived, the April 16 sit-in was the harbinger of things to come during that spring of 1970. Antiwar feeling was heating up. In March, 129 male students had signed a letter to the editor of the *MacWeekly* declaring their opposition to the draft and commitment to refuse to serve if called up.[42] Elsewhere in the nation, mid-April saw fifteen hundred students and other antiwar demonstrators marching on Harvard University, smashing windows and lighting fires. Yale was to be the next target, but thanks to a less autocratic institutional response, the demonstration in New Haven on Friday, May 1, remained peaceful. The difference in administrative responses is instructive. During the Harvard demonstration, the institution locked the campus gates in an effort to keep the demonstrators at bay. The demonstrators, finding the gates locked, unleashed their anger on the physical plant itself, causing some one hundred thousand dollars in property damage. In contrast, Yale president Kingman Brewster, counseled by Archibald Cox, who had presided over the Harvard fiasco, decided to keep the campus open and remain in dialogue with some of the demonstration leaders. Though antiwar sentiment loomed large, the main issue at Yale was the impending trial of three Black Panther members for the murder of a young New Haven man supposedly mistakenly identified as an informer. Panther leaders urged violence, but African American student leaders at the institution called for a peaceful demonstration and remained in dialogue with Brewster as the day approached. The goal of these and other campus demonstrations was to effect a general strike against the campus—to shut the campus down by convincing all the students to abandon their classes and take to the street. With national press focused on the campus, Yale student leaders broadcast a call for a nationwide strike.[43]

Demands for campus strikes immediately radiated across the country, fueled by concern and dread sparked by an announcement made that weekend by the president of the United States. On April 30, the day before the New Haven demonstration, Richard M. Nixon announced that troops were to be sent into Cambodia in an effort to cut off North Vietnamese supply lines. Another 150,000 troops would be needed to execute the new offensive, stepping up the Selective Service to new highs. For most Americans, and particularly college students, the advance into Cambodia meant an unprecedented incursion into a previously neutral country.[44] Former president Lyndon Johnson urged support for the new administration's plans.[45] In view of the news of the impending military escalation, campus strikes afforded students a rare, if disruptive, opportunity to express their concern, moral outrage, and fear in a way that would actually have an impact on institutions that many closely associated with the governmental offices that were pursuing and prolonging the war. Across the nation and in the Twin Cities, students took to the streets. On Monday, May 4, University of Minnesota students rallied at the Coffman Union calling for a strike, their numbers spilling out over Washington Avenue and down the mall to Northrop Auditorium. Minneapolis police used tear gas to disperse the crowd and reopen the street. Hamline University students also called a strike.[46]

At Macalester, a more specific target for student anger existed than simply the college administration. In 1969, as the Lyndon Johnson administration left office, DeWitt Wallace and a group of twelve other donors created the Hubert H. Humphrey Professorship in International Affairs, a joint position between Macalester and the University of Minnesota.[47] Humphrey himself, having just served as vice president under Johnson, had been appointed the first chair holder.[48] Opposition to the chair itself, in reaction to its being funded in part by an industrialist with substantial holdings in South Africa and on Humphrey's own complicity in the war, had erupted almost immediately on the announcement of the position in spring 1969. James F. Holly, Macalester's head librarian, who had come to Macalester from the University of Oregon at Arthur Flemming's urging and was serving as the expanded educational opportunities interim coordinator, wrote Humphrey expressing concern over the government's inability to bring hostilities to an end.[49] Other criticism focused on Humphrey's perceived support for Richard Daley's shoot-to-kill order during the Chicago Democratic National Convention demonstrations in 1968.[50] At least one faculty member charged Humphrey with abusing his Macalester position for personal gain and abdicating his responsibility to "serv[e] students enrolled in his classes."[51]

On the morning of May 4, Humphrey's secretary arrived at his office in Old Main to find the door barricaded with barbed wire and guarded by a student. According to a flyer printed by the students who formulated the protest, the barricade "voiced the discontent of many members of this community against the presence of Hubert Humphrey in our midst." The unique method of protest, the flyer explained, was chosen in part because of its nonviolent character. The message carried a call for students, and presumably faculty who similarly opposed the presence of the former vice president on campus, to assist in maintaining and guarding the barricade. Humphrey's secretary wrote that though tempted to tear the barricade down herself, she instead tried to reach President Flemming, but he remained unavailable all day.[52] Humphrey himself had departed the day before for Tel Aviv to accept an honorary degree from the Weizman Institute of Science.[53] The secretary went home in frustration, having been told by the dean that some decision on what to do about the barricade would come by afternoon. By afternoon, however, no decision had been made. Throughout the day, the group of seven or so students who had erected the barricade attempted to recruit support for the protest, but few joined. A single student guarded the blockade. Later that evening, twenty-eight Macalester students went to the office and removed the barricade, over the protests of those who had erected it.[54]

Earlier in the afternoon, however, word of an unimaginable tragedy had spread: four students had been shot to death by National Guardsmen during a demonstration at Kent State University in Ohio. What little chance the faculty and administration had of keeping students calm and in classes evaporated instantly. Traumatized students came together in large numbers as they tried to understand the situation—how, many asked, could a democratic, republican government open fire on its own people? Reaction was widespread nationally, with some two hundred campuses across the country being closed by student demonstrations. In the Twin Cities, Hamline University and the University of Minnesota were shut down by students. On the Macalester campus, students, faculty, administrators, and many neighborhood residents took to Grand Avenue, which sliced through the heart of the campus, closing the street between 7:00 and 9:30 P.M.

Here, too, the sympathetic attitude of many campus leaders, including many who connected their activism to deep commitment to public service, resulted in alignment between students and institution rather than conflict. During the evening rally, several faculty members spoke to the gathered crowd, and Chaplain Alvin Currier urged the crowd toward a potentially more productive activity. Describing the situation to doctoral student George Stevenson in 1972, he remembered that "two or three faculty spoke and then I took over the microphone and said, 'We're going to Washington. You can sit in the street all you want. I'm not sure it will work, but the place to try is not Grand Avenue, but Washington.'"[55] According to Stevenson, during the street demonstration, the Macalester campus security officer, under orders from Flemming, worked with the St. Paul police to divert traffic around the area rather than escalating the situation by trying to disperse the crowd.[56]

The suggestion of going to Washington, D.C., immediately caught on, and as rain began to fall, a group of students began planning a trip to speak with

Minnesota senator and former Macalester student Walter Mondale. They collected donations, and some thirty students made the trip the next morning. Faculty and students also met that day to decide a course of action: classes would be cancelled for the rest of the week. While the strike was thus successful in demonstrating some students' ability to influence campus activity, not all students agreed with the action. Some felt that working within political channels was a more effective strategy than public demonstrations. Many simply wanted to complete their course work for the semester and have the grades they had earned recorded. If such demonstrations were serving the public good, they were also disrupting another central mission of the college: academic study.

Christianity and a Country at War

In these turbulent days, Flemming often looked to the chapel for assistance in communicating with students. Yet here, too, turmoil brewed. The new chapel building, erected in the midst of the main quad of the campus, spurred discontent. Chaplain Maxwell Adams retired in 1968, leaving assistant chaplain and Macalester alumnus Alvin Currier to head up the office until a replacement could be found. Currier actively supported the antiwar movement, arguing in a short-lived student magazine that the war was harming Christianity itself, stating, "It is the immorality of the Vietnam War that is rotting out the Judaeo-Christian [*sic*] humanism that brought this nation to the greatness it has attained."[57] His compassion for students compelled him to also use the chapel to distribute information on the draft and provide counseling to male students likely to be called up. Unlike the situation during World War II, when the college provided reams of information to students on the draft, on what to expect when they went into service, and on how to prepare for service, during the Vietnam War, a shroud of official silence hung over Macalester and many other campuses. Institutions did not want to be seen as aiding the unpopular war by providing information. Currier and a few faculty members provided what little support there was for students facing this harrowing situation.[58] At one point, a student who had not reported for duty when his number was called asked to use the chapel as sanctuary when he was to be arrested. Currier passed his request to Chaplain Bodo, who denied it, saying that though he personally opposed the war, the chapel could not be used to make a political statement. Nevertheless, Currier's support for this student and others continued.

A year after the demonstrations protesting the bombing of Cambodia, the warm spring days of May brought another round of antiwar protests in commemoration of the Kent State deaths. In the early morning of May 6, several Macites participated in a march on the Old Federal Building in Minneapolis. The arrest of ten students and Currier during the course of the demonstration for obstructing entry into the building hit the newspapers like a storm surge. Ultimately, the charges against Currier and one student were dismissed; the remaining nine students were fined twenty-five dollars each. Hate mail flowed into Currier's office despite that the charges against him were dropped. Currier, Christian clergymen, and Macalester itself were vilified as encouraging disorderly conduct and violence.

Caught up in the culture of protest, Currier struggled to articulate political dissent within a Christian framework to a student body less and less interested in religious life. In a powerful sermon delivered in September 1973, Currier brought together the Christian story of Martha and Mary and the Heavenly Twins of the Macalester seal—Nature and Revelation—to make the point that the college, its administration, faculty, and students, caught up in the Martha-like busy-ness of "lectures, labs, and library," had turned away from Revelation, that is, "the revelation of God in Jesus Christ, as demonstrated through compassion, humaneness, and love." The crux of his message was that to regain these, one must listen to Christ's message to Martha: "You've lost your sense of perspective, of priorities." He continued,

> All of Martha's hyper-energetic activity is worthless unless enlightened by that one thing. Grades are ultimately meaningless, titles are empty, degrees are plastic window dressings, even all the knowledge in the curriculum and library stacks adds up to nothing unless it moves mankind toward easing human suffering. . . . A knowledge institution serving a knowledge society is idolatrous blasphemy unless the knowledge imparted reaches to touch the least of these, our brothers and sisters; the hungry, the thirsty, the homeless, the naked, the sick and imprisoned, wherever they may be from the room across the hall to the hovel across the continent, from the office next door to the ends of the earth.[59]

Though the sermon did not specifically mention activism, its casting of education back within the context of Christian service to others had deep roots in the college's history, even though that context was rapidly losing its perceived relevance. According to a survey of fifty students done in spring 1970, 50 percent identified themselves with a religious denomination: 35 percent Lutheran, 20 percent Presbyterian, 20 percent Methodist, 10 percent Catholic, 5 percent Jewish, and 5 percent Unitarian. These figures approximate those from 1968, which reported that among the entire student body of 1,981 individuals, about one-half indicated a religious preference: 421 (21%) Presbyterian, 311 (16%) Lutheran, 167 (8%) Catholic, and 33 (6%) Jewish. Students who responded to the 1970 survey overwhelmingly indicated that for the church to be more influential, it should enhance its "social relevance." Reporter Jostein Mykletun wrote of the responses that "the need for replacing ceremonies with social action appeared to a common complaint." The article also noted that of the twenty-five students who indicated that they had attended a chapel service at Macalester, 82 percent reported having a "favorable impression of the service," citing its "diversity, concern for current issues, and appeal to Macalester students" as positive elements of the services they had attended.[60] This approval was largely attributable to Currier's interests and efforts. The Presbyterian Church itself, however, was less willing to address contemporary issues head-on. It would be another two years before the Presbyterian Church would take a public stand against the war, a move that helped spur the separation of the Presbyterian Church in America and the Presbyterian Church (USA).

The situation of higher education, then, had changed radically over the first three quarters of the twentieth century. Though the elite model of learning and intellectual reflection pursued in a bucolic rural haven, popularized among eastern schools in the early nineteenth century and emulated by such educators as Edward Duffield Neill in the late nineteenth century, still obtained in spirit, if not in fact, in the early twentieth century, it lost cultural capital rapidly in the post–World War II era. We have seen that over the course of the twentieth century, Macalester students were never insulated from the calamities of the world—they heard about situations in China, for instance, and used the outlet of Christian missionizing to focus their own involvement and efforts to ameliorate the lives of Chinese peasants. We have seen that both World War I and World War II elicited pacifist responses from some students. We have seen students motivated by Christian understandings of fairness and justice and dedicated to providing service to humanity in a variety of ways. We have also seen the many ways in which curriculum and student life were affected by World War II and how Macalester students were encouraged by the administration and government alike to "do their part" to support and advance the war effort.

By the late 1960s, the flow of information on critical world and national situations had increased severalfold. Macalester students, like those across the country, were continually blitzed by the issues faced by the nation: war, racism, economic equality, industrial expansion. As members of the American democracy, they had a responsibility to engage with those issues, and Macalester men of draft age had a distinctly personal stake in their outcome. Furthermore, the college itself, with a long history of engaging in international dialogues and striving for service and Christian values, was also compelled to address these national emergencies. The mission of the college again proved sufficiently flexible yet focused to guide the institution's work with respect to these national and international situations; the real challenges to institutional unity would come from other directions—from the rapidly changing shape of student life and from the unanticipated alteration of the college's financial situation.

12

Challenges and Dashed Hopes

THROUGHOUT THE 1960S, as we have seen, Macalester was renegotiating its role in a world that was rapidly changing but doing so in a way that retained a semantic framework consistent with previous articulations of the college's mission. The newly articulated goal of academic excellence in the liberal arts built on the earlier conceptions of the role of the liberal arts that had engaged such themes as vocation and democracy. The dedication to service, now articulated in distinctively political contexts, similarly carried on the vocabulary, if not the same meaning, of earlier times, and the new discussion of internationalism, now imbued with cold war sensibilities and concerns, built on decades of interest in and engagement with the broader world.

One additional central difference that distinguished the period of the 1960s from earlier times at Macalester, however, was its newly found financial security and expectation of continuing donor largess. As the relationship between the college and the largest of those donors, DeWitt Wallace, developed in the 1950s and 1960s, the mission and identity of the college were very much at stake. At the same time that faculty and students were attempting to reconcile the college's mission with the ongoing national crises, that mission was also being negotiated at higher levels by the leadership coalition discussed in the last chapter. As we shall see, when that coalition fell apart, the mission and identity of the college itself was dangerously threatened.

Macalester Paradoxes

There is no doubt that Macalester forged ahead academically in the 1960s. With Lucius Garvin providing the intellectual and scholarly leadership, Paul

Davis providing information on best practices across the country, Arthur Flemming providing academic ideas and administrative guidance, and DeWitt Wallace providing money, expectations were riding high. Yet there were some snags. The selection and hiring of faculty, which had traditionally been done by the president, had, of course, been turned over to Garvin, who, following advice from Davis, hired several star faculty members, luring them with individual incentives and salaries higher than department averages.[1] As these salary disparities became known, longtime faculty, not surprisingly, were outraged, and morale dipped precipitously in some departments. Garvin described the situation to Flemming in April 1966: "Dissatisfaction on the part of the 'Old Guard' has, I am afraid, reached a new peak this year, particularly in the past couple of months since the announcement of salary increases which were smaller than in recent years because of limitations on available funds. Charges are heard that there have been created 'two cultures' among the faculty. Favoritism toward recent appointees is alleged. Students have joined the refrain, criticizing the 'new emphasis' on the Ph.D. degree and scholarly research."[2]

Indeed, higher education was professionalizing nationally, and new, more rigorous requirements for faculty performance were being adopted across the country, causing significant disruptions within institutions. If Macalester was to achieve a position of national leadership, a transformation in faculty culture would be required, something not easily accomplished. That transformation would also bring a shift in the mission and identity of the college. With the hiring of PhDs, a new emphasis on research seemed, in the view of many, to threaten the teaching focus of the college. Would these new faculty members, as some students feared, shift the college's priorities away from teaching and toward research?

Even more problematic was the presence of President Harvey Rice, who was rapidly falling out of favor. Rice's difficulties had begun from his first year in office. Wallace, as we have seen, had very high hopes for Rice in 1958, believing that he could take the college to national prominence by providing innovative thinking and action. Rice plunged into the job wholeheartedly, immersing himself immediately in the details of the college and in Wallace's ongoing correspondence. By fall of that first year, trustee David Winton expressed concern to Wallace that Rice was "overworking to the point of injuring the quality of what he is doing, finally almost impairing his health."[3]

The bad news that Winton did not share with Wallace was that he had just learned that the operating budget would end the year with a deficit of $145,000. Deficits were nothing new at Macalester. The previous president, Charles Turck, as we have seen, had struggled almost every year with the threat of a deficit in the operating budget. As president, he shouldered the onerous task of finding donors to balance the budget and was successful throughout his tenure as president. Whereas Turck no doubt planned for this each year, Rice, new to the position in 1958, was likely caught off guard. Turck, who had left office in July, was astounded to learn of the deficit later that fall. Suspecting an auditor's error, he asked repeatedly to be sent exact budget figures.[4] Whether he ever received them is not known. Winton, knowing that Rice was becoming overwhelmed, suggested to board president Arnold Lowe that the board take on the task of raising the amount of the shortfall or finance it out a few years. Winton himself contributed ten thousand dollars toward the deficit, and his sister likely contributed as well.[5]

During the Rice administration, the college would continue to post and carry forward operating budget deficits at the end of each year through the late 1960s.[6] Apparently, DeWitt Wallace frequently made up the shortfall at the end of the fiscal year, stepping in to balance the budget. He was not happy to do so, however. Wallace wanted to fund innovative programs, not college operating expenses. Weaning the college from Wallace's ongoing operating support ranked seventh on a list of priorities for 1967 that Paul Davis wrote up for Wallace.[7] As the yearly deficits grew larger, Wallace became more concerned, and the trustees persuaded Rice to turn the financial affairs of the college completely over to the new vice president for finance, John Dozier, just as he had earlier turned the academic affairs of the college over to Garvin. Nevertheless, the deficits continued.

The ongoing deficits pointed to a paradox at the heart of the so-called new Macalester. On one hand, the college was receiving tens of millions of dollars for specific programs and projects and was perceived by many to enjoy lush financial support. On the other hand, its regular income did not cover its operating expenses. Today, institutions, now well aware of the hidden costs of running special programs, work assiduously to convince funding agencies to cover these "indirect costs" to the institution. In the late 1960s, however, operating expenses were met primarily by tuition, endowment income, and individual unrestricted donations. Though operating expenses were rising rapidly, what with new buildings, new grounds, large numbers of students, and more staff, donor gifts were being directed into more academic areas of college programming.

College officials, Paul Davis feared, did not fully grasp the difference between Wallace's efforts to support programs and the college's ongoing situation. Indeed, some individuals at the college, including some trustees and the president, seemed to take Wallace's largess for granted. Davis revealed in a confidential letter to Arthur Flemming in 1967 that he felt that Rice "tends to be profligate," and there was "ever present the hazard the Macalester people might become easy spenders," a situation he felt would "ruin the college."[8] Wallace was so concerned that Macalester leaders took his largess for granted that, Davis reported, "a couple of years ago the Wallaces seriously considered saying, 'We have given enough,' and let Macalester swim or sink."[9] Thus, whereas public perception was one of great abundance at the college, the major benefactor had serious reservations about the use of his funds by the mid-1960s. Public perception of Macalester's relationship with its major donor and that donor's view of Macalester did not align.

But this was not the only problem. Neither Wallace nor the Macalester administration was particularly adept at accounting. DeWitt and Lila Wallace were in the habit of sending checks and stock certificates with, paradoxically, either minimal instructions as to their purpose or with highly detailed instructions. Financial office head Buddy Budolfson, a close friend of DeWitt, kept track as best he could and reported to Wallace, often in person, about expenditures and account balances. Wallace trusted Budolfson implicitly, but when Budolfson retired and John Dozier was hired as what we would now call chief financial officer, Wallace, and particularly Davis, pressed for more accurate and transparent accounting of Wallace's many contributions. Dozier, like Budolfson before him, had his hands full with the haphazard influx of gifts in the form of checks, stock assignments, and interest on investments. Wallace, for his part, does not seem to have kept any accounting of the amounts he sent to the college. He likely felt he did not need to under Turck and Budolfson. But by the mid-1960s, he was growing increasingly concerned about the college's ability to keep track of the monies.[10]

A situation with even greater potential for disaster, however, was also developing. Like most large donors, Wallace wanted to know what impact his contributions were having at the institution. Were his dollars being used effectively and producing real results? During the early years of Wallace contributions, President Turck kept Wallace well informed about the results of his gifts, sending him yearly financial reports along with regular updates on who was doing what with the money. Yet there was no systematic approach to reporting. When Harvey

Rice took office and larger gifts rolled in, the college struggled just to keep track of the financial end of the gifts; processes for evaluating the programs were not in place. Wallace's requests for such information, usually made through Davis but occasionally in personal letters to Rice and Garvin, became increasingly frequent after the huge expenditures of the mid-1960s. Garvin shouldered this responsibility, but new to the field of evaluation, he admitted that he was only just learning what information Wallace wanted to see in the reports. Explaining how a program was executed was not difficult; discussing the results was less straightforward.[11] Not surprisingly, Garvin turned to Davis for advice on how to proceed, and Davis recommended hiring Dr. Gilbert Wrenn, then trustee of the college and founder of the University of Minnesota's counseling psychology program. Wrenn, who was retained in late 1967, worked with faculty to carry out the various programs coherently. Despite this measure, the lack of evaluative reporting on the more than twenty million dollars in gifts during the middle to late 1960s would have significant ramifications.

By 1967, the situation was becoming untenable, and Wallace looked for a new solution. Davis, Flemming, and others expressed a lack of confidence in the president.[12] New blood was needed in the position. Rice tendered his resignation on October 25.[13] Though Rice had his troubles at Macalester, his contributions should not be overlooked. During his ten years at the college, he became the institution's congenial public face. His tartan sport coat became iconic—a tool gauged to attract attention and appeal to new and old friends of the college alike. Although he excelled in neither scholarship nor finance, fund-raising was another matter. He also oversaw the construction of the Janet Wallace Fine Arts Center and the Olin Science Hall. As an ambassador for the college, giving lectures across the country, he was instrumental in raising the profile of the college nationwide and particularly within the local business community.

Throughout summer 1967, the trustees' presidential search committee as well as Davis, Flemming, and Wallace had quietly queried their friends and colleagues for suggestions for a new president for Macalester. Numerous names were brought forward and investigated, but Flemming's rose to the top.[14] Given the central role that Flemming had played as a consultant in the development of the thirty-three programs and as a member of the board of trustees in the restructuring of the administration of the college and in creating a vision of progress for the institution as leader of the Flemming Committee, it is not at all surprising that the trustees offered him the presidency early the next year.

Just what sort of carrots were used to clinch the deal may never be fully known. Surely Flemming was offered some kind of guarantee of financial support for discretionary programs. According to historian John Heidenry, that promise consisted of a "special fund of $7 million," although Flemming agreed to accept only one dollar in yearly salary. Flemming's wife and biographer mentions no such fund but does say that Lila Acheson Wallace offered Flemming a car, chauffeur, and housekeeper and that DeWitt offered him a salary of one hundred thousand dollars a year for ten years.[15] While none of these claims can be corroborated through documents available to this author—indeed, any such promises were most likely oral agreements—it is clear that Wallace had very high hopes for Flemming and a track record of backing up his aspirations with large amounts of cash. As a Macalester trustee, as architect of many of the projects liberally funded by DeWitt Wallace in the previous three years, and as president of a university that had benefited significantly from Lila Wallace's generosity, Flemming was no stranger to Wallace largess. Yet, again, this largess was of the restricted variety. Flemming, like Rice before him, would soon be caught in various paradoxes—that though the college had lavishly funded academic programs, its operating budget was inadequate throughout the 1960s, and that though its public reputation was of a well-funded institution, internally troubles were simmering.

Escalating Concerns, Growing Divisions

Wallace, then, had been concerned for years about two things: (1) the shortcomings in reporting on both financial and programmatic evaluation surrounding his restricted donations and (2) the continuing deficits in the operating budget of the college, which he had been covering for years. During summer 1969, Davis and Wallace attempted to get specific information on both these areas from the college; Wallace was rethinking his philanthropic activities.

Clearly evaluative reporting on programs remained insufficient. Consultant Gilbert Wrenn had worked for over a year at Flemming's suggestion to reorganize the thirtysome individual proposals into a "new unified proposal," which in the end was never submitted to Wallace. Working with faculty on the various projects, Wrenn became increasingly aware that the short-term character of several projects and the uncertainty of renewed funding meant that project participants had little interest in evaluating the programs with an eye toward improving them in the future.[16] His job was made even more difficult by the fact that evaluative measures had not been built into each program, and in many cases, faculty and other participants ended up giving what he called "subjective evaluations" of completed programs.[17]

Reporting on the financial side was no better. Davis and Wallace repeatedly asked John Dozier for accountings of Wallace-funded projects currently under way and completed and of Wallace's obligations with respect to the Challenge Grant pledge of 1963. Information from Dozier was slow to arrive, sometimes not forthcoming at all.[18] On March 13, 1970, letters from Davis and Dozier passed in the mail, with Davis again asking for information and Dozier finally providing information in response to a telephone conversation between the two men that had taken place the day before. Dozier's letter compared salary expenditures for faculty, administration, and staff in the 1968–69 and 1969–70 academic years, along with total college expenses and the per-student cost of education in both years. Davis, on receiving the report, noted in the margin that the data demonstrated that in the 1969–70 academic year, 114 new positions were added to the payroll, representing an increase of $1,355,931 to the college's operating expenses. Of these positions, twenty-nine were faculty positions, seven were "combined" positions (most likely faculty-administrative appointments), forty-four were administrative positions, and thirty-three were staff positions. Davis also noted that the cost per student had risen by $590. The letter with Davis's marginalia was sent to Wallace. In a note to Wallace at the top, Davis suggested that given the size of the cost per student, the recent tuition increase of two hundred dollars seemed insufficient. Wallace, returning the letter with his own comments, wrote, "Extraordinary salary increases in one year!"[19]

Indeed, Wallace was seriously rethinking his giving to the college. In April 1970, Davis approached Macalester trustee Granger Costikyan in his efforts to obtain information from the college and pointed out in a letter to him that Wallace, who had to date given some forty-five million dollars to the college "and has set a new world's record for college gifts by a living donor," was "likely to cut his Macalester life time giving to the bone." Davis also noted that his and Wallace's major concern was the deficit and suggested that the college must "adjust its spending plans downward or its gift procurement upward" before it was "too late to adjust."[20] The trustees thus were warned.

Flemming's view of and response to the situation are difficult to ascertain from existing records. Davis clearly felt that Flemming was not taking the steps necessary to address the situation, noting that Flemming had recently assured the faculty that Wallace's level of giving would continue unchanged and had urged those who were aware of the situation that, in Davis's words, "opinions of probable cuts be kept confidential."[21] But rumors were already flying. A reporter for the *MacWeekly* noted that concerns were being expressed that "the college is not raising enough money to meet heavy commitments to the Expanded Education Opportunities [EEO] . . . and other programs." Flemming responded that the college was "fiscally sound" and that it had applied for a U.S. government grant "in six figures" that, if approved, would fund EEO.[22]

By summer, Davis assured Wallace that Wallace had no further legal obligation toward the college and that his many contributions since 1963 more than covered his pledge to the Ten Million Dollar Challenge Program. Furthermore, there was over one million dollars in the college's Wallace Reserve Fund awaiting dispersal into programs yet undesignated, and he had just urged the trustees to close the Macalester Foundation for the Advancement of Higher Education, given that the federal government had just opened similar units at several large universities better equipped than Macalester to do the work needed to reform education, an action that would add another million to the fund. Regarding future gifts, Davis opined, "The decision of whether or not you give additional funds to Macalester rests solely with you. There are no legal, moral, or ethical reasons which compel your making further gifts to Macalester. You have already magnificently met any and all Macalester obligations." He continued, "I wish that Macalester had been equally punctilious in meeting the College obligation to you by adhering to the terms of your gifts, by avoiding waste, and by obtaining more reasonable performance results."[23] The same letter outlined a scenario of impending crisis caused, in Davis's view, by Flemming, who did not make sufficient "use" of his "two able Vice Presidents" and whose "administration neglects both Trustees and donors." Furthermore, Davis charged, the college was diverting funds from the High Winds Fund real estate endowment to other uses.[24]

Dozier immediately responded to the charges regarding diversion of High Winds funds, stating that any errors with the fund had been addressed. The college had used the funds to "create a site for the Janet Wallace Fine Arts Center," with the understanding that the purpose of the fund was to "acquire land adjoining the campus for when and if the College requires additional space for new projects." Once it had become clear that Wallace did not intend the fund to be used to acquire building sites, Dozier explained, the college had remedied the situation. Also at issue over the High Winds Fund were the below-market rents charged to faculty and neighbors' concerns that the sidewalks were not shoveled and the lawns not mowed. Dozier indicated that some of the complaints were thinly veiled disapproval of the fact that African American staff members occupied six of the houses, integrating a previously all-white neighborhood.[25]

But Wallace had yet other concerns regarding the use of High Winds. Part of the contention over the High Winds Fund was its use to buy houses adjacent to the campus that were then demolished or relocated to erect the Janet Wallace fine arts building and parking lot. In particular, the parking lot took 112 Cambridge Avenue, a craftsman-style bungalow that DeWitt and Lila had bought in 1933 and secretly outfitted for DeWitt's father, James, and aunt-turned-stepmother, Miriam Wallace. The house, according to trustee Donald Garretson, was moved off the lot and relocated several miles away, off Summit Avenue.[26] Wallace, according to Macalester history professor James B. Stewart, expressed his disappointment over this action in a letter.[27] The location of the former president's home—his father's house—was now a parking lot.

Devastating news continued to roll in that summer. On July 20, Davis reported to Wallace that "inside sources" were estimating a $1.2 million deficit in the college's operating budget for the year and an $800,000 deficit in the physical plant fund, with no expenditure cuts in sight.[28] Wallace was apparently shocked, though his views during this period are almost impossible to ascertain from the few letters that are currently available. What is clear is that two points were in contention: (1) had Wallace's 1963 capital campaign pledge been fulfilled, de facto, by his generous programmatic giving since then? and (2) had Macalester inappropriately spent funds from the capital campaign on programs and operating costs? On the first point, Davis argued that Wallace had fulfilled his obligation, and college officials were in no position to suggest that their generous benefactor "owed" the institution money, although Dozier did suggest exactly this at least once to Davis. The second point was more problematic, springing in part from varying understandings of the definition of *capital fund*. Did the term denote endowment or capital projects? Wallace seemed to understand that the funds raised in the capital campaign were earmarked for endowment. Trustee George Dayton noted that all the gifts that Wallace had matched over the years had "gone into 'capital'" but did not define the term.[29] Davis then explained to Wallace that the Macalester trustees and administration, including Dayton, had spent "every penny" denoted as "capital" on "buildings, alterations, and improvements."[30]

By fall the 1969–70 audit was completed, showing a deficit of $2,576,801.[31] It also stated that just over half a million was spent "in support of certain restricted programs," for which the anticipated financing from a contributor (Wallace) had not been realized. In effect, Wallace had begun cutting back on his contributions in early 1970. To cover the $2.5 million deficit, the trustees authorized loans from unrestricted endowment-fund principal over a three-year period, with interest to accrue beginning in January 1971. They also authorized the loan of another two million dollars to cover operating costs for the 1970–71 academic year; again, these loans would begin accruing interest in January.[32] Flemming, Garvin, and Dozier began to make significant cutbacks. The largest spending area, faculty salaries, which had increased rapidly under the expectation of Wallace's continuing largess, was the first target. All salaries were frozen and new positions were prohibited; soon, faculty positions would be cut. Staff positions were also examined and trimmed.

The Leadership Coalition Collapses

By late fall 1970, everyone on campus knew that the college was in troubled financial waters. But in this, Macalester was not unlike colleges across the nation, which were being significantly affected by the loss of return on their endowment dollars and of alumni support caused by the growing recession and a growing aversion to the student unrest that had swept the country. In fact, the economic crisis in higher education led to the closing of many small colleges during this period, and though no one seems to have been concerned that Macalester would close, campus attention was riveted on the situation.[33]

A startling announcement came in early December. The *MacWeekly* published a brief article by Paul Davis that began, "Fifteen years ago DeWitt Wallace asked me to estimate the amount of additional gift money required to raise Macalester College to the top ranks of American education. After an extensive review, I advised it would take twenty five million dollars and ten years. I was wrong. It required nearly thirty six million dollars of Mr. Wallace's money and fifteen years."[34] With that opening, Davis claimed Macalester's success, attributing its current leadership in such areas as international affairs and forensics and its high ranking in faculty salaries (in the top ten in the nation) and number of national merit scholars (more than any other college in the nation) to Wallace's dollars. But what Wallace wrought, he could also take away, and the crux of the article was that the college's major benefactor had decided to "focus his future giving on . . . other philanthropic programs."[35] Macalester, having been the beneficiary of gifts that "exceed those of any living donor to any four year college in the world," had become "extravagant" and was attempting to do too much. Its academic focus needed to be tightened. "An austerity period," Davis wrote, "will provide an additional element of realism [to the college] which will be beneficial."[36] Hovering on the page above the article appeared two large portrait photos of Wallace and Davis.

A little over a month later, on Tuesday, January 19, Davis arrived in Minneapolis to attend, as a nonvoting delegate, the meeting of the Macalester Board of Trustees scheduled for Thursday. On his arrival, he contacted the local newspapers to repeat his announcement: Macalester benefactor, noted publisher DeWitt Wallace, would be terminating his donations to the college for the near future.

The Twin Cities community awoke the next day to Davis's bombshell on the front pages of the *St. Paul Pioneer Press* and the *Minneapolis Tribune*. Davis was quoted as saying that the college's significant financial troubles and large deficit (various accounts put it at eight hundred thousand dollars) for the previous year motivated Wallace's decision. The press quoted Davis as saying that Macalester had become "too affluent" and even "extravagant," that it had "spread itself too thin," and that in his opinion, "a small college endeavoring to be excellent in a large number of fields is an extravagant use of resources." Elaborating on the theme, he suggested that Macalester's extravagance resulted in poor education, for the college was "trying to turn out doctors and, at the other end of the spectrum, students who barely got through high school." In the middle group, Davis opined, "are students with no particular direction, who might end up pumping gas or what not when they get out, or be secretaries or typists."[37] Two papers contacted college officials for a response, with the *Tribune* quoting a college spokesman as pointing out that Macalester's education was indeed expensive, in large measure because the college had achieved what it set out to do in 1961. "It has raised faculty salaries to the top 10% in the nation; it has beefed up the faculty to the point where 81 percent hold doctorates; it has lowered the faculty–student ratio to about 1 to 11; and it has extended financial aid to 65% of the student body."[38] Those high aspirations, fueled by Wallace's enthusiasm and financial support, had been accomplished. So what was it about the results that soured Wallace to the enterprise? A scapegoat was already being identified in the press: the EEO program, which, the *Minneapolis Star* noted, cost $827,000 in the previous year (it also noted that the deficit for the year was $800,000), would be identified as the chief culprit by both reporters and others looking for an easy answer to a complex problem.[39]

The trustees met in a closed meeting later that week; the major piece of business on the table, however, was not Davis's revelation but Arthur Flemming's: he would resign the presidency, leaving office no later than August. In his statement to the trustees, Flemming urged them to work to continue the many programs that had been launched in recent years, arguing that they exemplified "the pursuit of excellence in the liberal arts" and also made the college "stand out as one of the colleges that is endeavoring to be responsible to the pressing needs of society." Furthermore, he stated, the current direction of the college was linked directly to its Christian heritage. Regarding political activism, Flemming praised the students, faculty, and administrators who were "seeking answers in the field of human rights and dignity," saying, "I believe they are trying to listen to the spirit of a living God."[40] Anticipating a growing controversy over EEO, he singled out the program for comment, saying that he particularly hoped the college would continue the program, which exemplified the college's effort to be "true to its Christian heritage."[41] Later in the day, Flemming addressed students, receiving a warm ovation, and in a separate meeting he addressed faculty to a similar ovation.[42]

What Went Wrong?

The withdrawal of the Wallaces' financial support and the loss of Arthur Flemming's leadership plunged the institution into a crisis of morale, identity, and mission that would shape internal and external perceptions of the college for years to come. Many in the Macalester community have asked why this happened, and theories citing a range of single events that sparked Wallace's decision have been proposed to this author. None of these theories, however, fully accounts for the complexity of aspirations, motivations, actions, and reactions that occurred over the thirty-two years of Wallace's relationship with the college. The roots of the crisis, as we have seen, stretch deep into the institution's past. Potential contributing factors exist in abundance. We are unlikely to ever learn precisely why the eighty-one-year-old Wallace decided it was time to throw in the towel in 1971; he issued no statement explaining his actions at the time.[43] If we consider a number of contexts, however, Wallace's decision seems far less surprising than it may have seemed in January 1971.

On one level, the rupture between DeWitt Wallace and the college can be understood as a fairly classic situation of donor alienation. Wallace, as we have seen, was intimately involved in directing the use of his monies at Macalester.

Charles Turck had been highly skilled at keeping Wallace informed and in line with the college goals as Turck defined and developed them. Wallace continually put pressure on him to move in other directions, but Turck was quite brilliant in keeping Wallace on board, accepting some of his ideas, while distracting him from others. Turck was most enthusiastic when Wallace was preoccupied with some nonthreatening building or landscaping project, cheerleading outfits, or the like. Nevertheless, he put an enormous amount of time and energy into keeping Wallace on board but not strongly influential in curricular matters. Moreover, the benefits of Wallace's donations in these early years were tangible— improvements in the physical plant, faculty pensions, and so forth—and readily reported to Wallace.

When Harvey Rice came on board, things changed. Wallace was determined to become involved in the educational and pedagogical side of the college. By the time Rice became president, Wallace's education adviser Paul Davis was well entrenched in the Macalester system, and between Davis's education experience and Wallace's deep pockets, Rice did not have a chance of keeping the two at bay. Rice, more beholden to Wallace for his job and less forceful than Turck, could do little to keep Wallace from meddling in curricular matters. What had been a college run by its presidents (Turck, Acheson, Bess, Hodgman, and Wallace going back) became a college enormously influenced by its major donor. Of course, faculty, Lucius Garvin, and some trustees were involved, but Wallace's largess to faculty members was a means of ensuring that they would follow his lead.

Rice's limitations fueled Wallace's deeper involvement. Yet as Wallace's influence and donations increased, he moved no nearer the real work of the college—the academic core. Just what were the "outcomes" of his donations? The hiring of new faculty was fine, but what did they do to enhance the college? How did the many new programs tangibly advance the college? When Flemming came on board as president, things changed again. Once again, the college had a strong president who was well liked and respected by the faculty. Furthermore, Flemming had a vision of the college that built on a Christian ideal of service that resonated deeply with many students and faculty alike. Flemming and the faculty, with their growing sympathy with liberal causes, had the potential to seriously undermine Wallace's goals. Campus participation in antiwar demonstrations could not have been palatable to Wallace, and spring 1970 had witnessed unprecedented disruption.

The crux of the rupture, however, focused without doubt on the ongoing deficits in the Macalester operating budget. Those deficits had increased yearly throughout the Rice administration, and Wallace hoped, and probably assumed, that Flemming would eliminate them and balance the budget. This did not happen. Moreover, Flemming, not only willing but eager to advance the college into a position of national leadership, made the faculty hires and salary increases needed to re-create the school and pursued programs—EEO, among others—that had the potential to boost the college into the national spotlight. Even Wallace apparently was surprised at the extent of spending increases: payroll increases alone totaled over \$1.3 million between the falls of 1968 and 1969.[44]

As he had done since the early 1960s, Wallace covered the college's deficits for both 1968 and 1969, Flemming's first two years in office. By 1970, however, he had had enough. This decision did not come out of the blue. As we have seen, Wallace, disgusted with the college's spending and angered by administrators and trustees whom he felt took his benevolence for granted, considered ending his contributions in the mid-1960s.[45] Deciding, however, to continue on with the effort to make the college "one of the top ten," he stepped up his efforts to obtain adequate reporting on the use of his donations, being stymied in the effort by insufficient reporting and inadequate assessment. And he continued to give for many years. But by 1970, with the new president well settled in, there was no sign that the college had its operational budget under control. The time had simply come to quit.

But Wallace's disillusionment with the college may have gone deeper than its deficit spending and inept financial reporting and assessment practices. For ten years Wallace had been urging college leaders to improve the school in ways that would propel it into a position of national prominence. Throughout the 1960s, the college seemed to be moving steadily, even rapidly, in the right direction. It was developing a more respected professorate and bringing in stronger students and was becoming known overseas. But 1970 brought some sobering realities. First, the well-connected Flemming proved less successful than was hoped in securing funding for Macalester programs. Foundation gifts were particularly disappointing, suggesting that Macalester under Flemming was not the national player that many hoped it would become.[46] Second, a major federal project creating centers for the advancement of higher education overlooked Macalester, which had aspired to be a leader in precisely this area. Wallace, perhaps better than most people, understood that success attracts further success, and despite his and others' efforts, Macalester had not achieved a position among those schools the federal government naturally turned to in its efforts to support higher education.

The relationship between Flemming and Wallace must also be taken into account. Had there been a secret deal between the two men? Seven million dollars in discretionary funds? Some other figure? Flemming's expansion of the faculty and staff and of the minority education program can be readily explained by such an agreement. When Wallace announced that he would no longer support the educational programs, Flemming took it as a breach of promise and resigned, perhaps thinking that with himself out of the picture, Wallace would return and continue support.[47] Wallace, however, stayed his course, walking away from the school to which he had given over thirty-four million dollars, a decision that he had been contemplating, according to Paul Davis, since the mid-1960s.

Paul Davis himself was another complicating factor in the situation. Davis shaped Wallace's vision of what the college might become, counseled him to curtail his contributions, and announced that decision in the college newspaper and later the Twin Cities press in a manner designed to embarrass the institution by exposing its financial troubles to public scrutiny. It was Davis's effort to publicly humiliate the college that many in the Macalester community found most troubling. Gilbert Wrenn, for instance, found Davis's actions inexplicable for someone who had supported the college for so long and had been so fully involved in its recent development. John Dozier, however, who had been through a year of tussling with Davis, was, according to Wrenn, "bitter" and had nearly warned Davis off the campus.[48] S. Decker Anstrom, student president and student representative to the board of trustees, condemned Davis's comments about Macalester students and suggested that he withdraw from the trustees.[49]

Flemming, like Wallace, kept his views on Davis to himself. Although they were close friends in the mid-1960s, it was perhaps difficult for some to distinguish just who was king and who was the kingmaker. Davis had worked hard to get Flemming into the Macalester presidency. Whether he expected some consideration in return is unknown. He was, however, invited to join the board of trustees as an at-large member as Flemming took office. Though Davis had close ties with the board through the Rice years as an educational consultant, he had not served as a member prior to 1969. As a member of the board, Davis in effect became a member of Flemming's corporate boss. According to Bernice Flemming, Davis became increasingly persistent in giving Flemming advice and critiquing his actions in the first year of his presidency, frequently attempting to dictate Flemming's activities and decisions.[50] As Davis put greater pressure on

Flemming through 1970, while at the same time beginning to suggest to Wallace that he distance himself from the college, he drove a wedge between the two men.

Davis's motives for doing this remain unclear. Wrenn confided to Garvin that he felt that Davis, having done so much public damage, should stay away from the campus, but, he predicted, "he is likely to take this as a challenge and to come back again."[51] Wrenn proved correct in his prediction. By April, Wallace had notified trustee John Driscoll that Davis would stay on campus because "I need his counsel," and he sent a check to cover Davis's full-time salary for a year.[52] Wrenn was also correct in saying that Davis's "usefulness" to the college "is almost zero." No one trusted him, faculty were suspicious of his continual efforts to pump them for incriminating information about administrators, and those students who were aware of his presence simply hated him. Yet Davis remained on the Macalester payroll, paid directly by Wallace, for three more years.[53]

By 1973, Davis's reports to Wallace were becoming increasingly negative, eventually accusing administrators of deliberately, and presumably fraudulently, redirecting restricted funds for purposes other than those intended. Historian John Heidenry reports that Davis outlined for Wallace several actions that he might take to curtail this "pattern of fund diversion and 'political trickery.'"[54] In August 1973, according to Heidenry, Davis wrote Macalester trustee Carl B. Drake suggesting that over one million dollars from the Wallace reserve had been withdrawn without authorization. Wallace, who had recently learned that at least two trusted friends had cheated him of perhaps millions, was understandably concerned.[55] Trustee chair John Driscoll categorically refuted Davis's accusations and warned him that pursuing the accusations would result in scrutiny of Wallace's strings-attached donation record, which "violated both the spirit and the letter of federal gift-tax laws" and, in Driscoll's words, would "place the tax treatment of these gifts in serious jeopardy."[56] Wallace dropped the issue. Davis, for his part, resigned from the college payroll, parting from the college with one final, bitter statement: "Macalester College doesn't have a chance of becoming one of the dozen or so private colleges which are needed and can be significant in pure liberal arts."[57] His dreams, whatever they had been, were shattered.

The other key player, of course, was Flemming, at whose feet many laid the blame for the fiscal extravagance that propelled the college into turmoil. As we have seen, there is no doubt that spending levels rose significantly during the first two years of his administration, the majority of increases in salaries and programming. Many in the Macalester community point to what they viewed as Flemming's uncontrolled spending as the cause of the rupture with Wallace, and the view was tested publicly in an article in the *Minneapolis Star* that claimed that Flemming was something of a gadfly, given his many government and educational positions, who found budgets "a bore."[58] Yet Flemming seems to have been confident that the funding for these increases was forthcoming. In 1968, he launched a wide-reaching effort to approach organizations and foundations for programmatic grants. Whereas in 1969 the college posted nearly $260,000 in external grants, 1970 brought in none. Nevertheless, Flemming had guarantees from both the trustees and Wallace for funding. As mentioned earlier, we do not know what Wallace had privately guaranteed Flemming, but the trustees had pledged nine hundred thousand dollars for the EEO program. Flemming had been hired to lead the institution into a bright new future, but he had made it clear before he accepted the position that it would cost money, and he operated on the assumption that those promised funds would be forthcoming.

Complicating the picture at least somewhat may have been the changing economic situation in the country in general. The inflation rate had doubled between 1965 (2.2%) and 1968 (4.5%), and 1969–70 saw a mild recession, causing President Richard Nixon to impose wage and price controls. Prices continued to rise, and by 1971 institutions of higher education across the country were reporting deficits. Though the growing recession would have a significant impact over the next few years as Macalester tried to recover its financial footing, the early stages of the impending financial crisis may well have affected the giving patterns of both individual donors and the federal and nonfederal organizations and foundations on whose support Flemming had been counting.

The role of the trustees in the situation is similarly difficult to pin down, but it appears that once Flemming was in office and was perceived to be a strong and capable leader at the helm, the trustees, who just a few years earlier had for the first time become deeply engaged in college educational policy by overseeing the creation of the thirtysome educational programs, were content to acquiesce to his command. Approving deficit budgets for years, and since 1969 approving endowment loans to cover deficits, the trustees, like Flemming, relied on and likely took for granted Wallace's ongoing largess. With Paul Davis serving on the board beginning in 1968, it is likely that many trustees assumed that the college's relationship with its primary donor was in fine shape.

Thus Wallace's decision to curtail his donations can be linked to growing disconnects among the expectations, assumptions, past actions, secret promises, and personal aspirations of several players within the college community. Nevertheless, in the turbulent, politically charged atmosphere of the period, speculation on Wallace's reasons for abandoning the college were rampant and often had little to do with finance. Some students were convinced that the appearance of the "*f*-word" in the *MacWeekly* sent Wallace over the top. Others were convinced that Wallace's conservative political views were at such odds with the publicity the college had been getting regarding the antiwar movement that he ended the relationship. That the talk-show airwaves in the Twin Cities were abuzz with criticism of sexual permissiveness and drug use at the college was also suggested as contributing to Wallace's decision.[59]

Those closest to the centers of power, however, pointed to the budget crisis. Lacking information on the long history of deficits, many interpreters blamed the most public and admittedly most costly of the many new programs on campus, the EEO. The *Minneapolis Star* first intimated this view in its report on January 20, which contained the two eight hundred thousand dollar figures. In an effort to leverage some power on campus, the African American campus organization BLAC announced at a press conference that Flemming had been forced out of office because of his support for EEO, which presumably the trustees and Wallace opposed.[60] Many individuals, both on and off campus, were only too eager to place this setback at the feet of the program that had brought African American students to the neighborhood, resulting in a series of complaints over the loud music and unkempt yard of Black House. Fueled by resentment, critics charged that the beneficiaries of the program, young men and women from the ghetto who should have been grateful and austere in their habits were buying stereos, toiletries, and airline tickets home with their financial aid dollars—acting, in effect, exactly like their white peers.[61] In fact, the main reason that this program was singled out both by critics and BLAC was spurious: the coincidence that the cost of the program in 1970 was similar to the cost of the physical plant deficit. The two figures, of course, had nothing to do with each other.

More than anything, the sudden announcement of Wallace's intention marked the fact that a transformation had occurred: Macalester was not the same school it had been a decade earlier. *MacWeekly* editor Dave Lapakko noted on the front page of the February 5, 1971, issue that

You can still find Macalester College in the white pages of the telephone directory. Old Main has not come tumbling down. Students still go to class occasionally.... Professors, most of them, at least—are still on the payroll. Administrators of all sorts still sit in their thickly carpeted alcoves.... Contrary to popular belief, Macalester College still exists. To be sure, however, things have changed a bit lately.[62]

Whereas Lapakke focused on the recent changes, we can take a broader perspective and, taking into consideration the dozen years since Charles Turck had presided over the college, understand that things had changed far more than "a bit." The blended vocational–liberal arts curriculum had been stripped of its vocational elements; professors were now highly educated PhDs with research agendas and professional commitments that often took them away from the classroom; students were often more focused on navigating the social contexts of sex, drugs, and rock 'n' roll in which they found themselves than working toward a future career; service to society took the form of critique of political figures and national decisions; and Christianity was no longer assigned the role of student character building—indeed, it, too, was put to service as political critique.

Some Macites, including many alumni, viewed these changes and saw loss. The security of the campus, the security of their future roles in the world, the security of trusted decision makers above them, all of which they had taken for granted as students, no longer abided and never would again. Others viewed these changes and saw opportunity and responsibility. The 1960s and Wallace funds presented the opportunity for the college to re-create education in ways that made it relevant to the changing world, just as Turck had embraced the opportunity to make the campus relevant to the post–World War II world. Worlds had changed, and so, too, had Macalester. Yet change itself cast the institution's identity into doubt—just what did Macalester stand for now? What was its mission now? Flemming left office emphasizing an ongoing continuation of the Christian spirit of the founders, yet it was clear that even that was fading rapidly. While the liberal arts, service, and internationalism remained intact for the time being, the loss of Wallace's support cast doubt on whether even those themes could be sustained.

13

Countercultural
Campus

IN THE EARLY 1960S, all freshmen entering Macalester College were required to read a preselected book during the first few weeks of the fall term. Discussions of the text, both formally arranged and informal, ensued. In 1962, the book selected for the freshmen was B. F. Skinner's *Walden Two*; a year later, freshmen read Albert Camus's *The Plague*; and in 1964, the selection was William Golding's *The Inheritors*. These books—the first portraying an experimental communitarian society attempting to develop a way of life outside of the consumer-oriented, capitalist context of modern life; the second a reflection on free will, authority, and individual responsibility within the context of an overpowering civil threat; and the third depicting an essential inhumanity and brutality at the core of human existence—raised themes that Macalester students, along with young adults across the nation, were debating at the time.[1] Echoing the theme of the new Man and His World course, which in 1963 took the place of one required religion course, each of these books invited extended reflection on the role of the individual within social, political, and cultural contexts in which traditional sources of meaning and foundations for moral action are impotent or absent.

While student life by the late 1960s is frequently remembered as characterized by radical critique, rebellion, experimentation, and hedonism, at the heart of all these responses was an ongoing philosophical questioning of seemingly bankrupt norms and traditions and a desire to find new ways of being in and knowing the world that cut across many areas of campus life—a search for meaning wrapped up in, as one student put it, "the spiritual cry . . . the social cry . . . and the intellectual cry."[2] To address these "cries," young adults rejected traditional mores and authorities, developing alternative philosophies and ways of life that felt more authentic, fulfilling, and humane. Pursuing such ideals, students, hippies, artists, druggies, and others created a counterculture movement that significantly shaped student life at Macalester in the late 1960s and 1970s.

Packing "Relevance" into Education

Education itself was among the first targets of countercultural critique—a natural outgrowth of the student movement. At the same time as the professor-ate, especially at Macalester, was attempting to raise its credentials and profes-sionalize, the traditional structures and methods of the university came under fire by students. The desire for a meaningful—"relevant," in the parlance of the period—intellectual life permeated education across the United States and at Macalester during this period. Traditional knowledge and ways of learning were increasingly seen as divorced from the problems and issues of real life.

The development of the Interim term during January 1964 was a direct response to students' lobbying for "relevance" in the curriculum. The term was meant to be spent in serious study of topics of unique concern to students. In the words of Don Gemberling and Art Ogle (class of 1964) in their underground newsletter *Right and Left in the Ivory Tower*, it "should well have been an answer to all our complaints . . . a lack of fulfillment of the liberal arts education—intellectually, spiritually, and socially."[3] Yet while idealism motivated many stu-dents, not all shared the enthusiasm for self-directed inquiry. Events such as a field trip to a Greek Orthodox church were canceled "for lack of interest," voluntary chapel meetings were "almost deserted," the library stood "almost empty," and the campus itself was "de-populated" on weekends, "as the suitcasers rush home to better food and better social life." Faculty were perceived as no deeper in their commitment to learning, "desert[ing] the place by noon."[4]

With Interim, the slippage between the ideal, offering a unique educational opportunity, and the reality, that such opportunities would never be fully em-braced by students eager for a range of experiences, became readily apparent. And this slippage between lofty goals and mundane reality, between an idealistic striving for new goals and acceptance of traditional ways, created a tension that infused student life throughout the era.

The Interim term was only the first of several educational experiments aimed at fostering a more experientially based educational environment at the college. As debates about the artificiality of grades and traditional course requirements swept the country, and as the Macalester faculty themselves eliminated the physical education and language requirements and relaxed the liberal education requirements in the late 1960s, students lobbied for even more radical change. The student-run Macalester Free College (MFC), launched during spring 1968, consisted of students teaching courses and leading discussions on a host of topics viewed as more relevant to contemporary life. As Wallace Cason, a senior who chaired the MFC, explained to a *St. Paul Dispatch* reporter, the Free College was conceived as "a cooperative student effort to self-educate on an informal basis, making learning a social thing."[5] According to Cason, the Free College offered a radical critique of education at the college. In his view, "the faculty is at fault for failing to meet the new social outlook of each new wave of freshmen. The students are at fault for failing to meet the faculty halfway to tell the faculty what we, students, are interested in NOW."[6]

In describing the Free College to students, promotional material explained that "Mac's Free College is set up to involve you in new learning experiences. It is based on the premise that Interim is too good a thing to do only one month out of the year. We will help you to meet new circles of people much more homogeneous and specialized for your interests than school classes can be."[7] A host of courses were offered by several students, including Love and Sex (Erick Markusen), Kazantzakis (George Meyn), The Political Philosophy of Nietzsche (Robert Fitzgerald), Chess (Mauricio Torres), Aggression (George Toth), Folk Music of the Depression, Mac Book Service, Mysticism (Steve Wright), The Occult Sciences, Centralizing and De-Nationalizing the World Political System (John Olmsted), Edgar Cayce: The Sleeping Prophet, Sensitivity Group: Group Therapy, Oceanography, Esperanto, Environmental Pollution, Intelligent Life in the Universe, Effects of Technology on Value Structures, Geo-chemistry, Evolution, Social Comment and Sacrilegious [*sic*] Music Machine, Bridge, Creative Writing, and Urban Studies. There would be no grades or other artificial incentives for learning. The Free College aimed at simply bringing together people curious about a topic and willing to learn about it together.

But the Free College was also a means of critiquing both the traditional education system and ongoing situations in American society. As Chaplain Al Currier argued in the opening convocation for the Free College, "It is the immorality of the Vietnam War that is rotting out the Judaeo-Christian [*sic*] humanism that brought this nation to the greatness it has attained. It is the racism of this society that is making a mockery of the Declaration of Independence which promised liberty and justice for all."[8] Opposition to these sociopolitical circumstances was seen as requiring a countering force, a new approach to learning and thinking about and ultimately addressing vital social problems of the day.

By participating in the Free College, students demonstrated their commitment to taking responsibility for their own education and for their role in society. The sessions raised questions about the role of the faculty: if faculty were out of touch with student interests and students could learn on their own, were faculty really needed? In a period in which traditional authorities of all types were being challenged, faculty were in an uncomfortable position. Some, particularly more senior faculty, identified strongly with the traditions and standards of their disciplines and of academia in general; some of the newer, younger faculty, however, were quite willing to question old authorities and redefine the role of the academy. Journalist Steven Van Drake pointed to these questions in his series of columns on the Free College, asking whether the Free College was a serious critique of teaching techniques that students found ineffective or merely a showy assertion of student power.[9] Macalester faculty advisors for the Free College, Ernest R. Sandeen (history) and Michael Obsatz (education), asserted that the project had merit. Encouraging independent student inquiry aligned well with the general philosophy of personal responsibility that pervaded the campus during the period.

Similar questions about the purpose of education, the role of faculty, and the responsibilities of students informed another educational experiment developed by Macalester students and launched in fall 1969: the Inner College, a live-in, communal experiment in individualized learning. The seeds of the idea to develop a communal educational experiment were planted when students attended a Free University conference in Kansas and learned about Bensalem experimental college, located across the street from Fordham University in the Bronx. Bensalem, named for the "island academy in Francis Bacon's poem, *The New Atlantis*,"[10] was an effort to move outside the box of institutional education by bringing graduate students and junior faculty together in both living arrangements and free-ranging intellectual exploration. Topics of study were to be selected by consensus; students developed portfolios of work that they would evaluate qualitatively together with faculty.[11] The idea captured students' imaginations across the country, and Macalester students began to develop a communal college.

As organizer James Thompson explained in the *MacWeekly*, the effort grew out of student frustrations with both education and social life. Specifically, he pointed to the instigating factors as "an irrelevant curriculum detached from any reality other than that of graduate school requirements, anti-educational barriers between faculty and students as well as between students themselves, and a grading and credit system that could hardly have been more detrimental to learning if it had been designed with that in mind," and as a lack of community on campus: "people at Macalester have trouble relating to one another."[12]

During fall 1969, Inner College occupied two houses on Summit Avenue, where some twenty-eight participating students lived with faculty advisor Alvin Greenberg (English), his wife, Marsha, and their St. Bernard dog, Bernard. Students could attend Inner College for a semester. There were no requirements and no grades. Students wrote evaluations of their work over the period of time, working with a faculty member to decide how many credits the work would satisfy. By the end of the first semester, commitment to the college had grown. Dr. Gerald Friedberg of the Fordham Bensalem College visited to learn about the Macalester college and deliver a lecture titled "The Traditional College vs. the New College."[13] Among Inner College's accomplishments was the cohosting, along with the Education Affairs Committee of the Macalester Program Board and the chapel, of a conference in November titled "Careers in Social Change." Topics examined during the two-day event included economic institutions, women's liberation, war and the draft, education, communal living, media, and city problems.[14]

Yet, as with most experiments of its kind, Inner College endured only briefly. Though a few students thrived under the situation, others produced only average work, and many produced little at all. Student evaluations of the experience were uniformly positive, but importantly, most dealt less with what they had learned over the course of the semester than with the interpersonal relationships among the Inner College residents. Many indicated that the ideal interpersonal relationships they had hoped would develop remained elusive and that social life among their communal comrades was no more authentic than among students on campus—a topic that, as we shall see, was of key importance to students during the period.

Redefining Social Relationships through Counterculture

As vital as educational questions were during this period, and as pressing as a host of political issues were as well, the search for more authentic personal relationships arguably claimed more student energy and time. For many, college life presented a host of obstacles to making friends at the same time that it touted community as a defining feature. Students cited cliques, inhospitable gathering places (including the union), and the lack of social events as hindrances to establishing satisfactory relationships.[15] In describing the student-run Macalester Community Council, charged with organizing student activities, Professor Hildegard Johnson reportedly argued to "eliminate the unrealistic 'community'" in the organization's title as it did not seem to apply to the fractious group. Indeed, the word *community* was among the most debated concepts of the period, and the educational experiments mentioned previously all included significant efforts to foster authentic communities.[16]

The very foundations of interpersonal relationships were changing dramatically, requiring every individual to reassess just how to interact with others. Foremost among those changing foundations were understandings of and attitudes toward sex. Whereas earlier generations of students had clear rules for social interaction among men and women that, while bendable, did guide behavior, young people in the 1960s were frequently more adrift, dealing with the growing independence of youth and the sexual revolution. Further raising the stakes on interpersonal communication was concern that if human communication on an interpersonal level could not be perfected, the solutions to conflicts among peoples nationally and internationally would never be found. The personal was very much the political, a phrase that would become popularized in the 1970s by historian Sara Evans. For Macalester students, like those around the nation, the foundation of social life was the countercultural triumvirate—sex, drugs, and rock 'n' roll.

New sexual mores were emerging on campus throughout the 1960s, resulting in visible policy shifts and the relaxing of en loco parentis regulations concerning living arrangements. Men's dormitory hours were eliminated early in the decade, with women's dorm hours being relaxed as well. Dorm visiting hours were also expanded again and again over the course of the decade, so that by 1969, men's dorms were entirely open to visitors and most women's dorms had very liberal visiting hours. The adoption of coed dorms, however, signaled a new era in student housing. At Macalester the advent of coed housing was hailed by students as a radical new advance in interpersonal relations. As Tim King pointed out in an article announcing the plans for the new policy, Mac was hardly a leader in this regard, following a number of campuses that had already adopted coed housing policies that "incorporate homogeneous men's living units in which were formerly women's dorms and vice versa." Mac, however, according to King, was going further, with its 1969 plan for "heterogeneous living units (men and women on the same floor or wing with roommates of the same sex)."[17]

Whether these housing arrangements encouraged more intimate relations among students is difficult to ascertain, but clearly many young people of the period felt that they were on the cutting edge of a new era of freedom in gender and sexual relations that earlier generations would never understand. Many national commentators on coed dorms argued that they were simply a means of making sexual relations more convenient in an era in which birth control pills diminished the likelihood of pregnancy significantly. Coed dorms seemed like giving free license to students to have sex. As anthropologist Margaret Mead observed on a visit to the Twin Cities in April 1971, "Today's [older] adults were simply brought up—the most of them—that if you were left alone in your room with a man, that meant sex."[18] Many young people, however, felt that having men and women living in closer proximity to one another was important for breaking down artificial barriers that separated people and developing more honest, authentic relationships. In fact, concern about social relationships on campus ran deep. A report presented to the board of trustees noted, regarding coed housing, that "the social life has loosened up and boys and girls are doing more things together."[19] Despite this official observance, however, concern among students about the lack of social life at the college continued, indicating that the new housing arrangements were not solving that particular problem.

Recreational drug use was another countercultural practice that flourished at Macalester, again, in many cases, as a means of addressing the problems of social life and relating to one's peers. "Dope hit the campus in 1967," remembered Chaplain Al Currier.[20] The year of the "summer of love" in Haight-Ashbury found some Macalester students adopting the psychedelic aesthetic of hippy counterculture along with the social use of marijuana. By the following spring, other supposedly mind-expanding pharmaceuticals had arrived, including LSD. According to research by University of Minnesota graduate student Donald Arden Chipman during the 1970–71 school year, some 57 percent of the 607 Macalester students surveyed had tried marijuana, with 44 percent describing themselves as "currently using" marijuana, figures that were comparable, though on the high side, to those found at other colleges and universities by other researchers.[21] Those numbers were distributed fairly evenly by sex but demonstrated something of a bell curve with respect to year in school, with first-years and seniors reporting less usage than sophomores and juniors. Though the study did not focus on other drugs, a few questions did gather preliminary data indicating that whereas the use of stimulants (Benzedrine, Dexedrine, diet pills, and methedrine) was in the single digits (4%, 7%, 7%, and 5%, respectively), hashish use registered at 38 percent, LSD at 11 percent, mescaline at 18 percent, and psilocybin at 14 percent.[22]

Apart from these figures, which may or may not be reliable given that they were self-reported, the study offers insight into students' attitudes toward not only drug use but also a number of other issues on which they were invited to comment. Several students asserted a difference between marijuana use, which they considered relatively harmless, and the use of "harder" drugs that were more "dangerous."[23] Moreover, several students located their use within social contexts. One young man commented, "The communion-like spirit that is present when people smoke dope is the thing I think I value the most, for everyone is united under a common bond."[24] That common bond functioned within a context of potentially powerful peer pressure. According to one young woman, "I'm a freshman and there are 10 other frosh [*sic*] on my floor. When we started in Sept. none of us had ever used drugs, some wanted to but hadn't had the opportunity, now only two of us don't use drugs."[25] The presence of "prestige attached to progressively higher levels of hallucinogens" was also noted by one student, indicating that participation in this social activity was perhaps not as uncoerced as some would think.[26] In any event, students were well aware of the complications of locating oneself within the prominent social structures vis-à-vis this particular activity.

Coping with the presence of drugs not only on campus but throughout society became a necessary skill for college students. Articles in the *MacWeekly* and other student publications addressed issues related to drugs. For instance, an article titled simply "Pot" appeared in the December 12, 1969, issue of the *MacWeekly* and consisted of a reprint of a national article discussing the pervasiveness of marijuana and efforts to weaken and eliminate laws in Canada that banned its possession and use. Another student publication, *Imani*, created by and for African American students at Macalester, carried articles on cocaine by editor Randolph R. Royals. In these articles, Royals mentions the increased interest in cocaine with the popularity of the film *Superfly* in 1972 and examines the problems associated with the drug.[27] Articles such as these provided both information and perspective as students negotiated the questions of drug use.

As the presence of drugs became a fact of life at educational institutions across the country, acknowledgment of that fact at Macalester was fairly public. A liberal attitude toward drug use, and particularly marijuana, was shared by some faculty, particularly younger faculty close to their own graduate school years. The presence of marijuana at parties attended by both faculty and students was commonplace and rarely a point of contention. Yet for students who were not interested in the drug scene, this faculty participation was problematic. At least one nonusing student in the survey commented on faculty drug use and advocacy, asserting that such individuals abdicated their "moral responsibility," ignoring their duty by encouraging students.[28]

While marijuana clearly played a role in campus social life, alcohol was an even more central factor. In response to Chipman's question, "Do you drink beer, whiskey, wine or other alcoholic beverages?" 85 percent of the students answered in the affirmative.[29] At the time of Chipman's study, the legal drinking age in Minnesota was twenty-one, but it would be lowered to eighteen in 1973 when concerns about drafting individuals who could not vote forced the lowering of the age of majority. That same year would see the origins of an annual social event on campus that would survive in some form, though in the view of many, only as a shadow of its early glory, to this day: Springfest.

Springfest, an all-day, all-campus outdoor celebration well lubricated with beer and marijuana, was the brainchild of two graduating seniors in 1973, Lance Rigg and Michael Knoche. According to Paul R. Dambert (class of 1987), in March of that year, they began organizing an all-campus party to take place in the Kirk Hall courtyard in April. Beer would be the centerpiece of the event, with a Hamm's beer truck accommodating the participants. Dean of Students Earl Bowman leant an official stamp of approval to the party but placed two restrictions on the event: first, the party must stay within the courtyard, and second, minors were not to be served alcohol. A new security force, just established that academic year, would keep order.[30]

This first Springfest was a low-budget affair, costing under five hundred dollars. Music was provided not by the live bands of later years but by the Macalester radio station, KMAC, which aired party tapes that Rigg and Knoche had prerecorded. During the event, according to Knoche, "We just told everyone to turn their stereos or radios out the window and turn them up. It was great . . . we had four walls of sound."[31] Students paid a three-dollar cover charge and were allowed all the beer they could drink.

While an all-day beer party was not a particularly uncommon event in the

Upper Midwest at this time, what made Springfest into a countercultural legend was the open distribution of marijuana cigarettes during the day. A pound of marijuana was obtained by organizers, rolled into joints, and handed out—three per person—during the event.[32] This public distribution of marijuana, to which the administration seems to have turned a blind eye, firmly located the event in the context of the counterculture—a latter-day Woodstock, briefer and without the mud, but clearly following in the same vein of bringing together people to share a unique, communal experience.

The first Springfest proved popular, and the event grew steadily over the next several years. The organizing of the second Springfest, with originators Rigg and Knoche having graduated and thus out of the picture, became a somewhat more formal activity. Planning began in fall 1973. The event was expanded considerably and was moved to Shaw Field. A two-thousand-dollar budget, much of it solicited from local merchants and from dorms, brought in not only the beer and joints of the previous year but also souvenir T-shirts, a rented circus tent, and live bands in the afternoon and evening: anthropology professor David Mc-Curdy's band, the Heaven Hill String Band (later the Mouldy Figs); the Eugene Stump Group; and Lamont Cranston (which would later achieve national recognition). By 1975, Springfest was advertised as a citywide party, with a budget of twenty-three hundred dollars and seventy-five kegs of beer, but this model, which attracted many underaged partygoers, was abandoned the next year when the drinking age rose to nineteen. Springfest would remain an event exclusively for Macalester students and their guests. Growth took off after the third year, and by 1979, the budget had ballooned to fifteen thousand dollars.[33]

Significant change occurred in 1978, when the organizing of Springfest, which had become a yearlong process of planning, raising funds, and making preparations, was incorporated as an activity under the Community Council. This status allowed Springfest organizers to use Macalester facilities without paying a fee and released them from having to secure private insurance for the event. Other changes were in the offing as well, particularly with respect to marijuana. The new dean, William Sverluga, expressed strong concerns about the presence of controlled substances at a party hosted by an official student organization, a situation that seemed to put the stamp of administration approval on the event. Furthermore, party organizers were increasingly concerned that the event would be targeted by the St. Paul Police Department. Springfest organizers, proceeding with their original plans to continue the marijuana distribution as in previous years, took precautions, distributing the marijuana among themselves so that they would never have more than an ounce of marijuana on their persons at any one time to avoid being charged with a more serious crime than the misdemeanor that possession of up to an ounce incurred. Dean Sverluga, according to organizer Andrew Bloom, decided not to pursue the marijuana issue, at least not that year.[34] Nevertheless, the 1978 event would be the last at which the open distribution of marijuana by organizers would take place, although, as Dambert observed in his 1987 study of the history of Springfest, "the availability of controlled substances on campus always increases immediately prior to Springfest," and many students in his experience at Macalester "obtain[ed] marijuana privately and use[d] it at Springfest."[35] Thus the distribution and use of marijuana at Springfest, the primary countercultural element of the event, did continue, though more deeply "underground" than in the event's earlier years. As a result, the event retained something of its deviant or transgressive reputation.[36]

Nevertheless, in the 1980s, the focus of Springfest was very much on the music, with organizers inviting nationally known bands to campus for the event, and on the all-day, all-campus, beer bash aspect of the gathering. As the counterculture movement passed from the public stage and Springfest lost its transgressive character, the legend of its earlier glory remained, resulting in a certain nostalgia among some Macites for what seemed to be a more genuine and simple, and more demonstrably transgressive, event.[37]

Negotiating Culture through Personal Expression

Among the strategies that students used to negotiate the complexities of campus and national life during this period was self-expression through self-published newspapers. Countless student newspapers were printed, containing personal, political, and artistic works. *Phaez 3*, among the first of the Macalester student publications, appeared in fall 1964 on mimeographed sheets that explained its purpose as "an independent discussion paper managed and operated by a few Mac students with the intention of offering not only Macites but other area college students the opportunity to read and air uncensored ideas in a new form dedicated to the ideal of academic freedom."[38] The articles in *Phaez 3* dealt primarily with issues of race and discrimination. Van Drake, for instance, wrote a piece titled "Dixie Is Discrimination" about the experiences of the Macalester international students who had toured the South during the summer on an Ambassadors for Friendship junket.[39] A later issue included an anonymous personal reflection in the form of a letter dated September 6, 1964, on teaching at a Freedom School in Mississippi.[40]

Mongoose, like *Imani* and *BLAC*, was a publication produced by African American students that provided information on how some students viewed their experiences at Macalester in negotiating complicated racial terrain. The first issue of *Mongoose* explained its title, a metaphor for struggle in a hostile territory:

Do you know what a mongoose is? It is an animal, though not a very large one, say only as big as my clenched fist, it is usually brown or black in complexion, sleek and awesome in its strength and desire. Its usual habitat is the jungle area, a dense overly populated area where only the strongest survive. To survive, it must meet and conquer some of the most overwhelming circumstances known to exist, the mongoose daily existence [*sic*] depends on his ability to defeat the most powerful, venomous snake in the world, the hooded cobra, a deadly merciless animal who has been known to swallow its victims, also making them invisible to the world but plainly visible through the skin of the cobra, the cobra's venom can knock a man dead in a matter of minutes, it is wily and deceptive, darting in and out, feigning injury only to strike again. By nature the mongoose should fear the cobra, but it is by nature that the mongoose must survive, the mongoose attacks the cobra, the mongoose wins. God, let me be a mongoose.[41]

The two surviving issues located in the Macalester College Archives contain prose and poetry by Macalester students struggling with the educational, social, cultural, and emotional circumstances they were experiencing.

Imani took a more news-oriented approach, producing an alternative newspaper on the *MacWeekly* model. Its issues included in-depth profiles of African American faculty, including Luther Stripling (music) and James Bennett (English, class of 1964), both of whom were encouraging the college to launch a black studies program. It also reported on stories of interest, such as students' experiences at the National Third World Student Organization conference in Terre Haute, Indiana, in 1973, and Angela Davis's visit to the University of Minnesota. *Imani* also ran articles by local civil rights activists, such as Mahmoud El Kati (history), and pieces on local issues in the Twin Cities, including coverage of desegregation in St. Paul schools and an opinion piece by Broderick Grubb on the implicit racism in editorials in the *St. Paul Dispatch*.[42] With these types of publications, Macalester students not only communicated with one another but distributed their thoughts widely through the Twin Cities community.

Student Life and College Identity

Student activities such as those mentioned earlier—coed dorm life, alcohol and drug use, rock 'n' roll, self-expression, and of course, political activism—merged to form a powerful public image of higher education nationally. In the Twin Cities, a region that was home to several colleges and universities, Macalester College became something of a standout, known for radical student behavior. Many people speculate that this was in part because the college was readily accessible to local reporters, who looked to Macalester first for campus-oriented stories—stories which were frequently negative. This understanding of the "bad press" that Macites, and particularly Macalester leaders, felt as an increasing burden during the period has some merit to it, for local newspapers did run a raft of negative stories on the college. Yet at least one other factor should also be taken into account: the extent to which student activities came to define the identity of the college in the early to mid-1970s.

By the early 1970s, as the college administration faced a financial crisis that threatened the college's existence and all but silenced public discussion of the college's direction and goals among the institution's leaders, the student activities mentioned earlier not only captured headlines in local newspapers but also were proudly touted by the students themselves. Although some administrators may have lamented the situation, many students were recharacterizing Macalester as a progressive, forward-thinking campus. According to a 1973 survey of some 254 first-year respondents, in which they were asked to check those items that pertained to themselves in a list of possible reasons why they selected Macalester, the top-ranked choice among men was the progressive atmosphere of the campus; among women, the progressive atmosphere came in second behind the college's academic reputation (which ranked second among the men). The progressive atmosphere of the campus also ranked first and second among transfer women and men, respectively.[43]

Of course, it was not only student activities that contributed to this new identity. Administrative decisions, such as those regarding housing, the new curriculum, and the various educational experiments, contributed as well. Yet the student atmosphere, more than at any previous time in the history of the college, had become a prominent factor in the identity of the college. Embroiled in a deepening financial crisis, college administrators and trustees, seemingly cast adrift ideologically by the resignation of Arthur Flemming as well as financially by DeWitt Wallace, articulated no alternative vision of the mission of the college. With few alternative messages about the institution's identity being cast into the public arena during this period, the countercultural identity of student life took root both inside and outside the college.

14

Negotiating Institutional . Democracy

MANY OF THE STRUGGLES this book has covered can be traced to questions of power, authority, and influence. Who owns a college? Who gets to make the important decisions? Whose authority, whose say, counts? Should institutional governance be top down? Bottom up? Centralized somewhere in the middle?

We have seen the answer to such questions at Macalester shift distinctively, even dramatically, from time to time. Edward Neill's negotiations with the Minnesota Synod of the Presbyterian Church were over whose say counts. In that case, the very founder of the college found himself forced to relinquish his position as Macalester president as a condition, in effect, for the college to open in the first place. Finding his say ranking below that of the new president and the board of trustees, he spent the rest of his life attempting to influence decisions made by both. With Neill essentially out of power, the board of trustees pursued new strategies for opening the college. The Presbyterian Synod of Minnesota gained influence, installing Thomas McCurdy as president, a man who saw the college's first mission as preparing Minnesota men for the seminary. As his decisions and actions regarding scarce financial resources and faculty positions met with increasing opposition from faculty members like James Wallace, he found resignation a more attractive option than remaining at the institution.

Beginning with Wallace, Macalester launched a period of strong, not to say autocratic, presidents that would last over fifty years. During these years, the role of the trustees narrowed significantly from what it had been in those early years of struggle, when they had assumed financial and ideological leadership of the institution. The burdens of having say rested with presidents: Wallace, Bess,

Hodgman, Acheson, and Turck. What these men decided went. Faculty, though meeting diligently, had relatively little influence over curriculum matters and no real say. Indeed, the faculty was viewed by both presidents and trustees in the category of "hired help," more often than not. Students, even lower on the say scale, had little voice and were easily silenced when their views—for instance, on the question of U.S. neutrality during World War I and II—were considered out of line by the administration. Over time, however, students did successfully lobby for a variety of important amenities that made life at Macalester more bearable: a gymnasium, a skating rink, and the right to hold dances on campus. Moreover, their personal interest in literary societies eventually reshaped the curriculum itself.

In the post–World War II period, a new voice emerged, that of DeWitt Wallace, a person who insisted on having say because of the financial support he could provide for the institution. Under a particularly strong president, Charles Turck, Wallace's efforts to have say could be subordinated—nicely—without rancor. Under a new, less forceful president, Wallace's say grew. But as much as Wallace wanted say, he was uncertain about wielding it and so turned to a lieutenant, Paul H. Davis, to advise him on what to say. The scheme worked under Harvey Rice, but when a new president with enormous force of will and personality took office, a struggle for power ensued.

During these years, other figures also wielded significant say, among them the deans. Though technically members of the faculty, Clarence Ficken and later Lucius Garvin both functioned more like the previous presidents (Ficken in the absence of the president and Garvin in place of a weakened president) than any earlier faculty members, hiring and firing faculty and staff. Like the deans, a few faculty members, usually holders of PhDs, gained some say, particularly as efforts to strengthen the college's national reputation were launched. Under Paul Davis's influence, a small number of trustees, brought together on the Educational Committee, gained significant say over curriculum.

These contests for authority within the college occurred within a changing cultural milieu during the post–World War II period, in which previously "silent" groups struggled to achieve recognition and influence—that is, say—within the public sphere. The civil rights movement succeeded in achieving federal legislation designed to ensure the rights of African Americans and other minority groups. The antiwar movement brought the voices of people from many walks of life to the fore and provided a catalyst for the passage of the Twenty-sixth

Amendment to the Constitution in 1971, extending the right to vote in federal elections to all adults over the age of eighteen. The civil rights and black power movements cast the voices of minority groups struggling for social and economic justice into the public arena. The women's movement—or what is more accurately known as the second wave of the women's movement—brought another group into the struggle for influence in the public arena.

As a result, the number and variety of groups on campus demanding say in institutional decisions rose precipitously. Students in particular, coming from all walks of life and being pressed into national crises involving war and race, wanted say in campus decisions. Yet unlike the situation at many other campuses, the Macalester administration was quite willing to increase student autonomy and participation in decision making. At Macalester, the students and administration were not in conflict with one another, at least not during the Flemming years, a point that George W. Stevenson makes in his 1972 study of the college.[1] The new Student Rights and Responsibilities charter from the late 1960s, for instance, approved by the faculty and administration, codified various rights of students to oversee their own activities on campus. Perhaps most important is that the Students Rights and Responsibilities allowed students to attend and serve on a number of college committees, including the faculty assembly, hiring or search committees, and the board of trustees. Student attendance at faculty committees soared as controversial subjects were taken up by the faculty, suggesting that students believed that faculty wielded significant power to effect policy change.

The reality was somewhat different. As we have seen, Macalester faculty had never wielded significant authority, particularly when it came to policy decisions. Strong presidents, a strong donor, and the board of trustees had guided the direction of the college for decades. Yet as we have also seen, the new faculty recruited in the middle to late 1960s were better educated and more willing to understand their role as including institutional leadership responsibilities beyond simply sitting on committees. Activism extended beyond the streets and voting booths into the classroom and the committee room.

In fact, faculty themselves began participating in campus decisions in unprecedented ways. The professorate itself was changing at Macalester and elsewhere. As more PhDs were hired into the Macalester faculty and as high salaries (among the highest in the country for liberal arts colleges) attracted ambitious and talented individuals, demands for say deepened significantly among the faculty, particularly after 1971, when professors saw both the administration and the trustees floundering during the financial crisis. Faculty did not, however, speak with a single voice. Consequently, when the college faced a major turning point, several constituencies would be involved in the decision-making process, constituencies that had never fully worked out processes for interaction or shared activity. And just as those new interest groups began to challenge established authorities, those authorities themselves vanished. As a result, just when crisis loomed and some unifying component was desperately needed, the college community was fragmented.

Women Faculty's Struggle for Equal Rights

Foremost among those faculty members who embraced an activist voice vis-à-vis institutional policy were women faculty, who, in the early 1970s, brought second-wave feminist agendas to the college. The question of women's appropriate role or roles in society, as we have seen, had been addressed on campus throughout the twentieth century. Second-wave feminism, precipitated in part by Betty Friedan's groundbreaking book, *The Feminine Mystique*, of 1963, launched an era of consciousness raising and critique of the numerous cultural and social limitations placed on women, from low expectations regarding their intellectual and physical capabilities to discriminatory hiring practices and salaries.

Women faculty members at Macalester were well aware of the disadvantages they faced as scholars and employees. The hiring of the 1960s had strongly favored male candidates; for instance, over three-quarters of all hires in 1967–68 were men. By the 1970s, on the assistant professor level women made up only 12 percent of the cohort. Moreover, the salaries of women were significantly lower than those of their male peers. Astonishment rocked the college in 1970 when an unauthorized copy of faculty salaries on which those of women faculty were circled was distributed across campus. Many were appalled by the raw data, particularly by the fact that one of the most nationally and internationally respected professors on campus, Dr. Hildegard Johnson, was paid significantly less than male faculty in lower ranks. Indeed, in every rank, women were in the lower half of the salary scale.[2] The salary disparity between two PhD political scientists, one male, one female, both hired in 1968, was thirty-four hundred dollars, with the man's salary about one-third higher than the woman's, was also controversial.[3] The documents also made clear that women's promotions took longer than did men's.

Across the nation, women were working to address these economic disparities and the social disparities that also obtained. Efforts to establish equal rights for women had been given an unexpected boost in 1964, when Title VII of the Civil Rights Bill, intended to eliminate racial discrimination, was modified by its opponents to include gender discrimination, a provision added in the cynical belief that its inclusion would make its passage impossible. Surprisingly, the amendment was approved, providing a new tool with which women could challenge discriminatory practices—though in reality, gender discrimination was perceived nationwide as of significantly less importance than racial discrimination, and it would be years before gender discrimination suits would meet any significant success.

Just how women should participate in society was being widely discussed, and the salary disclosure catalyzed discussion at Macalester. The Women's Faculty Caucus was formed to gather information about women on campus. As work progressed, concern developed that the influential college years were in fact inhibiting women's full participation in society. English professor Patricia Kane noted, "There's evidence that something happens to women in college.... Somewhere along the line they begin to fear success." Betsy Newell (economics) agreed, saying, "There are subtle socialization processes that go on on campus that can break down your plans.... Women come into college wanting to be something exciting, and end up doing something not exciting at all."[4]

To address these questions, three faculty members, Dorothy Dodge (political science), Patricia Kane (English), and Virginia Schubert (French), received a ninety-eight hundred dollar research award from the Department of Health, Education, and Welfare to study undergraduate women's career aspirations. They used the funds to organize the HEW Career Seminar for Women, three-day seminars held in both 1972 and 1973, which brought to campus local and national women to discuss "attitudes toward careers and the role of women in our society today."[5] During the first year, panels were offered on government employment and public service, medicine and science, media, communications, law, social welfare and public service, arts, professional business careers, and academic administration. Featured speakers included Eugenie Anderson, who had been the first woman to be appointed a U.S. ambassador (to Denmark) and was currently the ambassador to the United Nations and a representative on the Trusteeship Council; Aida S. Khalafalla, a senior principal research scientist in the Aerospace Division of Honeywell Inc.; Marlene Johnson (class of

1968), who cofounded an advertising and public relations firm (she would go on to become lieutenant governor of Minnesota from 1983 to 1991, under Rudy Perpich); Wilma Aufderheide, vice president and controller at Dayton's; Mary Brodbeck, dean of the Graduate School at the University of Minnesota; as well as three local attorneys, an architect, and many other professional women. The highlight of the seminar was a keynote address by well-known author and cultural critic Kate Millett, whose book *Sexual Politics* had been both praised and vilified throughout the country.[6]

Widely reported in the press—though rather negatively and, in the *Pioneer Press*, in the Family Life section—the seminar was a success. The one theme that seemed to unite the various speakers was the feeling that, as former ambassador Anderson put it, "women have to work harder than anyone else; harder than the men do."[7] Nevertheless, in an era when all public job announcements were designated as either male or female, each speaker had carved out a career and was willing to serve as a model for young college women considering their own futures.

The seminar also achieved some consciousness raising among faculty as well as some institutional change. President James Robinson, who had arrived on campus from the more progressive Ohio State University in fall 1971, had expressed his concern that Macalester was not treating its women faculty fairly, providing another impetus to effect change. Soon the faculty passed a requirement that at least one woman serve on all committees, a requirement that, though welcome, placed a significant burden on the handful of full-time women faculty available to serve.[8] The grant also brought some curriculum change as well when Kane focused a literature course on women authors, a strategy that many had argued was impossible because of what was then perceived as a dearth of women writers. Furthermore, the seminar opened up opportunities for a deeper critique of Macalester hiring, promotion, and salary processes. Seventeen of the 153 full-time faculty were women in 1972, down three from the previous year.[9]

These critiques negotiated between two different models of advancement: individual advancement through merit and group advancement through the elimination of discriminatory practices. On one hand, salaries, these women argued, should not be decided on the number of dependents a person had to support; rather, they should be decided on merit and accomplishments. Hiring and firing decisions—and the college had just experienced a significant number of firings due to the budget crisis—should be based on merit, not on preconceived gender notions such as the idea that married women who are let go or not hired will be supported by their husbands and that single women are better off finding a husband than joining the workforce.[10] On the other hand was the position that women as a group should be better integrated into the systems of the college. Women PhDs should be interviewed for new positions, and stereotypes that limited women's advancement should be addressed and challenged.

The feminist movement brought this tension between individual and group advancement to the fore. Detractors focused on individuals, arguing, for instance, that the fact that the college had employed women since Julia Johnson was hired in 1897 indicated that institutional obstacles to women's advancement were a fiction. If Johnson and the other individual women who had been employed by the college had not expressed concerns, the contemporary concerns were unmerited. Feminism, on the other hand, took a group approach, examining the systemic treatment of women as a group vis-à-vis men as a group, and thus unmasked multiple forms of privilege and consideration to which the former group had no access. For both groups, the few exceptions—women who had been able to carve out careers in the college—proved the rule(s), opposite though they may be.

Expanded Educational Opportunities and Students of Color Challenge of Dominant Authorities

At the same time that feminist efforts to achieve equal treatment challenged traditional authorities and ways of thinking, fragmenting the faculty, the struggle of students of color on campus similarly challenged entrenched ideas about race and education, further fragmenting the campus community. The desire for a level playing field on which each individual would excel to his or her own abilities challenged the informal structures that had previously held the college together, whether religious preference (Presbyterian, or at least Protestant), gender privilege (male), or racial privilege (white). Substituting competition for privilege, the academy (not just Macalester) pitted not only faculty member against faculty member but also department against department and, in some instances, students against faculty. But the desire for group advancement challenged the institution even more, and this was precisely what students of color on campus were demanding. At the same time, some interpreters blamed the deepening financial crisis on, if not the actual presence of minority students on campus, the costly Expanded Educational Opportunities (EEO) program that had brought many of them to Macalester. Here was fragmentation of a particularly insinuating and destructive kind. To understand this highly polarizing interpretation of the financial crisis, we need to reexamine the EEO program more closely within the context of the struggle for minority rights both nationally and on campus.

As we have seen from the previous chapter, EEO was developed and initiated with resounding support throughout the campus. The Kerner Report, the social gospel, and liberal confidence in merit created an extraordinary and powerful convergence in the idea of opening the gates of Macalester to young men and women of color from poor urban neighborhoods—ghettos, as they were called at the time. Macalester would admit a specific number of such students, provide them with remedial education during the summer to get them up to speed, and place them in the classroom in the fall to compete on a now supposedly level playing field with the other students. Advisors and counseling staff would be available to help the students of color make the transition to life in this upper Midwest, mostly white community.

The Kerner Report catalyzed the development of EEO programs similar to this one at several liberal arts institutions across the country, including Oberlin. Most barely got off the ground. Macalester's program, however, ran fairly vigorously for nearly a decade and served as a national model. Although woefully naive in its idealism, its understanding of African American cultural contexts and social strategies, and its belief that people just want to get along, the EEO program is most significant not in its spectacular failure, as many have contended over the years, but rather in its astonishing, against-the-odds success. The factor that most tipped the odds against the program was that EEO was based on the theory of meritocracy and its counterpart, the melting pot model of cultural pluralism. What made it successful was the group identity and solidarity of the student participants.

In summer 1969, seventy-five young men and women of color, mostly African American but some Hispanic and Native American, from across the country, with particularly strong representation from the Chicago area, attended summer classes in subjects designed to increase their academic skills where necessary and to orient them to life on the campus.[11] The students then went home for two weeks to decide whether Macalester was right for them. Almost all returned in September. That fact in itself is astonishing. These students' desire for education superseded their discomfort and disorientation in the new environment. Their commitment mirrored that of the college. The next year, 85 percent of the first class returned and another cohort of seventy-five was enrolled. The payoff would be seen years later. By the fourth year, half of the first cohort of students graduated, a figure comparable with the 54 percent graduation rate for all students who entered that year.[12] By spring 1975, 302 students had been enrolled through the program and 134 had graduated, 14 in fewer than four years.[13] In a situation in which the odds were decidedly against any kind of success, a majority of EEO students clung tenaciously to this rare opportunity; they also transformed the campus in important ways. For these students, individual advancement in a seemingly meritocratic environment might offer true opportunity.

But neither the college nor broader society was in reality meritocratic. The civil rights movement of the post–World War II period had made gains in education, voting rights, and human rights that had eluded the grasp of individual African Americans for generations. The fostering of racial identity had succeeded in making gains for all African Americans, not just a few, and African American students at Macalester (as well as throughout the country) understood very well that their individual presence was not only seen by whites as symbolic of an entire people but that their individual advancement came through privileges that were denied to many. Furthermore, by the early 1970s, as Richard Nixon's so-called southern strategy was increasingly withdrawing federal enforcement of antidiscrimination legislation passed in the 1960s and supporting white southerners determined to overcome such legislation and retain white power, African Americans throughout the country were well aware that gains achieved by the movement were eroding. Education was a particular touchstone. In Chicago, the home of many EEO students, controversies over the desegregation of public schools through busing were escalating, with the city being declared out of compliance with Illinois regulations in August 1972.[14] African American students at Macalester, both EEO and non-EEO, forced into a racial identity by the stares of Twin Cities whites as well as by the policies of national, state, local, and institutional governments, had few options but to join the struggle to expand what privilege they could to the broader group.

But that group identity was far from unified or monolithic. Just as the college was beginning to experience a new range of voices claiming influence, or at least some say, in decision making, EEO diversified but also fragmented the campus in completely unexpected ways. As we have seen, Macalester had admitted African Americans and other students of color well before EEO, but EEO, with its distinctive financial support package—essentially a full ride, along with some personal stipends—not only created a distinctive group on campus but also sparked new academic stereotypes informed by the category of "under-privileged." Academic expectations for these new students among both faculty and non-EEO students were low. Rumors flew even before the program began that admission standards would be lowered to bring in EEO students and that once admitted to classes, EEO students' work would be held to lower standards than the work of other students.[15] Thus EEO students and non-EEO students of color were perceived—and perceived themselves as being perceived—through a double lens of stereotypes, racial and academic. As senior Broderick Grubb put it in 1973, "We were not treated as people, we were treated as poor, deprived, black, 'things' that needed help. There was no self-identity, whether one was an EEO or not, everyone thought it—an EEO Scholarship was for the Black Dummies and not for Black Scholars. Differences in treatment were apparent everywhere."[16] Non-EEO students of color in particular resented being lumped under these stereotypes, which, of course, slandered many of the EEO students themselves, who had gotten into the program because of exceptional potential they had demonstrated in high school. Here again, the tension between individual merit and group identity worked against the EEO cohort.

The odds were not in their favor in other ways as well. As we have seen, African American students had formed BLAC years earlier precisely because they found comfort in one another as they faced the mostly white campus in the mostly white area of St. Paul. EEO students facing the same situation, with the addition for many of a new socioeconomic environment, had no easy task in carving out an education and a life at Macalester. On top of the homesickness that most students endured, there were real cultural differences in the way people treated one another and in interpersonal relationships; in shared background; in the use of language; and in food, clothing, music, and so on that continually reminded these and other "minority" students that they really were living in a culture that was very different from that of their home. Furthermore, African American culture itself was going through cataclysmic change during this period in an ongoing struggle for social, political, and economic voice. The black power movement, which had peaked a few years earlier, was in decline, and, as mentioned earlier, previous advancements seemed to be disappearing. Justice seemed to be slipping further from the grasp of people of color. Thus at the heart of EEO and all black students' experience on this campus was an ongoing negotiation of the treacherous waters between individual advancement and group solidarity within a national context of perceived and real loss of ground.

In negotiating this territory, students of color applied the tactics of protest and demonstration widely used throughout the country as well as on campus to issues they wanted to advance. Faculty meetings, which students were now allowed to attend, provided a ready stage for airing grievances and pursuing new agendas such as adding African and African American history to the college's course offerings. Tensions rose palpably as faculty felt intimidated by student behaviors at these meetings. Chaplain Alvin Currier, commenting on a particularly tense faculty meeting in 1971 when several students of color made their ideas known in a highly forthright, even intimidating manner, shouting and standing on tables, observed that though the students were "rough" and "rude," the history of black–white relations in the nation had prepared them for no other means of affecting institutions. A storm of racial negotiation was brewing, he predicted, and white faculty needed to move beyond their "insulated academic barometers," which could not sense its approach. Currier, for one, argued for weathering the impending storm together—a fight for survival, as he saw it—which would make the institution stronger.[17] His words, as we will see, would be prophetic.

Institutional Financial Crisis or Ideological Backpedaling?

This fragmentation occurred just as the college entered the financial crisis caused by the withdrawal of DeWitt Wallace's support. By fall 1971, the trustees had hired a new president, their third choice, James Robinson, the thirty-nine-year-old provost of Ohio State University. His appointment was something of a landmark in the history of the college in that he was the first president whose religious background was not touted as a central element in the selection.

Robinson's charge was to fix the financial crisis, to balance the budget. Tuition income plunged as enrollments plummeted from 2,093 in 1970 to a low of 1,637 in 1975, a decline of 22 percent.[18] With the loss of both Wallace funding and substantial tuition income, expenditures needed to be cut back. As the largest area of expenditure was salaries, jobs were the first item on the line. A faculty committee presided over the sad task of terminating forty-four faculty and staff employees during the 1971–72 academic year. Departments, forced to cut their teaching faculty, were in turmoil. New hires watched the process with trepidation. Some faculty left for new posts; some retired early, vacating their positions to allow newer faculty to remain on the payroll. Trustees stepped in to guarantee the payroll. Morale plummeted. Women faculty, who, as we have seen, tended to be grouped in the lower ranks within department hierarchies, were particularly hard hit by the terminations, and the percentage of full-time women faculty dipped to 13 percent by 1976.[19] By 1974, some thirty faculty positions and sixty staff positions had been eliminated.

That first year of cuts, 1971–72, brought other reductions as well. The instructional and departmental research budget, which included salaries, was slashed by 16 percent. The Wallace-sponsored programs that had attracted so much attention to the college, including the faculty book budget, travel stipends, and other faculty-oriented programs, were gutted by 93 percent. The library budget was cut by 6 percent and physical plant operations by 4 percent. General administration, including staff salaries, was cut by about 73 percent. On the income side, tuition went up about two hundred dollars, and a few federal and nonfederal grants came in. The August 1972 audit showed a year-end deficit of $32,277, as compared to $2,734,675 the year before.[20]

Only two budget lines showed increases that year, both concerned with student well-being: organized activities went up $84,989, just over 10 percent, and student services went up $33,000, or just over 6 percent, increases due in part to the third cohort of new EEO students (forty) who had enrolled in fall 1971. That year, however, the college also took in $245,000 in restricted federal, foundation, corporate, and individual gifts to support the program, a figure almost double that of the previous year, and the college put in $102,000 (down from $166,000 the year before).[21] The next year, restricted gifts and grants for EEO programs amounted to $187,000, and college support rose to $162,000.

While these measures moved the college's balance sheet toward the black, two factors remained problematic. First, even with the cuts, the college borrowed against its unrestricted endowment to pay the bills and balance the budget. By 1973, it owed the endowment almost $4.5 million. Second, the nation's economy was faltering. Productivity fell in the early 1970s and economic growth slowed to 2.3 percent annually. Double-digit inflation loomed. From 1970 to 1972, the administration had admitted more students in an effort to increase tuition income—raising the total student body to highs of 2,093 and 2,097 in 1970 and 1971, respectively—but sharp declines occurred in 1972 (2,021) and 1973 (1,877) when tuition raises averaged two hundred dollars per year. In 1974, as the national economic crisis deepened, tuition was once again raised, and the student body declined again to 1,748. Efforts to trim the budget resumed, this time with faculty and staff agreeing to pay cuts. The same faculty that in the late 1960s had led the nation in salary now trailed some thirty liberal arts colleges, including four Associated Colleges of the Midwest schools (Lawrence, Grinnell, Carleton, and Colorado colleges).[22]

Acting on the news that over one hundred admitted students were not intending to enroll, college administrators met in August 1974 to once again roll back expenditures. This time, EEO, both programs and financial aid, was cut by sixty-six thousand dollars, or 22 percent. Among the specific components most affected was the Black Education Institute (or Institute for African Education), an elementary education program operated by Macalester education students and community partners, which was to be terminated. At least two staff positions were to be cut as well.

African American, Hispanic, and Native American students who had benefited from the EEO program rallied quickly, fearful that the cuts sounded the death knell of the college's previous commitment to minority education. As students arrived back on campus, they were greeted by demonstrators. Administrators' and trustees' efforts to reassure the students that the cuts were temporary and the college remained committed to minority education were unconvincing. As Dan Gearino (class of 1998) points out in his history of EEO, during these early discussions the administration and trustees focused on the fiscal situation. In their view, the cuts were a reasonable and necessary financial measure required in the face of an ongoing institutional fiscal crisis. They had nothing to do with the merits of the programs, just as the budget cuts shouldered for several years by the academic departments had nothing to do with the merits of those departments. From the students' point of view, however, the merits of the program were paramount. Caught again between their own individual privilege and the need to demonstrate racial solidarity by struggling for the continuation of the programs from which they had benefited, EEO students, supported by many non-EEO students of color and some white, escalated their protest in the second week of September. Before dawn on the morning of Friday, September 13, some twenty-two EEO students entered the campus administration building, known as "77 Macalester," locked the doors, and denied access to anyone attempting to enter for twelve days.[23]

Resolution, of Sorts

The students occupying the building issued a statement: "We believe the Macalester administration has not only killed the liberal commitment to Minority students, but has not had or even presented an adequate proposal to aid Minority youths in gaining the right of a liberal education."[24] The budget cuts, in their view, "will lead to assured elimination of the EEO Program," and they called for a six-year commitment on the part of the college to a "program for Minority people over the United States." This prologue located the protest squarely in the context of group identity. This was a racial action, a last-ditch effort to save a program for future students of color. The specific demands included the retention of a position in the education department previously held by a woman of color, the reinstatement of twenty-two thousand dollars to the EEO program budget, the continuation of the Institute for African Education, and the continuation of programs for Hispanic students.

Vice President for Academic Affairs Charles W. McLarnan responded to the student document point by point on September 14. He restated the college's commitment to continuing EEO and recruiting forty students for 1975; he explained that even with the cuts, minority students were served by programs costing some $250 each, whereas the student body in general (including minorities) were served by dean of students programs costing about twenty-five dollars per student; regarding the Institute for African Education, he implied that a committee would review the situation; and he explained that Hispanic students would "continue to be included in the Minority program; and that the college would recruit a bi-lingual education specialist for the Department of Education to help meet the counseling needs of Hispanic students."

On Monday, the two sides met, but negotiations did not go smoothly. The students felt that their views regarding the future of the program were being ignored by the administrators, who talked only about the numbers. Recriminations followed, and though efforts were made to continue a dialogue, talks soon broke down entirely. A moderator was needed. On Friday, September 20, Earl Craig, an African American social policy consultant who had run for the U.S. Senate against Hubert Humphrey four years earlier and who was at the time teaching political science in the Carleton College Afro-American studies program, agreed to step in and mediate the negotiations. Through the effective intervention of Craig, an agreement was carved out and signed by both sides: EEO would be cut only by fourteen thousand dollars, two staff positions would be saved, including those of a half-time Puerto Rican and a half-time Mexican American counselor, forty full-tuition EEO scholarships would be offered each year for another five years, and charges would not be pressed against the students who occupied the building.[25] The students unceremoniously left the building during the evening of September 24, and a group of staff entered to assess the damage. Their report estimated damages at twenty-three dollars. The students, as Gearino points out, seemed to have "won a tremendous victory." Two weeks later, however, the trustees rejected the settlement on the grounds that its prime signatory, President Robinson, had no authority to guarantee the agreement.[26]

In a way, all history boils down to personalities or, more accurately, how historians assess the various personalities and perspectives at odds in any particular conflict. This situation is no different. Many people have blamed President Robinson for being inflexible, not attuned to students' views, unsympathetic, and even intimidated by the students. Others have blamed the students themselves, for selfishness in the face of the institutional crisis. Still others have blamed Arthur Flemming for launching the program in the first place. And many have blamed EEO itself for "ruining" the college. In regard to this latter accusation, what is clear in hindsight was that over the first six years of the program, total costs to the college, excluding external funding, amounted to between $2.7 and $2.8 million. The growth of institutional debt over the same period reached seven million dollars.[27] So though EEO was a component in the college's financial problems, it was by no means the only nor even the predominant cause.

Yet perhaps the fundamental paradox in the interpretation that places primary responsibility for the institution's financial crisis on the failure of EEO, and by extension on the supposed failure of the students involved in the program, is that just what its success would have looked like seems to have been rarely if ever discussed. In hindsight, one can easily discern that engaged participation in institutional decision making was a mark of success. Surely the production of numerous literary and informational newsletters, such as *Imani*, *BLAC*, and others, was a mark of success. Surely the development of networks of mutual support in an alien place was a mark of success. Surely retention rates and graduation rates were marks of success. Of course, some students did not flourish and dropped out; of course, some aggressively pursued agendas; but such instances did not mean the program was a failure, an interpretation that grew entrenched in college lore over the ensuing decades. EEO, in fact, succeeded quite well in providing an educational opportunity to a number of students of color who had few educational choices available to them, and those students who pursued that opportunity in turn made the program successful by their participation, commitment, flexibility, and tolerance. How did college leaders define success? Well-intentioned but culturally naive administrators and faculty hoped, it seems, to reshape the EEO students into clones of earlier generations of authority-acquiescing white students. In that task, they clearly failed.

The Center Will Not Hold

It was not just the challenges presented by various interest groups, however, that fragmented the Macalester community. Another vital component was the loss of a central shared vision of the mission and identity of the college. To understand this situation, we would do well to hark back to a somewhat similar concern faced by Charles Turck in the late 1930s, as the college embraced the liberal arts. Then, as in the 1970s, the choice seemed to be between a shallow materialism, enslavement to the bottom line, versus a value-filled and principle-guided educational policy. Turck argued for the values inherent in the liberal arts themselves, which would, he felt, provide a safeguard against materialism. He also broadened the understanding of Christianity during his tenure and linked Christian service to national ends. This vision of Christian education in the service of democracy and justice inspired students, faculty, trustees, and alumni during the two decades that Turck was in office.

But such idealism, a view of education as in the service of broader social and political needs, had faded among college leaders in the utilitarian 1960s, as the aspirations of the wealth of DeWitt Wallace and the business models for advancement propounded by Paul Davis guided the institution. Eying the prize of national educational leadership and recognition, Macalester's purpose became highly pragmatic and instrumental in a self-referential way. In all the material and letters of the 1950s and 1960s having to do with the effort to raise Macalester in the national rankings, none but the most general discussion of why this goal was important appears. Its desirability was deemed self-evident to the college's leaders, although a few faculty members did question the aspiration for national recognition and encourage continued focus on regional students. The extension of the international programs was understood within a context of national service, but that, too, was never fully fleshed out, and soon the anti-Communist underpinnings of the effort to advance American values overseas were challenged by the antiwar movement.

Furthermore, the Christian context of the earlier understandings of service had all but vanished by the 1970s. As mentioned in chapter 10, Yahya Armajani's response to Lucius Garvin's 1967 "Steeples of Excellence" speech outlined his analysis of the growing distance between the college and the church and lamented what he saw as the community's unwillingness to discuss the ramifications of this move.[28] If the church-related component of the college's identity were abandoned, what, he asked, would replace it as the college's central unifying factor? Indeed, the *function* religion had previously served as informing the college's underlying purpose had never been fully addressed, much less replaced by a new central component, either intellectual or ethical. As the college worked to tighten admissions and improve faculty credentials, the discussion of values shifted to a secular concern for achievement and national recognition for its own sake and for the sake of the financial well-being of the institution. Garvin's "steeples" speech had begged the question of purpose, taking pride in accomplishments but not dealing with why those accomplishments were important. Furthermore, as Armajani's analysis portended, the mere identification of several categories or steeples would have a difficult time providing a unifying mission for the institution. The metaphor itself suggested an apt lesson, as the steeples that graced Christian churches, creating a vision of Christian unity in nineteenth-century city and village landscapes, were themselves public statements of denominational competition that was frequently fierce. Height indicated social prominence, or at least aspiration, in a religious marketplace marked by competition for members; architectural style masked central theological, ideological, and social divisions. Similarly, science, internationalism, and the other strengths mentioned by Garvin, though seemingly unifying themes, would soon become lighting rods for division. Even service, that fulcrum of Macalester's fortunes, had become a steeple. By the mid-1960s, service as individual volunteerism prevailed. Volunteer Day promotions encouraged students to sign up to participate in a variety of community projects, but institutionally the rhetoric of service was rarely heard.

The few years during which Arthur Flemming manned the helm were an extraordinary exception. Flemming, something of a throwback to mid-century, believed that education in the service of society was central to the college's purpose. It is not a coincidence that the federal award named after him is the Flemming Award for Public Service. For students thirsting for some sort of "relevance" in their education during a time of social and political crisis, Flemming's rhetoric of principles and service to society placed their four years at Macalester in a broader context of intellectual responsibility to society that many found inspiring in the same way that earlier Christian students had found Turck's or John Acheson's or even James Wallace's vision inspiring. The category of service answered the why questions: Why develop an international curriculum? For the service of the world. Why develop a multicultural curriculum? For the service of society. By the early 1970s, in a country and institution wracked by tension,

Top, Homecoming bonfire in Shaw Field. Photograph 1946. Courtesy Minnesota Historical Society.

Bottom, Macville, temporary housing for students who had served in World War II and their families. Photograph 1946. Courtesy Macalester College Archives, DeWitt Wallace Library.

Opposite, top, Residents of Macville. Mr. and Mrs. Martin Wiebusch and Mr. and Mrs. William Bowell. Photograph 1946. Courtesy Macalester College Archives, DeWitt Wallace Library.

Opposite, bottom, Macalester student supporters of Ohio senator Robert Taft's bid for the Republican presidential nomination in 1948. Taft, a staunch conservative who had opposed entry into World War II and Franklin Roosevelt's New Deal, lost the nomination to the more moderate Thomas E. Dewey. Photograph ca. 1947. Photograph by Philip C. Dittes, courtesy Minnesota Historical Society.

Above, Macalester student supporters of Democratic presidential candidate Adlai Stevenson. Photograph October 1952. Courtesy Macalester College Archives, DeWitt Wallace Library.

Top, Macalester supporters of Progressive Party presidential candidate Henry Wallace (second from right). From left, Professor Mary Gwen Owen, student Walter Mondale, President Charles Turck. Photograph 1948. Photograph by Eugene Debs Becker, courtesy Minnesota Historical Society.

Bottom, Charles Turck, Hubert H. Humphrey, and student Walter Mondale. Photograph ca. 1948. Courtesy Macalester College Archives, DeWitt Wallace Library.

Top, Macalester College cheerleaders wearing the Scottish outfits designed by Mainbocher. Photograph 1955. Courtesy Macalester College Archives, DeWitt Wallace Library.

Bottom, Macalester Bagpipe Band. Photograph 1955. Photograph by Norton and Peel, courtesy Minnesota Historical Society.

Above, Lila and DeWitt Wallace in Phoenix, Arizona. Photograph ca. 1955. Courtesy Macalester College Archives, DeWitt Wallace Library.

Opposite, top, Political science professor Dorothy Dodge (right) and Macalester student Janice Pagel (class of 1960) with United Nations project during Political Emphasis Week. Photograph 1958. Photograph by Ivan Burg, courtesy Macalester College Archives, DeWitt Wallace Library.

Opposite, bottom, Macalester students Caddie Thomson and Keith Avery browse a book display during Religion in Life Week. Photograph ca. 1950. Photograph by Marilyn Bruette, courtesy Macalester College Archives, DeWitt Wallace Library.

Above, Macalester College chaplains Alvin Currier and Maxwell Adams. Photograph ca. 1964. Courtesy Macalester College Archives, DeWitt Wallace Library.

Opposite, Political science professor Theodore Mitau in his office. Photograph ca. 1960. Photograph by Ivan Burg, courtesy Macalester College Archives, DeWitt Wallace Library.

Above, President and Mrs. Harvey Rice with DeWitt and Lila Wallace and an unknown individual. Photograph 1965. Courtesy Macalester College Archives, DeWitt Wallace Library.

Opposite, top, Flying Scots, with airplane donated by DeWitt Wallace. Photograph ca. 1958. Courtesy Macalester College Archives, DeWitt Wallace Library.

Opposite, bottom, Professor Mary Gwen Owen (seated, center) with student actors. Photograph ca. 1965. Courtesy Macalester College Archives, DeWitt Wallace Library.

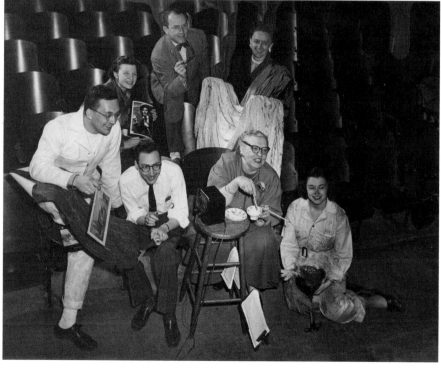

Opposite, top, Vietnam War symposium, Weyerhaeuser Memorial Chapel, Macalester College. Photograph ca. 1970. Courtesy Macalester College Archives, DeWitt Wallace Library.

Opposite, middle, Vietnam War memorial on campus outside Turck Hall. Photograph 1970. Photograph by Tom Nelson, courtesy Macalester College Archives, DeWitt Wallace Library.

Opposite, bottom, Macalester students participate in anti–Vietnam War march on Washington, D.C. Photograph 1970. Photograph by Tom Nelson, courtesy Macalester College Archives, DeWitt Wallace Library.

Above, Yippie leader Jerry Rubin (center, with beard) during Macalester College appearance. Photograph 1970. Photograph by D. Schuster, courtesy Macalester College Archives, DeWitt Wallace Library.

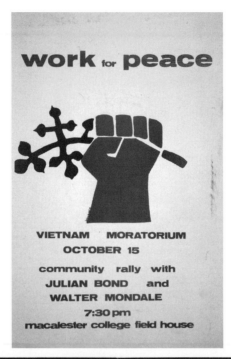

Top, Peace moratorium poster. 1969. Artist unknown. Courtesy Minnesota Historical Society.

Bottom, Cover of *BLAC,* Macalester African American student publication. 1968. Courtesy Macalester College Archives, DeWitt Wallace Library.

Top, Unidentified journalist interviewing Melvin Collins (class of 1975) during EEO occupation of the administration building at 77 Macalester Street. September 1974. Courtesy Macalester College Archives, Dewitt Wallace Library.

Bottom, Seated from left: Melvin Collins (class of 1975), Earl Craig, James Robinson, and Larry Craig (class of 1975) negotiating settlement. Standing: David Hersey (Director of Admissions and Financial Aid) and unidentified journalist. September 1974. Courtesy Macalester College Archives, Dewitt Wallace Library.

Top, Professor Gerald (Jerry) Webers (far left) and his students in Antarctica. From the left: Curt Hudak, John Craddock, Larry Rosen, and Pat Gould. Photograph 1979. Courtesy John Craddock.

Bottom, John B. Davis and DeWitt Wallace. Photograph ca. 1975. Courtesy Macalester College Archives, DeWitt Wallace Library.

unrest, and disruption, such idealism was easily targeted. Hard-nosed fiscal realism was needed after a presidency undone by fiscal crisis, and Jim Robinson, the new search committee agreed, seemed capable of delivering it. It was time for pragmatics, not ideals.

Thus a mission-oriented educational philosophy was not the victim of the 1970s crisis; it had disappeared much earlier, returning for a brief final act during the Flemming years. Its absence would be felt acutely in the turbulent 1970s, when the college was forced to make difficult choices. The students of color who protested the EEO cuts wanted to be told just where the college's commitments lay, what its priorities were, but answers to those questions were not forthcoming. Macalester had similarly been forced to make hard financial decisions on many previous occasions, indeed from well before the institution's doors actually opened. Those earlier decisions, however, as we have seen, were made in the context of general agreement on the purpose of the institution itself—as a Christian institution, as a liberal arts institution, as a participant in American democracy, as a vocational institution, and so on. In each period, the educational philosophy emerged in conversation with national and international situations and contexts, and the leaders willingly articulated the college's position.

The Disappearing Christian Identity

One historically prominent component that was clearly missing from the institutional discussions of mission and purpose in the 1970s was the Christian character of the college. By 1975, an official religious presence on campus was deemed all but dead. Chaplain Alvin Currier, who had taken a leave of absence in 1974, was not replaced, leaving the college without a chaplain that year. Currier would not return, and as the 1975 academic year opened, the college unknowingly returned to its pre-1947 state, with no chaplain. The question was raised as to whether one was needed. A survey taken among faculty soliciting opinions on retaining or eliminating the office showed that feelings were not strong in either regard. Thirteen percent identified retaining the position as a "top priority," while 11 percent labeled it a "low priority" or "unnecessary." Those claiming the middle ground, or "medium priority," represented 18 percent of the sixty-one faculty and staff members who responded. Another 17 percent indicated that a part-time chaplain was preferable. Opinions, thus, were widely variable.[29]

The relationship with the synod was similarly ambiguous. Though Macalester's annual reports to the synod continued to ensure the importance of religion to the college's mission, synod contributions to the college, which had peaked in the early 1960s at around twenty thousand dollars per year, had tapered off significantly in 1971—down to $985 from $8,646 in 1970—and had dwindled to $641 in 1975. Denominational support from the Presbyterian Board of Christian Education had nosedived from a high of $65,077 in 1969 to nothing in 1974 and 1975.[30] The next year would bring a turnaround, though. The Synod of Lakes and Prairies recommended raising the Macalester allocation to ten thousand dollars for 1976, and a report by two visiting reviewers to the synod indicated that they found "interest to develop a stronger campus ministry, make worship opportunities available to desiring students, and provide an environment of spiritual expression that is non-constraining and constructive."[31] The review team likely had access to the faculty survey, though it is interesting to note that their interpretation of the role of campus ministry differed distinctly from that envisioned by the survey. Whereas the review team cited fostering worship and spiritual expression as the activities of interest, the survey cited pastoral counseling, fostering student religious groups, and pastoral ministry as the primary roles of the chaplain's office. Of those who felt that the office should be continued, 29 percent ranked "pastoral counseling with students" the top priority of the office; "fostering student religious groups" was cited as the top priority by 25 percent, and 22 percent cited "pastoral ministry with students" as top. Seventeen percent identified providing "a Christian presence" in college life as the most important function of the office.

This disparity between the synod review team's recommendations and the faculty survey results pointed to two different understandings of college chaplaincies, the first equating the role with that of the clergy or a church leader, focused on worship and spiritual development, albeit with an ecumenical flavor, and the second equating it with the counseling role. No longer was the pastoral role focused exclusively on the individual's relationship with God; it had, for decades, as we have seen, adopted the strategies of modern psychology to address the individual's relation with the world. By the 1970s, as students were increasingly stressed by global situations on top of pressure to succeed and new responsibilities for their own and the institution's success, counseling was a growing area of need, and chaplains across the country stepped in to assist, aided by a new focus on counseling in seminary training. As the Macalester survey showed, the need for counseling was the primary reason for maintaining the office—even a respondent who identified himself as a "committed secularist" indicated that he had "no objection to a chaplain-counselor in some role in relation to student developmental needs."[32]

Providing opportunities for worship and pastoral counseling were a long way away from the focus of earlier Macalester chaplains. Adams had come closest to focusing on worship, but his main occupations were fostering a strong religious identity of the institution itself, bringing in Christian speakers, community service, and Bible teaching. Russell Wigfield similarly had focused on service and advancing the Christian identity of the college. John Bodo and Al Currier, in particular, focused on integrating Christian philosophy into the political issues of the day in an effort to maintain the religion's relevancy to students concerned about world issues, but also found themselves increasingly involved in counseling. Though all the chaplains had offered some worship opportunities and some counseling, these never defined the core of their work. Now these two aspects were being touted by two different groups—the synod, on one hand, and the faculty, on the other—as central to the office. If Macalester were to retain the office of chaplain, it would look very different from its previous character. In fact, several of the faculty comments suggested seeking a young woman to fill the position, a perspective consistent with the widespread Christian practice at the time of channeling women candidates for the ministry into counseling positions rather than church leadership positions.[33]

By the end of the 1974–75 academic year, the decision had been made to keep the office. Furthermore, a faculty and staff task force was created to reaffirm the relationship between the college and the synod, a task predicated in part on the adoption of a new "Statement of Mutual Responsibilities" by the United Presbyterian Church (USA). That statement presented separate lists of responsibilities for each institutional category: church and college. Responsibilities on the college side cited by the document included instruction in and emphasis on human values and service to individuals and society; making its "knowledge, skills, and related education resources available to the church"; offering courses "in religious studies, with emphasis on the Judeo-Christian tradition"; and providing a catalog statement of the institution's relationship with the church. On the church side, responsibilities included regarding the colleges as "extending the outreach of the church" but "not under the control of the church"; encouraging the colleges toward the "responsible exercise of academic freedom"; helping to "strengthen" colleges "though active concern, through a variety of services, and through the sharing of leadership"; and to provide financial and other support and "encourage such support from individuals, congregations and other agencies."[34]

With two distinctive paths set out for the college and the synod, and the college relinquishing its earlier responsibility for religious education, the fundamental context for the meaning and purpose of the institution needed to be rethought and rearticulated. The college had lost the religious legitimacy of its prophetic voice but had put nothing in its place. The shared Christian view no longer held sway, as the new faculty represented a diversity of religious and nonreligious perspectives, and the student body questioned the moral authority of religious organizations unwilling to address the current issues of the day. The college had moved into a post-Christian period just as it faced significant institutional challenges, financial, social, and intellectual.

Bereft of a clearly articulated vision and conviction of shared purpose and challenged by the rise of new group identities and agendas at the same time as a fiscal crisis loomed, the college community fragmented and, probably for the first time, questioned its contribution to society. Similarly, as cultural critics have argued, the idealism of the 1960s generally dissolved into individualism and instrumentalism in the next decade. The election of 1972 pitted the supposedly idealistic George McGovern against the realistic Richard Nixon, producing one of the largest landslides in U.S. political history. Steeped in a financial crisis, lacking the supporting purpose of a unifying mission, and struggling with increasing numbers of groups demanding a voice in the processes of institutional decision making, the college by the mid-1970s was fraught with deepening fragmentation and disillusionment. Negotiating institutional democracy was proving a significant challenge.

15

Peaks, Pluralism, and Prosperity

THE SNOW-COVERED GRANITE PEAKS of the Heritage Range of the Ellsworth Mountains in Antarctica have peered out over the continental ice for hundreds of millions of years. One of those peaks, Mount Macalester, juts an impressive 7,972 feet into the frigid sky. Just how a mountain in the Antarctic came to be named after a small liberal arts college in Minnesota is one of the too rarely told stories of this period.

Scientific exploration of the Antarctic was given a boost in the 1960s with the worldwide expansion of science. In the United States, the National Science Foundation (NSF) and the U.S. Navy supported several expeditions to the frozen southern continent, and in 1979 Macalester professor Gerald Webers of the geology department snared a major NSF grant for an expedition, an unusual coup for such a small institution. With the help of the navy, Webers and four Macalester students traveled in November to Antarctica, where they were joined by forty-two other geologists and support people from all over the world, including Japan, the USSR, and New Zealand. The expedition was well equipped, with twelve snowmobiles, three twin-jet helicopters (no more than two in the air at a time), and a camp—fondly named Camp Macalester—consisting of five Quonset huts, complete with kitchen, mess hall, shower, and two flush toilets.

The purpose of the expedition was to study the geological sediments of the continent—three hundred million years of Antarctic history compressed in layer upon layer of bedrock, granite, and sediment. Webers, the students, and the other geologists spent each day at different sites in the Ellsworth Mountains taking ground samples. Cold weather, it turned out, was not much of a problem, for during the period, the Antarctic summer temperatures ranged between five degrees below zero Fahrenheit to thirty degrees above. The twenty-four hours of sunlight each day, though, took some getting used to, according to Webers. The group's research resulted in a stratographic column, or vertical map of the layers of sediment, that remains definitive to this day. And perhaps of even more long-lasting significance, Webers, as head of the expedition, had the honor of naming some of the prominent formations; he dubbed what was then considered the highest peak in the Heritage Range "Mount Macalester."[1]

Mount Macalester stands like a beacon for the college's recovery. No one knew this better than Webers, who four years earlier had served on the search committee for a new college president. At that time, the college was at a particularly low point, having been battered by fiscal cutbacks that required letting go of significant numbers of employees and the loss of many others who found more attractive employment elsewhere. Departmental budgets had been cut to the bone. Long-distance phone calls were permitted only on a case-by-case approval basis. Teaching materials were scarce and teaching techniques that required expenditures were out of the question. This was not a situation conducive to attracting talented leadership, as the search committee quickly learned. But the committee was fortunate and foresightful; their decision would send the college in a new direction—not, certainly, to the top of Mount Macalester but clearly well up from despair.

Back from the Brink

"Macalester is on the edge of the last opportunity for survival," claimed John B. Davis as he was inaugurated into the office of the president in November 1975. The college, which had celebrated its one hundredth anniversary a year earlier, had come full circle, back to the reality of contingency that had characterized its first half-century. The college, Davis warned, may well not survive "without 'redefining its reason for being.'"[2] Over the next two decades, Macalester would in fact negotiate just such a redefinition, moving in a direction that would continue to take the college far from its original roots.

John Davis's warning, coming in November, was a touch anticlimactic, at least financially speaking. The preceding Robinson administration had had little success in stabilizing the college's financial situation. Indeed, by November 1974, the college had reached the end of its credit, carrying a two million dollar loan, and did not have sufficient cash and income to meet the payroll. Trustee John Driscoll personally guaranteed a loan to meet payroll that month. The next month, across-the-board salary decreases were again instituted.[3] That winter, institution leaders knew their last hope lay in finding an effective president who could mend the fences with their estranged donor. As they courted John Davis that spring, he delayed his decision until he had spoken with DeWitt Wallace, which he did on two occasions that summer. Out of those conversations, Wallace agreed to release seven million dollars in restricted endowment funds (held in the Wallace Reserves), to be applied to the college's growing debt. By the end of August, Macalester had repaid the bank the two million dollar note that had come due and had repaid its own endowment about five million dollars in loans borrowed against it. Out of debt, the college that Davis agreed to lead was presented to him with something of a clean financial slate.

Davis was an unexpected and not uncontroversial choice for president, for his background was in secondary, not higher, education. As superintendent of the Minneapolis public schools, Davis had earned a reputation as an effective and progressive administrator. He had spearheaded programs for minority students, kept the budget in line, and opened up dialogue among contentious groups. Nevertheless, many observers wondered how Davis, who held a doctoral degree in education from Harvard, would handle the shift to higher education. As it turned out, Davis did so with a grace and diplomacy that would became characteristic of his leadership and that earned him the legacy of being the most respected college leader since Charles Turck. But where Turck was a singular, sometime autocratic leader, Davis's times called for a very different approach, and he developed effective means of diffusing authority, working with faculty, students, staff, and trustees on issues. This is not to say that he avoided making decisions; on the contrary, he made several very difficult ones, but did so based on input from the various affected constituencies.

Listening, in fact, was Davis's forte. He astonished students by showing up unannounced at events, in the student union, and even in the dorms, chatting with them and learning their views and concerns. No president in the history of the college was as accessible as Davis. Though Flemming and Robinson had held open office hours for student conversations, Davis went out to the students. His interaction with faculty was similar; moreover, he embraced the task of boosting faculty morale, which, after five years of firings, cutbacks, and salary loss, was, to put it mildly, fairly low. The entire campus, Davis observed early in his tenure at the college, had little community feeling. "With all of our campus diversity, independence and different backgrounds, we need more of a people spirit," he said. "I went to a football game last weekend and couldn't find the Macalester cheering section. . . . We must find common bases for communication."[4]

Davis's focus on communication and community soon produced results. Both faculty and students, for instance, praised the way he mediated a dispute between students and administration fiscal authorities regarding the assigning of dorm rooms. A two-year Faculty Renewal Program, developed by professors Charles Green (political science) and Walter Mink (psychology) and launched in 1974 with support from the federal Fund for the Improvement of Post-Secondary Education, continued to encourage faculty collaboration across disciplines and foster a broadening of teaching skills and expertise. Davis's new fiscal team, headed by faculty member Paul Aslanian (economics), established more sophisticated accounting techniques and brought order to the informal and largely ineffective accounting procedures that had led to much of the confusion over expenditures and income in the previous decade. No longer did a "sense of inevitable financial chaos and doom" pervade the campus, and for the first time in decades, college officials and department heads were reassured that the college was functioning within its means.[5] By spring, an external review of the college reported that despite the setbacks of the previous years, the atmosphere on the campus was one of "expectation rather than fulfillment." One faculty member even went so far as to describe the atmosphere as "euphoric."[6] *Relief* might have been a more accurate description.

Uncertainty and a New Chapter

Although Davis had succeeded in inspiring a more positive ethos on campus, another feeling remained present—a feeling of uneasiness or, as one faculty committee described it, "uncertainty" with respect to the purpose of the college. The Curriculum Survey Committee cited "uncertainty" in their discussion of student attrition, noting that the "College's uncertainties about itself make students uncertain of their own future at Macalester."[7] It went on to argue that revision of the curriculum that would clarify its "design and purposes" would go far to dispel at least students' uncertainty and to counter attrition. Faculty uncertainty was another thing entirely, however, for the very mission of the college, its purposes and goals, were no longer stable and could not be taken for granted.

Under review for accreditation in spring 1976, the college community demonstrated little unity with respect to the purpose and goals of the college—little unity, that is, apart from universal agreement that the purposes and goals were not "clear, unambiguous, consistent" or widely agreed on.[8] The review committee took this to mean that the college was undergoing transition, observing that "the present is a time for consolidating, re-thinking, re-focussing," or as one person put it, "a chapter has ended and a new chapter has begun."[9] Given Davis's approach of diffused authority and institutional broad participation in decision making, the shape of that new chapter would be negotiated through the engagement of many diverse voices and perspectives. Many argue that a clear consensus on the purpose and goals of the institution, on its identity and mission, has remained elusive to this day. Others point out that a strongly unified vision of education pervades the campus, even though those who swim in its atmosphere, like fish in water, may not be able to fully perceive it. Indeed, angst over the college's history and identity has emerged over the years as a kind of recurring theme, with the subtext often being that if the institution could just get beyond the "failure" of the Flemming years, it would emerge with a unified community and identity. Contrary to this view, it appears to this author that in looking back at the college's history, one can readily construct a narrative emphasizing a relative consistency of identities and institutional themes that informed earlier eras in an institution's life and that, as argued in the previous chapter, the Flemming years continued. What was new was the diversity of voices and participants in the formation of institutional identity through which, by the middle to late 1970s, the Macalester community members—faculty, students, and administrators—constructed a view of the college as diverse and progressive but not necessarily unified around a single goal. Establishing a shared identity was relatively straightforward in the early decades of the college, when it encompassed a fairly homogeneous community, but the new diversity required a commitment to pluralism, to a dialogue among multiple voices, and to the realization that a shared identity may no longer be a relevant goal.

The College–Synod Compromise

The Presbyterian denomination remained one of the multiple voices involved in the college. By the early 1970s, as outlined in the previous chapter, the college and synod had agreed to formalize their relationship with a covenant that described their complementary, though distinctively different, responsibilities with respect to the college.[10] Over the next several years, the general model of identifying responsibilities of each party persisted, while the list of responsibilities grew. Among the new college responsibilities recommended by the 1981 Presbyterian General Assembly of the Synod were "being sensitive to priority issues and mission concerns of the denomination," including "peace studies and economic justice," areas of interest that had been adopted by the General Assembly as early as 1971 as part of the church's mission and, in particular, its corporate social responsibility and investment guidelines. These guidelines were integrated in the 1981 covenant between the college and the church, which outlined several responsibilities and commitments of each party, based in large measure on the General Assembly document.[11]

The legalistic flavor of both the General Assembly recommendations and the covenant—the latter duly signed by the president of the board of trustees, the college president, the chaplain, the moderator of the synod, the synod executive, and the stated clerk—witnessed to the delicacy with which each party entered into the effort of defining the relationship. It was to Macalester's advantage to retain the relationship because significant endowment resources had been left in trust to the college but were administered by the church (the Bleodel and Synnott trusts). There was also significant feeling that the historical connection to the church and the goodwill generated among Presbyterian churches was of significant value to the institution. On the synod's part, retaining a relationship with the college advanced the educational component of its religious mission and provided an important site for integration with the culture and, in particular, with young people. The college, concerned about academic freedom and unwilling to advance a particular religious position in a period of increasing religious diversity among students, nevertheless needed to keep the church at arm's length. The synod, which had distanced itself from the college significantly during the troubles in the early 1970s, also had concerns about outside perceptions of the relationship between the two institutions. The next time the covenant would be renegotiated, during renewal in 1995, the differing spheres of influence of each and their differing purposes were clearly outlined prior to a discussion of areas of "common affirmation."

Though the covenant described an idealized vision of the relationship between the two institutions, the chaplaincy, and particularly the personal interests of the chaplain, guided the actual role of religion and of Presbyterianism on campus. In 1978, Chaplain Kristine Holmgren initiated a number of new chapel programs addressing social and religious issues, including the "Movements in Theology" series, which featured faculty speakers, and the Church Explorers program, begun a few years earlier, which took interested students on visits to different churches each Sunday. Services continued to be held Sunday evening.[12] A few years later, then chaplain Russell Wigfield took the chapel in a more political direction, becoming deeply involved in the national draft registration controversy that arose in the early 1980s under the Jimmy Carter administration and in nuclear disarmament. His successor, Brent Coffin, emphasized interfaith dialogue, given the growing reality of religious pluralism on the campus, as well as social action in areas such as AIDS awareness and humanitarian intervention in Nicaragua, Guatemala, and El Salvador. Hebrew House, a college-sponsored home for both Jewish and non-Jewish students interested in participating in a variety of Jewish domestic practices, gained a new foothold during this period, having almost closed in 1981, and Rabbi Bernard Raskas taught courses on Hebrew Bible and Judaism in the religious studies department and functioned as an associate chaplain. The Muslim Student Association organized a room in the chapel lower level as a mosque, and Quaker services were held in the building on Sunday mornings. A number of Christian student organizations also flourished.

Religious life at Macalester, as at many colleges across the country, was once again becoming a more grassroots, student-directed activity, returning, one could argue, to an early-twentieth-century model of being not so much led by campus religious officials as fostered by them. As before, student religious organizations intersected with other student organizations in the areas of ethics and service. Ethical commitments, religiously and philosophically based, united students in any number of service activities, from contributing to blood banks and homeless shelters to forming the Macalester chapter of Habitat for Humanity. By the mid-1990s, new shifts in emphasis would again occur with the chaplaincies of Donald Meisel and Lucy Forster-Smith, which emphasized a more Christian worship-centered chaplaincy and student counseling, respectively.

Just how the college functioned, then, as a church-related institution lay in the details, under the surface, rather than as a measure of its public persona. Religious perspectives, particularly on ethical matters, remained of prominent interest, particularly in the Coffin years. But fewer students were interested in organized religious activities, and many were surprised to be reminded from time to time that the college maintained a formal relationship with the Presbyterian Church.[13]

In terms of the religious identity of the college, then, our story is all but complete, though, of course, the role of religion continues to evolve to this day.

The identity of the college itself as Presbyterian, however, had all but disappeared. Most enrolled students, it is safe to say, know little if anything about the historical Presbyterian roots of the college, much less its current relationship with the church. Even the synod no longer suggests that the college is in any way Presbyterian. This is not to say that there is no religious life at the college. Student interest groups dedicated to many religious perspectives flourish, religious services of various types are held in the chapel, and Hebrew House remains successful. In this student-directed environment, the role of the chaplaincy became more responsive than proactive, particularly in the 1990s. And with the development of the covenants, the relationship between the college and the church took on a bracketed character that comfortably separated it from the heart of on-campus religious activities, that is, the student organizations.

This brings us back, then, to the question of what this college's experiences suggest regarding processes of secularization. The most profound shift in the role of Christianity vis-à-vis the college occurred not in the 1960s and 1970s, as the college removed its various religious requirements from the curriculum, but rather in the pre–World War I period, when the belief that knowledge of Christianity was a necessary foundation for all knowledge waned in the face of scientific and social scientific inquiry and methods. Although the twin sisters of the Macalester seal, Revelation and Nature, still conversed, their respective realms of authority separated. Christianity now provided the ethical grounding of the college in the idea of service, whereas science went its own way to learn about the world. Meanwhile, the college took steps toward establishing a chaplaincy precisely because the belief in the Christian foundation of knowledge no longer obtained. Religion had become a separate area of activity and thus needed separate, cocurricular structures to foster it. At the heart of the process was the liberal Protestant perspective, for as the college leadership deevangelicalized and later de-Christianized, the liberal commitment to religious tolerance, service, and justice remained stable and central to the college's identity, while Presbyterianism was increasingly relegated to a separate sphere. In this way, Macalester, like many other formerly church-related colleges, participated in redefining *both* the religious and the secular by relocating the former within new institutional structures and by infusing the latter with values previously connected, in their experience, to Christian creeds. In this example, no secularization process eliminated religion; instead, the two arenas were redefined in relation to one another.

Recent covenants between Macalester and the synod acknowledge that these transformations have occurred and that though each institution—the college and the church—generally pursues its work now in a different arena, doing so does not preclude continuation of the conversation. Nature (in the form of science education) continues to dialogue with Revelation, particularly on topics related to tolerance, service, and justice, but no longer is their relationship codependent.[14]

The Final Wallace Legacy

DeWitt Wallace, age ninety-one, died in his home High Winds in Pleasantville, New York, on March 30, 1981. Lila Acheson Wallace died three years later, on May 8, 1984, at the age of ninety-four. A year before he died, Wallace had given the college two large gifts totaling 5,530 shares of *Reader's Digest* stock, which were to be administered by a supporting organization charged with holding the money in trust and distributing the earnings. Those shares yielded the college about one million dollars in income per year, earmarked for faculty salaries. With this gift, Macalester was able to close a nearly decadelong period of faculty stagnation by hiring new people.

During the 1980s, the college was able to regain some ground and stature in the academic world. A renewed focus on academic distinction was the quest of President Robert Gavin, who took office in 1985. The next year, the college created the new DeWitt Wallace Distinguished Visitors program, bringing to campus top scholars, including Norman Dorsen, president of the American Civil Liberties Union; Harry P. Gray, founder of the field of mathematical physical chemistry; cultural critic Robert Jay Lifton; historian Mary Beth Norton; and Antonin Scalia, constitutional expert.[15] Under Gavin, admissions standards were once again tightened and the college became more selective, resulting in a decline in admission rates from around 80 percent in the early 1980s to between 50 and 60 percent in the 1990s.[16] By 1989, Macalester was listed as an up-and-coming college "worth a closer look" by *U.S. News and World Report.*[17] But everything was about to change.

At Wallace's death, Macalester owned about ten million shares of *Reader's Digest* stock, which Wallace had set aside for the college's use over the many years of his association with it. On Valentine's Day 1990, a chunk of *Reader's Digest* stock went public for the first time. Originally valued at ten to fifteen dollars per share, when the stock went public it quickly split at twenty to one. Macalester's ten million shares were suddenly worth the astonishing figure of three hundred million dollars. Macalester's endowment, which was $65 million in 1989, soared, the national press crowed, to around $320 million.[18]

Things were good, but not that good, for the college did not control the *Reader's Digest* shares, which remained administered by the supporting organization (SO) mentioned earlier. The SO represented eight nonprofit organizations to which the Wallaces had left substantial legacies: Macalester College, the Sloan-Kettering Memorial Hospital, Hudson Highlands (an environmental organization), the New York Zoological Society, Community Funds, the Lincoln Center, the Metropolitan Museum of Art, and Colonial Williamsburg.[19] Representatives of the boards of each served on the SO. Thus Macalester's windfall was in dividends on the stocks, which had also increased significantly since the late 1970s.

Nevertheless, Macalester was substantially better off in mid-1990 than it had been for over a quarter of a century, and perhaps ever. And things began to change quickly. Returning students were greeted by new tile and energy-saving bathroom fixtures in Bigelow, new carpeting and furniture in the Kagin Dining Hall, and the start of renovations to Carnegie. Having put into motion immediate renovations to the rapidly deteriorating physical plant, which had had little attention since the Rice administration, Gavin and other college leaders took stock of the many ways in which the new income could benefit the college, launching a series of conversations throughout the fall. The changes put in place—the hiring of new faculty, the construction of new buildings, the development of new programs and curricula, the purchase of new equipment, and so forth—would transform the college in new ways.

For most of its history, Macalester had been financially strapped. Now, with the Wallace legacy, it was on yet another new financial path, one that the institution itself could guide. As Provost Betty Ivey observed, the college was "laying track into uncharted territory." It would be another decade before the college would wrest control over the *Reader's Digest* shares away from the SO. In the meantime, the shares would lose much of their earlier value as the stock price declined. Nevertheless, the income boost of the early 1990s and Gavin's new policies raised the national visibility of the college and helped to better its position in national rankings of colleges, moving it up into the top twenty-five institutions. Thus, with this legacy, Wallace's vision of Macalester as a nationally prominent college was finally achieved.

A New Era

The Macalester College that I came to know when I became a visiting faculty member in 1998 seemed quite confident in its identity and mission, at least from the perspective of an outsider. A stable, well-funded, politically conscious institution with fine academic standards, Macalester attracted good students from across the county and across the world. Its faculty members were, as a group, dedicated to teaching, but many were also engaged in the production of knowledge, and some were doing cutting-edge research. Students did fine in their courses and were likely to spend their free time engaged with local or national issues, particularly in the areas of environmentalism and social and economic justice.

But what became clear to me after teaching at the college for a couple years was that the Macalester community, particularly the faculty, was neither confident nor certain about the institution's identity. Just what did the college stand for? What held everyone together in a community? Indeed, was there a coherent community at the college? Such questions were often raised in hallways and in meetings. With the advent of the new financial situation, the college entered a period of taking stock, of reassessing itself, of deciding whose voices would be heard and what values would be privileged. Launched about the time I joined the college by President Michael McPherson with a series of discussions on the college's core values, this process of institutional reflection continues to this day. For as the culture has shifted—economically, politically, and socially—in the past decade, so, too, has the college. It will be many years before historians will be able to look back on this period to identify patterns and priorities, to evaluate the process and the influences on it. When they do, however, they will no doubt tell a new story about a college positioning itself within changing local and global contexts and addressing the challenges of the twenty-first century. One theme that is likely to remain, however, is an ongoing effort to construct the education offered at Macalester College in such a way that it engages as fully as possible with those contexts.

Epilogue

THIS BOOK BEGAN with some reflections on the nature of history making: the creation of narratives by selecting certain events and circumstances and interpreting them in particular ways to illustrate a general continuity or disrupt-edness. Is this story of the changing institutional identity and commitments of Macalester College a narrative of continuity or a narrative of disruptedness? Or has this story blazed a path between the two poles, and if so, does that path lead to knowledge and understanding?

. I have chosen to end the narrative just as the college embarked on a new period of financial well-being and renewed drive for academic excellence and national recognition; many new discontinuities would characterize the next decade, but up to this point, a few continuities linking the first half-century of the college with the second stand out. The strongest is that of a dedication to service, the fulcrum on which the college balanced throughout the century. Although the underlying justifications for engaging in service to the region, nation, and world changed over the course of the century, the institution remained dedicated to the idea that it had a responsibility beyond providing classroom education to its students—that it was preparing students to be active citizens, concerned with and about issues of justice, charity, and human rights, and that a complete education includes the development of empathy with and concern for others and that radical individualism and single-minded pursuit of personal gain are not legitimate ways of being in the world.

This commitment to service has been closely linked throughout the century with another thread of continuity, interests and outlooks whose scope goes beyond the local and national to include the international. Internationalism at the college was the offspring of the evangelical concept of service—missionizing and Christianizing the world—that prevailed in the early years of the twentieth century. By mid-century, justification for the study of the world moved far afield from those original roots, just as the justification for service would also step beyond its original Protestant roots. Yet both threads, service and internationalism, remain to this day distinctive features of the institutional commitment and identity of the college.

In those changing justifications, however, significant disruptedness is apparent. Most obviously, the college no longer maintains an institutional outlook based on a particular religious perspective, despite the fact that it does continue to maintain a formal relationship with the Presbyterian Church. The reasons that the college let go of the institutional Presbyterian identity are relatively clear. Most important, that identity began to give way in the interwar period as a result of the deevangelicalization of the institution. In large measure, the purpose of founding a Presbyterian (or a Protestant nonsectarian) institution of higher education was to advance the mission of the church and evangelical Christianity itself. By educating citizens to be good Protestants, the college would spread Christianity through its graduates. Thus the purpose of the college was to evangelize. By the 1930s, however, the evangelical outlook was being rejected by many people associated with the college. When Charles Turck became president, he not only deemphasized the former missionizing goal but also translated the service and international themes to which it had given rise into a new national language of democratic participation. Service and internationalism in the interest of democracy were based, to be sure, on principles of brotherhood and justice, informed by Turck's understanding of Christianity, but that understanding did not include allegiance to the exclusivity claims of the former evangelical position. Embracing a more liberal theology, Turck welcomed all comers to the table, and his championing of the United Nations became a fitting symbol for his inclusivist religious as well as political convictions.

This liberal Protestant perspective itself would recede in the 1960s, as the college pursued a new goal of academic excellence and leadership. During these years, service remained linked to a general Christian understanding of doing good for others, but the religious perspective no longer drove the administration's or the trustees' institutional agendas. With respect to internationalism, a new type of missionizing arose, linking the purpose of studying international situations with the spread of U.S. democratic systems globally. Moreover, the suspicion that religious commitments hampered rigorous academic advancement grew markedly. Classes in the religion department, particularly, came under great scrutiny, and the courses in religious education, which had traditionally been little more than Sunday school instruction designed to confirm the largely Protestant student body's beliefs, were eliminated. Precisely because of this shift in institutional commitment to Protestantism, the college and the synod reconstructed their relationship, drafting formal agreements that outlined their distinctive, separate spheres and a few areas of shared interest. The language of the "church-related college and the college-related church" was floated, but rarely did the respective religious or academic purposes of the two institutions truly join or inform one another.

This is not to say that religious perspectives would no longer be evident at the college. But they would never again drive the agendas. Even when ordained Methodist Arthur Flemming connected the college's minority programs to a broadly Christian agenda, he did not speak for the college itself, which had pursued Expanded Educational Opportunities not out of a distinctively Christian perspective but rather from a political understanding of social justice that, though perhaps once informed by Christianity, was by the late 1960s itself a distinctively secular concept. And Flemming was the last of the Macalester presidents to make an effort to link agendas to religious concepts or outlooks. The college successfully transformed the previously religious conceptual foundations for its endeavors into nonreligious concepts and contexts, while maintaining many of the endeavors themselves, including internationalism and service.

Disruptedness is apparent in other areas as well, as other elements of the pre–World War II Macalester identity faded in the 1960s and 1970s. Shortly after World War II, Mary Gwen Owen rightly characterized the college's context as "white, Republican, and Presbyterian," a description that had applied to the institution since its founding. By the 1990s, these descriptors no longer obtained, not because there were no individuals left who claimed these categories but rather because the Macalester community was more racially, politically, and religiously diverse and, more important, because the institution was no longer committed to retaining the privileged position of these groups.[1] Other voices and perspectives gained predominance; a commitment to multiculturalism, liberal social and political agendas, and religious pluralism supplanted the earlier categories.

Though these ideological, social, and political disruptions and transformations were critical in defining the changing character and identity of the institution, underlying them were significant periods of financial crisis, each of which also played a significant role in defining the college. Had Edward Duffield Neill and the early trustees been able to amass significant funding from eastern or local supporters in the 1870s, the college would have opened without the Presbyterian imprimatur. Because it did, and because of the ongoing financial crisis, particularly after the turn of the century, underscoring its Presbyterian identity became an expedient choice. As the crisis waned and the financial situation grew somewhat better with the help of new donor DeWitt Wallace in the late 1930s, independence from that denominational identity became possible. Though Turck did not pursue such independence, he did refuse to acquiesce to denominational policies, shaping the Presbyterian college around a liberal Protestantism that was partially but not entirely embraced by the church itself. By the 1960s, another spurt of Wallace dollars, along with a new aspiration for educational leadership in the national context, significantly reshaped the college's identity yet again. And when those dollars were no longer available, a distressing period of uncertainty settled on the institution. Thus, in this story of one institution's negotiation of educational priorities and institutional mission and identity, these important categories are closely linked to changing financial situations. In this regard, Macalester's history is quite like that of countless other small colleges for whom the wolf at the door was a frequent visitor and failure often loomed.

Overall, then, perhaps more than either continuity or disruptedness, this story is one of continual change and contingency. Education must necessarily change to remain relevant to changing social, political, economic, and cultural circumstances. Indeed, change in education can, in some cases, lead change in other areas. Institutions also experience change, but it is contingency that best characterizes a great deal of institutional change. Time after time in the preceding material, we have seen the college change—move in new and unexpected directions—despite carefully laid plans and periods of consensus. Unforeseen circumstances arise, and the responses can shift the goals, the mission, and even the identity of a college.

In the late 1990s, after the Wallace legacy had arrived, after the physical plant had been spruced up, after admissions standards had been tightened, and after procedures to ratchet up promotion and tenure decisions for faculty had been put in place, all under the administration of then president Robert Gavin, the college once again had the luxury of reexamining itself, taking on the project of defining its core values under the leadership of the next president, Michael McPherson. Those discussions picked up the thread that had been dropped in the despair of the 1970s. Concern for purpose, now couched in philosophical rather than religious terms, reemerged. The college was providing an increasingly excellent education to students, but just why was it doing so? What were the institution's underlying goals now? These questions needed attention. Quite naturally, the thread of service provided a starting point for discussion and action, with the college becoming involved in a variety of new civic engagement initiatives, to use the contemporary phrase. Under McPherson, the college became involved with Project Pericles, a national group organized to cultivate engagement between institutions of higher education and communities, and with the Lilly Endowment Program in the Theological Exploration of Vocation, a national initiative that, at Macalester, took the form of a five-year exploration of work and values.

Macalester's identity at the turn of the twenty-first century was once again bound up in a search for values, for meaning, for purpose. Although meaning and purpose were more readily identified in the earlier decades of the college, when Christianity provided the informing ideology, and although institutional articulation of alternate ideals faltered in the post-Christian period, concern for the underlying meaning of education remains the defining characteristic of the college. Edward Neill's seal for the college, the Heavenly Twins, Nature and Revelation, remains relevant, if secularized, as the Macalester community remains committed to, in McPherson's words, a "sense of all good things go together"; the institution must be "receptive to scientific and humanistic knowledge."[2] The search for values, mission, and purpose will no doubt carry the college for many more decades.

Notes

1. *Identity and Change*

1 Edward D. Neill to Board of Trustees of Macalester College, May 13, 1892, copybook, Neill Family Papers, Box 6, Folder 1, Minnesota Historical Society.

2 E.g., James Burtchaell, a Catholic scholar, adopts the secularization thesis, arguing that colleges founded on Christian principles lost or abandoned their Christian aspects through a variety of internal and external pressures to secularize. See Burtchaell, *Dying of the Light.* Historian of evangelicalism George Marsden suggests that colleges founded on Christian principles and moral values retained many of these elements but divorced them from their Christian roots as secular society grew hegemonic. See Marsden, *Soul of the American University.* Historian Merrimon Cuninggim modified this narrative, suggesting that the distancing that occurred between colleges and denominations was unsurprising, given the rocky character of those relationships, which he calls "uneasy partnerships." See Cuninggim, *Uneasy Partners.* Countering these narratives, Conrad Cherry, Betty DeBerg, and Amanda Porterfield have challenged the idea that former church-related colleges are now in fact oceans of unbelief, citing abundant evidence of ongoing and, indeed, vigorous engagement with religion among students on college campuses. See Cherry et al., *Religion on Campus.* Similarly, historian David Hollinger, pointing to the diversity of religious outlooks now visible in institutions of higher education, has argued that institutional change over the twentieth century is best characterized not as a "secularization," which has been, by now, associated with strongly negative connotations of loss, but rather as a "de-Christianization," which has been beneficial and democratic, opening up college education to non-Christian, and particularly Jewish, faculty and students. See Hollinger, "The 'Secularization' Question."

3 Eamon Duffy, "Back to the Cross," *Times Literary Supplement,* August 5, 2002, 25.

4 Ibid.

5 Ibid.

2. Christian Education and Institution Building in St. Paul

1 On early St. Paul history, see Wingerd, *Claiming the City*, 19–22. See also Hoffmann, *Church Founders*, 119–20.

2 Hoffmann, *Church Founders*, 25.

3 Biographical details of Neill's life appear in Dupre, *Edward Duffield Neill*, 24–26; [Janssen], *Edward Duffield Neill*, typescript, n.p., ca. 1937, Macalester College Archives; Johnson, *A Journey of Hope*, 9; and "Dr. Neill Is Dead," *St. Paul Pioneer Press*, September 27, 1893. Neill was sent as a missionary to the white population, but he was not the first Presbyterian missionary in the region. Two Presbyterian brothers, Gideon and Samuel Pond, had been working among the Dakota since 1834.

4 On the early founding of the state, see Folwell, *A History of Minnesota*.

5 Tewksbury, *Founding of American Colleges and Universities*, 55.

6 See ibid., 32. Princeton's original name was the College of New Jersey.

7 "The Yale Report of 1828, Part I, Liberal Education and Collegiate Life," http://www.collegiateway.org/reading/yale-1828a.html, 4. See also Rudolph, *Curriculum*, 65–67.

8 Dupre, *Edward Duffield Neill*, 14, quoting Richard Salter Stores, class of 1839, quoted in Hammond, *Remembrance of Amherst*, 100.

9 Rudolph, *Curriculum*, 27, quoting Kelley, *Yale*, 70.

10 Dupre, *Edward Duffield Neill*, 14, quoting Stores from Hammond, *Remembrance of Amherst*.

11 Amherst students had organized a missionary society during the 1820s, which was still functioning during Neill's time on campus.

12 Neill's mother was particularly influential in his decision. Her grandfather, father, and several brothers were noted ministers. See Neill Family Papers, Box 1, Folder 2, Minnesota Historical Society.

13 On Andover, see Williams, *Andover Liberals*, 1–14.

14 Congregationalism, which developed in the eighteenth century, traces its roots to seventeenth-century New England Puritanism, which grew from efforts to reform the Church of England. Similarly, Presbyterianism developed in mid-seventeenth-century Scotland, Ireland, and England in response to elements in Anglican theology, polity, and worship practice.

15 Williams, *Andover Liberals*, 13, quoting Henry K. Rowe, *History of Andover Theological Seminary* (Newton, Mass.: n.p., 1933), 35.

16 On New School and Old School Presbyterians, see Balmer and Fitzmier, *Presbyterians*, 47–49.

17 Neill Family Papers, Box 1, Folder 3, Minnesota Historical Society.

18 *Journal of the Council during the First Session of the Legislative Assembly of the Territory of Minnesota* (St. Paul, 1850), 68–69, as quoted in Dupre, *Edward Duffield Neill*, 37–38.

19 Dupre, *Edward Duffield Neill*, 44–47.

20 See List of Subscribers to the Preparatory Department of the University of Minnesota, Neill Family Papers, Box 1, Folder 6, Correspondence 1850–52, Minnesota Historical Society.

21 Neill, *History of Minnesota*, 642–43. Historian James Gray sneers at Neill's complaint regarding "stamps and stationary" and attributed his resignation to a fit of temper. Given the struggle to support his family and the lack of state funding for its flagship educational institution, Neill's pique is understandable. See Gray, *University of Minnesota*, 23.

22 Gray, *University of Minnesota*, 23. Neill was not entirely unsuccessful in his work with the university, though evidence of success would come only years after he left the position. During his tenure as chancellor, Neill had rigorously argued that the state legislature owed the new university a significant grant of land, in addition to the original parcel that had been granted the so-called territorial university years earlier. The new state university had received no land and, in Neill's estimation, deserved another parcel. Though during the economically tight years of the 1850s and 1860s, the legislature refused to agree with this perspective, several years after Neill left the office, the legislature did in fact make the second grant, consisting of two additional townships. See also Roberts, "An Early Political and Administrative History."

23 Neill, *History of Minnesota*, 512, 520, 522. Castle, *History of St. Paul and Vicinity*, 455, 490.

24 Minnesota Neill, "Sketch by Miss Minnesota Neill," January 17, 1930, typescript, p. 2, Neill Family Papers, Box 7, Folder 7, Minnesota Historical Society.

25 Ibid., 3–6. The framed chapel was short-lived, burning to the ground the next spring. Within a few months, it was replaced with a brick church at the corner of Third and St. Peter.

26 Neill's offspring were Minnesota (b. 1850), Samuel (b. 1852), Henry (b. 1855), Edward Jr. (b. 1858), and John Selby Martin (b. 1860).

27 Edward D. Neill to Nancy Hall Neill, June 20, 1850, Neill Family Papers, Box 1, Folder 6, Minnesota Historical Society. On this early period, see also Edward D. Neill, "Historical Discourse," *Minutes of the Synod of Minnesota*, vol. 1, St. Paul, 1870.

28 Baldwin's biographer notes that Barnes and Baldwin were "lifelong friends." Calkins, *Memorial of Matthias W. Baldwin*, 26, 43, 162. Baldwin's name appears on an undated list of donors to the construction of a Presbyterian church in St. Paul, which is likely from Neill's 1851 trip to Philadelphia to secure funds for that purpose. See Neill Family Papers, Box 8, Folder 2, Minnesota Historical Society. Baldwin may have also known Neill's cousin, George Duffield, who wrote an obituary on Baldwin at his death. See George Duffield, *American Presbyterian*, September 27, 1866, cited in Calkins, *Memorial of Matthias W. Baldwin*, 41n.

29 Despite the term *college* in the name of the school, the Baldwin School contained a primary school and the equivalent of a high school or prep school. College courses would not be offered in any Neill school until the opening of Macalester. Matthias

W. Baldwin to EDN, January 4, 1852, Neill Family Papers, Box 1, Folder 6, Minnesota Historical Society. See also Edward D. Neill to Matthias Baldwin, undated, Neill Family Papers, Box 1, Folder 7, Minnesota Historical Society.

30 On the Baldwin School, see Neill, *History of Minnesota*, 587.

31 The importance of this toasting ritual is indicated by a large, highly decorated porcelain punch bowl, brought to St. Paul by Henry Sibley and now housed in the collection of the Minnesota Historical Society. That this fragile artifact was carefully transported to the region by one of these eastern exiles indicates the significance of the social ritual. The toasting itself consisted of the assigning of toast topics by the host. Each speaker then received a slip of paper on which the topic had been written and was called on to make his oration. Toasting speaks to the rhetorical skills these men would have developed during their college years.

32 "Addresses at the Supper," in *Addresses Delivered at the Dedication of the Edifice of the Preparatory Department of the Baldwin School, Saint Paul, Minnesota Territory; and Catalogue for 1853* (St. Paul: Owens and Moore, 1854), 18–19.

33 Ibid., 21.

34 Ibid., 27.

35 Edward D. Neill, "Dedicatory Remarks," in *Addresses Delivered at the Dedication*, 9–10.

36 Ibid., 39.

37 Ibid., 10.

38 Ibid., 10–11.

39 Ibid.

40 Years later, Neill wrote to Baldwin to say that he had "exhausted my wife's little patrimony in my efforts to [advance?] religion and education." Edward D. Neill to Matthias Baldwin, January 23, 1864, Neill Family Papers, Minnesota Historical Society.

41 Joseph Cretin to Lyons Propagation of the Faith Society, February 22, 1854, and March 14, 1855, as quoted in Hoffmann, *Church Founders*, 337.

42 Joseph Cretin to Lyons Propagation of the Faith Society, February 22, 1854, and March 14, 1855, as quoted in Hoffmann, *Church Founders*, 337.

43 Neill, *History of Minnesota*, 586n1.

44 Ibid., 586–87.

45 Neill, *Nature and Importance*, 3, 6–8. Among Neill's other charges were that Catholic education was controlled by Rome and that students "chiefly receive oral instruction," which left them "unable to read or write" and thus unfit for public office (7).

46 Among Catholics' concern regarding the Bible were differences in translation, but of greater importance was the idea that whatever version was used, it was corrupted by Protestant interpretation. Furthermore, teachers' use of the Bible—giving students a number of verses to read on their own without commentary or explanation—was an approach antithetical to the Catholic requirement that lay readers look to clergy for biblical interpretation.

47 Neill, *Report of the Committee on Schools*, 7; italics in original.

48 Edward D. Neill, "Official Decision," *St. Paul Pioneer and Dispatch*, August 7, 1860, 1. Neill was certainly not alone in holding these opinions, which were relatively widespread among Protestants during the period. These positions and use of the term *sectarian* owed a great deal to debates over church and state questions addressed in the East in previous years. In 1844, Neill's hometown of Philadelphia erupted in public controversy when Catholics challenged the use of the King James Bible in public schools. Nativism and Know-Nothingism spread quickly among Protestants, and the American Republican Party in the city sponsored several "Save the Bible" rallies and issued a platform statement championing the neutrality of the King James version: "Resolved, that the Bible, without note or comment, is not sectarian—that it is the fountainhead of all morality and all good government, and should be used in our public schools as a reading book." See Boston, "When Christians Killed Each Other." Shortly after this, Philadelphia exploded in anti-Catholic riots that left several people dead and two Catholic churches burned. Whether Neill was present in Philadelphia that summer is not known; he had recently graduated from Andover Seminary and began teaching in Virginia within a few months. Nevertheless, given his growing interest in religious education, he no doubt was in communication with family, friends, and Presbyterian clergy who apprised him of the situation.

49 "The Dedicatory Services at Macalester College," *Northwest Chronicle*, September 24, 1885.

50 *Addresses Delivered at the Dedication*, 21.

51 Ibid.; italics in original.

52 Ibid., 22.

53 Neill, *Report of the Committee on Schools*. See also Dupre, *Edward Duffield Neill*, 64–65.

54 Neill's use of the term *college* to indicate a boys' prep school has led to confusion that the 1874 charter renaming the Baldwin School Macalester College indicated that the enterprise would now be devoted to higher education. Although Macalester College, when it eventually opened, was devoted to higher education, the institution also retained a preparatory school for boys and girls, variously referred to as Macalester College and the Baldwin School.

55 On the Neill home and Summit Avenue, see Sandeen, *St. Paul's Historic Summit Avenue*, 1–2.

56 Folwell, *A History of Minnesota*, 1:363–64. See also Wills, *Boosters, Hustlers, and Speculators*, 80–81, 89–96; Wingerd, *Claiming the City*, 28–29.

57 See Theron Baldwin to Edward D. Neill, January 6 and May 16, 1857; and May 5 and 19, 1858, Neill Family Papers, Minnesota Historical Society.

58 On the founding of House of Hope Church, see Johnson, *A Journey of Hope*, 9–10.

59 Folwell, *History of Minnesota*, 3:84, 360. Neill, *History of Minnesota*, 650; Dupre, *Edward Duffield Neill*, 66–67.

60　It is possible that Neill resigned due to decreases in chaplains' salaries. See his undated manuscript, "The Constant Effort to Lower the Salary and Thus the Standard of Chaplains in the Army," Neill Family Papers, Box 9, Folder 2, Document 19, Minnesota Historical Society.

61　Edward D. Neill to Nancy Hill Neill, July 18, 1862, Neill Family Papers, Box 2, Folder 3, Minnesota Historical Society.

62　Edward D. Neill to Nancy Hill Neill, February 2, July 18, July 25, and July 26, 1862; Alexander Ramsey to Edward D. Neill, February 19, 1862, Neill Family Papers, Minnesota Historical Society. Given that Ramsey was a good friend of the Neills, along with Nancy's proximity to him in St. Paul, one wonders whether she had a hand in persuading the governor to act on behalf of her husband. An interesting fictional account of the financial hardships endured by a wife of a home missionary minister during the period appears in Beecher, *From Dawn to Daylight*.

63　Edward D. Neill to Nancy Hill Neill, January 22, 1864, Neill Family Papers, Minnesota Historical Society.

64　Matthias Baldwin to Edward D. Neill, February 12, 1864; see letters with a similar theme, Baldwin to Edward D. Neill, January 17 and 19, 1865, Neill Family Papers, Box 3, Folder 1, Minnesota Historical Society. See also undated letter from Neill to Baldwin, Box 3, Folder 3. On January 20, 1865, Baldwin asks Neill to intervene in a problem he is having with Washington legislators and offers him 33% of the profit to be gained (or about twenty thousand dollars) if the problem is smoothed out. Neill seems to have attempted to address the situation, but whether he met with any success is unknown.

65　Letter signed by ten men, March 11, 1865, Neill Family Papers, Box 3, Folder 2; see also undated letter from Ramsey to Lincoln, Neill Family Papers, Box 3, Folder 1, Minnesota Historical Society. President Andrew Johnson appointed Major General Oliver Otis Howard, who had established a reputation as being one sympathetic to African American advancement. Though Howard's career would remain primarily military, he would become a founder of Howard University and, later, a noted historian of the West.

66　The exact amount of this "Baldwin Fund," as Neill called it, is unclear. Neill maintained in later years that it totaled twenty-five thousand dollars. See Neill, *Historical Notes*, 21. An earlier document put the donations to the Baldwin School (excepting those from Baldwin) at eight thousand dollars. See Edward D. Neill, *History of Macalester College* (n.p.: ca. 1873), bound with several other pamphlets by Neill. Edward D. Neill, *Neill Historical Pamphlets, 1863–88* (n.p., n.d.), Macalester College Archives.

67　Neill's specifications for the Baldwin Lectureship appear in a letter from Edward D. Neill to "My Dear Judge," May 3, 1869, Neill Family Papers, Box 3, Folder 4, Minnesota Historical Society.

68　Neill, *English Colonization of America*.

3. *The Idea of a Christian College*

1   Edward D. Neill, "Memorandum in re Macalester College," manuscript, Neill Family Papers, Box 10, vol. 3, 7, Minnesota Historical Society. It should be noted that Neill and the Baldwin trustees had made some attempt at reopening the college in 1864, when they petitioned for, and were granted, a change in the original Baldwin School charter by the state of Minnesota. In the March 3, 1864, act of the legislature, the name "Baldwin School" was changed to "Baldwin University," to which all the assets, rights, and privileges previously granted to the College of St. Paul were conveyed. See Edward D. Neill, Appendix, *Brief History of Macalester College*, bound in *Neill Historical Pamphlets*, undated, Macalester College Archives.

2   Henry M. Knox to Edward D. Neill, March 21, 1871, Neill Family Papers, Box 3 Addendum, Minnesota Historical Society.

3   Neill, "Memorandum." This and the preceding quotation present a negative view of the situation, which is in part influenced by the financial difficulties of the 1880s, the period during which Neill was writing this memoir.

4   Ibid.

5   Technically, this should be considered a "reopening." As discussed in the previous chapter, the Baldwin School had initially opened through Neill's efforts in 1853, with 125 students, both boys and girls, and funded by Matthias Baldwin. Baldwin died in 1866, leaving no legacy for the school, which closed shortly after.

6   "Letter to Hon. Eugene M. Wilson, Mayo of Minneapolis," circular letter from Edward D. Neill, November 1, 1872, Neill Family Papers, Minnesota Historical Society.

7   Jesus College Handbill, Neill Family Papers, Box 3, Folder 5, Correspondence, 1870–71, Minnesota Historical Society. Handbill is stapled to a letter dated December 21, 1871, from the second assistant secretary, Department of State, Washington, D.C., to Neill. See also *Statement of the Object of Jesus College*, pamphlet, Minnesota Historical Society.

8   "Letter to Hon. Eugene M. Wilson."

9   Thomas A. McCurdy, "*History of Macalester College, Saint Paul, Minnesota* by the Rev. Professor Henry D. Funk, Reviewed by Rev. Thomas A. M'Curdy, D.D., LL.D., President, Macalester College, 1884–1890," typescript, [1910], 3, Macalester College Archives.

10 Edward D. Neill, *Jesus College, Its Aim and Name*, Minneapolis, Minn., 1872.

11 Ibid.

12 Ibid.

13 On Charles Macalester, see http://www.glenfoerd.org/history/history1.html. On Charles Macalester's financial dealings, see Gatell, "Spoils of the Bank War," 40n26, 42, and Hamilton, "Texas Bonds and Northern Profits," 587, 591. On his political influence, see Fowler, "Congressional Dictation," 37.

14 See "Dr. Neill Is Dead," *St. Paul Pioneer Press*, September 27, 1893, regarding the relationship between Neill and Macalester.

15 Charles Macalester to Edward D. Neill, June 4, 1873, Neill Family Papers, Box 3, Folder 6, Minnesota Historical Society.

16 Macalester died on December 1, 1873. On the bequest, see Probate document, July 11, 1877, Neill Family Papers, Box 7, Folder 4, Minnesota Historical Society. See also Jno. B. Gest to Neill, December 23, 1873, Neill Family Papers, Box 3, Folder 6, Minnesota Historical Society.

17 Neill's frustration with the Baldwin School trustees is mentioned by his sister. See Emily [Neill] to Neill, October 10, 1872, Neill Family Papers, Box 3, Folder 6, Minnesota Historical Society.

18 Edward D. Neill to Mrs. Berghman, December 31, 1873, Neill Family Papers, Box 3, Folder 6, Minnesota Historical Society.

19 S—— Berghman to Edward D. Neill, January 8, 1874, Neill Family Papers, Box 3, Folder 6, Minnesota Historical Society.

20 Macalester College historian Henry Daniel Funk reports that the Berghman letter was entered into the Minutes of the Trustees of Macalester College, Record "A," 18–19. The present location of these minutes is unknown. The transcript of the Berghman letter is taken from Funk, *History of Macalester College*, 43. Funk, who did not have access to the Neill letter and was unaware of Neill's role in the creation of the Berghman letter, inaccurately traces the school's nonsectarian character and Presbyterian representation on the board of trustees to Berghman and, by extension, to Macalester himself. (Neill's daughter Minnesota did not donate Neill's papers to the Minnesota Historical Society until around 1916.)

21 Guelzo, *For the Union*, 3.

22 David Cummings, as quoted in Guelzo, *For the Union*, 206.

23 See George D. Cummins to EDN, January 13, February 16, February 17, March 2, March 19, July 9, July 28, and August 11, 1874, Neill Family Papers, Box 3, Folder 6, Minnesota Historical Society.

24 On the Reformed Episcopal Church, see Guelzo, *For the Union*.

25 Dupre, *Edward Duffield Neill*.

26 Edward D. Neill, *Some Principles of the Reformed Episcopal Church, Stated in a Letter to the Presbytery of St. Paul, April 10, 1874*, bound in EDN, *Neill Historical Pamphlets, 1863–1888*, Macalester College Archives. A good indication of Neill's preference for worship appears in the order of worship of the Jesus College chapel service. That order closely follows the Presbyterian order used during the period, beginning with a responsive reading and moving on to the doxology; the confession of sin; the Lord's Prayer; a responsive reading from the Old Testament; a praise song such as the Te Deum Laudamus, Magnificat, or Benedic Anima Mea; a New Testament reading; a congregational chant such as Luke 1:68–71 or Psalm 67 or 23; the Apostle's Creed; prayers by the minister; the sermon; and the benediction. See *Jesus College Chapel Service Arranged by the Provost, Rev. Edward D. Neill* (n.p., n.d.), bound in *Neill Historical Pamphlets, 1863–1888*, Macalester College Archives.

27 Ibid.

28 See A. Milton Baker et al. to EDN, August 16, 1877, Neill Family Papers, Box 4, Folder 1, Minnesota Historical Society.

29 Neill, *Thoughts on the American College*, 5n.

30 On anti-Catholicism in the antebellum period in the United States, see Lannie and Diethorn, "For the Honor and Glory of God," 44–106; Higham, *Strangers in the Land*; and Franchot, *Roads to Rome*.

31 Neill, *Thoughts on the American College*.

32 "Dedicatory Services at Macalester College."

33 Neill's dislike of Catholicism is evident in some of his writings, including his article "Maryland Not a Roman Catholic Colony; Stated in Three Letters" (Minneapolis: Johnson and Smith, 1875), a revisionist article arguing that it was not Catholic political leaders who had established the concept of religious tolerance in the colony of Maryland, granted by James I in 1632 to the Catholic Calvert family as a proprietorship, but, as he argued, Protestants, who made up the majority population in the colony and the legislature. Neill also berated the Catholic doctrine of transubstantiation. See an undated manuscript sermon, Neill Family Papers, Box 9, Folder 2, Document 24, Minnesota Historical Society.

Neill was not alone in his anti-Catholicism. The Reverend David James Burrell, whom Neill knew as the pastor of Westminster Church in Minneapolis from 1887 to 1891 and who served as president of Macalester from 1890–91, published an anti-Catholic pamphlet titled *The Roman Catholic Church vs. the American Public School* around this period. In it, he argues that the hierarchy of the Catholic Church threatens republicanism and the focus of that threat is in the public schools, which will collapse, along with the republic, if Catholic efforts to eliminate the religious (Protestant) foundation of lessons are successful. He urges his Protestant readers to take heed and speak out against Catholic efforts and to be on guard against Catholic "blarney" (duplicity) presented in the form of efforts to work with Protestants—he uses the example of St. Paul's archbishop John Ireland working with the National Education Association. Though such individuals seem to be well-meaning, he warns, they are concealing a "dagger" with which they intend to eviscerate the entire school system.

Neill seems to have had some contact with Archbishop Ireland. Ireland, for instance, read Neill's work on Maryland and critiqued it in a letter to Neill. See John Ireland to Edward D. Neill, February 21, 1881, Neill Family Papers, Box 4, Folder 2, Minnesota Historical Society.

34 The late-nineteenth-century connotations of the term *sect* have a good deal in common with late-twentieth-century connotations of the term *cult*. Both were frequently understood to suggest a hierarchically organized group whose leadership wielded inordinate power over congregants.

35 Manuscript, July 7, 1874, Neill Family Papers, Box 7, Folder 4, Minnesota Historical Society.

36 Manuscript resolution, July 14, 1874, Neill Family Papers, Box 7, Folder 4, Minnesota Historical Society.

37 During the same period, the synod saw an increase in Presbyterian church membership of 5,731 (for an 1880 total of 8,090). The number of Presbyteries increased by one and the number of churches by approximately fifteen. Edwards, *History of the Synod*, 117, 118.

38 See, e.g., Knox to Neill, March 21, 1871, Neill Family Papers, Box 3, Folder 5, Minnesota Historical Society.

39 *Minutes of the Synod of Minnesota, Presbyterian Church in the U.S.A.*, vol. 1, 1870–84.

40 John B. Gest to Edward D. Neill, January 5, 1875; George H. Kyd to Edward D. Neill, February 27, 1875, Neill Family Papers, Box 3, Folder 7, Minnesota Historical Society.

41 H. [K...] Taylor to unnamed recipient, April 22, 1875, Neill Family Papers, Box 3, Folder 7, Minnesota Historical Society.

42 Edward D. Neill to Rev. H. A. Boardman, April 18, 1877, Neill Family Papers, Box 4, Folder 1, Minnesota Historical Society.

43 Edward D. Neill to H. A. Boardman, April 18, 1877, Neill Family Papers, Box 4, Folder 1, Minnesota Historical Society.

44 H. A. Boardman to Neill, April 28, 1877, Neill Family Papers, Box 4, Folder 1, Minnesota Historical Society.

45 See *Minutes of the Synod of Minnesota*, September 30, 1872, 79.

46 Ibid. See also Synod of Minnesota, Ed. Ctte. Reports, October 14, 1876, 183, and October 15, 1877, 218.

47 Edwards, *History of the Synod*, 87. The synod apparently revisited the question during 1879, as well. See David R. Breed to Neill, March 24, 1879, Neill Family Papers, Box 4, Folder 1, Minnesota Historical Society.

48 Edwards, *History of the Synod*, 86–95.

49 H. L. Moss to Trustees of Macalester College, September 27, 1880, Neill Family Papers, Box 4, Folder 2, Minnesota Historical Society.

50 Ibid.

4. *Twin Cities Rivalry*

1 See Wingerd, *Claiming the City*, 34–41.

2 Wills, *Boosters, Hustlers, and Speculators*, 199–200; see also Wingerd, *Claiming the City*, 34.

3 See Wingerd, *Claiming the City*; see also Kunz, "An Excess of Zeal," 4–8.

4 H. L. Moss to Associate Trustees of Macalester College, September 27, 1880, Neill Family Papers, Box 4, Folder 2, Minnesota Historical Society.

5 Ibid.

6 Ibid.

7   Ibid.

8   Edwards, *History of the Synod*, 149–51.

9   "Presbyterian Doings," *St. Paul and Minneapolis Pioneer Press*, October 17, 1880, 1–2.

10 Minutes of the General Assembly, 1882, 91, as quoted in Funk, *History of Macalester College*, 87. Macalester historian Henry Daniel Funk points out that the Congregationalists were well ahead of the Presbyterians in advancing education in the West, having organized their college aid society in 1844 and having accumulated some $1,352,000 for their twenty-six colleges by 1882. See Funk, *History of Macalester College*, 89.

11 The Winslow House, with over one hundred rooms, was poorly designed for a school. Its construction was relatively unsafe, and the interior was nearly impossible to heat. Furthermore, its location in the busy mill district rendered it unusable as a college. See "The College Hospital," *Minneapolis Tribune*, March 20, 1885, 3. The Winslow House was used as the college hospital for a few years, but by 1888, it had been sold to the city of Minneapolis, which razed the building to put up the Exposition Building.

    Regarding the other sites considered for the college, the University Avenue land, a parcel of sixty acres, was owned by Girart Hewitt, E. F. Drake, A. DeGraff, Alexander Ramsey, Holyoke, and D. A. Robertson, with Ramsey being a trustee of the college. The St. Anthony Park land, a parcel of thirty acres, was owned by the Knapp, Stout, and Tainter logging company of Menomonie, Wisconsin, and William Marshall, governor of Minnesota and trustee of Macalester. Girart Hewitt to E. D. Neill, November 16, 1875, Neill Family Papers, Box 3, Folder 7; Henry M. Rice to E. D. Neill, March 17 and March 27, 1876, Neill Family Papers, Box 3, Folder 7; William R. Marshall to E. D. Neill, April 18, 1876, Neill Family Papers, Box 3, Folder 7, Minnesota Historical Society. The Calhoun site is mentioned in an undated document, Neill Family Papers, Box 8, Folder 1, Minnesota Historical Society.

12 On Summit Avenue, see Sandeen, *St. Paul's Historic Summit Avenue*.

13 See William R. Marshall to Trustees of Macalester College, January 25, 1881, Neill Family Papers, Box 4, Folder 2, Minnesota Historical Society. Cf. manuscript agreement in Neill's hand, February 10, 1882, Neill Family Papers, Box 7, Folder 6, Minnesota Historical Society. The location of the land is described as "the West half of Southeast quarter Sec. four (4) Township no. Twenty Eight (28)."

14 Dr. D. F. Dunsmoor had made a bid of forty thousand dollars on the building with the intention of turning it into a hospital for the college. Documentation as to whether this bid was accepted is inconclusive. The synod reported the bid in its minutes of 1881. See Edwards, *History of the Synod*, 354. See also Thomas Cochran to Edward D. Neill, August 30, 1881; D. F. Dunsmoor to the Committee on the Sale of the Macalester College Building, September 15, 1881, and November 17, 1881, which report negotiations in the asking price. See also William W. Porter to E. D. Neill, October 21, 1881, Neill Family Papers, Box 4, Folder 2, Minnesota Historical Society, which responds to Neill's request for a rewritten deed. A later source reports a sale price of sixty thousand dollars, although the accuracy of this claim is uncertain. See "The

College Hospital," *Minneapolis Tribune*, March 20, 1885, 3.

15 Charles E. Vanderburgh, January 21, 1882, manuscript document of the "Special Committee," Neill Family Papers, Box 4, Folder 3, Minnesota Historical Society.

16 Manuscript agreement in Neill's hand, February 10, 1882, Neill Family Papers, Box 7, Folder 6, Minnesota Historical Society.

17 Edward D. Neill to James McNair, March 30, 1882, Neill Family Papers, Box 4, Folder 3, Minnesota Historical Society. McNair's quote, a response to Neill's inquiry, is penciled in at the bottom of this letter.

18 The *Globe* article is quoted in Sandeen, *St. Paul's Historic Summit Avenue*, 9. See also Zellie and Peterson, *St. Paul Historic Context Study*, 6–11.

19 Edward D. Neill to McNair, March 30, 1882, Neill Family Papers, Box 4, Folder 3, Minnesota Historical Society.

20 Hodgson and Son, architects to the Building Committee of Macalester College, January 26, 1883, Neill Family Papers, Box 4, Folder 4, Minnesota Historical Society.

21 One street is named for John Witherspoon, a Scottish Presbyterian divine, who was president of Princeton from 1768 to his death in 1794 and who supported the American struggle for independence, signing the Declaration of Independence and serving in the Continental Congress from 1776 to 1782. "Geneva Street" refers to the home of Reformation theologian John Calvin and "Baldwin Street" to Matthias Baldwin, the early supporter of Neill's educational efforts. "Hamilton Street" may refer to William Stirling Hamilton, a Scottish philosopher of the Common Sense school.

22 On St. Anthony Park, see Lanegran, *St. Anthony Park*, 2–13.

23 Zellie and Peterson, *St. Paul Context Study*, 7.

24 On the seminary, see "St. Thomas Aquinas Seminary," *Inter-Urban Graphic*, June 2, 1888, 2.

25 On the development of trolleys in the area, see Young and Lanegran, *Grand Avenue*, 18–21, and Lowry, *Streetcar Man*, 117–18.

26 "St. Paul Real Estate," *Northwest Magazine*, April 1886, 17. See also *Northwestern Chronicle*, October 8, 1885.

27 Thomas A. McCurdy, "History of Macalester College, Saint Paul, Minnesota by the Rev. Professor Henry D. Funk, Reviewed by Rev. Thomas A. M'Curdy, D.D., LL.D., President, Macalester College, 1884–1890," typescript, n.d. (ca. 1910), 3, Macalester College Archives.

28 Funk, *A History of Macalester College*, 109.

29 Ibid., 85, quoting the minutes of the Synod of Minnesota, 1882, 388.

30 McCurdy, *History*, 5. McCurdy, in this memoir, argued against college historian Funk's view that stronger efforts on McCurdy's part to raise funds in the East would have been successful, given that other colleges in the West, including Carleton, had recently had some luck in doing so. McCurdy points out that comparing the cases of Macalester and Carleton was not illuminating in that their situations were very different. He argued that "while Macalester had a divided support of its denominational

constituency; Carleton had the united support of its denominational constituency supplemented by aid from Presbyterians; Macalester was, in the judgment of many Presbyterians, not needed; Carleton, in the judgment of the Congregationalists, was needed."

31 Ibid., 4.

32 Ibid., 5.

33 Ibid., 8.

34 Ibid., 12.

35 Ibid.

36 Ibid.

37 Ibid., 13.

38 Ibid., 14–15.

39 Funk suggests this was so, and at least one letter exists indicating that Neill felt compelled to apologize for his behavior. See D. Blakely to Neill, February 13, 1880, Neill Family Papers, Box 4, Folder 2, Minnesota Historical Society.

40 On the opening of Macalester College, see Funk, *History of Macalester*, 113–28, 136.

41 Edward D. Neill, as quoted in ibid., 117.

42 Ibid., 136, 138. On the number of college prospects in attendance, cf. James F. Holly to Thurlow G. Burbank, November 28, 1961, Alumni Box—Class of 1889–Class of 1930, Folder 4, Macalester College Archives.

43 These figures are quoted in Funk, *History of Macalester*, 162–63. He cites Record B of the board of trustees, a document that was not available to this author.

44 Ibid., 166.

45 J. C. Whitney to EDN, October 1, 1885, Neill Family Papers, Box 4, Folder 6, Minnesota Historical Society.

46 Haebig, "What's Historic about This Site," 35. See also Macalester College, *A Century and Beyond*, 15.

47 The letter appeared in the *St. Paul Pioneer Press*, June 24, 1890. On July 3, the trustees voted to censure Neill for this action, stating, "Resolved that the President of this Board be requested to communicate to Professor Neill its displeasure at the evidence of disrespect and insubordination evinced by the article published in the *Pioneer Press* of June 24th, and its sense of the injustice done Dr. McCurdy by the false inferences necessarily drawn from that publication." Neill Family Papers, Box 5, Minnesota Historical Society.

48 W. M. Tenney (Bd of Trustees) to E. D. Neill, July 10, 1889; H. Knox Taylor to Neill [typewritten], July 5, 1890, Neill Family Papers, Box 5, Folders 3 and 4, Minnesota Historical Society. On Kirkwood, see James Wallace to Neill, July 18, 1889, and H. L. Humphrey [attorney at law, Hudson, Wisc.], July 20, 1889, Neill Family Papers, Box 5, Folder 3, Minnesota Historical Society.

49 Neill Family Papers, Box 5, Minnesota Historical Society.

50 A full accounting of the college's financial situation and donors during this period

is available in Funk, *History of Macalester College*, 137–96. Information on the Oliver bequest appears on pp. 164–65.

51 "Resolution Adopted by the Trustees of Macalester College," July 7, 1891, Neill Family Papers, Box 5, Minnesota Historical Society.

52 See various correspondences in Neill Family Papers, Minnesota Historical Society, including a note in Neill's hand, dated July 30, 1887, saying that Macalester's requirements for the junior class in history were not up to the standards of other schools: in the first term, Hamline, seven hours each week, the University of Minnesota, five hours each week, and Macalester, zero hours per week; in the second term, Hamline, seven hours, University of Minnesota, five hours, Macalester, zero hours. See also a letter from B. F. Wright [trustee] to Neill, August 9, 1887, thanking him for his communication regarding the study of history at Macalester and saying he will present it at the next meeting of the Committee on Instruction. Letter from Neill to the trustees, August 11, 1887, which includes a report recommending new curricular hours in history and literature for all classes. B. F. Wright to Neill, August 16, 1887, saying the Committee on Instruction did not owe Neill an apology. B. F. Wright to Neill, September 7, 1887, saying that the committee wished it could immediately make the curriculum changes in the requirements for history, English literature, and political economy that he proposed but that, lacking a teacher, they must wait a year. Neill Family Papers, Box 5, Folder 1, Minnesota Historical Society.

53 Edward D. Neill to Robert F. Sample, April 2, 1892, Neill Family Papers, Box 6, Folder 1, Minnesota Historical Society.

54 Over a period of nearly four years, Neill was forced to write the trustees several times to request that his salary be paid. See Thomas Cochrane to Neill, May 20, 1890; David E. Platter (Macalester treasurer) to Neill, February 3, 1891, March 4, 1891, and June 4, 1891. Neill to D. E. P. [David E. Platter]; Platter to Neill, June 2, 1891; David Platter to Neill, June 26, 1891; Platter to Neill, July 29, 1891; Platter to Neill, August 5, 1891, Neill Family Papers, Box 5, Folders 6 and 7, Minnesota Historical Society; Neill to David Platter and Board of Trustees, July 4, 1892; Platter to Neill, August 12, 1892, Neill Family Papers, Box 6, Folders 1 and 3, Minnesota Historical Society.

55 Edward D. Neill to Rev. Dr. [Adam] Ringland, March 13, 1893, Neill Family Papers, Box 6, Folder 3, Minnesota Historical Society.

56 Note in Neill's hand, May 11, 1891. [W . . .] [Sundberg] to the Faculty of Macalester College, undated, Box 5, Folder 6, Minnesota Historical Society. Among the clothing Sundberg needed was likely a silk hat, a fashion statement popular among young men of the period. See Joseph W. Cochran's reminiscences on the first graduation in 1889 in Joseph Wilson Cochran, "The Uninjurable Man," June 11, 1939, Alumni Box 1, Class of 1889–Class of 1930, Macalester College Archives.

57 Gus L. Heegaard to Edward D. Neill, September 8, 1891, Neill Family Papers, Box 5, Minnesota Historical Society. Neill's *Historical Contributions* (later *Macalester Historical Contributions*) were collections of his essays printed privately on an occasional basis

between 1863 and 1890. James J. Hill funded the printing of at least one volume. See W. A. Stephens (private secretary to James J. Hill) to Neill, January 1, 1890, indicating that Hill would pay to print the *Contributions*. Neill Family Papers, Box 5, Folder 4, Minnesota Historical Society.

58 George W. Achard to Edward D. Neill, September 24, 1889, Neill Family Papers, Box 5, Minnesota Historical Society.

59 See George W. Achard to Edward D. Neill, May 13, 1891, Neill Family Papers, Box 5, Minnesota Historical Society.

60 Edward D. Neill to Henry Vanderburgh, December 4, 1889, Neill Family Papers, Box 5, Minnesota Historical Society.

5. College Life and Identity at the Turn of the Century

1 Only two other categories were available for self-identification between 1905 and 1917: "other," which in 1905 garnered forty-six students, and "no preference," with thirty-one students.

2 On Presbyterianism's reactions to modernism and evolution during this period, see Marsden, *Understanding Fundamentalism*. On New School Presbyterians, see Marsden, *Evangelical Mind*, and Balmer and Fitzmier, *Presbyterians*.

3 See, e.g., Higham, *From Boundlessness to Incorporation*.

4 *Macalester Echo*, November 1, 1893, 11.

5 James Wallace to Edward D. Neill, June 18, 1893, Macalester College Archives, James Wallace Papers, Box 6, Folder 4, Macalester College Archives.

6 This author has not been able to corroborate this position. Anna Dickson may have been the daughter of new trustee Thomas Dickson. A Miss Ringland, perhaps the daughter of the president, appeared in a Hyperion Society performance in the fall of 1894 and was thus presumably a college student at the time; I have not been able to ascertain the date of her admission, however. Nevertheless, this argument was put forth by one trustee and thus carries some weight.

7 Margaret Stewart to Edward Duffield Neill, November 21, 1892, and Edward Duffield Neill to Margaret Steward, November 22, 1892, Neill Family Papers, Box 6, Folder 2, Minnesota Historical Society.

8 Edward D. Neill to James Wallace, September 19, 1893, Box 6, Folder 4, Minnesota Historical Society.

9 Ringland to Neill, September 23, 1893, and Neill to Ringland, September 23, 1893, Box 6, Folder 4, Minnesota Historical Society.

10 Obituary, Edward Duffield Neill, *St. Paul Pioneer Press*, September 27, 1893.

11 "The Last of Earth," *Macalester Echo*, November 1, 1893, 1.

12 "Obituary," *Macalester Echo*, November 15, 1893, 4.

13 Edwards, *History of the Synod*, 215.

14 *Macalester Echo*, November 1, 1893, 13.

15 [Daniel Rice], "A Plea for the Higher Christian Education" (n.p.: [1882]), 12, Presbyterian Historical Society. Late-twentieth-century criticism and analysis of such views abound, starting with Said, *Orientalism*.

16 Rice, "A Plea," 12.

17 Ibid.

18 Ibid., 13.

19 Ibid., 14.

20 Minutes of the Trustees, Record B, 246–47, as quoted in Henry Daniel Funk, *History of Macalester College, Its Origin, Struggle, and Growth* (St. Paul: Macalester College Board of Trustees, 1910), 208. The tendency for families in the Midwest to invest in their daughters' educations over their sons' was not uncommon and deserves more scholarly attention.

21 "The College Year," *Macalester Echo*, November 1, 1893, 5.

22 Anna M. Dickson, "The Progressive Woman," undated, 3, Alumni box, Alumni, Class of 1898 Folder, Macalester College Archives.

23 Ibid., 6.

24 On Janet Davis Wallace, see Kagin, *James Wallace*, 37–68. On Wallace's support for women's ordination, see James Wallace, "On the Woman Overtures," *Presbyterian Banner*, March 6, 1930, 11–12. In this piece, Wallace argues that women, just as men, may be called on by God to preach the Gospel and lead the church, citing Salvation Army founder Evangeline Booth and English preacher and suffragist Agnes Maude Royden as examples. He also cited a number of biblical verses illustrating women's leadership in the ancient church. The Presbyterian Church's position that God would never call a woman to preach or lead, he concluded, denied women's equal position to men and was unbiblical.

25 Electives themselves were fairly new in U.S. higher education, having been hesitantly borrowed from the German university in the 1860s and then championed by Harvard reformer Charles Eliot in the 1870s. Macalester introduced elective choices in languages in 1886, rejecting the prescribed curriculum it had adopted in its first year. Until the early twentieth century, however, electives were limited to choices among several languages or among the natural sciences. By 1910, available choices included "expression" and a variety of history and literature courses. Incorporating cocurricular activities as curricular electives was by no means unique to Macalester. The migration of cocurricular activities into the curriculum occurred throughout higher education from the mid-nineteenth century on. See Rudolph, *Curriculum*, 140–50.

26 Occasional references to the assistance of one Miss Morton suggest that the societies or the college may have employed her to help train the speakers.

27 "Early Days at Macalester," *Macalester Echo*, January 15, 1894, 6.

28 A fourth society, Athenian, which was limited to men, appeared within a few years. See Dewitt Wallace to Janet Wallace, September 22, 1907, Macalester College Archives.

29 *Macalester Echo*, March 1, 1894, 5.

30 *Macalester Echo*, December 15, 1893, 10.

31 *Macalester Echo*, April 16, 1894, 1.

32 "Mrs. J. M. Johnson, Educator, Dies Here," *St. Paul Dispatch*, [1935], clipping; "Oliver Towne, 'Son of the General!'" *St. Paul Dispatch*, March 12, 1869, clipping; Gareth Hiebert, "Mac's 'Mystery Man' Sleuthful," *St. Paul Dispatch*, undated clipping; Julia Johnson, unprocessed Box 2 of 5, Macalester College Archives.

33 Letters from several 1910 alumni to other 1910 alumni, Alumni Box, Class of 1889–Class of 1930, Folder 9, Alumni class of 1901–1910, Macalester College Archives. Mildred Phillips Kindy, "Give What Our Hearts Dictate," *Macalester Today*, October 1951. Kindy reports that at that time, a total of $3,295.75 had been raised toward the $10,000 goal to furnish the Julia M. Johnson memorial room.

34 Braude, "Women's History Is American Religious History," 87–107.

35 Faculty meeting minutes, bound volumes, President's Office, Macalester College. Will Reeves, "'86, Grad to Fete Mac Alumni Day," *St. Paul Dispatch*, undated, Alumni Box—Class of 1889–1930, Folder 4—Alumni Class of 1890, Macalester College Archives. After graduating from Macalester, Kirkwood was invited to teach at Macalester but was let go in 1893 because of the college's financial situation. He went on to become a journalist, teaching writing and editing for the University of Minnesota School of Agriculture. He earned an MA in journalism from the University of Missouri in 1922 and continued to teach writing and editing at the University of Minnesota, offering the first reporting courses at the university and laying the groundwork for what would become the School of Journalism. See "Summary Information," William Paul Kirkwood Papers, 1893–57, University of Minnesota Archives. The Reverend William Kirkwood, who taught mental science and logic at the college until 1890 (see previous chapter), may have been this Will Kirkwood's father.

36 Faculty meeting minutes, bound volumes, President's Office, Macalester College.

37 "Dancing Tends to 'Spoonery,'" *St. Paul Pioneer Press*, March 15, 1903, 1.

38 Ibid. See also James Wallace, Annual Report of the President to the Trustees of Macalester College, June 9, 1903, James Wallace Papers, Macalester College Archives.

39 The letter appears below exactly as it was handwritten. I decided to make no corrections of spelling or grammar to present an accurate picture of this important alumnus's letter. Wallace, as a later chapter explores more fully, was far from a model student, and this letter testifies to his attitudes and abilities during the period. Dewitt Wallace to Janet Wallace, February 28, 1908, James Wallace Papers, Box 2, Folder: Letters DeWitt Wallace, Macalester College Archives: "It was thusly: Sarah MacKnight decided to have a skating party and as she was inviting out-siders also we did not make any effort to keep the affair quiet. Therefore we did not think it at all likely that the Freshies would do anything. Still I was going to take due precaution and run no chances. So when I finished playing handball I came up and changed my clothes—putting on my old ones as if going to supper to change later for the party. However I did not expect to go near supper and I was just waiting for the Freshies to go to supper

before I would make record time in changing and getting away. I put on my hat to go to supper and I went down to Luke Brinks room. He was sure the Freshies werent going to do anything. I came out and happened to meet Roy Clark going down stairs. He eats at Edwards and I thot I would walk down stairs with him as a blind. All but 2 or 3 of the Freshman boys were waiting for me in the entrance way and after some scrap they tied me up. Meanwhile Luke came down and felt awful sore after telling me he didnt think anything was doing and I think he went back upstairs—where he met Noyes and Cardle going to supper. He told them what was on and they hiked back & down the fire escape and away. [Heed] the only other Soph in the dorm had gone to Mpls to meet a friend in the afternoon. They wanted to get me out of the way lest the Sophs should get together & raid the Freshies so 3 Freshies and I walked up and down then go Carson and Ellison at Edwards & Heed returning from Mpls ran right into them so they got him. They ties these 3 hand & foot & put them in the [Wallace] attic. I just had my hands ties but not enuf so that I couldnt eat pie. I carried on a very pleasant conversation with [Gracie] Clark & Johnson—the Freshies with me—for an hour and a half and then I told them Miriam was comming [*sic*] that night and I would like to meet her so they let me go on condition I wouldnt go to the party—They kept the others tied up until 10:00 oclock. I went to Mpls. but Miriam didn't arrive. I didn't see the river—to say nothing of a cave. It was just some of Fisks yellow journalism. And he certainly got it rubbed into him about that write up. It was all rank imajination [*sic*] work on his part."

40 Just where the cow came from is never addressed either. The closest farms at the turn of the century were about a mile to the southwest. By the time DeWitt Wallace was a student (1904 in the academy; 1907–8 in the college), even those were gone. Perhaps this is why the animal is reported by historian John Heidenry to have been a horse. He also suggests that Wallace was all but expelled for the prank. As Heidenry proves to be fairly careful in sticking to documentary evidence, I am not convinced that the episode did not happen. Heidenry had access to materials that I have been denied, and information on this episode may be among them. See Heidenry, *Theirs Was the Kingdom*, 28. The cow in the basement is reported in Kagin, *James Wallace*, 133.

41 Although I have found no documentation of the original cow story in the college's early years, a cow was definitely brought into the chapel in 1923, an event documented by several alumni reminiscences and the *St. Paul Pioneer Press*. This first documented occurrence is, however, long after the legend supposedly began. See "Dr. Sobrepena Recalls Cow in Drama Studio in Days Gone By," *MacWeekly*, October 29, 1948, 5; and Scot Hamilton, "Chickens, Cows Contribute to Chaotic Chapel," *MacWeekly*, January 20, 1978, 1.

42 George W. Wishard to T. M. Hodgman, June 7, 1911; and Hodgman to Wishard, June 13, 1911. "Minutes, Executive Committee. Trustees of Macalester College" with materials from June 1910 to December 1922, Macalester College Archives.

43 Grace Whitridge to T. M. Hodgman, June 15, 1911.

44 W. S. Walker to the Trustees, [July 14, 1915]—see reference and discussion in Executive Committee minutes of July 14, 1915.

45 Minutes of the Macalester College Board of Trustees, April 26, 1926.

46 *Secretary's Book, Class of '98, Macalester College*, Alumni Box—Class of 1889–1930, Folder 7—Class of 1898, Macalester College Archives.

47 "The Class of '08 Holds Reunion," *St. Paul Pioneer Press*, clipping, Alumni Box—Class of 1889–1930, Folder 9—Alumni class of 1901–10, Macalester College Archives. It is likely that the impetus behind the rock stemmed in part from a similar effort at the nearby Hamline University a few years earlier.

48 Glenn Clark to his parents, January 17, 1912, Glenn Clark Box, Macalester College Archives.

49 Ibid.

50 W. H. Swift (Board of Aid for College and Academies) to Messrs. Kirk and Jefferson, October 10, 1900, College Board Records, RG 32, Box 17, Folder 13, Presbyterian Historical Society.

51 James Wallace, Annual Report of the President to the Trustees of Macalester College, June 9, 1903, James Wallace Papers, Box 1, Folder 4, Macalester College Archives.

52 Ibid.

53 Hill, who had shared a personal relationship with Edward D. Neill based on their mutual interest in library development, had been assisting the college financially for years, making his first donation in 1888 (amount not recorded) and another of five thousand dollars in 1891. Between then and 1915, Hill had donated over $125,000 to the college, a sum that translates into 2007 dollars as approximately $2.5 million. Because Hill always refused public recognition for his all philanthropic work, his vital support of the college has never been fully acknowledged. Ledger books, James J. Hill Papers, Minnesota Historical Society.

54 "Generous Gifts to Macalester," *St. Paul Pioneer Press*, June 16, 1905, 4.

55 Hodgman to [no recipient named], March 26, 1910, College Board Records, RG 32, Box 17, Folder 15, Presbyterian Historical Society.

6. *Evangelical Engagement with Modernism*

1 Religious liberalism and conservativism are conceived of here as existing on a continuum of beliefs related to the relative influence of supernatural or divine forces in human life. Those on the conservative end give the divine—God—more weight in influencing human history and, in this case, salvation. Those on the left lean toward humanism, giving human rationality and action more weight in influencing history and conceiving of salvation in universalist terms. As liberal Protestantism and evangelical Protestantism staked out distinct ideologies along this continuum and eventually parted company entirely in the 1920s and 1930s, Presbyterians could be found on both sides of the spectrum. Indeed, some Presbyterians were among the

leaders in the development of ultraconservative or fundamentalist positions, and some were among the leaders of liberal Protestantism.

2   The most radical conservatives turned toward premillennial dispensationalism in their belief that God's intervention was needed to redeem society. This group forecast the imminent return of Jesus Christ in apocalyptic end-times scenarios. This view was not popular among Macalester faculty or supporters. On premillennial dispensationalism, see Sandeen, *Roots of Fundamentalism*; and Kilde, "How Did *Left Behind's*," 33–71.

3   T. Morey Hodgman, "Is Christian Education Vital to the Church and Society?" undated typescript, Charles Turck Box, Hodgman Folder, Macalester College Archives.

4   "The College Year," *Macalester Echo*, November 1, 1893, 5.

5   "YMCA Notes," *Macalester Echo*, November 1, 1893, 6.

6   "Local and Personal," *Macalester Echo*, June 1, 1894.

7   Joseph Koshaba became a naturalized citizen of the United States on April 15, 1896. The United States had established diplomatic relations with Persia in 1883.

8   See Zirinsky, "American Presbyterian Missionaries."

9   See "Roll of Alumni," *Macalester College Bulletin*, 1906, 99–104.

10 Either Petran or Schulyer was the associate editor of the *Echo* at the time. See "Editorial," *Macalester Echo*, March 20, 1894, 1.

11 These early twentieth-century students were quite unaware of late-twentieth-century critiques of missionary work as imperialistic. They believed strongly that by bringing Christianity to other parts of the world, they were doing service both to the individuals they converted and to God. On the function of missionary work as the "moral equivalent for imperialism," see Hutchison, *Errand to the World*, 91–143.

12 See, e.g., "Circular Letter from Charles Petran to Chairman of [illegible], Mac.," YMCA, July 25, [1895], Macalester College Archives.

13 See, e.g., "YMCA Notes," *Macalester Echo*, March 20, 1894, 10.

14 On the history of missionary thought in the United States, see Hutchison, *Errand to the World*, 91–95, 102–11.

15 The author wishes to thank Dale Johnson for the phrase. On Mott, see ibid., 119–21.

16 Reference to this article appears in "Alumni and Former Students," *Macalester Echo*, November 15, 1893, 11.

17 *In Memory of George Leck*, memorial book, undated, Alumni Box—Class of 1889–Class of 1930, Folder 6—Class of 1897, Macalester College Archives.

18 Charles Allen Clark, "Memories of Sixty Years," undated, Alumni Box—Class of 1889–Class of 1930, Folder 8—Alumni, Class of 1899–1900, Macalester College Archives.

19 The Memorial Arch in Tappan Square on the Oberlin campus was erected as a reminder of that loss.

20 "Macalester in the Orient," *MacWeekly*, April 13, 1915, 1; emphasis in original.

21 On ideal types, see Weber, *Economy and Society*.

22 Clipping from the *State* (Columbia, S.C.), February 3, 1974, Alumni Box—Class of 1889–Class of 1930, Folder 9, Macalester College Archives.

23 James Wallace to Andrew Carnegie, April 12, 1905, James Wallace Papers, Box 1, Carnegie Science Hall Folder, Macalester College Archives.

24 *St. Paul Pioneer Press* clipping, [1939], James Wallace Papers, Box 3, Folder "Newspaper Clippings," Macalester College Archives.

25 See, e.g., *Macalester College Bulletin*, May 1905, 27, and *Macalester College Bulletin*, April 1920, 39, which delineate preprofessional curriculum requirements in each of these three areas.

26 Will Reeves, "86, Grad to Fete Mac Alumni Day," *St. Paul Dispatch* clipping, undated, Alumni Box—Class of 1889–1930, Folder 4—Alumni Class of 1890, Macalester College Archives.

27 T. Morey Hodgman, Report to John McLain, February 8, 1913, 11, Macalester College Archives.

28 William Hutchinson suggests that missionary work in fact "fetishized" lay participation, an attitude that church-related colleges, including Macalester, would have fostered with their vocational programs. Among the national proponents of lay mission work was Sherwood Eddy, who delivered chapel lectures at Macalester no less than nine times between 1931 and 1956. On lay missionary work, see Hutchison, *Errand to the World*, 101–2.

29 Schmidt, *A History*, 29.

30 Ibid., 14.

31 James, *Varieties of Religious Experience*.

32 Ibid.

33 Porterfield, *Transformation of American Religion*, 199.

34 Schmidt, *A History*, 15.

35 Harper, *Trend in Higher Education*, 19, as quoted in Schmidt, *A History*, 27.

36 Coe, *A Social Theory*, 54, as quoted in Schmidt, *A History*, 22.

37 Schmidt, *A History*, 6.

38 Luther Weigle, as quoted in ibid., 83.

39 Shailer Mathews, as quoted in ibid., 73.

40 Ibid.

41 T. Morey Hodgman to Professors Wallace, Anderson, Alexander, Fun, Jones and Burgess, undated, James Wallace Papers, Box 1, T. M. Hodgman Folder, Macalester College Archives.

42 *Macalester College Bulletin*, April 1915, 36.

43 *Macalester College Bulletin*, 1894, 28.

44 "Social Service," *Macalester College Bulletin*, June 1919, 2.

45 Ibid.

46 Ibid., 1.

47 Ibid., 2.

48 *Prospectus of Macalester College* (Minneapolis, Minn.: Tribune Job Printing, 1885), 16.

49 Ibid.; emphasis in original.

50 *Macalester College Bulletin*, 1900–1, 49.

51 Just what constituted proper preparation for these religious vocations underwent significant examination and discussion during the period, precisely because perceptions of the role of Christianity in the world were changing. In the 1880s, students had to choose between one of three curricula: classical, philosophical, or literary. Each curriculum required that all students take two Bible courses every term (three terms a year during this period) in their freshman and sophomore years. Those courses, Bible Instruction and Biblical Geography, familiarized students with the texts and locations of biblical narratives. In the junior year, all students were required to take two terms of Evidences and History of Christianity, followed by a course in Literature of the Bible. In the senior year was the yearlong required course in History of Free Thought. Thus, in the earliest years of the college, students were steeped in the study of the Bible. As we shall see in the next chapter, the Macalester leadership adopted a decidedly optimistic, postmillennial view that expressed the conviction that Christianity could successfully address all human, social, and national problems and conflicts.

52 James Wallace, "Tribute to Doctor George W. Davis at the Memorial Service Held before the Students and Faculty of Macalester," December 14, 1936, James Wallace Papers, Box 1, George W. Davis Folder, Macalester College Archives.

53 James Wallace to Milton McLean, April 4, 1939, James Wallace Papers, Box 1, Faculty Folder, Macalester College Archives.

54 Minutes of the Trustees of Macalester College, April 26, 1926.

55 "Bible Department Offers New Courses," *MacWeekly*, January 12, 1927, 1.

56 *Macalester College Bulletin*, April 1930, 77.

57 James E. Clarke, "The Program for a Religious Education Department," typescript, [1927]. See also the attached documents: James E. Clarke to John C. Acheson, December 29, 1927, and [Acheson?], "Comments on Dr. James E. Clarke's Paper," John C. Acheson Papers, Box 2, James E. Clarke Folder, Macalester College Archives.

58 *Macalester College Bulletin*, 1907, 49.

59 *Macalester College Bulletin*, 1911, 53.

60 Riley, *Inspiration or Evolution*, 144–45.

61 Arthur G. Bailey to J. C. Acheson, July 3, 1926, Acheson 103 Box, Macalester College— Professors, Miscellaneous Business Folder, Macalester College Archives.

62 Ibid.

63 John C. Acheson to A. G. Bailey, July 19, 1926, Acheson 103 Box, Macalester College— Professors, Miscellaneous Business Folder, Macalester College Archives.

64 Ibid.

65 A. T. Gordon to E. B. Kirk, August 4, 1926, Acheson 103 Box, Macalester College— Professors, Miscellaneous Business Folder, Macalester College Archives.

66 [Arthur Bailey] to James P. Welliver, August 18, 1926, Acheson 103 Box, Macalester

College—Professors, Miscellaneous Business Folder, Macalester College Archives.

67 Arthur G. Bailey to John C. Acheson, September 7, 1926, Acheson 103 Box, Macalester College—Professors, Miscellaneous Business Folder, Macalester College Archives.

68 O. T. Walter to John C. Acheson, April 26, 1926, John C. Acheson Papers, Box 1, Professors, Miscellaneous Business Folder, Macalester College Archives. Jean Robertson Ernst (class of 1941), undated typescript, in the author's possession, Macalester College Archives.

69 John C. Acheson to O. T. Walter, April 28, 1926, John C. Acheson Papers, Box 1, Professors, Miscellaneous Business Folder, Macalester College Archives.

70 Editorial, "Ignorance vs. Science," *MacWeekly*, March 16, 1927, 2.

71 S. J. Duncan-Clark, "Extending the Frontiers of Life," typescript, June 15, 1927, John C. Acheson Papers, Box 1, Macalester College Archives.

72 Robert S. Wallace to John C. Acheson, June 7, 1928, Acheson Box 103, Field Representative—Promotion Department Folder, Macalester College Archives.

73 Marsden, *Understanding Fundamentalism*, 51–52.

74 "The Macalester Neutrality and Peace Association," undated, Folder: World War I, Macalaster College Archives. The text of the letter was published in the *St. Paul Daily News* on March 18, 1917.

75 "Charges Minnesota School with Betraying America," *New York Herald*, March 21, 1917.

76 "Macalester Peace Letter Denounced by Congressman," *Minneapolis Journal*, March 21, 1917. These words are not Hodgman's but are the newspaper's paraphrase of his point.

77 "War on Kaiser Is Urged Now at Macalester," *St. Paul Pioneer Press*, March 22, 1917.

78 Ibid. Of the eighty-seven students who signed the document, forty-three, according to the *Daily News*, were freshmen. Fifty-five of the signators would go on to serve in the U.S. military during the war.

79 Hodgman to Minnesota Neill, April 23, 1917, Neill Family Papers, Box 7, Folder 7, Minnesota Historical Society. In the letter, Hodgman complained that Wallace, Professor Anderson, and trustee Thomas Shaw would capitalize on his handling of some student decisions that made the newspapers—a likely reference to the peace letter and rebuttal—to oust him.

80 H. D. Funk, "S.A.T.C.," *Macalester College Bulletin*, January 1919, 13.

81 "Resolution Respecting the Study of German in Macalester College," undated typescript. A handwritten note at the top of the document puts the date at March 1918 and explains the procedure. James Wallace Papers, Box 3, World War I Folder, Macalester College Archives.

7. The Collapse of the Evangelical Consensus

1 James Wallace, "The Great Betrayal," *St. Paul Pioneer Press*, clipping, [summer] 1939, 4.

2 With respect to his religious ideology, Wallace labeled himself a "moderate conservative" and his colleague Edwin Kagin a "liberal conservative." James Wallace to Milton

McLean, April 4, 1939, James Wallace Box 1, Folder "Faculty," Macalester College Archives.

3   The importance of the nuances at the center of these religious and political extremes are explored by the contributors to Jacobsen and Trollinger, eds., *Re-forming the Center*.

4   John Carey Acheson to Ralph W. Harbison, March 12, 1937; John Carey Acheson to Fred Michel, June 24, 1937, Macalester College Archives.

5   On Clark's life, see Glenn Harding, "The Saga of Glenn Clark and Camp Farthest Out: A Chronicle of Fifty Golden Years, 1930–1980," undated typescript, Macalester College Archives; Clark, *A Man's Reach*; and Clark, *Glenn Clark*.

6   Glenn Clark to John Acheson, September 23, 1924, Macalester College Archives.

7   John C. Acheson to the Board of Trustees of Macalester College, January 25, 1928, Acheson Papers, Macalester College Archives.

8   Ibid.

9   Ibid.

10 John C. Acheson to B. Warren Brown, August 12, 1931, Macalester College Archives.

11 Ibid.

12 "Dr. Acheson Sought High Education Efficiency for Macalester in College Reorganization Report," *MacWeekly*, December 9, 1937, 2.

13 Ibid.

14 Ibid.

15 "Hoover Praises Small Colleges," *St. Paul Pioneer Press*, November 15, 1931, 2; "Hoover Praises Small Arts Colleges of U.S.," *Minneapolis Tribune*, November 15, 1931, 2.

16 See the description of the club in the 1934 *Macalester College Bulletin*, 22. Carnegie funds are mentioned in the program for "Greetings from the International Relations Club of Macalester College" High School Day, May 19, 1934, Campus Clubs Box, International Relations Club Folder, Macalester College Archives.

17 Program, "Meeting of the International Relations Clubs of the Twin Cities under the Auspices of the Macalester College International Relations Club," February 14–17, 1934, Campus Clubs Box, International Relations Club Folder, Macalester College Archives.

18 See, e.g., clippings from the *St. Paul Pioneer Press*, the *St. Paul Daily News*, and the *Minneapolis Journal* in International Relations Club file, Macalester College Archives.

19 *Macalester College Bulletin*, March 1935.

20 "The College and World Citizenship," *Macalester College Bulletin*, March 1935, 3.

21 Ibid.

22 "Four Foreign Students to Speak Friday," *MacWeekly*, November 9, 1939, 1.

23 "Seamans, Jew-Christian Coordinator, Here Friday," *MacWeekly*, November 16, 1939, 1. Mitau was not the first Jewish student at Macalester; although records on religious affiliation of students are incomplete, it is clear that two Jewish students were enrolled in 1919 and 1927 and that five were enrolled in 1928. Others may well have been

overlooked by these and other counts. Mitau would go on to become a distinguished faculty member at Macalester and head of the political science department.

24 "Inquiry on Current Finances of the College," attached to letter from John E. Bradford to [John C. Acheson], October 7, 1933, Acheson Papers, Macalester College Archives.

25 Harold M. Robinson to John Acheson, March 23, 1933, College Board Records, RG 32, Box 18, Presbyterian Historical Society.

26 John C. Acheson to C. C. McCracken, April 25, 1936, Layman's Missionary Movement, Box 2, Macalester College Archives.

27 Roy William DeWitt Wallace was born to James and Janet Davis Wallace on November 12, 1889, in St. Paul, Minnesota. He attended the Macalester Academy for a year and was then sent to revivalist Dwight L. Moody's Mount Hermon Boy's School in Northfield, Massachusetts. He was accepted by Macalester College in 1907, completed two years, and did not return, perhaps as a disciplinary measure. See Heidenry, *Theirs Was the Kingdom*, 25–28.

28 Ibid., 83.

29 See James Wallace to DeWitt and Lila Wallace, June 12, 1931, James Wallace Papers, Macalester College Archives.

30 "Macalester Endowment Fund Boosted by Million," *St. Paul Pioneer Press*, March 10, 1936, 1.

31 "The Reader's Digest," *Fortune Magazine*, November 1936, 121–24.

32 James Wallace to DeWitt and Lila Wallace, November 14, 1936, James Wallace Papers, Macalester College Archives.

33 Ibid.

34 The DeWitt Wallace correspondence has a troubling history. On his death, his papers were transferred from the Pleasantville, New York, offices of *Reader's Digest* to the Macalester College Archives. The papers have never been cataloged. John Heidenry reviewed the papers for his 1993 book on the Wallaces and *Reader's Digest*. According to Heidenry (and corroborated by Macalester sources), on the publication of the book, *Reader's Digest* representatives went to Macalester and repossessed some of the papers. *Reader's Digest* has since denied having any papers. Around the same time, and perhaps in response to this incident, historian James B. Stewart, then provost of Macalester College, gathered a folder of sensitive DeWitt Wallace letters and asked then president Robert Gavin to house them in his office. Gavin's successor, Michael McPherson, denied having these Wallace letters in an e-mail to the author. McPherson's successor, Brian Rosenberg, however, mentioned the folder during his address at a Macalester Founders' Day dinner in 2004, although he has refused this author's requests to view the papers.

35 James Wallace to DeWitt and Lila Wallace, December 25, 1936, James Wallace Papers, Macalester College Archives. James was not hesitant about requesting money from his son once he learned of the great wealth he had accumulated. On the basis of all those

years of fund-raising for the college and a sense of entitlement born of filial piety, James's requests were quite straightforward. See James Wallace to DeWitt Wallace, January 6, 1937, which may have been written in response to an inquiry from DeWitt. See also James Wallace to DeWitt Wallace, February 16, 1936, in which James explains that he recently learned that his own salary and later pension had been paid for years by Thomas Cochran and his son Thomas Jr. but that the expense was becoming a burden on the family. He immediately approached DeWitt, requesting his intervention in the situation. All letters in Macalester College Archives.

36 "Byram Foundation Donations Year by Year," Byram Foundation Folder, Macalester College Archives.

37 Louis Edward Holden to Harold M. Robinson, November 29, 1937, College Board Records, RG 32, Box 18, Presbyterian Historical Society.

38 "Dr. John C. Acheson," *Macalester College Bulletin*, March 1938, 15.

39 Ibid.

40 See, e.g., F. R. Bigelow's letter to James Wallace, May 7, 1938, James Wallace Papers, Box 2, Trustees Folder, Macalester College Archives.

41 "Faculty Studies Policies of Distinctive Liberal Arts Colleges of Nation," *MacWeekly*, March 3, 1938, 1.

42 William H. Boddy, "Some Suggestions as to the Future of Macalester College," undated. A printed notation at the top of the document indicates that these ideas had been "first expressed in a letter to Mr. Bigelow dated December 14, 1937." See also William H. Boddy to Charles C. McCracken, February 2, 1938, which summarizes these main points. Both documents are located in RG 32, Box 18, Folder 2, Presbyterian Historical Society. See also "Dr. Boddy's Ideal College, Excerpts from the Minutes of the Board of Trustees of Macalester College Held June 10th, 1938," James Wallace Papers, Box 1, Letters—William Henry Boddy Folder, Macalester College Archives.

43 Ibid.

44 Ibid.

45 James Wallace to Harold M. Robinson and Charles C. McCracken, November 22, 1937, College Board Records, RG 32, Box 18, Presbyterian Historical Society.

46 Charles C. McCracken to James Wallace, December 2, 1937, College Board Records, RG 32, Box 18, Presbyterian Historical Society; and James Wallace Papers, Box 1, Letters Folder, Misc., Macalester College Archives.

47 James Wallace to the Macalester College Board of Trustees, June 10, 1938, James Wallace Papers, Box 2, Trustees Folder, Macalester College Archives.

48 Margaret Doty to James Wallace, June 27, 1938, James Wallace Papers, Box 2, Trustees Folder, Macalester College Archives.

49 "Why Should the Denominational College Live?" undated, James Wallace Papers, Box 2, Trustees Folder, Macalester College Archives.

50 James Wallace to William H. Boddy, January 16, 1939, James Wallace Papers, Box 1, Letters—William Henry Boddy Folder, Macalester College Archives.

51 James Wallace to William H. Boddy, January 5, 1939, James Wallace Papers, Box 1, Letters—William Henry Boddy Folder, Macalester College Archives.

52 William H. Boddy to James Wallace, January 10, 1939, James Wallace Papers, Box 1, Letters—William Henry Boddy Folder, Macalester College Archives.

53 James Wallace to William H. Boddy, January 16, 1939, James Wallace Papers, Box 1, Letters—William H. Boddy Folder, Macalester College Archives. Nason went on to serve as president of Swarthmore and Carleton colleges.

54 Presbyterian Church (USA), College Board Records, December 3, 1937, December 28, 1937, December 29, 1937, RG 32, Box 18, Presbyterian Historical Society.

55 "Dean Ficken Sees Increased Attention to Individual Student from Half Million Grant," *MacWeekly*, March 2, 1939, 2.

56 Ibid.

57 Ibid.

58 Ibid.; emphasis in original.

59 Ibid.

60 Ibid.

61 Ibid.

62 Ibid.

63 Ibid.

64 "Frosh Rules Committee Is Planned," *MacWeekly*, September 30, 1937, 1. Hazing could and did become more brutal at times, with at least one student dropping out of the college due to mistreatment. See Macalaster College, *A Century and Beyond*, 44–45.

65 "Frosh Will 'Fry'! Next 'Fryday' under New 'Education Plan' Arranged by Student Council," *MacWeekly*, October 21, 1937, 3.

66 "'Higher Education,' 'Justice' Feature Lively Induction of Freshman Class," *MacWeekly*, November 4, 1937, 1.

67 "'Li'l Abner' Comics Start Real Sadie Hawkins Day—Maybe," *MacWeekly*, November 3, 1938, 3.

68 "Future Looks Very, Very Dim for 'Mac Quack,' Football Mascot," *MacWeekly*, November 4, 1937, 3.

69 During the 1920s, Presbyterian-identified students ranged from 33% to 48% of the student body.

70 Wallace, *Wallace-Bruce*.

71 According to material published by the St. Andrew's Society, it was founded in Philadelphia in 1747 as a charitable society for the "relief of distressed Scottish immigrants." St. Andrew's Society of Philadelphia, "About."

72 "Scottish Plaid to Be the Fad," *MacWeekly*, March 10, 1938, 1.

73 Ibid. The Macalester pipe band would not be organized until 1949.

8. *Liberal Arts in Service to the Nation and the World*

1   See "On Chapel," *MacWeekly*, May 11, 1927, 2.

2   "Dr. C. Turck to Speak Monday," *MacWeekly*, November 3, 1938.

3   On progressive Republicans in Minnesota, see Delton, *Making Minnesota Liberal*, 112–15.

4   Minutes of the Trustees of Macalester College, February 8, 1939, Macalester College Archives.

5   On Wallace's conservativism, see Heidenry, *Theirs Was the Kingdom*, 53–54.

6   The reason for the delay is not known. The trustees discussed the inaugural as early as September during Turck's first meeting with them as president of the college, but no action was taken at that time. Minutes of the Trustees of Macalester College, September 15, 1939, Macalester College Archives.

7   Charles J. Turck, "The Liberal Arts College in American Democracy," 5, Charles Turck Papers, Macalester College Archives.

8   Ibid., 6. See also "President Charles J. Turck Optimistic as 55th School Year Begins Here Today," *MacWeekly*, September 21, 1939, 1.

9   Turck, "The Liberal Arts College," 11.

10 Ibid.

11 Turck's views on the important relationship between religion, the state, and democracy are expressed in Turck, *Problems of Church*, which he wrote as a summary of discussions on the topic hosted by the Presbyterian Church during the summer of 1939. The positions taken in this document are informed by the views of Richard Niebuhr (*The Kingdom of God in America*), liberal theologian Harry Emerson Fosdick (*A Guide to Understanding the Bible*), and John Coleman Bennett (*Christianity and Our World*). In this document, Turck uses the postmillennial Kingdom of God language but expands the vision of that Kingdom to include all humanity, describing the Kingdom as "an organized society that will gradually evolve into a world of brotherhood founded on justice and dedicated to righteousness and peace" (2). As in his use of the word *service* in the inaugural address, his understanding of the Kingdom here is far more humanistic than that of the evangelical view of the previous generation. For Turck, as for individuals like Reinhold Niebuhr, religion must serve as a prophetic voice, providing a check on government that counters any antidemocratic tendencies or unjust actions.

12 *Macalester College Bulletin*, 1940, 14, Macalester College Archives.

13 Ibid.

14 Ibid., 14–15.

15 James Hastings Nichols, "College Should Train for Church Adjusting," *MacWeekly*, December 11, 1941.

16 "Macalester Replies in National Student Poll," *MacWeekly*, March 31, 1938, 2. See also "Why Conduct Survey of Student Opinion?" *MacWeekly*, April 7, 1938, 2, which states

that of 450 surveys distributed on campus, only 10 were not completed.

17 "America Urged Not to Lose Peace Ideals," *MacWeekly*, October 6, 1938, 2; "'Force' Nations Scored by Dr. Turck," *MacWeekly*, October 20, 1938, 3.

18 "Macite Attends Anti-war Meet," *MacWeekly*, January 11, 1940, 3; "Students Study Problems," *MacWeekly*, April 18, 1940, 3.

19 "Pacifist Movement Headed by Werbes," *MacWeekly*, October 24, 1940, 3. Werbes was appointed cochair of the Religious Emphasis Week committee during the fall 1940 semester.

20 This argument, echoing those of conservative Christian leaders, grew in part from the historical relationship between China and U.S. Christian churches. "My Views," *MacWeekly*, April 18, 1940, 2.

21 "Nichols Registers for Draft after Five-Day Protest," *MacWeekly*, October 24, 1940, 1.

22 "Willkie Favored 3 to 1 in Student, Faculty Poll," *MacWeekly*, October 25, 1940, 1. These figures can be compared with those gathered two years earlier by political science professor Marion Boggs, who reported that out of sixty-four papers written by freshmen on their political background and views, thirty-six were clearly in the Republican camp, whereas seventeen claimed the Democratic Party. One each opted for socialism and communism. "Republican Elephant Has Not Given Up Ghost, Boggs Finds in Political Questionnaire," *MacWeekly*, January 20, 1938, 2.

23 Charles J. Turck, "Freedom Is Your Choice," in *Enduring Ideals and Concerns for Changing Times from "The President's Corner,"* 1, Charles Turck Papers, Macalester College Archives.

24 "Isolationists May Be Right," *MacWeekly*, March 6, 1941, 2.

25 "At Student Meeting," *MacWeekly*, May 15, 1941, 1; Charles Turck to DeWitt Wallace, May 13, 1941, Macalester College Archives.

26 "Petition Is Point of Great Controversy," *MacWeekly*, May 15, 1941, 6; "Letter Urges Students to Write Senators, Representatives," *MacWeekly*, May 15, 1941, 6.

27 *Reader's Digest* had printed isolationist articles and had at least one editor who leaned toward isolationism. Wallace's view is more difficult to discern, however. His father's efforts to advance international cooperation may have influenced him to some extent. See Heidenry, *Theirs Was the Kingdom*, 125–28, 207–8.

28 Turck, "Reason for Clear Thinking," in *Enduring Ideals*, 2.

29 Bill Haverstock, "Letter to the Editor," *MacWeekly*, May 1, 1941, 6.

30 "Students Turn Democratic," *MacWeekly*, March 14, 1940; "First Step," *MacWeekly*, April 18, 1940, 2; "Student Gov't to Hold Open Forum," *MacWeekly*, January 16, 1941, 1; "Self-Government," *MacWeekly*, January 29, 1941, 2; Charles Turck, "The President's Corner," *MacWeekly*, May 15, 1941, 6.

31 See, e.g., the article by political science professor Marion W. Boggs, "If War Is Prolonged—U.S. Will Fight," *MacWeekly*, December 5, 1940, 2.

32 Charles Turck, "President's Corner," *MacWeekly*, January 15, 1943, 8.

33 "National Guard Claims Macites," *MacWeekly*, January 16, 1941, 3.

34 "Almost 50 Men Enlist in Military Services," *MacWeekly*, October 2, 1941, 1; "Students Urged to Write Men in Service," *MacWeekly*, October 9, 1941, 6.

35 "Faculty-Student Poll Reveals—United States Can Stay Out of War," *MacWeekly*, October 16, 1941, 1.

36 "Letter to the Editor," *MacWeekly*, October 2, 1941, 6.

37 "Hitler's Defeat More Important Than United States' Staying Out of War—Student Poll Shows," *MacWeekly*, December 4, 1941, 1.

38 Ibid.

39 An exception was Turck's pronouncement that the duty of religious colleges during the war was "to furnish the spiritual will, the religious purpose, the divine intent to put down evil and advance the good, to achieve victory, not for its own sake, but for the possibilities that this victory will bring of establishing the Kingdom of God on Earth." "Dr. Turck to Act on College Unit," *MacWeekly*, January 15, 1942, 1, 3. Given that this announcement, made at the Baltimore meeting of the National Conference of Church Related Colleges, did not characterize any later discussion of the war at Macalester, the effort to draw on the language of the previous generation strikes this author as perhaps more expedient than central to his thinking.

40 "Students Impressed by Canadian Philosophy," *MacWeekly*, December 4, 1941, 6. On the founding of the conference, see Charles Turck to Kenneth Holmes, January 15, 1963, Macalester College Archives.

41 "College Hits Stride in War Program—Summer Course Will Begin Here," *MacWeekly*, January 15, 1942, 3.

42 Charles Turck to DeWitt Wallace, February 2, 1942, Mr. and Mrs. DeWitt Wallace Papers, Box 1, restricted access, Macalester College Archives.

43 "College to Offer 8 New Courses in Wartime Setup," *MacWeekly*, January 22, 1942, 1. See also *Macalester College Bulletin*, 1942–43.

44 See George Scotton to "Dear Friend," March 12, 1942, and typescripts of "Letter A to Prospective Freshmen Already in Touch with the College"; Letter B, "General Mailing to Prep and High School Seniors"; I. Burg, "New Army and Navy Courses," March 20, 1942, World Wars I and II Box, Military Men—March 1942 Folder, Macalester College Archives. See also "Enlistee Courses Set Here," *MacWeekly*, March 26, 1942, 3.

45 George Scotton to "Dear Friend," June 30, 1942, World Wars I and II Box, Military Men—July–December Folder, Macalester College Archives.

46 "Turck Answers Editorial on Byram Scholarships," *MacWeekly*, December 5, 1940, 1. See also "62 Students Receive $4,323 in Scholarships," *MacWeekly*, September 25, 1941, 1; "Ten Highest Receive $50—Next Ten in Each Class Get $25," *MacWeekly*, October 2, 1942, 5.

47 See "'Mac' News for 'Mac' Men in Service," World Wars I and II Box, Military Men—July–December Folder, Macalester College Archives.

48 Charles Turck to DeWitt Wallace, January 2, 1943, Mr. and Mrs. DeWitt Wallace Papers, Box 1, restricted access, Macalester College Archives.

49 George Scotton, "Macalester's Contribution in Personnel to the War," March 13, 1943, Macalester College Archives. Scotton worked feverishly to keep track of Macites in the service. With few reporting procedures in place and information coming in sporadically, he was able to collect fairly reliable lists of those who served, went missing in action, and were taken prisoner.

50 Connie Cronon, "Dean Doty Says in Interview—Coeds Are Not Serious Enough," *MacWeekly*, January 22, 1943, 2.

51 "Coeds Work on Home Front," *MacWeekly*, January 15, 1943, 3.

52 "Macalester Women in Military Service," 1943, World Wars I and II Box, Military Roll, Macalester College Archives.

53 Mary Louise Harris, "U.S. to Draft Women before War's End," *MacWeekly*, April 9, 1943, 7.

54 See May, *Homeward Bound*.

55 "She's Perfect," *MacWeekly*, April 3, 1941, 1.

56 Margie Dixon, "Armed Forces Get Lesson in Glamor—Five Vie for Title," *MacWeekly*, March 5, 1943, 5.

57 "Only One Sweetheart Vote, but . . . Turck Picks Five," *MacWeekly*, March 12, 1943, 2; "Who Is Sweetheart?" *MacWeekly*, April 9, 1943, 2; "Polly Johnson Is Soldiers' Sweetheart," *MacWeekly*, April 16, 1943, 1.

58 Charles J. Turck, "A Statement to the Students of Macalester," World Wars I and II Box, Military "Roll of Honor" Folder, Macalester College Archives.

59 Charles Turck to DeWitt Wallace, June 27, 1941, Macalester College Archives.

60 United Nations, "History of the Charter of the United Nations, the Declaration of St. James Place," http://www.un.org/en/aboutun/charter/history/index.shtml.

61 "Citizenship," *MacWeekly*, September 25, 1941, 1.

62 These curricula would be criticized a generation later as complicit in U.S. imperialistic efforts to spread American culture and business through Europe.

63 United Nations, "History of the Charter of the United Nations, Moscow and Teheran," http://www.un.org/en/aboutun/charter/history/moscowteheran.shtml.

64 Clarence E. Ficken, "President's Corner," *MacWeekly*, November 12, 1943, 6.

65 "Hubert H. Humphrey, Interdependence Declaration Urged," *MacWeekly*, November 12, 1943, 6.

66 See Boggs, "If War Is Prolonged," 2; Boggs, "Attempts to Define."

67 Charles J. Turck to DeWitt and Lila Wallace, August 1, 1951, Macalester College Archives.

68 Alumni Oral Histories, May 18, 2001, Interview 4, Macalester College Archives.

9. DeWitt Wallace's Ambition

1   On Miss Wood's School, see Bell, *With Banners*.
2   Charles J. Turck to DeWitt Wallace, May 24, 1940. Here and throughout this chapter, all letters are from the Mr. and Mrs. DeWitt Wallace Papers, restricted acccess, Macalester College Archives.
3   Ibid.
4   See, e.g., Charles Turck to DeWitt Wallace, July 16, 1941, July 15, 1942, September 10, 1945, November 20, 1946, and December 15, 1947, Macalester College Archives.
5   Charles Turck to DeWitt Wallace, May 13, 1941; Charles Turck to Lila Wallace, March 28, 1945, Macalester College Archives.
6   DeWitt Wallace to Charles Turck, November 18, 1944, Macalester College Archives.
7   Charles Turck to DeWitt Wallace, September 25, 1942, Macalester College Archives.
8   Charles Turck to DeWitt Wallace, June 21, 1946, Macalester College Archives.
9   Charles Turck to DeWitt Wallace, September 10, 1945, Macalester College Archives.
10 Ibid.; emphasis in original.
11 Turck, "Present Challenge," 7, 8.
12 Charles Turck, "President's Interim Report" [to the Board of Trustees], October 10, 1947, Macalester College Archives.
13 Charles Turck to "The Faculty," June 1, 1955, Macalester College Archives. Turck's use of religious language should be noted here. Though in the 1930s he avoided religious language in public discussions of the college's mission, a resurgence in evangelicalism nationally may have influenced his use of the language here.
14 See, e.g., Charles Turck to Paul H. Davis, July 18, 1972, Charles Turck Papers, Macalester College Archives.
15 Turck, *Nature of a Liberal Education*, 4.
16 Ibid., 14–15; the quote appears on p. 15.
17 DeWitt Wallace to Charles Turck, November 25, 1955; Charles Turck to DeWitt Wallace, November 29, 1955, Macalester College Archives.
18 Paul H. Davis to Charles J. Turck, June 28, 1972, Charles Turck Papers, Macalester College Archives.
19 Turck, *Nature of a Liberal Education*, 13.
20 Charles Turck, "President's Interim Report" [to the Board of Trustees], October 10, 1947, Macalester College Archives.
21 Charles Turck to DeWitt and Lila Wallace, August 1, 1951, Macalester College Archives.
22 Charles Turck to DeWitt Wallace, September 25, 1954; Charles Turck to DeWitt Wallace, November 3, 1954, Macalester College Archives.
23 Davis served as general secretary at Columbia University from 1946 to 1949, when he was appointed vice president of development. He left Columbia in 1950.

24 See DeWitt Wallace to Charles Turck, December 24, 1955, Macalester College Archives. Author John Heidenry describes Davis as "a wealthy conservative from Los Angeles who had made his fortune by playing poker—always a good credential so far as Wally was concerned." See Heidenry, *Theirs Was the Kingdom*, 366. Peter Canning describes him as a former vice president of Columbia, whom the Wallaces met when *Reader's Digest* was doing a series of articles on Dwight D. Eisenhower's work as the president of Columbia University. He describes Davis as a Presbyterian who had "flown De Havilland planes during World War I, then wing-walked his way through Stanford University; before coming to California, he had overseen San Francisco's Depression-era relief programs, managed a utility company in Brazil and [became] a sought-after consultant on college financing and administration." See Canning, *American Dreamers*, 106. The story that circulated around Macalester explaining how Wallace became interested in Davis was that as Davis was writing letters one evening, he inadvertently placed two letters in the wrong envelopes, sending Wallace the letter he meant for a close friend describing his wife's cancer treatments. Wallace was supposedly moved by the letter and sent Davis a check. Thus began the relationship. This story has not been verified.

25 Paul H. Davis to Gordon Gray, October 30, 1953, Mr. and Mrs. DeWitt Wallace, 1939–55, Macalester College Archives. Davis apparently gave Wallace a copy of this letter.

26 Paul H. Davis, "Colleges Need Salesmanship," *Los Angeles Times*, January 28, 1953. Mimeograph of article in Macalester College Archives, Mr. and Mrs. DeWitt Wallace, 1937–55.

27 See DeWitt Wallace to Charles Turck, July 1, 1955; Charles Turck to DeWitt Wallace, July 12, 1955, Macalester College Archives.

28 Paul Davis to Charles J. Turck, December 10, 1955, Macalester College Archives.

29 It should be noted that DeWitt and Lila Wallace visited Macalester in late September 1955. This was only the second time Turck had met them, the first being in 1938. See Charles J. Turck to the Trustees of Macalester College, October 6, 1955, Macalester College Archives.

30 DeWitt Wallace to Charles Turck, December 24, 1955, Macalester College Archives; emphasis in original.

31 Charles Turck to DeWitt Wallace, December 19, 1955, Macalester College Archives.

32 Charles Turck to DeWitt Wallace, January 9, 1955, Macalester College Archives.

33 Charles J. Turck, "Memorandum—Conversation with De Witt Wallace," February 5, 1956, Macalester College Archives. Turck's ten-year plan and plan of giving have not been found.

34 DeWitt Wallace to Charles Turck, telegram, April 12, 1956, Macalester College Archives.

35 The quote was from a joint statement released by the cochairmen of the development program, Macalester trustees Benjamin G. Griggs and J. Cameron Thomson. "Macalester to Start Big Expansion," *Minneapolis Tribune*, October 14, 1956. See also

"Macalester Expands Its Program for the Future," *St. Paul Pioneer Press*, October 15, 1956; "Macalester Program," *Minneapolis Star*, October 17, 1956.

36 See "Wallace Sees Big Future for City as College Town," *St. Paul Dispatch*, January 31, 1957; press release, no title, January 22, 1957, newspaper clipping, Macalester College Archives. Peter Canning offers a psychological analysis of DeWitt's troubled relationship with his family, deduced primarily from remaining correspondence and suggesting strong Oedipal overtones in his relationship with his parents. More likely, DeWitt probably knew little of his father, who suffered from often severe depression during his son's childhood years. DeWitt's mother Janet was also frequently institutionalized for long periods of time. Heidenry, *Theirs Was the Kingdom*, 25–30; Canning, *American Dreamers*, 100–1.

37 Given Paul Davis's expertise in publicity, it is quite likely that he had a hand in concocting the sentimental story of Wallace and his father.

38 Paul H. Davis, "Should College Giving Be Designated or Unrestricted?" photocopy of typescript, April 1957, 3, Macalester College Archives.

39 Ibid.

40 DeWitt Wallace to Charles Turck, July 23, 1956, Macalester College Archives.

41 Charles J. Turck to DeWitt Wallace, November 25, 1957, Macalester College Archives.

42 "Gifts from Mr. DeWitt Wallace, Mrs. DeWitt Wallace, Reader's Digest Association and the Reader's Digest Foundation from May 29, 1956 to December 19, 1957," December 19, 1957, Macalester College Archives.

43 Charles J. Turck to DeWitt Wallace, August 12, 1957; DeWitt Wallace to Charles J. Turck, December 4, 1957; F. W. Budolfson to DeWitt Wallace, October 8, 1958, Macalester College Archives.

44 These deficiencies were reported publicly in J. Cameron Thomson's report to the board of trustees, August 13, 1957, although many trustees and Turck must have known of them earlier. See minutes of the Board of Trustees of Macalester College, August 13, 1957.

45 Charles J. Turck to the Faculty of Macalester College, December 3, 1957, Macalester College Archives.

46 DeWitt Wallace to Earle Savage, July 29, 1957, Macalester College Archives.

47 Charles J. Turck to DeWitt Wallace, October 12, 1957; DeWitt Wallace to Charles J. Turck, February 4, 1958, Macalester College Archives.

48 Charles J. Turck to DeWitt Wallace, June 10, 1957, Macalester College Archives.

49 DeWitt Wallace to Harvey Rice, December 17, 1958, Macalester College Archives.

50 DeWitt Wallace to Charles J. Turck, April 1, 1957, Macalester College Archives.

51 Photo, *MacWeekly*, May 23, 1958, 4; Charles Turck to Lila Wallace, April 5, 1957; Charles Turck to DeWitt Wallace, April 15, 1957; DeWitt Wallace to Charles Turck, April 29, 1957, Macalester College Archives.

52 DeWitt Wallace to Charles J. Turck, September 13, 1956; Charles Turck to DeWitt Wallace, May 2, 1956, Macalester College Archives.

53 DeWitt Wallace to Charles J. Turck, April 26, 1957, Macalester College Archives.

54 Charles Turck to DeWitt Wallace, May 2, 1956, Macalester College Archives. Wallace also expressed alarm over students' apparent sympathy for Socialist Party member Norman Thomas in 1948 during a mock election held on campus, in which Thomas garnered 140 votes out of 531. Harold Stassen, the Republican candidate, received a comfortable majority of 269 votes. Turck, assuaging Wallace's concern, explained that a last-minute plea for Thomas was made as a strategic move to draw votes away from Truman. Charles Turck to DeWitt Wallace, June 10, 1948, Macalester College Archives.

55 Charles J. Turck to Dwight D. Eisenhower, November 9, 1954, Dwight D. Eisenhower Presidential Library.

56 See Charles J. Turck to Dwight D. Eisenhower, May 28, 1954, March 12, 1958, August 22, 1958, and August 27, 1959, Macalester College Archives.

57 A letter critical of Nixon, written by Turck, appeared in the *Washington Post* in December 1952. Wallace, on learning this, immediately sent Turck an article presenting Nixon in a favorable light. DeWitt Wallace to Charles Turck, December 2, 1952; Charles J. Turck to DeWitt Wallace, December 9, 1952, Macalester College Archives.

58 Memorandum for Mr. Morgan from Robert Gray, January 11, 1953, Eisenhower Library.

59 J. B. Matthews, "Communism and the Colleges," *American Mercury*, May 1953, 111. The author is grateful to Don Wortman (class of 1950) for bringing this important citation to her attention.

60 Ibid., 124.

61 Heidenry, *Theirs Was the Kingdom*, 209.

62 Ibid., 210.

63 Ibid., 255.

64 Don Wortman, "President Turck and Macalester Confront McCarthyism," typescript, [2008], Macalester College Archives. This essay presents a detailed account of Turck's and the college's response to the accusations.

65 J. B. Matthews, "Reds and Our Churches," *American Mercury*, July 1953, 3–13. See also J. B. Matthews, "Red Infiltration of Theological Seminaries," *American Mercury*, November 1953, 31–38.

66 Charles J. Turck to DeWitt Wallace, February 19, 1957, Macalester College Archives.

67 S. W. Royce to DeWitt Wallace, November 15, 1957, Macalester College Archives.

68 See DeWitt Wallace to Charles J. Turck, October 15, 1957; cf. Charles J. Turck to DeWitt Wallace, June 12, 1955, Macalester College Archives, in which Turck informs Wallace that he plans to retire by June 1960.

69 Minutes of the Board of Trustees of Macalester College, January 2, 1958.

70 Charles Turck, 1947 report to the Trustees, Macalester College Archives.

71 See "Minutes of the Stillwater Conference, Hill Family Foundation, Five College Project. Lowell Inn, Stillwater, Minnesota, February 18–19, 1955," Macalester College Archives.

72 Armajani, "Four College Area Studies," 6.

73 This Stillwater location was a popular one for Macalester conferences. The area studies program was developed at a conference in Stillwater four years earlier. Later college conferences would also be held there, including the September 1961 conference discussed later in this chapter.

74 Interview with Harvey Rice conducted by Bill Hakala, April 4, 1985, transcript, Macalester College Archives.

75 Rice reports that he had been offered a position as vice president at the University of Texas–Austin that spring and delayed responding to the offer until after the board meeting, believing that if the board voted down the recommendations, he would likely be asked to resign. Hakala, interview with Harvey Rice.

76 In a survey of sixty-four faculty members, each of these categories received dissenting votes of four or fewer. See "Record of Vote and Comments on a Report of the Advisory Council on Aims, Practices, Policies, and Plans of Macalester College," Macalester College Archives.

77 "Additional Comments on a Report of the Advisory Council on Aims, Practices, Policies, and Plans of Macalester College," [December 1961], Macalester College Archives.

78 Ibid.

79 Ibid.; emphasis in original.

80 "Additional Comments."

81 "Macalester College Challenges the Future: A Summary," Macalester College Archives.

82 This is true of the summary document. No copy of the full document exists in the Macalester College Archives.

10. *The Religion–Education Intersection Transformed*

1 Minutes of the Meeting of the Board of Trustees of Macalester College, October 20, 1960, Macalester College Archives.

2 Minutes of the Meeting of the Minnesota Synod's Committee on Higher Education, January 24, 1962, Macalester College Archives.

3 Ibid.

4 Ibid.

5 John Maxwell Adams to the Ministers of the Synod of Minnesota, March 16, 1962, Macalester College Archives.

6 J. M. Adams to the Curriculum Review Committee, May 18, 1962, Macalester College Archives.

7 Adams also taught Christianity courses in the religion department.

8 Harvey Rice to the Curriculum Review Committee, May 18, 1962, Macalester College Archives.

9 "Chapel Review Committee Statement," [April 1, 1963], Provost's Office Box, 1962–63, Advisory Council, 1962 Folder, Macalester College Archives.

10 Ibid.

11 Larry Demarest, "Protestants and Angels," *MacWeekly*, November 2, 1962, 2.

12 "Chapel Proposal Hurdles Council Tangle," *MacWeekly*, March 1, 1963, 3.

13 Minutes of the Meeting of the Minnesota Synod's Committee on Higher Education, January 24, 1962, Macalester College Archives.

14 Harold H. Vieham to William J. Van Dyken, October 15, 1965, Macalester College Archives.

15 William Van Dyken to Harvey Rice, October 1, 1965, Macalester College Archives.

16 Harvey Rice to William J. Van Dyken, October 4, 1965; see also John Maxwell Adams to Ernest Sandeen, February 16, 1967; and John Maxwell Adams, "Macalester College and the Presbyterian Church: Some Items from the History," November 17, 1969, Macalester College Archives, both of which reiterate the historical narrative, developed by Adams, that Rice presents in the earlier letter.

17 *Macalester College Bulletin*, 1940.

18 Figures on the number of Presbyterian-identified students were not found for the years 1966, 1967, and 1969–77.

19 "Report of Higher Education Committee on the Relationship between Macalester College and the Synod of Minnesota," [May 1967], Macalester College Archives.

20 Ibid.

21 Robert McAfee Brown briefly discusses his time at Macalester in his memoir *Reflections on the Long Haul*, 75–77.

22 J. Donald Butler, "Religion at Macalester," September 12, 1967, typescript, 1, Macalester College Archives.

23 Ibid., 3. See also J. Donald Butler, "Recommendations to the Department of Religion toward an Eventual Revision of Our Program of Study," September 12, 1967, typescript, Macalester College Archives.

24 On the development of the discipline of religious studies, particularly in the postwar period, see Porterfield, *Transformation of American Religion*.

25 John Maxwell Adams, "A Draft of Statements in Regard to Macalester College for Possible Incorporation in the 1967 Report of Synod's Committee on Higher Education," May 12, 1967, Macalester College Archives.

26 Students weighed in on both sides of issue. See "Speaking Out ... with Opinions," *MacWeekly*, March 11, 1966, 2.

27 Arthur S. Flemming to Harvey Rice, May 19, 1966, Arthur S. Flemming Papers, Dwight D. Eisenhower Presidential Library.

28 John Maxwell Adams to DeWitt Wallace, October 26, 1966, Chapel Files, Macalester College Archives.

29 John Maxwell Adams to DeWitt Wallace, March 17, 1967, Chapel Files, Macalester College Archives.

30 John Maxwell Adams to DeWitt Wallace, October 26, 1966, Chapel Files, Macalester College Archives.

31 DeWitt Wallace to Arthur Flemming, September 23, 1968, Chapel Files, Macalester College Archives. Concerns about Salisbury were raised in a letter from Mrs. Keith Adams to Harvey Rice, April 28, 1967, Chapel Files, Macalester College Archives; John Maxwell Adams to Mrs. Frederick Weyerhaeuser and Mrs. Walter B. Driscoll, March 20, 1976, Chapel Files, Macalester College Archives.

32 John Maxwell Adams to Mrs. Frederick Weyerhaeuser and Mrs. Walter B. Driscoll, March 20, 1976, Chapel Files, Macalester College Archives.

33 See "Speaking Out," *MacWeekly*, October 14, 1966, 2; "No Communication Concerning Chapel," *MacWeekly*, February 24, 1967, 2; "Speaking Out," *MacWeekly*, March 3, 1967, 2; "Speaking Out . . . Opinions, Comments, Criticisms," *MacWeekly*, March 10, 1967, 2; "Trustees, Administration Blasted: Better Communications Urged," *MacWeekly*, March 10, 1967, 1; George D. Dayton, "Trustee Explains Chapel Grant, Policy Development Process Told," *MacWeekly*, April 7, 1967, 2.

34 As quoted in "Chapel Issue Arouses Community," *MacWeekly*, March 10, 1967, 1.

35 See, e.g., John Maxwell Adams to Mrs. Frederick Weyerhaeuser and Mrs. Walter B. Driscoll, March 20, 1976, Chapel Files, Macalester College Archives.

36 Yahya Armajani, "What It Takes to Be a Christian College," September 19, 1967, Macalester College Archives.

37 Irwin Rinder, "Position Paper: In Favor of a Church-Affiliated College," April 29, 1969, Chapel Papers, Macalester College Archives.

38 Wayne Roberts, "People of Faith—Not Statements of Faith," [March 1970], Chapel Files, Macalester College Archives.

11. *New Approaches to Academics, Internationalism, and Service*

1 Leland D. Case to Charles W. Ferguson, February 27, 1957, Chapel Papers, Macalester College Archives.

2 On Flemming's hiring of Davis, see Arthur Flemming to Paul Davis, February 2, 1967; Mary Walker to Paul Davis, February 10, 1967, Arthur S. Flemming Papers, Dwight D. Eisenhower Presidential Library. On their friendship, see Paul Davis to Arthur Flemming, July 7, 1965; several letters between November 1965 and January 1966 regarding Davis's purchase of land on the McKenzie River, Arthur S. Flemming Papers, Dwight D. Eisenhower Presidential Library.

3 University of Oregon Libraries, Office of the President, http://boundless.uoregon.edu/digcol/clark/collectionBrowse.html.

4 See, e.g., Lila Acheson Wallace to Arthur Flemming, June 9, 1964; Arthur Flemming to Lila Acheson Wallace, December 15, 1964; Lila Acheson Wallace to Arthur Flemming, December 29, 1964; Arthur Flemming to Lila Acheson Wallace, January 6, 1965, Arthur S. Flemming Papers, Dwight D. Eisenhower Presidential Library.

5 Flemming's initial term ended within a year, suggesting that his appointment filled an existing vacancy. He was elected to a full three-year term in 1966.

6 Paul Davis to Arthur Flemming, June 7, 1965, Arthur S. Flemming Papers, Dwight D. Eisenhower Presidential Library.

7 Harvey M. Rice to Arthur S. Flemming, December 29, 1966, Arthur S. Flemming Papers, Dwight D. Eisenhower Presidential Library. The Wallace quotation appears in a handwritten note at the top of Rice's letter.

8 Immediately prior to coming to Macalester, Garvin was serving as chair of the philosophy department at the University of Maryland; from 1935 to 1952, he was a member of the philosophy department at Oberlin College. See "Maryland U Prof Will Take Over Duties August 1," *MacWeekly*, April 14, 1961, 1.

9 Lucius Garvin to Members of the Board of Trustees, September 1, 1966, Arthur S. Flemming Papers, Dwight D. Eisenhower Presidential Library.

10 This figure included a twelve million dollar transfer of funds from an unidentified program (SPREF) to the Restricted General Endowment. The purpose of this transfer and why it was recorded as a "program" are unknown. "Index and Summary of Proposals from Macalester College to Mr. & Mrs. DeWitt Wallace," November 8, 1965. See also Wallace Program Budgets, Macalester College Archives. Copies of all the programs exist in the Arthur S. Flemming Papers, Dwight D. Eisenhower Presidential Library.

11 Paul H. Davis to Lucius P. Garvin, January 31, 1966, Arthur S. Flemming Papers, Dwight D. Eisenhower Presidential Library.

12 Minutes of Special Meeting of the Executive Committee of the Macalester College Board of Trustees, February 4, 1966, Arthur S. Flemming Papers, Dwight D. Eisenhower Presidential Library.

13 See Paul Davis to Archibald Jackson, July 3, 1967, Arthur S. Flemming Papers, Dwight D. Eisenhower Presidential Library.

14 Arthur Flemming to David Winton, July 26, 1966, Arthur S. Flemming Papers, Dwight D. Eisenhower Presidential Library.

15 Arthur Flemming to Paul Davis, June 6, 1967, 3–4, Arthur S. Flemming Papers, Dwight D. Eisenhower Presidential Library.

16 See Lucius Garvin to Paul H. Davis, August 23, 1967; Lucius Garvin to Arthur S. Flemming, September 14, 1967; Lucius Garvin to Members of the Educational Projects Sub-Committee, September 18, 1967; "Summary of Consensus Decisions," October 11, 1967; Lucius Garvin to Arthur Flemming, David Winton, C. Gilbert Wrenn, and E. W. Ziebarth, October 11, 1967; Lucius Garvin and Louise F. Lowe to Members of the Educational Projects Committee of the Trustees, January 10, 1968; Harvey Rice to All Members of the Board of Trustees of Macalester College, January 31, 1968; Report of the Office of Educational Research and Experimental Innovation, undated; Memorandums 1–7 on individual programs, Arthur S. Flemming Papers, Dwight D. Eisenhower Presidential Library.

17 See "Macites Return from Abroad," *MacWeekly*, September 27, 1963, 1.

18 See "Ambassadors of Friendship Tour during Summer," *MacWeekly*, September 30, 1960, 4.

19 Bob DeBaugh, "Macites, Foreign Students Tour as Ambassadors for Friendship," *MacWeekly*, April 29, 1966, 4.

20 Heidenry, *Theirs Was the Kingdom*, 375–80. See also "Harry Morgan—Will Assume Mac Position in Sept.," *MacWeekly*, February 26, 1960, 1; "'Friendship Caravans' Will Embark April 9," March 11, 1960, 6; Kay Carroll, "12 Foreign Editors Will Spend Year at Mac," *MacWeekly*, June 30, 1961, 3.

21 After leaving Macalester, Flemming returned to public office in the Nixon administration.

22 Editorial, *Eugene Register Guard*, March 1962, as quoted in Flemming, *Arthur Flemming*, 232.

23 That same year, Macalester trustees prohibited Communist speaker Ben Davis from appearing on campus. See Thomas B. Thornton (class of 1941), letter to the editor, *MacWeekly*, March 22, 1963, 2.

24 This course seemed to have been offered by a community organization, perhaps a church or interfaith group. See Flemming, *Arthur Flemming*, 257. On the Gus Hall incident, see ibid., 235–43.

25 Macalester College press release draft, March 28, 1968, 3, Arthur S. Flemming Papers, Dwight D. Eisenhower Presidential Library.

26 See Donald H. Hughes to Harvey Rice, January 14, 1964; Harvey Rice to Donald H. Hughes, January 15, 1964; Donald Hughes to "Presidents and [illegible]," February 21, 1964; "Report: Inter-College Faculty Exchange Program," November 1966, Hill Foundation material, Macalester College Archives.

27 "Report: Inter-College," 7.

28 Harvey Rice, "How Small Liberal Arts Colleges Can Join in the Movement toward Equal Educational Opportunities," *Campus America*, 1965–75, Macalester College Archives.

29 See letters to the editor from Yolanda L. Ridley, Ron Weber, Marilyn Vigil, and Carol Huenemann, *MacWeekly*, October 19, 1962, 2.

30 Black Liberation Affairs Committee, undated, Macalester College Archives. This publication was intended to recruit other African American students to campus, for though the essays are painfully honest in the frustration they express, each one ends with the conviction that the individual is getting a first-class education at Macalester and that others would do well to come.

31 "President's Committee on Racism at the University, for Committee on Dormitory Staff Development," May 1, 1968, Arthur S. Flemming Papers, Dwight D. Eisenhower Presidential Library.

32 See Art Hughes, "The Legacy of the Morrill Hall Takeover," Minnesota Public Radio, http://minnesota.publicradio.org/display/web/2006/04/21/morrillhall/; and "African American and African Studies Celebrates 40 Years," *Reunion News*, http://afroam.umn.edu/anniversary.html.

33 See "Program to Expand Educational Opportunities," Trustee Materials, President's Office, Macalester College Archives. See also minutes of the Executive Committee, December 20, 1968, Macalester College Archives.

34 "Student Group Formed: EEO Solicits Student Pledges," *MacWeekly*, February 21, 1969, 1.

35 Gary Nash et al., *American People*, 982.

36 "Currier Joins Peace March with Religious Group in D.C.," *MacWeekly*, February 10, 1967, 1.

37 Author's interview with Paul Aslanian, February 27, 2003.

38 See "Mac Studies Take Business Office" and "College Reactions," *MacWeekly, Extra*, April 17, 1970, 1; Joan Henderson, "Trustee Meeting Set for Sixth," *MacWeekly*, April 24, 1970, 2.

39 This observation was made by several individuals interviewed for this history. See Roger K. Mosvick, "Remarks, Alumni of Color Reunion, EEO Vision, Purpose, Impact," June 4, 2005, Macalester College Archives.

40 In this view, racial justice demonstrations and race riots by definition indicated disrespect for the system and did not deserve to be rewarded by government or private efforts to ameliorate conditions. *Reader's Digest*, a bastion of white conservative popular writing, took this position. On *Reader's Digest*'s support for Goldwater, see Heidenry, *Theirs Was the Kingdom*, 281–82.

41 See Stevenson, "Social Control," 345–46, 360.

42 "We Are Committed," *MacWeekly*, March 13, 1970, 2.

43 The call for a nationwide strike of higher education originated at Brandeis University. See Philip W. Semas, "A Week of Tragedy: Disorders Flare, 4 Students Die as U.S. Action in Cambodia Inflames Many Campuses," *Chronicle of Higher Education*, May 11, 1970.

44 It was later revealed that the United States had been conducting secret bombing raids on the country for over a year.

45 "Johnson Urges Support for Nixon," *St. Paul Pioneer Press*, May 1, 1970, 2.

46 Gary Dawson, "U Rally Votes Peace Strike," *St. Paul Pioneer Press*, May 5, 1970, 1; "Hamline Students Call Strike," *St. Paul Pioneer Press*, May 5, 1970, 2.

47 See Ted Smebakken, "HH to Teach at Macalester and University," *Minneapolis Star*, December 13, 1968, 4A.

48 In February 1969, Humphrey was among the keynote speakers at a conference on urban affairs held at the college. See Paul Koniski, "Symposium Cites Urban 'Confusion,'" *MacWeekly*, February 28, 1969, 1.

49 Holly's letter was not found. See Hubert H. Humphrey to James F. Holly, March 1, 1969, Hubert Humphrey Box, "The New Deal" 1941 by HHH Folder, Macalester College Archives.

50 Macalester Committee for Peace in Vietnam, ". . . Humphrey, No!" flyer, undated, Hubert Humphrey Box, Political Science Faculty HHH Folder, Macalester College

Archives; "Time for Change in Humphrey Chair," *MacWeekly*, April 3, 1970, 2.

51 J. Michael Keenan to Hubert Humphrey, May 5, 1970; Hubert Humphrey to J. Michael Keenan, May 9, 1970, Hubert H. Humphrey Papers, Minnesota Historical Society.

52 Ruth [————] to HHH, May 5, 1970, Hubert H. Humphrey Papers, Minnesota Historical Society.

53 "HHH Arrives in Tel Aviv," *St. Paul Pioneer Press*, May 4, 1970, 22.

54 See Ruth [————] to HHH, May 5, 1970; List of Students, HHH Papers, Minnesota Historical Society.

55 Stevenson, "Social Control," 360–61.

56 Ibid., 362.

57 Alvin C. Currier, "The Emperor's Clothes," *Provo-cateur* 1, no. 2 (November 1968): 7. The piece is a reprint of Currier's address delivered at the opening program of the Macalester Free College, September 25, 1968, Macalester College Archives.

58 Ibid.; Alvin Alexsi C. Currier, personal interview with author, May 16, 2003.

59 All quotations in the preceding paragraph are taken from Alvin C. Currier, "Martha and Mary: A Sermon Preached Sunday, September 9, 1973, in Weyerhaeuser Chapel, Macalester College," Macalester College Archives.

60 "Jostein Mykletun," *MacWeekly*, March 13, 1970, 2.

12. *Challenges and Dashed Hopes*

1 Among the perks was a particle accelerator, which was used to attract a physicist. Author's interview with Truman Schwartz, July 12, 2002.

2 Lucius Garvin to Arthur Flemming, April 16, 1966, Arthur S. Flemming Papers, Dwight D. Eisenhower Presidential Library.

3 David Winton to DeWitt Wallace, November 5, 1958, David Winton Papers, Minnesota Historical Society.

4 See F. N. Budolfson to Charles J. Turck, November 21, 1958; Charles J. Turck to F. N. Budolfson, November 25, 1958; Charles J. Turck to F. N. Budolfson, December 4, 1958, Charles J. Turck Papers, Macalester College Archives.

5 David Winton to Arnold Lowe, November 5, 1958, David Winton Papers, Minnesota Historical Society.

6 See Macalester College Annual Reports, 1960–69, President's Office.

7 Paul Davis, "Seventeen Priorities for Macalester Suggested for Nineteen Sixty Seven," January 1, 1967, Arthur S. Flemming Papers, Dwight D. Eisenhower Presidential Library.

8 Paul Davis to Arthur S. Flemming, March 27, 1967, Arthur S. Flemming Papers, Dwight D. Eisenhower Presidential Library.

9 Ibid.

10 See, e.g., DeWitt Wallace to Harvey Rice, November 9, 1966, DeWitt Wallace Papers, International Center Folder, Macalester College Archives.

11 Paul Davis to Lucius Garvin, July 25, 1967, and Lucius Garvin to Paul H. Davis, August 7, 1967, Arthur S. Flemming Papers, Dwight D. Eisenhower Presidential Library.

12 See, e.g., Paul Davis to DeWitt Wallace, May 9, 1967; Arthur Flemming to Paul Davis, June 6, 1967; David Winton to George Dayton, January 26, 1967; David Winton to Arthur Flemming, January 26, 1967, Arthur S. Flemming Papers, Dwight D. Eisenhower Presidential Library.

13 John Heidenry indicates that Rice was "forced to resign over a personal matter" without revealing what that personal matter involved. See Heidenry, *Theirs Was the Kingdom*, 365.

14 See, e.g., Landrum R. Bolling to Paul H. Davis, June 28, 1967; Paul H. Davis to DeWitt Wallace, November 20, 1967; Paul H. Davis to Arthur Flemming, December 29, 1967; John L. Davis to Paul H. Davis, February 27, 1968, Macalester College Archives.

15 Heidenry, *Theirs Was the Kingdom*, 366; Flemming, *Arthur Flemming*, 276–77. Neither of these sources is completely reliable. Heidenry does not document his sources, so where he found the seven million dollar figure is unknown. He did have access to college documents that have been denied to this author, however, so it is not unlikely that his information is accurate. Bernice Flemming's account of her spouse, Arthur Flemming, is completely laudatory in its depiction of all aspects of Flemming's life.

16 C. Gilbert Wrenn to Lucius Garvin, November 13, 1970, DeWitt Wallace Papers, 1967–68, Macalester College Archives.

17 Ibid.

18 John M. Dozier to Paul H. Davis, July 11, 1969; Paul H. Davis to John M. Dozier, November, 17, 1969; Paul H. Davis to Arthur Flemming, February 10, 1970; Paul H. Davis to John M. Dozier, March 13, 1970; Paul H. Davis to Arthur Flemming, April 1, 1970; Paul H. Davis to Arthur M. Flemming, April 13, 1970; Paul H. Davis to Granger Costikyan, April 27 1970, DeWitt Wallace Papers, Macalester College Archives.

19 John Dozier to Paul H. Davis, March 13, 1970, DeWitt Wallace Papers, Macalester College Archives.

20 Davis to Costikyan, April 27, 1970, DeWitt Wallace Papers, Paul Davis File, Macalester College Archives.

21 Ibid.

22 "Mac to Issue Financial Report," *MacWeekly*, May 19, 1970, 2.

23 Paul H. Davis to DeWitt Wallace, June 21, 1970, DeWitt Wallace Papers, Macalester College Archives.

24 Ibid.

25 John Dozier, "The High Winds Program," July 6, 1970; Paul Davis to John Dozier, July 11, 1970, DeWitt Wallace Papers, Macalester College Archives.

26 Jeremiah Reedy interview with Donald Garretson, May 29, 2003, audiotape with transcript, Macalester College Archives.

27 This letter, along with several others from the period, is currently sealed by Macalester College. See chapter 7, n33.

28 Paul H. Davis to DeWitt Wallace, July 20, 1970, DeWitt Wallace Papers, Macalester College Archives.

29 George D. Dayton II to DeWitt Wallace, August 12, 1970, DeWitt Wallace Papers, Macalester College Archives.

30 Paul Davis to DeWitt Wallace, August 22, 1970, DeWitt Wallace Papers, Macalester College Archives.

31 Macalester College Audit, "Statement of Revenues and Expenditures, Current Funds, Year Ended August 31, 1970," Wilkerson, Guthmann, and Johnson, Certified Public Accountants, St. Paul, Minn., August 31, 1970, Exhibit B, Macalester College Archives.

32 Macalester College Audit, Wilkerson, Guthmann, and Johnson, Certified Public Accountants, St. Paul, Minn., August 31, 1971, 8, Macalester College Archives.

33 See Joan Henderson, "The Broken Down Budget: We Are Not Alone," *MacWeekly*, December 4, 1970, 1; Gina Cullen, "College Funding: A National Crisis," *MacWeekly*, December 11, 1970, 2. The University of Minnesota, e.g., terminated 168 faculty during the period, and many small colleges, including Reed and Antioch, came close to closing.

34 Ibid.

35 Paul Davis, "DeWitt Wallace at Macalester," *MacWeekly*, December 11, 1970, 1.

36 Ibid.

37 "Macalester Loses Fiscal 'Angels,'" *Minneapolis Star*, January 20, 1971, A15; Lewis Patterson, "Mac Losing Chief Donor," *St. Paul Pioneer Press*, January 20, 1971, 1; Greg Pinney, "Macalester Feels Shortage as Heavy Donor Stops Aid," *Minneapolis Tribune*, January 20, 1971, 1.

38 Pinney, "Macalester Feels Shortage."

39 "Macalester Loses Fiscal 'Angels.'"

40 Greg Pinney, "Resigning Head Asks Trustees to Keep Macalester Programs," *Minneapolis Tribune*, January 22, 1971, 11.

41 Ibid.

42 Lewis Patterson, "Flemming Gets Faculty Ovation at Macalester," *St. Paul Pioneer Press*, January 22, 1979, 1.

43 It is, of course, quite possible that among the documents closed by the college, further reasons for Wallace's decision were committed to paper. See chapter 7, n34.

44 John Dozier to Paul Davis, March 13, 1970, DeWitt Wallace Papers, Paul Davis File, Macalester College Archives.

45 Paul H. Davis to Arthur S. Flemming, March 27, 1967, Arthur S. Flemming Papers, Dwight D. Eisenhower Presidential Library.

46 In contrast, EEO was quite well funded, receiving $121,000 in federal grants in 1969–70. It continued to receive increasing amounts yearly through 1974. On federal and nonfederal support for EEO, see Macalester College, "Summary of EEO Program," August 4, 1974, Macalester College Archives. Foundation gifts increased significantly in 1970–71.

47 See Flemming, *Arthur Flemming*.

48 C. Gilbert Wrenn to Lucius Garvin, January 25, 1971, Dewitt Wallace Papers, 1967–68, Macalester College Archives.

49 Patterson, "Flemming Gets Faculty Ovation."

50 Flemming, *Arthur Flemming*, 291–302.

51 Wrenn to Garvin, January 25, 1971.

52 DeWitt Wallace to John Driscoll, April 19, 1971; and John Dozier to DeWitt Wallace, July 16, 1971, DeWitt Wallace Papers, Macalester College Archives.

53 This is perhaps the most perplexing aspect of the situation. College officials remained in contact with Wallace after the cessation of funds, but their confidence in Davis had vanished. Just what service Davis felt he could still do on campus is a mystery. Those faculty members who have suggested that he was nothing more than Wallace's "spy" are particularly correct with respect to the post–January 1971 period.

54 Heidenry, *Theirs Was the Kingdom*, 368, quoting Davis. The letter from which Heidenry took this quotation is not cited in the book. In private correspondence with the author, Heidenry claimed that the letter he used was in the Macalester College Archives when he did his initial research there. He thought that the letter could be among those removed from the archives by representatives of *Reader's Digest*. J. M. Heidenry, e-mail message to author, October 16, 2002. The current Macalester president, however, has indicated that it is in his possession. See chapter 7, n34.

55 See Heidenry, *Theirs Was the Kingdom*, 396–97.

56 Ibid., 369. Again, Heidenry's sources for this exchange were letters in the Macalester archives, which either no longer exist on campus or have been closed by the president. Until these documents are opened, Heidenry's account, which implies that Macalester officials may well have knowingly been making unauthorized withdrawals and that Wallace did not pursue legal measures against the college only because he was "fed up" with the school (369), must stand as authoritative.

57 Ibid.

58 *Minneapolis Star Tribune*, January 25, 1971, as quoted in "Flemming Eulogized," *MacWeekly*, February 12, 1971, 5.

59 For another treatment of the political and financial influences affecting the campus during this period, see Stevenson, "Social Control," 365–84.

60 Dave Lapakko, "The Search for a New President Begins," *MacWeekly*, February 5, 1971, 3.

61 Of particular concern was the fact that EEO students were allowed two paid trips home during the semester, whereas students on regular financial aid were allowed only one.

62 Dave Lapakko, "The Search for a New President Begins," *MacWeekly*, February 5, 1971, 1.

13. *Countercultural Campus*

1 James F. Holly, "Postscript: The Inheritors," *Phaez* 3 2, no. 2 (n.d.): 7, Macalester College Archives.
2 Don Gemberling and Art Ogle, "Right and Left in the Ivory Tower," broadside, [1964], Macalester College Archives.
3 Ibid.
4 Ibid.
5 Steven Van Drake, "The West Wind," *St. Paul Dispatch*, March 19, 1968, clipping, Macalester College Archives.
6 Ibid.; emphasis in original.
7 Tentative enrollment form for the student-operated Macalester Free College, Macalester Free College Folder, Macalester College Archives.
8 Alvin C. Currier, "The Emperor's Clothes" (address delivered at the opening program of the Macalester Free College, September 25, 1968), *Provo-cateur* 1 (September 1969), 7.
9 Van Drake, "West Wind."
10 Schroth, *Fordham*, 279.
11 Ibid., 279–80.
12 James Thompson, "Inner College Begins Its First Year," September 26, 1969, Macalester College Archives.
13 "The Traditional College vs. the New College," *MacWeekly*, December 12, 1969, 3.
14 "Careers in Social Change," November 24 and 25, 1969, broadside conference agenda, Inner College Box, Macalester College Archives.
15 See, e.g., Dan Lubin, "Perspectives on Transferring In and Out," *MacWeekly*, December 8, 1972, 13.
16 Anonymous broadside, [1964], Macalester College Archives (donated by Don Gemberling). The Community Council was often the organizer of campus activism.
17 Tim King, "Dorm Reorganized, Wally Goes Coed Next Year," *MacWeekly*, May 2, 1969, 1.
18 "Margaret Mead on Peace, Parenthood, and Co-ed Dorms," *MacWeekly*, April 30, 1971, 9.
19 Minutes of the Executive Committee of the Board of Trustees, Macalester College, June 20, 1968, Macalester College Archives.
20 Alvin Alexsi C. Currier, personal interview with the author, May 16, 2003.
21 Chipman, "Attitudes, Behaviors and Characteristics," 71, 11–33.
22 Ibid., 71, 162, 163. Antidepressants were also included but were reported as being used by less than a percentage point of the students surveyed. One must keep in mind that the data were collected through self-reporting surveys and follow-up interviews and that given the context of peer pressure, inaccurate responses may well have inflated the figures.
23 Ibid., 234.

24 Ibid., 237–38.
25 Ibid., 253.
26 This prestige factor also cast doubt on the figures obtained through self-reporting.
27 See Randolph R. Royals, *Imani* (Macalester College, Blackhouse Publications), March 23, 1973, 4, Macalester College Archives.
28 Chipman, "Attitudes, Behaviors and Characteristics," 255–56.
29 Ibid., 103.
30 Dambert, "Springfest," 5–10.
31 Ibid., 10.
32 Ibid., 9.
33 Ibid., 12–16, 22.
34 Ibid., 20.
35 Ibid., 38.
36 Ibid.
37 Dambert, e.g., argues that Springfest planning became "a somewhat fraternal/sororital phenomenon," essentially co-opted by the college administration (3) and by definition nontransgressive.
38 *Phaez 3*, undated, Macalester College Archives.
39 Steve Van Drake, "Dixie Is Discrimination," *Phaez 3* 2, no. 1 (n.d):3–4, Macalester College Archives.
40 "'Ole' Miss'—No Myth" *Phaez 3* 3 (n.d.): 5–6.
41 The *Mongoose*, March 14, 1969, 1, Macalester College Archives. On tensions between black and white students, see Stevenson, "Social Control."
42 Mahmoud E. Kati, "The Mass and the Media," *Imani*, March 23, 1973, 3; "All Oppressed Must Unite" and Michael Thompson and Lyle Foster, "Community Affairs—Desegregation in the St. Paul High Schools: The Black and White Sides," *Imani*, 3, no. 1 (1973–74): 3; Broderick Grubb, "'A Boost for Racism': A Rebuttal," loose pages, undated, Macalester College Archives.
43 Nan Burke, "Liberal Atmosphere Attracts Freshmen and Transfers," *MacWeekly*, March 23, 1973, 6.

14. Negotiating Institutional Democracy

1 Stevenson, "Social Control," 345–46.
2 There were two exceptions to this. See M. J. Hedstrom, "Dodge, Kane, Schubert, on Women, Aspirations, Goals, Careers, and Mac," *MacWeekly*, May 3, 1972, 6.
3 "Full Time Faculty Salaries 70–71," Virginia Schubert Papers, Macalester College Archives. Salary parity took decades to achieve, and faculty salaries came into alignment more quickly than did staff and administrative salaries. More than a decade and a half later, the average salary for male staff at Macalester was reported at twenty-six thousand dollars and for female staff at nineteen thousand dollars, statistics that

reflect the lower pay grades held by women and the two-thirds male majorities in the top three pay grades. See "Editorial," *MacWeekly*, May 1, 1987, 6. As in other schools, the percentage of women faculty at Macalester had declined significantly from earlier in the century. In 1927, for instance, Macalester employed thirty-eight faculty (twenty-six men and twelve women), with one-third being women. Their departments were predominantly languages, reflecting gender norms of the period: ancient languages (one associate professor), modern languages (two German, one Spanish, one unidentified, one French replacement), English (one full, one associate, and three assistants), and social and political science (one assistant with an MA degree).

4   Carol Lacey, "Freshmen Women Get Pep Talk at Macalester," *St. Paul Pioneer Press*, September 7, 1972, 19.

5   HEW Career Seminar for Women, October 4–6, 1972, Virginia Schubert Papers, Macalester College Archives.

6   Debby Hildebrand, Dan Lubin, T. James McKeown, and Gail Young, "Kate Millett: A Woman's Voice for Change," *MacWeekly*, October 13, 1972, 10–11; Joan Henderson-Roragen and Mary Vandemark, "Making It as a Woman," *MacWeekly*, October 13, 1972, 10–11.

7   "Eugenie 'Feared Error,'" *St. Paul Pioneer Press*, October 5, 1972, Family Life, 1. See also John Henderson-Roragen and Mary Vandemark, "Making It as a Woman," *MacWeekly*, October 13, 1971, 10–11; Carol Lacey, "No Turning Back for Women," *St. Paul Pioneer Press*, October 8, 1972, Family Life, 11; Marg Zack, "Kate Millett Says the News Media Try to Divide Women's Movement," *Minneapolis Tribune*, October 6, 1972, 2B.

8   Despite their presence on faculty committees, women faculty reported feeling that their contributions were frequently not taken as seriously or given the same consideration as men's contributions.

9   Hedstrom, "Dodge, Kane, Schubert," 7; Sue Kilian, "Macalester Professors Scrutinize Women's Career Attitudes," *Minnesota Daily*, October 4, 1972, 8.

10 The percentage of women faculty at the college in 2006 was approximately 42%.

11 The racial makeup of this class was sixty-five African American, five Latino, five Native American, and one white. Dan Gearino, "Exhuming EEO," typescript, 1998, 10, Macalester College Archives, quoting Dan Balik, "A Report on Minority Studies at Macalester College," 1983, Macalester College Archives.

12 Ibid., 13, 21.

13 "Report to the Synod of Lakes and Prairies," Spring 1975, Macalester College Archives.

14 G. Alfred Hess, "Renegotiating a Multicultural Society: Participation in Desegregation Planning in Chicago," *Journal of Negro Education* 53 (Spring 1984): 136.

15 "Rumors," *Expanded Educational Opportunities Newsletter*, March 10, 1969, 5, Chapel Files, Macalester College Archives.

16 Broderick Grubb, "A Black Senior," *Imani*, March 23, 1973, 9, Macalester College Archives.

17 Alvin Currier, "Some Afterthoughts on the April 29, 1971, Faculty Meeting," undated, Chapel Files, Macalester College Archives.

18 Marketing Report to Macalester College Board of Trustees, December 5, 1980, 5, Macalester College Archives. This report also notes that applications also plummeted from a high of over seven thousand in 1969 to a low of under three thousand in 1976 (17). As a result, admitted students' academic profile shifted significantly, with 90% of the class of 1970 graduating in the top 20% of their high school class to 51% of the class of 1979 having done so (20).

19 "Report to the Synod of Lakes and Prairies from Macalester College, St. Paul, Minnesota, April 1976 to March 1977," undated, President's Office, Macalester College Archives.

20 Macalester College Audit Reports, 1972, 1971, Macalester College.

21 Programmatic figures are exclusive of student financial aid. See "Macalester College, Summary of EEO Program," September 4, 1974, Macalester College Archives.

22 Untitled handout, quoting from the *AAUP Bulletin*, June 1974, Macalester College Archives.

23 Gearino, "Exhuming EEO," 23. Gearino's account and interpretation of the EEO situation is the most complete written analysis available. Though he does not consistently cite his sources, much of the information in the article is reliable and corroborated by sources I have found. In particular, Gearino provides information on the perspectives of the student protesters, gathered through interviews with key figures, including Melvin Collins, the spokesman for the students who occupied the building.

24 "Minority Student's Demand's [*sic*] for Continued Expanded Educational Opportunities," [September 13, 1974], EEO Box, Macalester College Archives.

25 Gearino, "Exhuming EEO," 27–28.

26 Ibid., 28.

27 Macalester College, "The Macalester College Institutional Self-Study Covering the Ten Academic Years 1965–66 through 1974–75," 75. External funding, federal and private, for EEO amounted to just over $1.4 million during the period.

28 Yahya Armajani, "What It Takes to Be a Christian College," September 19, 1967, David Hopper Papers, Committee on Church Relatedness Folder, Macalester College Archives.

29 Charles W. McLarnan to John B. Davis Jr., March 18, 1976, Macalester College Archives.

30 Minutes of the Synod of Lakes and Prairies Annual Meeting, June 10–12, 1975, 93.

31 Wayne Liljegren and Howard Dooley, "Visitation Report to the Synod of Lakes and Prairies on Macalester College," October 14 and 15, 1976, 3.

32 Statement by Walter Mink, as quoted in McLarnan to Davis, March 18, 1976, Macalester College Archives.

33 See Chaves, *Ordaining Women*.

34 The United Presbyterian Church U.S.A., *The Church and Related Colleges and Universities: A Statement of Mutual Responsibilities*, 1973, Presbyterian Historical Society.

15. *Peaks, Pluralism, and Prosperity*

1   Information on the expedition is from an interview with Gerald Webers by the author, March 12, 2003. Later measurements have identified another peak, Mount Bursik, at 8,282 feet, as the highest peak in the Heritage Range of the Ellsworth Mountains. Peaks were also named after Webers and each of the four students. E-mail from John Craddock to author, March 12, 2009, in author's possession.

2   John B. Davis inaugural address, as quoted by Charlotte Porter and Corey Gordon, "Davis Calls for Reevaluation, Change," *MacWeekly*, November 7, 1975, 1.

3   Author's interview with Paul Aslanian, February 26, 2003.

4   Beth Linnen, "Optimism Prevails at Mac as Davis Takes Over Presidency," *MacWeekly*, September 12, 1975, 1.

5   E. Graham Waring et al., "Report of a Visit to Macalester College, St. Paul, Minnesota, 26–8 April 1976 for the Commission on Institutions of Higher Information of the North Central Association of College[s] and Schools," 5, Macalester College Archives.

6   Ibid., 10.

7   Curriculum Survey Committee, Macalester College, "Interim Report," October 1975, 55, Macalester College Archives.

8   Waring et al., "Report," 9.

9   Ibid.

10 Presbyterian synods and colleges across the country drew up covenants during this period in an effort to clarify their respective relationships.

11 "A Covenant Describing Relationships between the United Presbyterian Church, USA (Synod of Lakes and Prairies) and Macalester College (Board of Trustees)," October 2, 1983, Macalester College Archives.

12 Scott Gibbs, "Chapel Programs Going Strong," *MacWeekly*, February 17, 1978, 2.

13 Alison Albrecht, "Religion at Mac: Presbyterians to the Hebrew House," *MacWeekly*, April 3, 1981, 7.

14 The relationship between religion and education on the Macalester campus is much different from what one finds on many public university campuses, where, although many student organizations offer a wide range of religious experiences and opportunities to students, the institutions themselves generally avoid involvement with any type of religious organization.

15 See Richard Shumann, "New Program to Bring Top Scholars to Mac," *MacWeekly*, March 15, 1986, 1.

16 Author's interview with Dan Balik, July 25, 2002.

17 Chris Hanchette, "*U.S. News* Notes Mac: Swarthmore Is Number One, They Say," *MacWeekly*, October 13, 1989, 3.

18 The author wishes to thank Dr. Paul Aslanian for sharing both information and

perspective on this period in the college's financial history. Author's interview with Paul Aslanian, February 27, 2003.

19 Heidenry, *Theirs Was the Kingdom*, 528.

Epilogue

1 Some may argue that the campus is not more politically diverse than in the pre–World War II period, having exchanged a predominantly Republican outlook for a predominantly Democratic one. Though in terms of party affiliation, this is accurate, in terms of political style and interests, diversity is much broader than in earlier periods.

2 Author interview with Michael McPherson, April 17, 2003.

Bibliography

Armajani, Yahya. "Four College Area Studies: A Cooperative Program in the Understanding of Other Cultures." *Association of American Colleges Bulletin* 43 (March 1957): 14–22.

Balmer, Randall Herbert, and John R. Fitzmier, *The Presbyterians* (Westport, Conn.: Greenwood Press, 1993).

Beecher, Eunice Bullard. *From Dawn to Daylight; or, The Simple Story of a Western Home.* New York: Derby and Jackson, 1859.

Bell, Marguerite N. *With Banners: A Biography of Stella L. Wood.* St. Paul, Minn.: Macalester College Press, 1954.

Bennett, John Coleman. *Christianity and Our World.* New York: Association Press, 1936.

Boggs, Marion W. "Attempts to Define and Limit 'Aggressive' Armament in Diplomacy and Strategy." PhD diss., University of Chicago, 1940.

Boston, Rob. "When Christians Killed Each Other over Religion in Public Schools." *Liberty: A Magazine for Religious Liberty,* May/June 1997. http://candst.tripod.com/boston3.htm.

Braude, Ann. "Women's History Is American Religious History." In *Retelling U.S. Religious History,* edited by Thomas A. Tweed, 87–107. Berkeley: University of California Press, 1997.

Brown, Robert McAfee. *Reflections on the Long Haul.* Louisville, Ky.: Westminster John Knox, 2005.

Burtchaell, James Tunstead. *The Dying of the Light: The Disengagement of Colleges and Universities from Their Christian Churches.* Grand Rapids, Mich.: W. B. Eerdmans, 1998.

Canning, Peter. *American Dreamers: The Wallaces and* Reader's Digest; *an Insider's Story.* New York: Simon and Schuster, 1996.

Castle, Henry A. *History of St. Paul and Vicinity.* Chicago: Lewis, 1912.

Chaves, Mark. *Ordaining Women: Culture and Conflict in Religious Organizations.* Cambridge, Mass.: Harvard University Press, 1997.

Cherry, Conrad, Betty A. DeBerg, and Amanda Porterfield. *Religion on Campus.* Chapel Hill: University of North Carolina Press, 2001.

Chipman, David Arden, II. "The Attitudes, Behaviors and Characteristics of Students at Macalester College, with Respect to the Use of Illicit and Exotic Drugs with Particular Emphasis on Marijuana." PhD diss., University of Minnesota, 1971.

Clark, Glenn. *A Man's Reach: The Autobiography of Glenn Clark.* St. Paul, Minn.: Macalester Park, 1977. First published 1949 by Harper and Brothers.

Clark, Miles. *Glenn Clark, His Life and Writings.* Nashville, Tenn.: Abingdon, 1975.

Coe, George Albert. *A Social Theory of Religious Education.* New York: Charles Scribner's Sons, 1917.

Cuninggim, Merrimon. *Uneasy Partners: The College and the Church.* Nashville, Tenn.: Abingdon, 1994.

Dambert, Paul R. "Springfest: Sex, Drugs and Rock & Roll on a College Campus." Honors paper, Macalester College, 1987.

Delton, Jennifer A. *Making Minnesota Liberal: Civil Rights and the Transformation of the Democratic Party.* Minneapolis: University of Minnesota Press, 2002.

Dupre, Huntley. *Edward Duffield Neill: Pioneer Educator.* St. Paul, Minn.: Macalester College Press, 1949.

Edwards, Maurice Dwight. *History of the Synod of Minnesota, Presbyterian Church U.S.A.* [St. Paul]: Synod of Minnesota, 1927.

Flemming, Bernice. *Arthur Flemming, Crusader at Large: A Memoir.* Washington, D.C.: Caring, 1991.

Folwell, William Watts. *A History of Minnesota.* 4 vols. St. Paul: Minnesota Historical Society, 1926.

Fosdick, Harry Emerson. *A Guide to Understanding the Bible.* New York: Harper and Brothers, 1938.

Fowler, Dorothy Ganfield. "Congressional Dictation of Local Appointments." *Journal of Politics* 7 (February 1945): 25–57.

Franchot, Jenny. *Roads to Rome: The Antebellum Protestant Encounter with Catholicism.* Berkeley: University of California Press, 1994.

Funk, Henry Daniel. *A History of Macalester College: Its Origin, Struggle and Growth.* St. Paul: Macalester College Board of Trustees, 1910.

Gatell, Frank Otto. "Spoils of the Bank War: Political Bias in the Selection of Pet Banks." *American Historical Review* 70 (October 1964): 35.

Gray, James. *The University of Minnesota, 1851–1951.* Minneapolis: University of Minnesota Press, 1951.

Guelzo, Allen C. *For the Union of Evangelical Christendom: The Irony of the Reformed Episcopalians.* University Park: Pennsylvania State University Press, 1994.

Haebig, Steve. "What's Historic about This Site? Macalester's Old Main and Its First Century." *Ramsey County History* 25, no. 1 (1990): 35.

Hamilton, Holman. "Texas Bonds and Northern Profits: A Study in Compromise, Investment, and Lobby Influence." *Mississippi Valley Historical Review* 43 (March 1957): 579–94.

Hammond, William Gardiner. *Remembrance of Amherst: An Undergraduate's Diary, 1846–1848.* New York: Columbia University Press, 1946.

Harper, William Rainey. *The Trend in Higher Education in America.* Chicago: University of Chicago Press, 1905.

Heidenry, John. *Theirs Was the Kingdom: Lila and DeWitt Wallace and the Story of the Reader's Digest.* New York: W. W. Norton, 1993.

Hess, G. Alfred. "Renegotiating a Multicultural Society: Participation in Desegregation Planning in Chicago." *Journal of Negro Education* 53 (Spring 1984): 132–46.

Higham, John. *From Boundlessness to Incorporation: The Transformation of American Culture, 1848–1860.* Ann Arbor, Mich.: William L. Clements Library, 1969.

———. *Strangers in the Land: Patterns of American Nativism.* New Brunswick, N.J.: Rutgers University Press, 2002. Originally published 1955.

Hoffmann, M. M. *The Church Founders of the Northwest: Loras and Cretin and Other Captains of Christ.* Milwaukee, Wisc.: Bruce, 1937.

Hollinger, David A. "The 'Secularization' Question and the United States in the Twentieth Century." *Church History* 70 (2001): 132–43.

Hughes, Art. "The Legacy of the Morrill Hall Takeover." Minnesota Public Radio. http://minnesota.publicradio.org/display/web/2006/04/21/morrillhall/.

Hutchison, William R. *Errand to the World: American Protestant Thought and Foreign Missions.* Chicago: University of Chicago Press, 1987.

Jacobsen, Douglas, and William Vance Trollinger Jr., eds. *Re-forming the Center: American Protestantism, 1900 to the Present.* Grand Rapids, Mich.: W. B. Eerdmans, 1998.

James, William. *The Varieties of Religious Experience: A Study in Human Nature.* New York: Modern Library, 1902.

Johnson, David W. *A Journey of Hope: The House of Hope Presbyterian Church, 1849–1999.* St. Paul, Minn.: House of Hope Presbyterian Church, 2000.

Kagin, Edwin. *James Wallace of Macalester.* Garden City, N.Y.: Doubleday, 1957.

Kelley, Brooks Mather. *Yale: A History.* New Haven, Conn.: Yale University Press, 1974.

Kilde, Jeanne Halgren. "How Did *Left Behind*'s Particular Vision of the End Times Develop? A Historical Look at Millenarian Thought." In *Rapture, Revelation and the End Times: Exploring the Left Behind Series,* edited by Bruce David Forbes and Jeanne Halgren Kilde, 33–70. New York: Palgrave, 2004.

Kunz, Virginia Brainard. "An Excess of Zeal and Boosterism—Few Holds Barred in Twin Cities Rivalries." *Ramsey County History* 25, no. 2 (1990): 4–8.

Lanegran, David A., with Judith Frost Flinn. *St. Anthony Park: Portrait of a Community.* St. Paul, Minn.: District 12 Community Council and St. Anthony Park Association, 1987.

Lannie, Vincent P., and Bernard C. Diethorn. "For the Honor and Glory of God: The Philadelphia Bible Riots of 1840." *History of Education Quarterly* 8 (Spring 1968): 44–106.

Lowry, Goodrich. *Streetcar Man: Tom Lowry and the Twin City Rapid Transit Company.* Minneapolis, Minn.: Lerner, 1979.

Macalester College. *A Century and Beyond.* St. Paul, Minn.: Macalester College, 1985.

Marsden, George M. *The Evangelical Mind and the New School Presbyterian Experience: A Case Study of Thought and Theology in Nineteenth-century America.* New Haven, Conn.: Yale University Press, 1970.

———. *The Soul of the American University: From Protestant Establishment to Established Nonbelief.* New York: Oxford University Press, 1994.

———. *Understanding Fundamentalism and Evangelicalism.* Grand Rapids, Mich.: W. B. Eerdmans, 1991.

May, Elaine Tyler. *Homeward Bound: American Families in the Cold War Era.* New York: Basic Books, 1988.

Nash, Gary B., Julie Roy Jeffrey, John R. Howe, Peter J. Frederick, Allen F. Davis, Allan M. Winkler, Charlene Mires, and Carla Gardina Pestana, eds. *The American People: Creating a Nation and a Society.* 2nd ed. New York: Harper and Row, 1990.

Neill, Edward D. *The English Colonization of America during the Seventeenth Century.* London: Strahan, 1871.

———. *History of Minnesota: From the Earliest French Explorations to the Present Time.* Minneapolis: Minnesota Historical Company, 1882.

———. *The Nature and Importance of the American System of Public Instruction: A Discourse Delivered on Sunday Morning, Sept. 25, 1853.* St. Paul, Minn.: Owens and Moore, 1853.

———. *Report of the Committee on Schools, of the Council, Accompanied by the Report of the Superintendent of Common Schools of the Territory of Minnesota.* St. Paul, Minn.: Owens and Moore, 1852.

———. *Thoughts on the American College; An Address Delivered in Macalester College Chapel, Snelling Avenue, Saint Paul, Minn., September 16, 1885.* St. Paul, Minn.: The Pioneer Press, 1885.

Niebuhr, Richard. *The Kingdom of God in America.* Chicago: Willett, Clark, 1937.

Porterfield, Amanda. *The Transformation of American Religion: The Story of a Late-Twentieth-century Awakening.* New York: Oxford University Press, 2001.

Riley, William Bell. *Inspiration or Evolution.* Cleveland, Ohio: Union Gospel Press, 1926.

Roberts, Norene Davis. "An Early Political and Administrative History of the University of Minnesota, 1851–84." PhD diss., University of Minnesota, 1978.

Rudolph, Frederick. *Curriculum: A History of the American Undergraduate Course of Study since 1636.* San Francisco: Jossey-Bass, 1977.

Said, Edward. *Orientalism.* New York: Pantheon, 1978.

Sandeen, Ernest R. *The Roots of Fundamentalism: British and American Millenarianism, 1800–1930.* Chicago: University of Chicago Press, 1970.

———. *St. Paul's Historic Summit Avenue.* St. Paul, Minn.: Living Historical Museum and Macalester College, 1978.

Schmidt, Stephen A. *A History of the Religious Education Association.* Birmingham, Ala.: Religious Education Press, 1983.

Schroth, Raymond A. *Fordham: A History and Memoir.* Chicago: Loyola Press, 2002.

Semas, Philip W. "A Week of Tragedy: Disorders Flare, 4 Students Die as U.S. Action in Cambodia Inflames Many Campuses." *Chronicle of Higher Education,* May 11, 1970.

St. Andrew's Society of Philadelphia. "About the St. Andrew's Society of Philadelphia." http://www.standrewsociety.org/index2.htm.

Stevenson, George W. "Social Control in Institutions of Higher Education: Administration Responses to Student Protest at the University of Minnesota and Macalester College (1967–1972)." PhD diss., University of Minnesota, 1972.

Tewksbury, Donald G. *The Founding of American Colleges and Universities before the Civil War.* New York: Teachers' College, Columbia University, 1932.

Turck, Charles J. *The Nature of a Liberal Education.* St. Paul, Minn.: Macalester College, 1955.

———. "The Present Challenge to the Colleges." *Association of American Colleges Bulletin* 33 (March 1947): 5–13.

———. *Problems of Church and Society.* Minneapolis, Minn.: Burgess, 1941.

United Nations. "History of the Charter of the United Nations, the Declaration of St. James Place." http://www.un.org/en/aboutun/charter/history/index.shtml.

———. "History of the Charter of the United Nations, Moscow and Teheran." http://www.un.org/en/aboutun/charter/history/moscowteheran.shtml.

Wallace, James. "On the Woman Overtures." *Presbyterian Banner,* March 6, 1930.

———. *Wallace-Bruce and Closely Related Families: Barefoots, Taylors, Wilsons, McKees, Douglasses, Liddells, Hendersons, Notestines, and Others: History and Genealogy.* Northfield, Minn.: Mohn, 1930.

Weber, Max. *Economy and Society: An Outline of Interpretive Sociology.* Edited and translated by Guenther Roth et al. 2 vols. New York: Bedminster Press, 1968.

Williams, Daniel Day. *The Andover Liberals: A Study in American Theology.* Morningside, N.Y.: King's Crown Press, 1941.

Wills, Jocelyn. *Boosters, Hustlers, and Speculators: Entrepreneurial Culture and the Rise of Minneapolis and St. Paul, 1849–1883.* St. Paul: Minnesota Historical Society Press, 2005.

Wingerd, Mary Lethert. *Claiming the City: Politics, Faith, and the Power of Place in St. Paul.* Ithaca, N.Y.: Cornell University Press, 2001.

Young, Biloine Whiting, and David Lanegran. *Grand Avenue: The Renaissance of an Urban Street.* St. Cloud, Minn.: North Star Press, 1996.

Zellie, Carole, and Garneth O. Peterson. *St. Paul Historic Context Study: Residential Real Estate Development, 1880–1950.* St. Paul, Minn.: St. Paul Heritage Preservation Commission, 2001.

Zirinsky, Michael. "American Presbyterian Missionaries at Urmia during the Great War." Paper presented at the International Roundtable on Persia and the Great War, Tehran, Iran, March 2–3, 1997. http://www.iranchamber.com/religions/articles/american_presbyterian_missionaries_zirinsky.pdf.

Index

Jeanne Halgren Kilde is director of the religious studies program at the University of Minnesota and former director of curricular activities for Macalester College's Lilly Project for Work, Ethics, and Vocation. She is the author of *When Church Became Theatre* and *Sacred Power, Sacred Space* and coeditor of *Rapture, Revelation, and the End Times.*

James Brewer Stewart is James Wallace Professor of History Emeritus at Macalester College.